The
EUDEMIAN
ETHICS
of ARISTOTLE

The
EUDEMIAN
ETHICS
of ARISTOTLE

Translated with Explanatory Comments by
Peter L. P. Simpson

Routledge
Taylor & Francis Group

LONDON AND NEW YORK

First published 2013 by Transaction Publishers

2 Park Square, Milton Park, Abingdon, Oxfordshire OX14 4RN
711 Third Avenue, New York, NY 10017

Routledge is an imprint of the Taylor & Francis Group, an informa business

First issued in paperback 2017

Library of Congress Catalog Number: 2012018214

Library of Congress Cataloging-in-Publication Data

Aristotle.
   [Eudemian ethics. English]
   The Eudemian ethics of Aristotle / translated with explanatory comments and accompanying translation of Aristotle's On Virtues and vices [by] Peter L. P. Simpson.
     p. cm.
     1. Ethics. 2. Virtues. 3. Vices. I. Simpson, Peter, 1951– II. Aristotle. De virtutibus et vitiis. English. III. Title.
B422.A5S56 2012
171'.3–dc23

                                2012018214

ISBN 13: 978-1-4128-4969-2 (hbk)
ISBN 13: 978-1-138-51585-7 (pbk)

To my Students and Colleagues at the City
University of New York

Contents

Introduction

Reason for the Translation and the Accompanying Commentary

Of the works on ethics in the Aristotelian corpus that have come down to us from antiquity there is now no significant dispute among scholars that the *Nicomachean Ethics* [*NE*] and *Eudemian Ethics* [*EE*] are authentic.[1] Of these the best known and most read and studied, by scholars as well as by general readers, is the *Nicomachean*. The *Eudemian* has, at least in recent years, come to be read and used by scholars as a helpful support and confirmation and sometimes foil for *NE*.[2] However, for all the attention recently paid to it, *EE* remains a largely neglected work in the study of Aristotle's ethics, both among scholars and among moral philosophers. Reasons are not far to seek. *EE* is more concentrated, even crabbed, in style and argumentation, and it is less adorned with engaging descriptions or enlarged by leisurely explanations. More, and worse, the Greek text is plagued with problems both of grammar and translation, whereas the text of *NE* is relatively free of them. Recent scholarly work has done much to help clear up these problems but more needs to be done. Further, translations of *EE* (in any language) are few and largely incomplete. For *EE* shares three books in common with *NE* (Books 4–6 of the former being the same as Books 5–7 of the latter), and these common books are usually found in translations only of *NE* and not in those of *EE*.[3] Finally, the particularities of doctrine in *EE*, because its argumentation is so concentrated and elliptical, are not easy to decipher, especially in comparison with the more expansive *NE*. Further, because the work as a whole has attracted less attention, these particularities have remained without the extensive commentary and explanation that *NE* has long enjoyed and that have rendered its doctrine and argumentation more open to view.

The translation and commentary offered here are meant to contribute toward rectifying this state of affairs. To begin with, the translation includes the common books. Second, it provides an analytical outline of the whole, together with summaries (not Aristotle's, of course, but the translator's) of each individual section, so as to make the overall structure and the detailed argument as clear and as intelligible as possible, or at least clear and intelligible enough that readers will be able to grasp, even on a first view, what is being argued where and why. Third, the translation contains many renderings of words and phrases, and many proposals for emending or not emending the text, that differ from what other translators and scholars have adopted. The result is that the meanings attributed to certain passages and arguments differ, sometimes markedly, from the prevailing consensus.[4] Whether these meanings are correct must be decided by reference to matters of philology and of logical analysis. The philology, wherever necessary, is discussed in the notes to the translation. The logical analysis, except where the point can be stated briefly, is discussed in the separate commentary.

Fourth, and apropos such commentary, the translation has aimed to be literal, without expansion or paraphrase, and yet also readable. An unreadable translation is useless, but a translation that strays too far from the original wording runs a like danger. The danger is all the greater in a text like *EE* where, more than usual in Aristotle's writings, the precise bearing of a philosophical claim or the exact logic of an argument turn on the peculiar wording or order.[5] There is, unfortunately, no way entirely to avoid such problems in a translation. The only way to do so is to provide extensive notes or commentary. The translation does contain notes here and there to aid intelligibility, but too often something much fuller than a note is required. The separate commentary is meant to serve that fuller purpose. This commentary would overwhelm the translation if it was made part of it. In addition it is, in the first instance, dispensable. The translation is meant to stand on its own and to be intelligible on its own, at least in general if not in all particulars. The commentary is only needed for those particulars, and also, from time to time, for placing together in a single view what the text itself leaves scattered or unfocused. The commentary is designed, therefore, to aid a deeper study of the doctrine and the argument, not for rendering or locating that doctrine or argument in the first place, which is rather the job of the translation and the analytical outline.

General Relationship between the Eudemian and Nicomachean Ethics

The main puzzle about Aristotle's ethical works that has exercised scholars is why he wrote two (or three or even four)[6] works covering very much the same ground. The puzzle is most acute with respect to *EE* and *NE* because, among other things, these works share three entire books in common. Why write two works to begin with, and why, if two works were really required, keep three books the same?

An initial, and an initially attractive, response to this puzzle is to say that one or other work is not, after all, by Aristotle. The response is attractive because the ancient evidence for the genuineness of both works, while real and extensive, is not unambiguous. Notably, *NE* was attributed hesitantly to

Aristotle's son Nicomachus by Cicero and positively by Diogenes Laertius, and *EE* was hesitantly attributed to Eudemus by Aspasius.[7] Doubts of a more extensive kind first began to be cast on some of Aristotle's ethical writings during the Renaissance when scholars puzzled over why Aristotle, notorious otherwise for his brevity, could have gone to the trouble of writing more than one major work on ethics that covered the same ground in pretty much the same way. Their suggested solution was to say that one or other of them was written by someone else, and since by then *NE* had achieved canonical status as *the* ethics of Aristotle, it was *EE* they cast into doubt.[8]

These doubts, while not altogether allayed, ceased to attract much attention until Schleiermacher raised them again in the early nineteenth century by propounding the controversial thesis that another ethical work attributed to Aristotle, the *Great Ethics* [*GE*], was the only genuine one. Schleiermacher argued for his thesis on the philosophical ground that only the *Great Ethics* was consistent and coherent because, unlike the *Nicomachean* and the *Eudemian*, it downplayed or ignored the so-called intellectual virtues and located morality where it properly belonged in the moral virtues.[9] Schleiermacher was challenged by Spengel, who responded with philological and historical arguments, such as references to *NE* in other genuine works of Aristotle, that *NE* was genuine and the only genuine ethics of Aristotle.[10] Spengel's view became the norm for most of the nineteenth century, though a few dissenting voices could be heard here and there.[11]

The next major stage in the controversy occurred in the early twentieth century when Jaeger popularized the developmental or chronological thesis about all Aristotle's works (and not just his ethical ones).[12] The thesis says that Aristotle's works as we have them are a compilation of disparate writings from different stages in Aristotle's career and reflect different stages in his intellectual development. About the ethical works, Jaeger held that *NE* was Aristotle's mature ethics and that *EE* was a less mature version from his younger years. Jaeger's thesis was immediately challenged by Von Arnim[13] but only as to its details and not its main point (that Aristotle's ethical works were different because they reflected different stages in chronological development). Despite the disagreement between these two scholars, and despite the severe criticisms that Jaeger's work in particular has been subject to,[14] the consensus still today is that Aristotle's writings reflect different periods of his career. The consensus is also that *NE* is later than *EE*, as well as philosophically superior.[15]

Since there is no longer scholarly dispute about the authenticity of *EE*, there is no need (as there is in the case of *GE*) for extended discussions of the nature and validity of arguments about authenticity. Something, nevertheless, needs to be said about relative dating, as well as about the problem of the common books. The question of relative dating, however, is closely connected with the question of authenticity, because the reasons scholars give for saying

EE is earlier, or later, are the same in kind as those they give that *GE* is not authentic, namely differences of style and content. The assumption in both cases is that the same author could not have written at the same time (in the case of *NE* and *EE*), or at all (in the case of *GE*), works that display differences of the sort in question.

Little argument is given in support of this assumption and none that is compelling. Differences in time of composition, or in authorship, of a given work can indeed explain peculiarities of style and content, but so can other differences, such as the audience addressed. That different works can differ because they have different audiences is a common enough idea, and we find it often to be the case in writings produced today. (Scholarly books are not like popular books, even if sometimes they have the same author, because they are aimed, as we say, at different "markets.") It is curious that scholars have not thought of appealing to this idea more often in their discussion of the differences between the several versions of Aristotle's ethics.[16] In any event, there are no differences between *EE* and *NE* that cannot be as well, or better, explained by the hypothesis of difference in audience than by difference in time of writing.[17] Since we know next to nothing about when Aristotle wrote what (all we have are suggestions and ingenious guesses, almost as numerous as the people who propose them; none of which is better founded on the available evidence than any other),[18] but we know a great deal about the audience addressed (for each work makes plain, either by explicit statement or by structure, argument, and design, whom the author has in mind), it seems the better part of valor to abandon attempts to distinguish *EE* and *NE* from each other by their time of composition and to distinguish them instead by their audience.

The thesis adopted here, then, is that *EE* and *NE* differ, as is evident especially, but not only, from their beginnings and endings (and as is argued in more detail in the commentary), because *EE* is directed primarily to philosophers and *NE* (which continues immediately into the *Politics*) primarily to legislators (which will include especially advisers to kings).[19] *EE* will thus constitute a sort of *apologia pro vita sua* for Aristotle and his closest friends in philosophy, while *NE* will be a sort of extended *vademecum* for legislators. This thesis does not require any accompanying hypothesis about the reasons for the names of either work, but if one is permitted to indulge in speculation (though in speculation that claims no more support in the evidence than any other speculation compatible therewith), a particular suggestion is as follows. *EE* has the name it has because it commemorates Eudemus of Rhodes, student and colleague of Aristotle, who established a school of philosophy at Rhodes after the fashion of the one established by Aristotle at Athens. Eudemus will thus be representing philosophers, which is why *EE* bears his name. *NE* has the name it has because it commemorates Aristotle's father and son (both named Nicomachus), the former of whom was physician and adviser at the royal court in Macedon (where Aristotle himself was also long an adviser), and the latter of whom was no doubt destined for a similar life at the same court. That he was to die young was unknown to his father who had already predeceased him. Nicomachus *père et fils* will thus represent wise legislators, which is why *NE* bears their name.[20]

Nevertheless, even the above thesis about the audience of *NE* and *EE*, while it does rely on evidence that actually favors it against its rivals (as opposed to evidence that is compatible with almost any rival), is ultimately dispensable. What matters in the case of both works is not when they were written or for whom, or even by whom, but what they say. It is the philosophical content that is of most interest. This content will remain what it is however much our views of its time or audience may change. The aim of this translation, and of the commentary, first and last, is to expose and expound this content as fully and as carefully as possible. Everything else is secondary.

The Question of the Common Books

The question of the common books is analogous and may be decided in an analogous way. To begin with, we must note that the textual tradition, as it has come down to us from antiquity, attributes these books equally to both *EE* and *NE*. In some of the extant manuscripts of *EE*, the text of these books is included, and where they are not included, reference is made back, to avoid duplication in the labor of copying, to the relevant books of *NE* copied out earlier.[21] There is, nevertheless, a question as to whether these common books belong more to one work than the other. Here, indeed, recent scholarship seems to have made advances and to have uncovered some good evidence that the common books belong, in style and structure, to *EE* rather than *NE*.[22] However, nothing of further significance follows from this result, whether the common books are properly part of *EE* rather than *NE* or of *NE* rather than *EE* or equally of both, or whether they were being written at the same time or earlier or later than either *EE* or *NE* or both. A whole variety of plausible explanations could be constructed to fit almost any hypothesis. For instance, perhaps Aristotle started *NE* first, completing the material we have in the books peculiar to it, but when he came to the material of the common books, he decided, for whatever reason, that a different style was preferable. Having used that style on the common books, he then decided that the style was preferable altogether (because it was simpler or briefer or tighter or the like), and so he wrote the rest of *EE* to fit them, relegating *NE* in the process.[23] Alternatively he wrote *NE* and *EE* at the same time but decided, as before, that the material of the common books should have *EE's* style, even though he intended these books to be as much part of *NE* as *EE*. Or, he wrote *NE* second but decided the common books did not need revising, or he intended to revise them but died before he could complete the task. Or, again, he did not write the common books at all, but his son Nicomachus did (perhaps using his father's notes), or his colleague Eudemus[24] wrote them or his successor, Theophrastus.

We could, for amusement if not for instruction, continue long in the same vein, coming up with a diversity of rival theories and writing scholarly articles and books in support of a favorite.[25] The point, however, is simple. Theories that save or are compatible with the evidence are legion; ways to decide between them are next to nil. Or rather there is one way: to follow the tradition as it has come down to us from antiquity and to accept that the common books, for whatever reason, are part equally of *NE* and *EE*. The tradition might be wrong, but it is the tradition and it must have its source, somehow or other, in the Lyceum and in Aristotle's actual texts. We should accept the tradition unless and until we have compelling reasons to reject it.[26] We have no compelling reasons. Indeed we barely have reasons at all.

The Question of On Virtues and Vices[27]

There is a fourth ethical work in the Aristotelian corpus, *On Virtues and Vices* [*VV*], and a translation of it appears here at the end of the translation of *EE*. The state of argument as to the authenticity of this work is, if anything, worse than the state of argument about the priority of composition of *EE* and *NE*. Scholars assert with confidence, sometimes with dogmatic confidence, that it is not by Aristotle.[28] But when looking for the reasons for this confidence, we are hard pressed to find any. Evidence there is aplenty that the book is peculiar in certain ways—ways that need explaining. The problem, however, is not the evidence; rather it is how to deduce from the evidence that Aristotle did not, or could not, have written *VV*. One such piece of evidence is that the work lists only one vice for each virtue and says nothing about the classic Aristotelian doctrine of the mean. But how does this evidence prove Aristotle did not write it? We need some such premise that Aristotle would not or could not write a book on virtues and vices that ignored his most distinctive doctrine. The problem with this premise is that it would force us to conclude that Aristotle did not write the *Rhetoric*, for the *Rhetoric* includes a discussion of virtues and vices that says nothing of the mean.[29] Scholars who reject *VV* because it does not talk about the mean should, in consistency, reject the *Rhetoric* too. Moreover, since scholars who reject *VV* nevertheless favor theories of development for Aristotle's writings, why could one not say that the theory of the mean was a development of Aristotle's mature years, not of his early ones, and that *VV* belongs to those early years?[30] Similar problems afflict the other evidence used to show that *VV* is not genuine, as that it begins with an appeal to the division of soul proposed by Plato, and that it is eclectic in character.[31] Aristotle, to be sure, did not accept Plato's division of the soul, or not in its totality, and he was moreover a Peripatetic and not an Eclectic. But again nothing of relevance follows from either fact. For what if *VV* was meant to be a collection of received opinions about virtues and vices (as the passages on virtues and vices in the *Rhetoric* seem to be), and what if these opinions included, as Aristotle typically would have meant them to, not only the opinions of most people but also the opinions of the few and wise? Would not Plato count as one of the few and wise, and would not his views deserve to be included in any collection of opinions, whether finally accepted by Aristotle or not? Further, if Plato's views would fittingly be included, so would the views of anyone else of note, and thus, by necessity, any collection of such views would have an eclectic character. For while Aristotle was no Eclectic, he certainly was eclectic; indeed few people before or since have been so industrious in collecting data and evidence and opinions from almost everywhere about almost anything.

The case against the authenticity of *VV* labors under this and the like problems. It has and can have no weight against the tradition from antiquity that *VV* is in the Aristotelian corpus because Aristotle himself wrote it. The tradition can, moreover, be given support from *EE* itself where, at 2.2.1220b10–11, Aristotle speaks of "a division, *en tois apēllagmenois* or *apēlegmenois* (a misspelling perhaps for *apeilegmenois*), of passions and powers and habits." In the part of the text where the phrase occurs, Aristotle is discussing moral character, and he has just concluded that characters are qualities in the soul brought about by custom or habituation. He adds that what must next be discussed is which qualities in what part of the soul. From what he stated earlier (at 2.1.1219b39–20a12, 29–37), as well as from what he has just concluded, he is able to say, in general terms, that these qualities are in accord with the powers, whereby people feel the various passions, and in accord also with the soul's customs or habits, whereby people are spoken of as being accustomed to feel or not to feel the several passions in some specific way. But such generalities are not enough. Aristotle needs to go beyond them and descend to details (in particular the details, in the next chapters, of the several virtues and that each virtue is a mean between two opposed vices). His method, as he has just recalled (at 2.1.1220a15–18, repeating what was said at 1.6.1216b30–35), is to begin with truths already known but unclearly, so as to reach truths that are clear. So the thing to do would be to appeal to the unclear truths about moral characters that we already have and use them to advance to what is clear, and it is at this point that Aristotle appeals to a division, *en tois apēllagmenois* or *apeilegmenois*, of passions and powers and habits.

What the term means is disputed. The prevailing scholarly suggestions are that it means "in the canceled version" or "in the separate section" or "in the finished works," that is, works separated off or released from further discussion.[32] But we can also add, not as substitutes to the latter two suggestions but as complementary to them, the further suggestion that the word means, or carries the idea of, "abstracts." For things "released" or "separated" (the literal meaning of the Greek word) are the sort of thing that abstracts are.

Abstracts also nicely fits the context of Aristotle's argument, since the work he is referring to would seem to be some set of summaries or abstracts of moral characters. If so, there seems to be little difference between reading "abstracts" *apēllagmenois* or "selections" *apeilegmenois*, since the sense turns out to be very much the same. Aristotle is referring to some set of selections or abstracts (which we might even gloss as "selected abstracts") that are relevant to his current argument.

More interesting and more important is the question of what writing Aristotle is referring to. The suggestion that this writing is the (lost) work on divisions[33] is certainly plausible, and not least because Aristotle says that the work contains a division, namely of passions and powers and habits. But we should look first for clues in the context, and especially in Aristotle's words that follow his mention of the division and of the writing that contains it (1220b12–20):

> I mean by passions such things as these, spirit, fear, shame, desire, things generally which are for the most part essentially followed by a perceptible pleasure or pain. And according to these there is no quality but there is active feeling. There is quality, however, according to powers. I mean by powers things according to which people are said to be active with respect to their passions, as the angry person, the un-irked person, the erotic person, the shame-faced person, the shameless person. Habits are all those things which are cause of these [sc. the powers or the passions] being either in accord with reason or the opposite, such as courage, temperance, cowardice, license.

If we judge by these comments, we should say that the work referred to should have the following features: First it should be about moral characters, for Aristotle's aim now is to find what sort of things, in what part of the soul, moral characters are, and so a set of abstracts or selections relevant to such a search should be of moral characters. Second, it should be of moral characters in such a way as to include some sort of division of passions (as spirit and fear), powers (as that whereby angry and shameless people are angry or shameless), and habits in accord with or against reason (as courage and cowardice). But, further, in view of what Aristotle immediately goes on to argue in the next chapter, this writing can contain no explicit statement of the doctrine of actions and passions being divisible into excess and defect and mean, nor of the accompanying doctrine that virtues are in the mean and are opposed by two vices each, one at either extreme. For these doctrines are the clearer truths that we do not yet possess and that Aristotle intends to argue for by using the less clear truths he here briefly summarizes, and so these less clear truths can hardly include the doctrines already. Aristotle confirms the point himself, for his examples of habits in accord with and against reason include only one of each: courage and temperance being opposed only to cowardice and license and not also to rashness and insensibility. Still, even if this writing contains nothing about the mean, it must contain something about reason being what separates the habits into opposites. It must also contain something from which the doctrine of the mean may be reached, which it will of course do if it contains a division of powers and passions and habits. For Aristotle's argument to the mean, which he gives and enlarges on with many examples in the next chapter, proceeds from the fact that the habits are qualities in the powers for exercising, or being active with, the passions in certain ways. Such action, he then continues, is change, and change is a quantity (a continuous quantity), and quantities admit of a mean and an excess and a deficiency, of which the mean for us as commanded by knowledge and reason is best. Hence the habits in the powers of passion, or moral characters, can be against reason in two ways: by excess and by deficiency.

Now, interestingly enough, *VV* answers very well to this description and so to the needs of Aristotle's argument. This work is a set of selections or abstracts; it is about moral characters, and it talks about them in terms of passions and powers and habits. It lists virtues against only one opposed vice, and it makes clear, in its descriptions, that the virtues are cause of rational behavior and the vices of irrational.[34] The fit, therefore, between *VV* and the work referred to in the crux phrase from *EE* is tight. Moreover the pieces of evidence, mentioned earlier, appealed to by scholars to show *VV* cannot be genuine (i.e., it fails to talk about the mean and the extremes in the case of actions and passions; it lists only one vice for each virtue; it begins with an appeal to the division of soul proposed by Plato; and it is eclectic in character), all turn on features of *VV* that make that work to be just the sort of writing *EE* is referring to here. Even the reference to Plato and the eclecticism fit, for the views of Plato and others will be among the unclear truths we are to begin from so as to get to truths that are clearer. Accordingly we have excellent reason to conclude that *VV* is the writing being referred to by the phrase *en tois apēllagmenois*. We thus have also excellent support for the universal witness of tradition that *VV* is one of Aristotle's genuine works. Hence, if for no other reason, a translation of *VV* is suitably appended here to the translation of *EE*.

Note on the Greek Text

The Greek text used for the translation of the *EE* (and of the common books from *NE*) is that of Bekker. The editions by Susemihl and the *Oxford Classical Text* have both had to be largely left aside for two reasons. The first and less serious of the two is that they indulge in many emendations to the text that, even if plausible, are seldom necessary and often misleading. Bekker is more conservative, perhaps excessively so, but at least he makes the original manuscript readings easier to see. His *apparatus criticus* is thin and needs to be supplemented by Susemihl's and the *OCT*'s. The second and more serious reason for largely setting aside the texts of Susemihl and the *OCT* is that both regularly get the Bekker line divisions wrong and so make exact reference to particular passages unreliable. We need to keep our references to Bekker numbers as accurate as possible if we are to continue enjoying the immense benefit they have conferred on us for the study of Aristotle. The *apparatus critici* of Susemihl and the *OCT* are indeed both invaluable and should be used; less so their texts.

Bekker's text can be downloaded online from Google Books.

Notes

1. Pakaluk (1998) seems to be the only one in recent years who has tried to revive the theory that *EE* is not by Aristotle. He was rightly taken to task by Buddensiek (1999: 30–36). No one, to my knowledge, has tried to revive the theory that *NE* is not by Aristotle since Elorduy (1939) who, in this regard, was expressly following Schleiermacher (1835).
2. As especially by Kenny (1978, 1992).
3. One exception is the recent translation of the *EE* by Kenny (2011) that does include the common books. Another will be the translation of *EE* by Brad Inwood and Raphael Woolf that is due for publication by Cambridge University Press (Cambridge Texts in the History of Philosophy).
4. Kenny's translation (2011) has a minimum of indication of structure and follows the prevailing consensus on how to render the text.
5. Van der Eijk (1989: 33n21) speaks (apropos 8.2 in particular) of Aristotle's "clumsy" way of writing. The word is too strong but captures something of the idea. Aristotle is certainly not bothering to make his meaning perspicuous.
6. If we include the *Great Ethics*, as well as *On Virtues and Vices*.
7. Cicero, *De Finibus* 5.5, Diogenes Laertius, *Life of Eudoxus* in *Lives of Eminent Philosophers* viii 88, Aspasius (*CAG* xix, pars 1, 151.18–27).
8. The details are in Dirlmeier (1958: 93–146; 1962: 109–143). Case (1596: 1–7) explicitly defended *GE* against these doubts, arguing that it served a different purpose and was for a different audience.
9. Schleiermacher (1835). His arguments have found echoes among contemporary scholars who have been engaged for some time in a debate about whether the *NE*, which they nevertheless hold to be genuine, is inconsistent in its argument about happiness and whether it is incoherently split between the practical life of moral virtue and the contemplative life of intellectual virtue. See the discussions in Buddensiek (1999: 104–47), Natali (2001: 111–14), and the extensive one by Caesar (2009).
10. Spengel (1841, 1843). His move to philological considerations from philosophical ones was compelling and enough to defeat Schleiermacher's thesis in the eyes of most scholars, despite the fact that, for instance, the references to the *Ethics* in other writings of Aristotle are to books of *NE* that it has in common with *EE*, Kenny (1978: 5–8). But Spengel's rejection of *EE* did not, ultimately, win as much favor as his support of *NE*.

11. For example, Thomas (1860).
12. Jaeger (1923).
13. Von Arnim (1924, 1926, 1927, 1928, 1929a, 1929b).
14. Notably by Wilpert (1946), but see also Buddensiek (1999: 23–36).
15. A notable exception is Kenny (1978, 1992), who is inclined to think that *EE* is later and superior; Allan, in Mansion (1961), expressed similar views.
16. Case definitely adopted this explanation for *GE* (1596: 1–7); Allan, in Mansion (1961: 303–304, 318) and Wilpert (1946: 132–35) suggest it as a general possibility; Schleiermacher (1835: 307–308) and Brink (1933: 15), see also Fahnenschmidt (1968: 21), raise the possibility and, rather peremptorily, reject it; Thomas (1860: 23–54), Von Arnim (1929b: 6–8), Elorduy (1939: 18, 65–69), and Helms (1954) all adopt it for *GE*, and Flashar (1965: 235) adopts it for *NE* and *EE*, as Kenny (1992: 141) is also inclined to do.
17. An interesting test case is Mills (1980), where every single difference he notes between *NE* and *EE* can be explained at least as well by difference in audience as by difference in time of composition.
18. Another interesting test case is Kenny (1978, 1992) and his challenge to the view that *EE* is earlier than *NE*, a view that Rowe (1971) considered settled. The arguments of neither scholar prove their respective hypotheses; the most these arguments do is show that the respective hypotheses are compatible with the evidence. But other hypotheses, no less plausible, may claim the same. A dating game thus conducted does not seem very promising.
19. Cf. Kenny (1992: 141) who suggests *NE* was designed "for a less professional audience" than *EE*.
20. These suggestions about the names, it must be stressed, are entirely speculative, for we do not know from ancient sources how any of them arose; see the discussion in Décarie (1978: 17–31).
21. Harlfinger (in Moraux and Harlfinger [1971: 38–50]), who says eleven MSS, out of the twenty we have of *EE*, contain the common books fully written out.
22. The evidence about style is given by Kenny (1978) and about structure by Von Fragstein (1974: 400–403; also 216, 230, 232n). Rowe (1983: 74) seems also now to endorse Kenny's results in this regard.
23. While the common books are closer in style and structure to *EE* than *NE*, their argumentation seems on the whole less compressed than in the rest of *EE*, though of course more compressed than in the rest of *NE*. The common books may be something of a mean between *EE* and *NE*, if closer to *EE*, and not fully comparable to either.
24. Spengel (1841, 1843) thought *EE* to be altogether by Eudemus. See also Natali (2007: 368).
25. Zürcher (1952) is a classic case in point. He wrote a whole book arguing that only about a quarter of the Aristotelian corpus was written by Aristotle; the rest was written by Theophrastus. The thesis has little to support it, but then the other theses that scholars from Jaeger on have favored about the dating and composition of Aristotle's works have also little to support them. See the pointed complaints of Wilpert (1946).
26. As Rowe (1971: 12) wisely remarks.

27. The material contained in this section is a reduced version of what I wrote defending the authenticity of *VV* in an article forthcoming in *Classical Quarterly*.
28. A particular instance is Rowe, who asserts its inauthenticity twice (1971: 9; 2002: 4), without argument and without reference to any scholarship where such argument might be found. See also Kenny (2011: xn1).
29. *Rhetoric* 1.9. The point was made by Gohlke, (1944: 16–18; 1949, 6–7), who defended the authenticity of *VV*, as did also Zürcher (1952: 259).
30. The theory actually adopted by Gohlke, ibid.
31. For example Zeller (1862: 2.2.73n1), Susemihl (1884: xxxi), Stock (1915: xxii–xxiii), Schmidt (1965: 16–21).
32. The first two proposals are from Allan (in Mansion [1961: 303–18, 312n4]) and the third from Dirlmeier (1962: 35–43).
33. Dirlmeier (1962: 35–43), followed by Von Fragstein (1974: 64). Some elements of the lost *Divisions* have perhaps survived; Rose (1863: 679ff.). Kenny (1978: 11) tentatively suggested that the reference was to an appendix containing material excerpted from the *EN*, which, if combined with his other suggestions that the *EN* is an earlier work than the *EE* and in some sense superseded by it, might fit Allan's proposal that *en tois apēllagmenois* means "in the canceled version."
34. *Rhetoric* 1.9 does not fit this description well. It is less full, says little about behavior being rational or irrational, says little about the passions (which are dealt with later and at large in the second book of the *Rhetoric*), and is not in the form of an abstract or separate selection but is an integral part of a larger work. The divisions printed by Rose (1863: 679), which may have an ultimate Aristotelian provenance, lack any indication that the virtues and vices differ by being in accord with or against reason.

Analytical Outline

1

Analytical Outline of Aristotle's *On Virtues and Vices*

Book One: The Science of Happiness

Chapter 1

Introduction to the Science
Worth, Nature, and Questions of This Science. *The pleasantest and the noblest and the best are not three things but one thing: happiness. The study of happiness is about getting it and requires asking what it is found in and how it is acquired: whether it is acquired by nature or learning or practice or divine inspiration or luck, and whether it is found in prudence or virtue or pleasure or all three.*

The man who in Delos before the god gave out his opinion wrote it down on 1214a1
the propylaeum of the temple to Leto's son, setting apart, as not all being found
in the same thing, the good and the noble and the pleasant, in these lines:

> What's justest is noblest; healthy is best; a5
> Most pleasant of all, love's object possess,[1]

but we do not go along with him. For happiness, which is noblest and best
of all, is most pleasant.

Of the many theoretical studies that have something puzzling about them 1214a8
and need examination as regards each thing and each nature, some tend only
to knowledge but others deal with getting and doing the thing. As regards
what is matter merely for theoretical philosophizing, then, we must discuss
what is proper to the study when the right time arrives.[2]

First, however, we must examine what living well is found in and how it is 1214a14
acquired, whether it is by nature that those who happen to be called happy
all become happy (as is the case with those who are big or small or stand out
in complexion), or by learning, supposing there to be a science of happiness,
or by some kind of exercise (for human beings get many things neither in a20
accord with nature nor by learning but by habituation—base things by base
habituation and good by good). Or whether it is in none of these ways but
in one or other of the following two, either as people are smitten by nymphs
and gods—being enthused by the inspiration of some spirit[3]—or by chance
(for there are many who say that happiness and good luck are the same thing). a25
That its presence among men is in all or several or one of these ways is not
obscure. For all comings to be fall more or less under these principles (for
even all doings of thought might be brought together under those of science).

Being happy and living blessedly would be found mainly in the three 1214a30
things that seem most worth preferring. For some say that the greatest

a34

b5

good is prudence, others virtue, and others pleasure. There are also those who argue about the weight these have for happiness, asserting that one or other of them contributes more, prudence being a greater good than virtue for some, virtue than prudence for others, pleasure than both for others. Further, some think happy living comes from all three, others from two, others from some one of them.

Notes

1. Theognis 255.
2. Probably not a reference to anything done within the *EE* but to what the gentleman does in worshipping and contemplating the god; see 8.3 below. Hence "first" in the next line does not mean "first of the things to be done in this treatise" but "first before the right time arrives for theoretical study."
3. The Greek is *daimon*.

Chapter 2

Review of Others' Opinions
Reason for Disputed Opinions about Happiness. *All who are able to choose how to live set up some target of living nobly, as honor or repute or wealth or education. But there is a difference between what living well consists in and what it cannot exist without, and it is this that leads to dispute about what happiness is.*

1214b6

b10

b15

So setting in place that with respect to these things everyone who can live by his own deliberate choice sets up some target of noble living, whether honor or repute or wealth or education, by turning to look at which he will do all that he does (on the supposition that it is a sign of much folly not to order one's life in view of a goal); we must first most of all define within ourself, and not in haste or lightly, which one of the things that are ours living well consists in and which ones it cannot exist among men without. For health and that which health cannot exist without are not the same. This holds in like manner of many other things too, so that neither is living nobly the same as what it is impossible to live nobly without.

1214b17

b20

Among such things some are not private to health nor to life but are, so to say, common to all states and actions (as that without share of breathing or waking or moving, we would have nothing good or bad at all); others of them, which should not be overlooked, are private rather to a particular nature in each case (for eating meat and walks after meals are not related to a good bodily state in the same way as what has just been said). For it is these things that cause

dispute about what being happy is and what it comes to be from, since some b25
think that what it is impossible to be happy without are parts of happiness.

Chapter 3

Which Opinions to Consider. *The opinions of children or the ill or the insane
are not worth examining, nor should the opinions of the many alone be focused
on. But the puzzles proper to the highest way of life and opinions about them
do need discussion, to show by refutation of the opposite what is true, and to
determine what hope there is of acquiring happiness, whether it is a matter of
chance or nature or of one's own effort.*

Now to examine all the opinions that someone or other has had about 1214b28
happiness is to overdo things, for there is much that appears even to small
children and to the ill and to the insane that no one with any sense would
puzzle over (for it is not words that these need but time to develop in the
one case and medical or political punishment in the others; for medication
is punishment no less than a beating). In like manner with these, neither b34
should the opinions of the many (for it is they who speak at random about
almost everything, and especially so) be "searched into about" alone.[1] For it
is absurd to bring reason to bear on those who need not reason but suffering.

Since, though, each undertaking has its own puzzles proper to it, plainly 1215a3
the greatest way of living and the best life must have them too. So to put these
opinions to the test is a noble thing, for the refutations of disputants are proofs
of the statements that oppose them. Not to let such things escape notice is
worth the effort, especially in regard to what all investigation should aim at
(what the sources are for being able to share in living nobly and well—if the a10
term blest living is rather invidious to use), and in regard to what hope there
might be about each of the decent things.

For if living nobly depends on what happens by chance or nature, then most 1215a12
people would have no hope of it (for it is not got hold of by care or by what is
up to them or by their own undertaking). But if it rests on what oneself and
one's deeds are like, then the good would be a thing more common and more a15
divine—more common because something more people can share in, and
more divine because laying down happiness for those who make themselves
and their deeds to be of a certain sort.

Note

1.   Following the Bekker text but putting a parenthesis and not a stop after
     tas tōn pollōn (the [sc. opinions] of the many) at 1214a34, and closing the
     parenthesis after *malista* (most of all) at 1215a1 (cf. the similar position of

kai malista at 7.10.1242a7). Taking also the *peri* (about) that immediately follows *malista* as going with *episkepteon* (should . . . be searched into) to form the nonce word *periepiskepteon* and so regarding *monas* (alone) as in agreement with the object *tas* (the [sc. opinions]), thus giving the sense "should the opinions . . . be 'searched into about' alone." The sentence is sarcastic in tone, and the suggestions here of how to construe it merely serve to heighten the sarcasm, both by the word order (the "most of all" and the "alone" are put, for emphasis, at the end of their respective clauses), and by the nonce word, which, if correct, will be so clearly made up for the occasion that we should perhaps exploit current English usage and put it in scare quotes. Aristotle's barb is aimed at sophists and rhetoricians and demagogic politicians who, to curry favor with their audience, put all their energy and ingenuity into repeated examinations (hence the *periepi* in *periepiskepteon*) and approvals of only popular opinions, which, since the many are most of all guilty of speaking about everything at random, is as silly as examining only the opinions of children or the ill or the insane.

Chapter 4

Summary of Opinions. *Disputes will be clear if it is determined whether happiness is a matter of the soul being of a certain sort or the deeds too. The ways of life people pursue are either those that are concerned with necessities, as the vulgar and mechanical arts and business; or those that are concerned with leisured pastime, as the lives of philosophy and politics, which are about truth and virtue; or the life of indulgence, which is about bodily pleasure and is unable to conceive how the other lives can be happy (as a story about Anaxagoras shows).*

1215a20   Most of the disputes and puzzles will be clear if there be given a noble definition of what one should think happiness to be, whether it is in only being of a certain sort in one's soul, as some of the sages and elders thought, or whether one must both be oneself of a certain sort but, more, one's deeds must be of a certain sort.

1215a25   Since ways of life fall into groups, and since some of these lay claim to being that kind of good time but are pursued as if for the sake of necessities—such as are those that are about the vulgar arts and business and the mechanical arts (I mean by vulgar arts those that people carry on just for glory, by

a30   mechanical arts those that are sedentary and for pay, and by arts of business those that relate to the market and to sales by trading)—while others of them are drawn up with a view to a happiness of cultured pursuits[1] and are three in number (those goods that were also said before to be the greatest possible for

men, virtue and prudence and pleasure);[2] we see that in fact there are three a35
ways of life that those who happen to be in power[3] all choose to live: the life
of politics, the life of philosophy, the life of indulgence.

Of these ways that of philosophy means to be about prudence and the study 1215b1
of truth; that of politics about noble deeds (these are the ones that come from
virtue); that of indulgence about the pleasures of the body (which is why it b5
gives the name happy to someone else, as was also said earlier).[4] Anaxagoras
of Clazomenae,[5] when asked who was happiest, said, "None of those you
are thinking of, but he would look to you an odd sort of fellow." Anaxagoras
answered in this way because he saw his questioner was unable to conceive b10
that it was not someone great and noble or rich who happens to have this
title. He himself, though, perhaps thought that one who lived without pain
and was pure as to justice or who shared in some divine contemplation, that
this man, humanly speaking, was blest.

Notes

1. The Greek is *diagōgē*, which can also carry the idea of a leisure spent in
   cultured pursuits, as it does particularly in *Politics* 5(8).
2. 1.1.1214a30–33.
3. The Greek at 1215a35 is *exousia*, which carries the meaning also of right
   and opportunity and even resources.
4. That is, to someone else other than the one held to be happy by the first
   two, namely to one who indulges in pleasure and not to one endowed with
   virtue. The reference back is to the opening quotation in the first chapter,
   1.1.1214a1–6, and also to the end of that chapter, 1214a30–b6.
5. The famous Pre-Socratic philosopher, 500–428 BC, and friend of Pericles, who had to escape from Athens when prosecuted on a charge of impiety.

Chapter 5

Discussion of Opinions
*The Different Ways of Life. Judging what makes life worth living is not easy,
as many of life's ills make not being born better than being born. The things
people are forced to do and undergo in life are such that even great length of life
would not make living preferable. The same goes for the pleasures of food and
sex, which some animals enjoy more than we, and for the pleasures of sleep,
which is to live like a plant or a child in the womb. In answer to such problems
some say it is the life of philosophy that is worth living, as Anaxagoras did, or
that it is the life of indulgence or that it is the life of noble deeds in politics.*

Now many are the things and different about which a noble judgment is 1215b15
not easy to make, but especially so about a thing that everyone thinks very

easy and for any man to know: what among the things in life to prefer and what, if one got it, would fill one's desire. For much of what happens that people throw away their lives over, as disease, anguish, storms, is such that it is plain the thing to prefer from the start, had someone given us a choice, would be, on account of these things at any rate, not to be born.

b20

1215b22 Add to this the way of life people lead while still children, for no one of good sense would put up with going back to that again. Further, many of the things that have in them neither pleasure nor pain, or have pleasure in them but not a noble one, are such that not to be is better than being alive. On the whole, if one were to bring together everything that everyone does or undergoes, but none of it voluntarily because not for its own sake, and were to add on an endless stretch of time, one would not for all these opt more for life than not life.

b25

1215b30 But not even would the mere pleasure of food or of sex, after taking away the other pleasures that men get from knowing or seeing or any other sense, make anyone put life first, unless he were an utter slave. For it is plain that it would make no difference to someone who made this choice whether he became a man or a beast (the ox in Egypt at any rate, which they honor as Apis, has privileges in more such things than many monarchs).

b35

1216a2 Likewise neither in the case of the pleasure of sleeping. For what is the difference between sleeping unawares from the first day to the last of thousands or any number of years and living as a plant? At any rate plants seem to share some such life, just as also do small children. For these too, on their first coming to be in their mother, go on as things begotten but sleeping the whole time. So it is evident from all this that what is good and well in life escapes us when we look into it.

a5

1216a10 Now Anaxogoras, they say, when someone was raising these sort of puzzles and was asking him why one would prefer coming to be rather than not coming to be, replied "so as to study the heaven and the order of the whole cosmos." So he thought that it was for the sake of knowledge of some sort that the preference for life was honorable. But those who bless Sardanapalus or Smindyrides the Sybarite[1] or some of the rest who live the life of indulgence all appear to line up happiness with enjoyment.

a15

1216a19 Certain others there are who would prefer neither any prudence nor the bodily pleasures rather than the deeds of virtue. Some at least take this option not only for the sake of glory but even if they are not going to be renowned. But the many among politicians do not truly have the title, for they are not politicians in the true sense. For the politician is one who chooses noble deeds for their own sake, but the many take hold of a life like this for the sake of money and getting more for themselves.

a25

1216a27 So from what has been said it is evident that everyone refers happiness to three ways of life: the political, the philosophic, and the indulgent.

How They Deserve Examination. *The pleasures of indulgence need no investigation save as to whether they or some other pleasures belong to the happy life. As for virtue and contemplation, everyone worth talking about attaches them to happiness. Socrates thought that it was enough to know virtue to be virtuous, but this idea holds only of theoretical sciences. Of practical sciences the aim is not to know the thing but to be it, as to be healthy or brave or just, and for this purpose it is necessary to know how the thing comes about and not just what it is.*

Of these ways of life, what the pleasure is that concerns bodies and in- 1216a29 dulgence, and what it is like and what are its sources, are not obscure, so that there is no need to look for what these pleasures are but whether they contribute anything to happiness or not, and how they do so, and whether, if there must be some pleasures attached to living nobly,[2] these ones must be, or whether, while it is necessary to share these in some other way, there a35 are different pleasures that make people think it reasonable that the happy man live pleasantly and not just painlessly. But these things must be investigated later.[3]

First let us study virtue and prudence, both as to what the nature of each 1216a38 of them is and whether they are parts of the good life, either themselves or the deeds that come from them; for even if not everyone attaches them to happiness yet all those men who are worth talking about do.

Now Socrates the elder[4] thought that knowing virtue was the goal, and 1216b2 he used to look for what justice was and what courage and what each of its parts. For he did this reasonably since he thought that all the virtues were b5 knowledges, so that knowing justice and being just happened at the same time. For as soon as we have learnt geometry and house building, we are also house builders and geometers. Hence he used to look for what virtue is but not for how it comes about or from what.

But this is what happens in the case of the theoretical sciences, for the job 1216b10 of astronomy or of natural science or of geometry is nothing other than getting to know and contemplating the nature of the things that are the subjects underlying the sciences (although nothing prevents them being accidentally b15 useful to us for many necessities). Whereas, with the sciences of making, the goal is something other than the science and knowing, for example, health is other than medicine, and good law or some other such thing is other than politics.

Now it is, to be sure, a noble thing to get to know each of the noble things, 1216b19 but yet, as concerns virtue at any rate, it is not knowing what it is that is most honorable but recognizing what it is from. For our wish is not to know what courage is but to be courageous, nor to know what justice is but to be just, in the same way as it is also our wish to be healthy rather than to recognize b25   what being healthy is, and to be in good condition rather than to recognize what being in good condition is.

Notes

1.   Sardanapalus, a mythical king of Assyria, and Smindyrides, from the Greek colony of Sybaris in South Italy, were both noted for their luxury.
2.   Reading at 1216a34 *kalōs* (nobly). If the MSS reading *kalas* is preferred the meaning will be: "if there must be some noble pleasures attached to living."
3.   In Book Six.
4.   The famous Socrates of Plato's dialogues. There was a younger Socrates who appears in the *Theaetetus* and its companion dialogues.

Chapter 6

The Science Proper

The Method. *Arguments must use the phenomena as evidence and cohere with what all men say, or will say if they are led on from the unclear truths they are already familiar with to things better known. The arguments must show the why, as well as the what, but the arguments must be proper to the subject, else one can get caught by empty and irrelevant arguments. One must also judge the conclusion separately from the reason given, both because one should follow the phenomena and because a false reason can yield a true conclusion.*

1216b26   The attempt to seek out something one can trust in all these matters must be done through arguments with the phenomena used as evidence and example. For the greatest thing is that all men be in manifest agreement with what we are about to say, or if not, that they do in a way at least wholly[1] agree

b30   with it, which they will do if they change as they go along. For each of us has some familiarity with the truth, and this must be the source for in some way showing how things are. For from what is said truly but not clearly, we will, as we go forward, also get clarity if we always exchange better known things for the confusions that are usually said.

1216b35   Arguments stated philosophically and not philosophically differ with respect to each method. So one should not think the sort of study to be wasted effort in political things either that manifests not only the what but also the why. For such is what is philosophic as regards every method.

1216b40   But this needs much care. For some there are who, because it appears the part of a philosopher to say nothing at random but to speak with reason, often deceive themselves by stating reasons that are foreign to the subject and empty (which they do sometimes from ignorance and sometimes from

a5   boasting). By these even the experienced and able in action happen to get

14

caught—by those who neither have nor are capable of thought for action or for rule in the arts. They suffer this effect because they are uneducated. For to be uneducated is to be unable to judge, in the case of each thing, what are the reasonings proper to that thing and what foreign to it.

Noble also is it to judge the statement of the reason separately from the 1217a10 thing shown, both because of what was just said—that one should not make everything depend on what comes through arguments but often rather on the phenomena[2] (as it is, when they cannot give a refutation they are compelled to believe what is said)—and because often what seems to have been shown a15 by the argument is true indeed, but not for the reason the argument says. For it is possible to prove a truth from a falsehood; the thing is plain from the *Analytics*.[3]

Notes

1. Such is what the MSS say at 1216b30, but a scholarly emendation, which may be correct, would change wholly (*pantōs*) to all (*pantas*).
2. Or, alternatively at 1217a12–13: "one should not pay attention in everything to what comes through arguments but often rather to the appearances."
3. *Prior Analytics* 2.2.53b7–10, 4.57a37–40.

Chapter 7

The Subject Matter: Happiness
What Happiness Is in General
Happiness Is the Best Thing Doable. *Happiness is the greatest and best of human goods—human because perhaps there is a divine happiness and because the other animals do not share in happiness. Some goods are doable and some are not, or doable only for those who are best. Doable goods are both the end for which things are done and the things that are done, so happiness is the best of things doable by man.*

With this too said as preface, let us speak beginning first from what is said 1217a18 first but, as was stated, not clearly, seeking after a clear discovery of what happiness is. That it is the greatest and best of human goods is agreed. I say human because there might perhaps be a happiness of some other better being as well, of god for instance. For among the other animals, which are worse in nature than human beings, none shares this title in common. For a horse a25 is not happy, nor a bird nor a fish nor any other being, that does not have by its name in nature[1] a share of anything divine, but by some other sharing in goods one of them lives better and another worse.

1217a29   But that this is how things are must be investigated later.[2] As for now let us say that some goods are doable for men and some are not. What I mean is this, that because some beings do not share in change, so neither do they in the goods,[3] and these are perhaps in nature the best. Some goods are doable but doable for things better than us.

1217a35   Since what is doable is said in two ways (both what we do things for the sake of and the things we do for the sake of them share in action, for instance health and wealth we place among things doable as well as the things done for the sake of them, the things of health and the things of business), plainly

a40   happiness too must be set down as best of the things doable by man.

Notes

1.   Or "in its nature." The Greek at 1217a27–28 (*en tēi physei*) is ambiguous as between nature as a whole and the nature of the thing in question. The same ambiguity recurs at 1217a34: "these are perhaps in (their) nature the best."

2.   A reference presumably to the biological works and to Book Six later.

3.   The human goods, that is; a reference back, perhaps, to 1.2.1214b17–24.

Chapter 8

This Best Is Not the Idea or the Common Good. *About the best there are three opinions. The first opinion is that it is the Idea of the Good, which is said to be both the best of goods and cause of the goodness of other things. But this opinion is (i) empty and merely logical; (ii) is of no use for life and action because (a) good is in all the categories, and (b) there is no single science of good in all the categories nor even of the good in one category; (iii) things that are ordered into prior and posterior have no common idea over them; (iv) to make the good eternal or separate does not make it better and prevents it being common; (v) the proof of the good itself is the reverse of what it should be; (vi) the proof that the one is the good because numbers desire it is meaningless and contrary to fact; (vii) there is no one good that all arts aim at, and the good itself is useless and not doable. Likewise as regards the second opinion, that the common good is best, for the common good is (i) neither good, for it would be the good even of a small good, (ii) nor doable, for no art aims at making a good that can be present in anything whatever.*

1217b1   The thing, then, to be examined is what the best is and in how many ways it is said. The best, then, seems to be in three opinions in particular. For they say that the good itself is best of all goods, and that the good itself is that which has belonging to it both that it is first of goods and that it is cause, by

b5   its presence, of the being good of other things. They say that both these (by

16

both these I mean being first of goods and cause, by its presence, of the being good of other good things) belong to the idea. For the good is said truly most of that, for the other things are good by sharing in it and having its likeness; b10 and it is first of goods, for when what is shared in is taken away, the things that share in the idea, which are referred to by their sharing in it, are also taken away, and this is how what is first is related to the later. Consequently the idea of the good is the good itself—for it is also separable, as are also the other ideas, from what shares in it.

To consider this opinion belongs to a time of study both different and of 1217b16 necessity in many respects more a matter of logic, for arguments that are at once destructive and common accord with no other science. But if we must speak briefly about them, we say first that to assert there is an idea not only b20 of the good but of anything else is a logical and empty statement. The matter has been examined in many fashions, both in exoteric discourses and in philosophical ones.[1]

Next, even if the ideas, and an idea of good, exist to the greatest extent 1217b23 possible, surely this is of no use either for a good life or for actions. For good is said in many ways, in fact in as many ways as being is. For being, as has been said elsewhere,[2] signifies the what a thing is, the what it is like, the how much, the when, and, in addition to these, the being changed and the causing change, and good is in each of these cases—in substance, intellect and the b30 god; in the what it is like, the just; in the how much, the due measure; in the when, the right time; about change, the teaching and the taught. So, as being is not something one in the cases mentioned, neither is the good.

Nor is there one science of either being or good. Nay, there is not even 1217b34 one science to study the goods that are said in the same category, as with the right time or the due measure, but one science considers the right time or measure in one case and another science in another. For instance, in the case of food, medicine or gymnastics considers the right time and measure, while in the case of deeds of war it is generalship, and thus another science b40 in the case of another action; hence it can scarcely be one science that studies the good itself.

Further, whatever things have in them the prior and posterior, there is 1218a1 not beyond them any common thing and that a thing separate. For then there would be something prior to the first. For the common and separate is prior because, once the common is taken away, the first is taken away too. a5 For example, if the double is the first of the multiples, it cannot be that the multiple that is commonly predicated be separate. For it will be prior to the double—if the common happens to be the idea, that is, if one were to make the common separate.

For if justice is a good and courage, then there is,[3] they say, some good 1218a9 itself. So the itself is placed as an addition to the common term. And what could this mean other than that it is eternal, that is, separate? But what is white for many days is no more white than what is so for one; consequently neither, then, is the common good the same as the idea, for a common thing is present in everything.

1218a15 They should, also, prove the good itself reverse to the way they now prove it. For now from things agreed to *have* the good, from those things they prove things agreed to *be* good[4]—from numbers that justice and health are good, for these are orderings and numbers, their assumption being that the

a20 good is present in numbers and monads because the one is good itself. But they should prove from what is agreed, as from health, strength, moderation, that in changeless things too the noble exists more, for all these things are order and rest. If so then the latter[5] are more, for they[6] belong to the latter more.

1218a24 Rash too is the proof that the one is the good itself because numbers desire it, for neither are these spoken of in any manifest way as desiring it (but the word is said too simply), and how can one suppose appetite to exist in what does not have life? There is need to deal with this and not assume in any unreasoning way things that even with reason are not easy to believe.

a30 And saying that all beings desire some one good is not true. For each thing has appetite for its own proper good, the eye sight, the body health, and thus other things other goods.

1218a33 That there is not some good itself, then, such are the difficulties. Also that it is not useful for politics but rather some good proper to it is, as is true also of the other arts, good condition, for example, being so for gymnastics. Further, there is what has been written in the discourse,[7] for the form itself of the good is either useful to no art or it is useful to all of them alike. Further, it is not something doable.

1218a38 Nor yet the common good likewise,[8] neither is it good, for it would even be present in a little good, nor doable, for medicine does not undertake to make present what is present to anything whatever but to make health present, and likewise also with each of the other arts.

This Best Is the End. The third opinion is that the best is the end "for the sake of which," something not manifest in changeless things or things that are not doable. The "that for the sake of which" is best, cause of what falls under it, and first (it itself falls under the controlling art of politics). Teaching shows the end is cause of what falls under it, because from the end one proves what is for the end, and no one proves that the end is good. But we must next examine in how many ways the end is the best.

1218b4 But the good is manifold, and there is something of it that is noble and one part is doable and another not doable, and doable is this sort of good, the "that for the sake of which," but it is not the one manifest in changeless things, because it is not the case either that the idea of the good is the good itself that is being looked for—nor is it the common good (for while the first of these is changeless and not doable, the second, while changeable, is not doable). The "that for the sake of which" as end is best and cause of what falls b10 under it and is first of all. So this would be the good itself, the end of things doable for human beings.

This is what falls under the art that controls all arts, and this art is politics 1218b12 and household management and prudence. For these habits differ from others by being of that sort (whether they differ with respect to each other must be stated later.)⁹

That the end is cause of things under it is shown by teaching. For it is by 1218b16 defining the end that people prove about the rest that each of them is good. For the "that for the sake of which" is the cause. For example, since being healthy is this, what is useful for health must be that. But the healthy thing is cause of health as moving cause, and then of the being of health but not of the being good of health.

Further, no one demonstrates that health is a good, unless he is a sophist 1218b22 (for these use extraneous arguments to make sophisms with), and not a doctor, just as no one demonstrates any other principle either.

But as regards the good as end for men and the best of things doable, we 1218b24 must, since this is best, examine in how many ways it is the best of them all, taking after this another beginning.

Notes

1. The reference to philosophical discourses must primarily be to the last two books of the *Metaphysics* but also *Nicomachean Ethics* (*NE*) 1.6; the reference to exoteric discourses will be to the *Great Ethics* (*GE*), 1.1.1183a24–b8, as well as perhaps to others of Aristotle's more popular works now lost.
2. As the *Categories* in particular, but also *GE*, 1.1.1183a5ff.
3. Reading at 1218a10 the *esti toinun* (then there is . . .) of one of the MSS and not the *eti toinun* (further, then . . .) of others and Bekker.
4. There is no need to follow scholars in adding at 1218a16 a "not" to the first occurrence of "agreed" in this sentence, for, if instead one emphasizes the words "have" and "be," then Aristotle's point becomes, not that they should not prove things agreed to be good from things not agreed to be good, but that they should not prove things agreed to *be* good from things agreed to *have* the good, as with proving that justice and health *are* good because they are orderings and numbers and orderings and numbers *have* the good because they have the one which is the good. Rather, from what it is that things agreed to be good *are*, namely order and rest, they should prove that things agreed to *have* order and rest, the changeless things, are good too.
5. That is, the changeless things.
6. That is, order and rest.
7. Possibly a reference to *GE* 1.1.1183a38–b8, or also or instead to *NE* 1.6.1096b35–7a13.

8.   Sc. taken as best. There is a reduplication of negatives in the Greek at 1218a38, the first of which, *oude* (nor yet) refers backward to what has just been said about the idea taken as best, and the second of which, *oute* (neither), refers forward to the next *oute* (nor). Other translations regard the *oude* as redundant or merely emphatic and take the Greek along these lines: "Likewise the common good is neither (the) good itself . . ."

9.   Book 5.8.1141b23–42a11.

Book Two: Virtue in General

Chapter 1

Virtuous Doing Is the Best End

Proof. *Goods are either within or without the soul, and those within the soul, as prudence and virtue and pleasure, are better. In the soul are habits and powers and the like. Virtue is the best habit of that of which there is some work, as of a cloak or a ship or a house, and so also of the soul. The work of the better habit is better. And the work, as being the end, is better than the habit. But work is twofold: a thing beyond the activity, as a house or health, or the activity itself, as seeing or contemplating. A thing's work is the work of its virtue when it is done excellently. The work of the soul is to live, and of the soul's virtue to live virtuously. The same is happiness, for happiness is best and the soul's ends are best. These ends are either the habit or the activity, and the activity is better and the best habit has the best activity. So this activity is best and happiness. But since happiness is something complete, it is activity of complete virtue in a complete life.*

Taking after this another beginning, we must speak about what next fol- 1218b31
lows. All goods, then, are either outside or within the soul, and of these the
ones in the soul are more to be preferred, as we have in fact distinguished in
our exoteric writings.[1] For prudence and virtue and pleasure are in the soul,
and of these either all or some seem to everyone to be the end. Of things within b35
the soul some are habits or powers and others are activities and changes. So
let these points be thus laid down.[2]

About virtue too, that it is the best disposition or habit or power of each 1218b37
thing of which there is some use or work. The thing is plain from induction,
for we make this posit about everything. There is, for example, a virtue of
a cloak, for there is a work and a use to it too; the best habit of a cloak is a
virtue. Likewise too with a ship and a house and everything else. So too with
a soul, for it has a work.

Let also, then, the work of the better habit be better; and as the habits are 1219a6
to each other, let the works from them also be like this to each other. And
of each thing the work is end. It is manifest from this, then, that the work is
better than the habit; for the end, as end, is best. For the best and the last, a10
for whose sake everything else is, was laid down as end.[3] So, then, that the
work is better than the habit and the disposition is plain.

But work is said in two ways. For of some things the work is something 1219a13
else besides the using it, as a house and not the act of building is of the

21

house-building art and health and not the act of making healthy or curing of the medical art; but of other things work is the using, as of the eye seeing and of mathematical science contemplation. So that necessarily, of things whose work is the using, the using must be better than the habit.

1219a18   Having determined these things in this way, then, let us say that the work is of the thing and of its virtue, but not in the same way. A shoe, for example, is the work of the shoemaking art and of the act of shoemaking, so if there is some virtue of shoemaking and of a good[4] shoemaker, its work is a good shoe.[5] The same too with the rest.

1219a23   Further, let a soul's work be making to live and using life and being awake, for sleep is a sort of not working and rest. Consequently, since the work of the soul must be one and the same as the work of its virtue, virtuous life would be virtue's work. This then is the complete[6] good, which was happiness.

1219a28   It is plain from what was laid down—for happiness was the best, but the ends in the soul are in fact the best of goods, and it is either the habit or the activity—that since the activity is better than the condition, and the best activity is of the best habit, and virtue is the best habit, activity of the virtue of[7] the soul is best. But happiness was also the best. Happiness then is activity of a good soul.

1219a35   But since happiness was something complete, and life is both complete and incomplete, and virtue likewise (for virtue is both whole on the one hand and a part on the other),[8] and the activity of incomplete things is incomplete, happiness would be activity of complete life according to complete virtue.

Confirmation of the Proof. *(a) To do well is to live well, which is to be happy, and these are activity; (b) no one is happy for a day or as a child but when he reaches his end, as Solon said; (c) praise and encomia are of deeds; (d) happiness is not praised but felicitated, because other things are praised because of it, and it is the end; (e) the virtuous and the base are not different when asleep because sleep is not activity (which explains why the nutritive soul is not part of virtue, though if there are imaginations in sleep those of the virtuous are better).*

1219a39   That we are nobly stating its genus and its definition is evidenced by what we all think. For doing well and living well are the same as being happy, each of which is a using and activity. I mean living and doing, for the acting art is the using art, for the bronze worker makes the bridle, but the horseman uses it.

1219a4   Also, the fact that a man is not happy for a single day nor a child nor at every age, whence that thing too of Solon is nobly said, not to call a living man happy but when he reaches his end. For nothing incomplete is happy, for it is not whole.

1219b8   Further, praise of virtue is for its deeds, and encomia are of deeds; and those are crowned who win but not those who can win but do not; and a judgment of what someone is like is made from his deeds.

Further, why is happiness not praised? Because the other things are praised 1219b11 because of it, either by leading up to it or by being parts of it. That is why felicitation is different from both praise and encomium. For encomium is speech of the deed done in a particular case, and praise is speech that he is like this in general, but felicitation that it is an end.

Also plain from these things is the puzzle sometimes raised as to why it is 1219b16 that the virtuous are nothing better than the base half their life (for they are all alike when asleep). Reason is that sleep is idleness of soul and not activity. That is also why, if there is some other part of the soul, as the nutritive part, b20 the virtue of this part is not part of whole virtue, just as neither is the virtue of the body. For in sleep the nutritive part is more active, but the perceiving part and the desiring part are incomplete in sleep. But to the extent they share in change in some way,[9] the imaginations of the virtuous are better, except b25 through sickness or injury.

What Happiness Is in Particular
The Content of Happiness
Parts of Soul. *Virtue belongs essentially to the soul and the soul has two parts that share in reason, one by commanding and the other by obeying. Whether these parts are parts or only powers does not matter. Parts of the soul that are natural, as the nutritive or the merely appetitive, and do not share in reason are to be dismissed. There are two kinds of virtue, intellectual and moral (for both are praised), of which the former belongs to the part of the soul that has reason and commands, and the latter to the part without reason that naturally follows the part with reason.*

After this we must study the soul. For virtue is of the soul non-accidentally. 1219b26 Since we are looking for human virtue, let two parts of the soul be laid down that share in reason, though not both sharing in it in the same way but one by commanding and the other by naturally obeying and hearing. But if there is a part that lacks reason in another way,[10] let this part be dismissed.

It matters not if the soul is partible, nor if it is not partible; it yet has dif- 1219b32 ferent powers, that is, the ones mentioned, as the concave and convex on a curve are inseparable from each other and as the straight and the white are, yet the straight is not white except accidentally, nor is it substance of the same.

Also, whatever other part of soul there is, the natural[11] for example, has been 1219b36 separated off, but the above mentioned parts of the human soul are proper (and hence the virtues of the nutritive and appetitive part are not proper) to man.[12] For if he is a man there must be present in him reasoning and rule and action; b40 but reasoning does not rule over reasoning, but over appetite and passions; so he should have these parts too. Also, just as good physical condition is a combination of the virtues part by part, so too is the soul's virtue, insofar as it is end.

1220a4 There are two kinds of virtue, the one moral and the other intellectual (for we praise not only those who are just but also those who are understanding and wise), for virtue, or its work, was laid down as praiseworthy.[13] These do not act, but there are activities of them.

1220a8 Since the intellectual ones are with reason, those of this sort belong to the part that has reason, the part of the soul that, insofar as it has reason, gives commands; while the moral virtues belong to the part that is without reason but that is by nature follower of the part that has reason. For we do not say what someone is like in their moral character because he is wise or clever but because he is mild or bold.

Virtue of Character
In General
What It Is
That It Is Caused by and Does the Best Things. *The search for what moral virtue is and what are its parts must begin from what is true but is not clear and proceed to what is both true and clear. So, the best condition of a thing is brought about by and does the best things, and the same things, differently applied, bring it about and destroy it. Virtue is the sort of condition of soul that is brought about by and does the best in the soul and is brought about by what, differently applied, also destroys it. (Its use is for what increases and destroys it, for which it puts us in the best condition.) A sign is that virtue and vice are about pleasure and pain (for punishments are through pleasure and pain).*

1220a13 After this we must first examine moral virtue, what it is and what parts it has (for this is the point reached), and through what it comes to be. Our
a15 search, then, must be made in the way everyone in other matters makes a search when they have got hold of something, so that we must use what is said truly but not clearly to try and grasp both the true and the clear. For now our hold on things is just as it would be if our hold on health was that it is
a20 the best disposition of the body or that Coriscus[14] is he in the marketplace with the darkest skin; for what each of these two is we do not know, yet our having this hold on it is of help for knowing what each of the two is of it.

1220a22 So let there be laid down first that the best disposition is brought about by the best things and that best things are done in the case of each thing from each thing's virtue. For example, best toils and diet are what good physical condi-
a25 tion comes from, and people toil best from good physical condition. Further, every disposition is brought about and is destroyed by the same things when these are brought to bear on it in some way, as health is brought about and is destroyed by diet and toils and seasons. The thing is plain from induction.

1220a29 Virtue also, then, is the sort of disposition that is brought about by the best movements in the soul and from which the best works and passions of the soul are done, and by the same things it is in one way brought to be and

24

in another way destroyed. (Its use is for the things by which it is increased and destroyed, for which it puts us in the best disposition.)

A sign is that virtue and vice are about things pleasant and painful; for 1220a34 punishments, which are cures and, as in other things, come about through opposites, are through these.

Notes

1. Likely a reference to *GE*, in particular 1.3.1184b1ff., but also to 1.2–3 more generally.
2. Marking a stop at 1218b37 after *hypokeisthō* (let be laid down), following Dirlmeier (1962: 221).
3. In the concluding section of the last chapter of the previous book, 1.8.1218b4–27.
4. The Greek at 1219a22 is *spoudaios*, which has the literal meaning of serious but is typically used as the adjective for virtue, to mean virtuous or good or excellent; cf. Dirlmeier (1962: 224).
5. An alternative way of translating this clause would be: ". . . if there is some virtue of shoemaking, then the work of a good shoemaker is a good shoe," as in Kenny (2011: 15, 155).
6. The Greek of the MSS at 1219a28 is actually *pleon* (full) and *teleon* (complete) is Bekker's plausible emendation. *Teleon* is from *telos* (end) meaning complete in the sense of final or fully reaching the end.
7. Accepting the emendation of the MS *energeia ē* (activity or) to *energeian*.
8. An alternative translation of the Greek at 1219a37 would be: "for the one is whole and the other is part," where "the one" and "the other" will refer to life or virtue, respectively. The sense will be that if the whole can be complete or incomplete and it is made up of parts, then the parts can be complete and incomplete as well.
9. Accepting at 1219b24 Casaubon's emendation of *mē* (not) to *pēi* (in some way).
10. As the nutritive part, just mentioned in the previous paragraph.
11. Victorius' plausible scholarly emendation at 1219b37 would change "natural" (*physikon*) into "vegetative" (*phytikon*). But natural can make sense here if it is taken as contrasting with rational.
12. Punctuating the Greek at 1219b38–39 as in the English translation.
13. Earlier in this chapter, 2.1.1219b8ff.
14. Coriscus of Scepsis was a student of Plato's and a friend of Aristotle's. Aristotle uses the name frequently in his writings to designate indefinitely some person or other, in the way we use the name John Doe.

Chapter 2

That It Is an Acquired Habit. *Moral virtue is moral character, as its name signifies, and comes about through custom. It is a quality in accord with reason that belongs to the part of the soul that can follow reason. The division in the abstracts of passions and powers and habits illustrates the qualities in the passions as well as the habits. Passions are things like spirit and fear. Powers are that whereby people are active with their passions, as being angry or erotic or shameless. Habits are that whereby the passions and powers accord with reason or not, as courage and cowardice.*

1220a38　That moral virtue, then, is about things pleasant and painful is plain. But since one's moral character, as its name also signifies, because it gets

b1　its increase from custom[1] and because what is under a guidance not innate gets to have a custom by being changed repeatedly a certain way, is now in this way the activating part (which we do not see in lifeless things, for even if you threw a stone upward ten thousand times it will never not do this by force), therefore let a moral character be this, a quality of soul in accord with a reason in command of a being-able to follow reason.

1220b6　We must say, then, what qualities in accord with what in the soul moral characters are. They will be in accord with the powers of the passions (in accord with which people are spoken of as passionate) and in accord with the habits (in accord with which people are spoken of with respect to these passions by feeling them in a certain way or not feeling them).

1220b10　After this there is the division, in the selected abstracts,[2] of passions and powers and habits. I mean by passions such things as these, spirit, fear, shame, desire, things generally that are for the most part essentially followed by a perceptible pleasure or pain. And according to these there is no quality but

b15　there is active feeling. There is quality, however, according to powers. I mean by powers things according to which people are said to be active with respect to their passions, as the angry person, the un-irked person, the erotic person, the shame-faced person, the shameless person. Habits are all those things that are cause of these[3] being either in accord with reason or the opposite,

b20　such as courage, temperance, cowardice, license.

Notes

1.　The Greek for moral character is *ēthos* and for custom *ethos*, so that the two words differ only by a slight change in their first letter.

2.　The Greek at 1220b11 is problematic. The MSS have either *apēllagmenois* or *apēlegmenois* (a misspelling perhaps for *apeilegmenois*), the first of which means something like "in the things released or separated off" and the second "in the things picked out or selected." The first looks like a reference to a set of abstracts and the second to a set of selections (hence the combined translation of "selected abstracts"). The reference in either case would seem to be to *On Virtues and Vices* (*VV*), which is precisely such an abstract or selection of passions and powers and habits, or also or instead to Aristotle's lost work *Divisions* (some elements of which have perhaps survived; Rose [1863: 679ff.]).

3.　Sc. the powers or the passions or both.

Chapter 3

That It Is a Mean. Everything continuous and divisible has an excess, a defect, and a mean, and action is something continuous. The mean with respect to us is best and makes the best habit, for opposites destroy each other and the mean is opposite to both extremes, so that virtue must be a mean. The kind of mean is to be studied from the table showing the excesses on either side: as angriness is excess and not being annoyed defect in anger; rashness excess and cowardice defect in fears; license excess and insensibility defect in desires; gain excess and loss defect in takings; boasting excess and self-deprecation defect in making claims for oneself; flattery excess and hostility defect in praising; luxury excess and passivity to ill defect in suffering pain; vanity excess and smallness of soul defect in thinking oneself worthy; prodigality excess and illiberality defect in expenses; shabbiness defect and extravagance excess in what is fitting; unscrupulousness excess and simpleness defect in where one takes more from for oneself; envy excess and something nameless defect in pain at prosperity. That these things are essentially and not accidentally such goes without saying. The passions fall into kinds too according to time or amount or causes, as those who feel anger too quickly or too much or keep it too long or inflict too great punishment, and so also with passions of eating. But some passions are bad by themselves, as adultery and wanton violence, and not by amount.

Having made these distinctions, we must grasp the fact that in every 1220b21 continuous and divisible quantity there is an excess and a deficiency and a mean, and these relative either to each other or to us, as in gymnastics, in medicine, in house building, in helmsmanship, and in any action whatever, whether scientific or unscientific and whether artful or un-artful (for change b25 is continuous and action is change). In all of them, the mean relative to us is best, for this is the way science and reason command. And everywhere this is also what makes the best habit. This indeed is plain from induction and b30 argument. For opposite things destroy each other, and the extremes are opposite both to each other and to the mean. For the mean is either to either, as that the equal is greater than the less but less than the greater. Consequently, moral virtue must be about certain means and be a certain mean state.

We must grasp, then, what sort of mean state virtue is and what sort of 1220b35 means it is about. So, for example's sake, let us take and study each item from the outline:

Angriness	Dullness to Pain	Mildness[1]	
Rashness	Cowardice	Courage[2]	
Shamelessness	Shamed Shyness	Shame	a1

License	Insensibility	Temperance[3]
Envy	(nameless)	Righteous Indignation
Gain	Loss	Justice[4]
Prodigality	Illiberality	Liberality[5]
Boasting	Self-Deprecation	Truth
Flattery	Hostility	Friendliness
Fawning	Disagreeableness	Dignity
Softness	Passivity to Ill	Endurance
Vanity	Smallness of Soul	Magnanimity[6]
Extravagance	Shabbiness	Magnificence
Unscrupulousness	Simpleness	Prudence[7]

(a5, a10 markers appear in left margin beside Prodigality and Vanity rows respectively)

1221a13   These and suchlike passions happen to souls,[8] and all are said either by being excessive or deficient. For he is angry who gets angry more and quicker than he should and with more people than he should, and he dull to pain who is deficient both as regards whom and when and how. Also he is rash who neither fears what he should nor when nor how, and he coward who fears both what he should not and when he should not and how he should not.

a20   Likewise too he is a licentious man who is desirous and goes to excess in everything he can, and he is insensible who falls short and does not even have desire for as much as is better and is in accord with nature but is unfeeling like a stone. He is gainer who takes more for himself from every place, and he loser who takes from no source or from few. He is boastful who pretends

a25   to more than he has and he self-deprecatory who pretends to less. He is a flatterer who joins more in praise than is fine and he hostile who praises less. And fawning is being too much for pleasure while disagreeableness is being little so and scarcely.

1221a28   Further, he who puts up with no pain, not even if it is better, is soft, and he who puts up with every pain alike is simply speaking nameless but by transfer of words he is called stiff and hardened and wretched. He is vain who thinks himself worthy of greater things and he small-souled of less. Further, he is prodigal who is excessive in every expense and he illiberal who is deficient in every expense. Likewise with the shabby and the swaggerer, for the latter

a35   exceeds what is fitting and the former falls short of what is fitting. And the unscrupulous man is a taker of more for himself in every way and from every place, but the simple man not even from where he should. He is envious who is pained by more cases of prosperity than he should be (for even those who deserve to do well cause pain, by doing well, to the envious man). The opposite

a40   is rather lacking in a name but is he who exceeds in not being pained, not even at the well-doing of the unworthy, but is easygoing (like gluttons with respect to their food), while the other is harsh in his envy.

That things are not accidentally thus in each case is superfluous to define, for no science, whether theoretical or productive, either speaks or acts by making this an additional determination, but this is directed against the arts of sycophancy in logic. So let things be determined simply in this way but more accurately when we come to speak about the contrasting habits.[9] 1221b3

Of these affections[10] themselves kinds are named from differences in respect of excess either of time or of more or in relation to one of the things that produce the passions. I mean for instance that a man is quick-tempered by feeling the passion quicker than he should, and hard and spirited by feeling it more than he should, and bitter by preserving his anger, and a brawler and an abuser by retaliations from anger. Gourmands and gluttons and wine bibbers are so-called because their power of passion for indulgence in the respective food of each is opposed to reason. 1221b9 b15

One should not fail to notice that some of the things mentioned are not in how one takes them if how they are taken is by having the passion more. For instance, one is not an adulterer by consorting with married women more than one should (for one is not, but this is a kind of wickedness). For the passion is spoken of when both it and one's being such are taken together;[11] and likewise with wanton violence.[12] That is why people also protest, saying, in the one case, that they had intercourse but denying that it was adultery (they did it in ignorance or were forced), and, in the other case, that they did strike but not in wanton violence. So too in other such cases. 1221b18 b20 b25

Notes

1.   *VV* 4.1250a39ff., 6.1251a4ff.
2.   *VV* 4.1250a44ff., 6.1251a10ff.
3.   *VV* 4.1250b6ff., 7.1251b16ff.
4.   *VV* 5.1250b15ff., 7.1251a30ff.
5.   *VV* 5.1250b24ff., 7.1251b4ff.
6.   *VV* 5.1250b34ff., 7.1251b16ff.
7.   *VV* 4.1250a30ff., 6.1250b43ff.
8.   *VV* 8.1251b26ff.
9.   Book Three.
10.   The Greek at 1221b10 is *pathēmata*, which is cognate with *pathē*, the usual word for passions.
11.   That is, one is called an adulterer just by having a passion for adultery, no matter how much.
12.   The Greek at 1221b23 is *hubris*, which can also carry the connotation of rape.

Chapter 4

That It Concerns Pleasures and Pains. Moral virtue is in the desiring part of the soul and hence moral character is good or bad by the pleasures and pains it pursues or flees. The divisions of passions, powers, and habits make the point plain. That moral virtue is about pleasures and pains is also plain, because these are what make the soul better or worse, because people are base by pursuing or fleeing these wrongly, and because everyone's ready definition is that virtue is a state of rest about pleasures and pains and vice the opposite.

1221b27   Having grasped these things, we must say after this that since there are two parts to the soul, and since the virtues are divided according to these parts, and since those belonging to the part that has reason are intellectual
b30   virtues (whose work is truth, whether about how things are or about coming to be), and since the other virtues belong to the part that lacks reason but possesses appetite (for not any part whatever of the soul, if the soul is divisible, has appetite), then necessarily moral character is base and virtuous
b35   by pursuing and fleeing certain pleasures and pains. This is plain from the divisions[1] of the passions and powers and habits, for the powers and habits are of the passions, and the passions are distinguished by pain and pleasure.

1221b37   Consequently, because of this, and because of the positions laid down before,[2] it happens that every moral virtue is about pleasures and pains. For by what sort of things any soul naturally tends to become worse and better, in
b40   respect of those things and about those things is its pleasure found. And we say that people are base because of pleasures and pains, by pursuing and fleeing either those they should not or as they should not. That is why everyone has ready to hand as a definition that the virtues are a state of unfeeling and rest
a5   with respect to pleasures and pains, and that the vices are from the opposites.[3]

Notes

1.   Another likely reference to *VV*.
2.   Probably a reference to 2.1.1220a22–37.
3.   Cf. *VV* 8.1251b26–28, 37.

Chapter 5

That the Mean Is Not a Middle. Since virtue is that whereby people do the best and this is what accords with right reason and is a mean, the mean will be in pleasures or pains or both. The extremes are opposite to each other and the mean, but sometimes one extreme is more manifest than the other because further from the mean, as toil and abstinence are closer to health than no toil and indulgence, so that the latter seem to be the opposites. In the soul the extreme that is opposite is what we or the many err more toward and the other happens too little to be noticed, as anger is opposite to mildness, and few fall into the extreme of no anger.

Since virtue is laid down as the sort of habit from which people do the 1222a6 best things and according to which they are most well-disposed with respect to the best, and since what accords with right reason is both best and most well, and since this is the mean between excess and deficiency relative to us, necessarily would moral virtue in every case as such be a mean state, a10 or about certain means, in pleasures and pains and in pleasant and painful things. The mean state will sometimes be in pleasures, for so also are excess and deficiency, and sometimes in pains, and sometimes in both. For he who goes to excess in feeling joy goes to excess in the pleasant, and he who does a15 so in feeling pain does so in the opposite, and either simply so or with respect to some definite mark (for example, when not in the way the many do; the good man does as one should).

Since there is a habit by which he who has it will be of the sort on the one 1222a17 hand to accept the excess and on the other the deficiency of the same thing, necessarily, since these things are opposite to each other and to the mean, the habits must also be opposite in this way to each other and to the virtue.

It happens, however, that sometimes all the contrasts are rather manifest, 1222a22 sometimes those that go to excess, and at other times those that are deficient. Reason for the difference is that there is not always the same degree of inequality or likeness with respect to the mean, but a transition to the mean a25 habit may be quicker sometimes from the excess and sometimes from the deficiency, to which he who is further off seems more opposed. In the case of the body too, for example, excess in toil is healthier than deficiency and nearer the mean, while deficiency in food is healthier than excess, so that habits of a30 choice favoring physical exertion will favor health more as they accord with each preference: those who toil more being so here and those who are more restrained being so there, and the one who does not toil, and not both,[1] being here opposed to the mean and to what reason says, and there he too who is a35 indulgent and not he who goes hungry. This happens because our nature from the start is not at like distance from the mean in all cases, but we favor toil less and indulgence more.

Things are similar as regards the soul too, and we set as opposites[2] the habit 1222a38 that we and that the many err more toward, while the other is not noticed as if nonexistent, because its rarity makes it imperceptible. For example, anger is opposite to mildness and the angry man to the mild man, and yet there is b1 an excess also in the direction of being gentle and accommodating and not getting angry when hit, but few people are like this and everyone's bias is more toward the former (which is also why spirit is not a flatterer).

Summary. *The collection of habits and passions and the excesses and defects and the mean (which accords with right reason) make plain that virtues and vices are about extremes of pleasures and pains. But the best habit is the mean, so virtues are mean states.*

1222b4 But now that the collection of habits as regards each of the passions has been grasped, and the excesses and the deficiencies of the opposing habits too which people are in accord with when they are in accord with right reason (what right reason is, and what the mark is that, by looking off to, we should assert the mean, must be examined later[3]), it is manifest that all of the moral

b10 virtues and vices concern excesses and deficiencies of pleasures and pains, and that pleasures and pains arise from the stated habits and passions. But the best habit is the one that is the mean in each case. So it is plain that the virtues, either all or some of them,[4] will belong to mean states.

Notes

1. That is, both extremes (both he who avoids toil and he who toils too much).
2. That is, opposites to the mean. Reading at 1222a39 *enantia* (opposites) with the MSS and not *enantian* (opposite [habit]) with Bekker.
3. In Book Five.
4. A reservation, perhaps, in favor of justice, which is about a mean (the equal between gain and loss) but is not a mean state between two vices (for while he who takes more is unjust, he who takes or has less is not unjust but a victim of injustice).

Chapter 6

Through What It Comes to Be
That Man Is Voluntary Cause of Actions and Habits. *All substances are naturally principles and generate after their kind, as men men and animals animals. Man is also principle of actions. Principles that are cause of change are controlling principles, but principles without change, as in mathematics, are not (except by a certain likeness), and man is cause of change. If the principle changes, so does all that follows from it (as with triangles and quadrilaterals). So if some things change, their principles too must change; and man is principle of many such things, as of what he does and makes. Virtue and vice and the works they produce are praised and blamed and thus are about things where men are cause and principle. Men are cause and principle of what they do voluntarily and by choice, so virtue and vice are voluntary.*

Let us take, then, another beginning for our advancing investigation. So all 1222b15
substances are naturally principles, hence also each of them is able to generate
many things of like sort, for example a man generates men and generally an
animal generates animals and a plant plants. Additionally man, alone among
animals, is a principle of certain actions too (for we would not say that any
of the other animals acts).

All principles such as to be source whence changes first result are called 1222b20
controlling principles, and those most justly so from which there is no possibility of being otherwise (which is perhaps the principle the god rules by).
In the case of unchanging principles, as in mathematics for example, the element of control is not found, though by a likeness it is at least said to be, for b25
there too, if the principle changed, all the conclusions proved from it would
alter very greatly (but they do not cause themselves to alter if one of them
is assumed under the other, except by assuming the hypothesis and proving
through that). Man is a principle of change of a sort. For action is change.

Since, as in other things, the principle is cause of the things that exist and 1222b29
come to be because of it, we must think of it the way we do in demonstrations. For if, when the triangle has two right angles, the quadrilateral must
have four, clearly the cause of this is that the triangle has two right angles.
But if the triangle changes there must be change in the quadrilateral too—for b35
example, if three, six, and if four, eight—and if there is no change in it, but it
is of the sort it is, the former must be of the sort it is too.

That what we are maintaining is necessary is plain from the *Analytics*[1] (but 1222b37
now it is not possible either to deny or to affirm accurately more than this
much, for if nothing else is cause of the triangle being as it is, this would be b40
principle and cause of what comes after). Consequently if some of the things
that are can be in the opposite state, their principles also must be of that
sort, for the outcome of things by necessity is necessary but the outcomes of a1
these can be opposites. And men possess, in respect of what is up to them,
many such opposites, and of such opposites are they principle. So it is clear
that man can come to be or not[2] as regards all actions he is principle of and a5
controls, and that it is up to him whether at least those actions, whose being
and not being he has control of, come to be or not. But all things where it is
up to him to produce or not to produce, these things he is cause of; and all
he is cause of, up to him.

Since virtue and vice and the deeds they are the source of are some 1223a9
praiseworthy and others blameworthy (for they are blamed and praised), not
because of things that obtain by necessity or chance or nature but because of
what we ourselves are causes of (for what someone else is cause of, he gets
the blame and the praise for), it is plain that virtue and vice are about things
where one is oneself cause and principle of actions.

We must grasp, then, what sort of things those are where one is one- 1223a15
self cause and principle of actions. Now we all agree that whatever is

voluntary and accords with each man's choice he is cause of. But whatever is involuntary he is not cause of, and whatever he does having chosen to, he plainly also does voluntarily. Plainly, then, virtue and vice would be of things voluntary.

Notes

1. *Posterior Analytics* 1.1.
2. Sc. come to be active. Taking at 1223a5 "man" and not "actions" to be the subject of *ginesthai*.

Chapter 7

The Voluntary and the Involuntary

That They Are Not According to Appetite. *The voluntary would seem to be in accord with appetite or choice or thought, and the involuntary the opposite. Appetite is will or spirit or desire. It is not with desire because, on the one hand, the involuntary is forced and painful but desire is pleasant and so voluntary, and also the incontinent man is unjust and acts by desire and injustice is voluntary, so acting by desire is voluntary; but, on the other hand, to act voluntarily is to do what one wants, and the incontinent man does by desire what he does not want, so he acts involuntarily; and also the continent man is just, and acts against desire and justice is voluntary, so he acts voluntarily; so they act voluntarily and involuntarily at the same time, which is impossible. It cannot be spirit for the same reason, since continence and incontinence are in spirit as well as desire, so that what is done by spirit will in the same way be voluntary and involuntary at the same time. Hence, if this is impossible, the will more than either spirit or desire must be voluntary. But it cannot be will because the incontinent man is unjust and does what he does not want, but injustice is voluntary, so if will is voluntary, incontinence makes a man not unjust, which is impossible.*

1223a21   We must grasp, then, what the voluntary and the involuntary are and what choice is. First, since virtue and vice are defined with them, we must examine the voluntary and involuntary. So, they would seem to be one of these three things, either in accord with appetite or with choice or with thought, the voluntary being in accord with one of these and the involuntary contrary to one of them; but, further, appetite is divided into three things: will and spirit and desire. Consequently these[1] must be divided, and first in accord with desire.

1223a28   It would seem that all that is in accord with desire is voluntary. For the involuntary all seems to be forced and the forced painful, and all that men do or suffer under necessity, as even Evenus[2] says:

Every forced thing is by nature grievous

so that if something is painful it is forced and if forced painful. But what is against desire is all painful, for desire is of the pleasant, so that it is forced and involuntary. What is in accord with desire, then, is voluntary, for these are opposites to each other.

Further, all wickedness makes one more unjust, and incontinence seems 1223a36 to be wickedness. But the incontinent man is such as to act according to desire against calculation, and he is incontinent whenever he acts according to it; and acting unjustly is voluntary; so that the incontinent man will act b1 unjustly by acting according to desire. He will act voluntarily, then, and what accords with desire will be voluntary; for it is odd indeed if they who become incontinent will be more just. So from these considerations it would seem that what is according to desire is voluntary.

But from the following considerations it would seem that it is the opposite. 1223b4 For everything that someone does voluntarily he does wanting to do it, and what he wants to do he does voluntarily. But no one wants to do what he thinks is bad. But the incontinent man does not do what he wants, for to be incontinent is to do because of desire the opposite of what one thinks best. The same man, then, will turn out to be acting voluntarily and involuntarily at the same time. But this is impossible.

Further, the continent man will do what is just, and more so than inconti- 1223b10 nence will. For continence is a virtue, and virtue makes people more just. But one is continent when one acts contrary to desire in accord with calculation. Consequently if doing what is just is voluntary, as doing wrong is too (for both b15 these seem to be voluntary and, necessarily, if one of the two is voluntary, the other is as well), but acting against desire is involuntary,[3] then the same man will do the same thing at the same time voluntarily and involuntarily.

The same argument applies to spirit too, for incontinence and continence 1223b18 seem to be also about spirit, just as about desire too. Also, what is contrary to spirit is painful, and being held in check is forced, so that if the forced is involuntary,[4] that which accords with spirit would all be voluntary. In fact Heracleitus seems to have his eye on the strength of spirit when he says that holding it back is painful. "For it is hard," he says, "to fight with spirit; for it buys with its soul."[5] But, if it is impossible for the same thing to do at the b25 same time things voluntary and involuntary in regard to what accords with the same part of the thing, what is in accord with will, more than what is in accord with desire and spirit, will be voluntary.

But here is a sign: we do many things voluntarily without anger or desire. 1223b27 So it remains to examine whether the willed and the voluntary are the same. But it appears that this too is impossible. For we laid it down and it appears b30 that wickedness makes people more unjust, but incontinence appears to be a certain wickedness. But the opposite will result. For no one wants the things he thinks are bad, but he does do them when he becomes incontinent. If then doing wrong is voluntary, but the voluntary is what accords with will, when he becomes incontinent he will no longer be doing wrong but will be more just than before he became incontinent. But this is impossible.

1223b36   That the voluntary is not acting according to appetite, then, nor the involuntary acting against appetite, is manifest.

Notes

1. Probably a reference back to all the things mentioned and not just to the three kinds of appetite.
2. Poet and philosopher from the island of Paros and an older contemporary of Socrates.
3. This statement appeared earlier in the first argument on the other side, at 1223a33–35.
4. This statement, or at least its converse, also appeared in the first argument on the other side, at 1223a29–30.
5. Frag. 85. Heracleitus is the famous Pre-Socratic philosopher of the sixth century BC from Ephesus.

Chapter 8

That They Are Not According to Choice. *We do things voluntarily when willing (and also when not willing) and we do suddenly many things when willing, but no one chooses suddenly.*

1223b38   That the voluntary is not according to choice either is again clear from the following. For it was proved that what is according to will is not involuntary but rather all that is willed is in fact voluntary (but this has alone been shown, that it is possible also when not willing to act voluntarily). But we do suddenly many things when willing and no one chooses anything suddenly.

That They Are According to Thought
Force
Impulse and Reason and Appetite. *So the voluntary must accord with thought in some way. But force must be examined too as being akin to the subject. Force and necessity oppose both the voluntary and persuasion, and are found in lifeless things when they undergo something against their natural impulse, as a stone being carried upward, and also in animals. Things are more complex where reason and appetite, which need not agree, are involved. The continent man forces himself against appetite, and the incontinent man against calculation, yet the latter acts with pleasure and the former with persuasion, both of which are voluntary. The solution is that here the impulse is from within, not from without, and so it is not by force. Also, both are in pain as well as in*

pleasure (pleasure or pain in the present act and pain or pleasure in future expectation), so that they seem to be forced as going against an inner impulse. But this is only true of a part of their soul and not the whole, which does act voluntarily, because calculation and desire are each natural and so both act according to nature, though a different nature.

If one of these three things must be the voluntary, either in accord with appetite or with choice or with thought, and it cannot be two of these, what is left is that the voluntary lies in acting with thought in some way. But let us take the argument a little further still and put an end to our determination of the voluntary and the involuntary. For it seems that doing something by force and not by force is akin to what has been said. For the forced is involuntary and the involuntary is, we say, all forced. Consequently we must first examine the forced, what it is and how it relates to the voluntary and involuntary. 1224a4 a10

So it seems that the forced and the necessary, and force and necessity, are opposed to the voluntary and to persuasion in the case of people acting. The forced and the necessary we universally assert also of lifeless things, for we say that a stone is carried upward and fire downward by force and under compulsion. But when they are carried according to their nature and their own impulse, they are not said to be forced, nor indeed are they said to be voluntary, but the opposed state is nameless; and when they are carried contrary to it, we say they are forced. Likewise in the case of living things and in the case of animals we see that they suffer and do many things by force, whenever something from outside moves them contrary to their impulse within. 1224a13 a20

In lifeless things the principle is simple, but in living things it is multiple. For appetite and reason do not always go together. Consequently, in the case of the other animals, what is forced is simple as in the case of lifeless things (for they do not have reason and an opposed appetite but they live by appetite). In men, however, both are present—at a certain age, that is, the age to which we also attribute action; for we do not say that a child acts (nor that a beast does), but when he is already acting through calculation. 1224a23 a25

So it seems that everything forced is painful, and no one acts by force and with joy. That is why there is very great dispute about the continent and the incontinent man. For it is when he has impulses opposed to himself that each acts, so that the continent man, they say, drags himself off from pleasant desires by force (for he is in pain dragging himself off against the opposing appetite), and the incontinent man drags himself off against calculation by force. But he seems to suffer pain less. For desire is of the pleasant, which he follows with enjoyment, so that the incontinent man is more voluntary and not under force because he is not in pain. But persuasion is opposed to force and necessity, and the continent man drives toward what he is persuaded of 1224a30 a35 b1 and proceeds not by force but voluntarily, but desire drives without having persuaded, for it does not share in reason.

1224b2 That these alone, then, seem to act by force and involuntarily and for what reason, namely because of a certain likeness to what is forced (a likeness in accord with which we also speak of lifeless things), has been stated. Nevertheless if one adds here too the additional element lying in the definition, what is said is solved. For whenever something from without sets a thing in motion or brings it to rest contrary to its inner impulse, we say this is by force, and whenever not, not by force. In the continent and incontinent man his own impulse present within is what draws him (for he has both), so that neither b10 is forced, but each would, for this reason at any rate, act voluntarily and not under necessity. For we call necessity the principle from without that either stops him or sets him in motion contrary to his impulse, as if one were to take another's hand, who was resisting both in will and desire, and strike someone with it. But when the principle is within, it is not by force.

1224b15 Since, also, both pleasure and pain exist in both—for the continent man is pained when he is already acting against appetite, and he is enjoying the pleasure of hope that he will be later advantaged, or that he is being already advantaged, by being healthy, and the incontinent man too rejoices when, by b20 being incontinent, he gets what he has an appetite for, but is pained by pain from hope, for he thinks he is doing a bad thing—so that to say each of the two of them is doing something by force has reason behind it, as well as that each of them sometimes acts involuntarily because of desire and because of calculation, for each of these two, being separate things, is beaten out by the b25 other. Hence people transfer it to the whole soul as well, because they see something of the sort among things in the soul. Now it is possible to say this of the parts, but the whole soul of both the incontinent and the continent, being voluntary, is what is acting. Neither of the two acts by force, except for some part in them (since in fact we naturally have both parts).

1224b29 For, also, reason, being by nature ruler when generation is still being allowed and is not maimed, will be present within, as well as desire, because at once it follows and is present from birth. By these two things pretty much we define what is by nature, by whatever follows on us all as soon as we come to be and by whatever happens in us after coming to be has been allowed to proceed straight on, as gray hair and old age and other things of the sort. Consequently each of the two does not act according to nature, though simply each does act according to nature, a nature not the same.

1224b36 Now the puzzles about the continent and incontinent man are about whether both or one of them acts by force, so that either they do not act voluntarily, or they act by force and voluntarily at the same time and, if what is forced is involuntary, they act voluntarily and involuntarily at the same a1 time. But it is pretty much plain from what has been said how we must meet these puzzles.

Threats and Passion and Argument. *Force also refers to doing something under threat of greater evil. But this is voluntary since one can refuse and suffer the evil; or the end one does the thing for is voluntary but not the thing one does itself, which instead is by force. Passions of love or of spirit, or natural things, or strong pain, can also be by force if they are too great for nature to bear. The same can be true of enthusiasm and prophecy and passion and argument if they are too strong for us.*

Also in another way, although reason and desire are not out of harmony, 1225a2 people are said to act by force and under necessity, when they do what they suppose to be painful and base but there are floggings and imprisonments and deaths if they do not do it. For they say that they did this under compulsion. Or is this not so but they all do voluntarily this thing itself, for they are able not to do it but to abide the former suffering?

Further, perhaps one might say it is so in some of these cases but not in oth- 1225a8 ers. For as to all such things as must be up to oneself whether they are or are not, everything one does that one does not wish one does voluntarily and not by force. But as to all such things as are not up to oneself, one does them by force in a way though not at any rate simply so, because one does not choose the thing itself that one does but what one does it for—since there are differences here too.

For if one kills someone to stop him catching one in a game of blind man's 1225a14 bluff,[1] it would be ridiculous to say one did it by force and under necessity. On the contrary, there needs to be a greater and more painful evil that one will suffer if one does not act. For being thus under necessity and not under necessity,[2] one will act by force, or not by nature, when one does an evil for the sake of a good or for release from a greater evil—yes, and involuntarily, for these things are not up to oneself.

That is why many lay down that love too is involuntary, as well as some 1225a19 cases of spirit and natural things, because they are strong and beyond nature. We are even forgiving, supposing them naturally able to force nature. Also, one would seem more to be acting by force and involuntarily to avoid a strong pain than a mild one and, on the whole, to avoid pain than to avoid enjoyment.[3] For that which is up to oneself—and it wholly turns on this—is a25 what one's nature is able to bear. But that which one's nature is not able to bear, and which does not by nature belong to one's appetite or calculation, is not up to oneself.

Hence, as regards those in a state of enthusiasm and prophecy, even though 1225a27 they are doing a work of thought, nevertheless we deny that it is up to them either to say what they say or to do what they do. But neither do they do it a30 because of desire. Consequently certain thoughts, as well as passions, or the actions in accord with such thoughts and calculations, are not up to us but, as Philolaus[4] said, some reasons are too strong for us. Hence, if it was necessary to examine the voluntary and involuntary in relation also to the forced, let it a35   be thus distinguished (for these, as cases of acting by force but voluntarily, are getting most in the way of the voluntary).[5]

Notes

1.   The Greek at 1225a14 is literally "that he not catch him when feeling for him" (*psēlaphōn*), which is likely a reference to blind man's bluff or something similar.

2.   Inserting at 1225a17 a comma after the second occurrence of *mē* (not); without a comma little sense can be made of the Greek and emendations have to be adopted.

3.   Keeping at 1225a25 the *mē* (not) of the MSS before *chairēi* (enjoy), and not deleting it with Bekker. The reference is presumably to the continent, who go against desire and yet act voluntarily.

4.   A Pythagorean philosopher and contemporary of Socrates.

5.   The Greek of this phrase (1225a35–36) is obscure and perhaps corrupt. The meaning seems to be that those people or cases most get in the way of understanding the voluntary where action appears both forced and voluntary, as with choosing the lesser of two evils or being affected by internal impulses too strong for nature; hence the need to examine force in the context of examining the voluntary.

Chapter 9

Thought. *The voluntary is opposite to the involuntary, and the voluntary is to know the circumstances of the act, and the involuntary is not to know them; hence the voluntary is to act with knowledge when the action is up to oneself and the involuntary to do the same in ignorance. But knowledge is found both in having and in using, and lack of either can be ignorance and involuntary, provided the ignorance is not through carelessness or pleasure or pain.*

1225a36   Since this discussion is now at an end, and since the voluntary is defined neither by appetite nor by choice, it remains then that it be defined as what accords with thought. So it seems that the voluntary is opposite to the involuntary, and that to know whom or with what or for the sake of what (for sometimes one knows that it is one's father but one's aim is not to kill but to save, as in the case of the daughters of Pelias;[1] or one knows that this is a drink b5   but as a love-potion and wine, whereas in fact it was hemlock[2]) is opposite to not knowing, by non-accidental ignorance, whom and with what and what. But that which is done through ignorance of what and with what and whom is involuntary; the opposite then is voluntary. Everything therefore that one does of oneself and not in ignorance when it is up to oneself not to do it must b10   be voluntary, and this is what the voluntary is; but everything that one does in ignorance and because of ignorance one does involuntarily.

Since science and knowledge are double, one being the having and the   1225b11
other the using of the science, he who has it but is not using it would in one
way justly be said to be ignorant but in another way not justly, for example
if because of carelessness he did not use his knowledge. Likewise even
someone who does not have it would be blamed if it is because of carelessness   b15
or pleasure or pain that he does not have what is easy or necessary. These
things therefore are to be added to the definition. So let this be the way to
define the voluntary and involuntary.

Notes

1.   The daughters of Pelias cut him up and boiled him, having been tricked
into believing that this would restore his youth.
2.   The story—about a woman who gave her lover hemlock thinking it was a
love-potion—is told more fully in *GE* 1.16.1188b31ff.

Chapter 10

Choice
What Choice Is Not. *Choice is not appetite, for (a) desire and spirit are also
in animals; (b) choice can be without either of these; (c) these can be without
choice; (d) these are with pain but choice need not be; (e) will can be of things
impossible and of what is not up to us but choice cannot be. Choice is not
opinion, for (a) opinion is also of what is not up to us; (b) opinion is true or
false but choice is not. Choice is not opinion and will because these are also
of the end but choice is not.*

Let us speak after this of choice, raising puzzles first about it in argument.   1225b18
For one might be in doubt what genus it naturally belongs to and what sort of
thing it should be placed in, that is, whether the voluntary and the choosable
are not the same thing or are the same thing.

What choice is said above all to be by some, and it might seem to be so   1225b21
as one looks into it, is that it is one or other of two things, either opinion or
appetite, for they are both manifestly things that follow along with it. That,
therefore, it is not appetite is manifest, for it would be either will or desire   b25
or spirit; for no one has appetite for anything unless he has felt one of these.
Now spirit and desire are also found in beasts, but choice is not. Further,
even in the case of those who have both of these, they choose many things
without either spirit or desire; and when they are in states of passion, they
are not choosing but enduring. Further, desire and spirit are always with pain,   b30
but we choose many things even without being in pain. Moreover, neither
is it the case that will and choice are the same. For some things people want
knowing them even to be impossible, for example to rule over all men and to

41

b35   be immortal as well,[1] but no one chooses the impossible unless he does not know it is impossible; nor generally does anyone choose a thing that, though possible, he does not think is up to him whether to do or not do. So this, then, is clear, that the choosable must be something in what is up to oneself.

1226a1   It is likewise plain that choice is not opinion either, not even when someone is simply thinking something, for it is plain the choosable is something in what is up to oneself, but we have many opinions even about things that are not up to us, for example that the diagonal is commensurable. Further, choice is not true or false. So neither is it opinion about doable things up to us (the opinion whereby we happen to be thinking that we should do or not do something).

1226a6   The following is common to opinion and will, that no one chooses any end but what is for the end. I mean, for example, that no one chooses to be healthy but to walk about or to sit down for the sake of health; nor does anyone choose

a10   to be happy but to do business or to run some risk for the sake of being happy. On the whole, in fact, a chooser always makes plain what he is choosing and for what, and the "for what" is that for the sake of which he chooses something else, and the "what" is that which he chooses for the sake of something else. But he wants the end above all and thinks[2] it necessary both to be healthy and

a15   do well. Hence it is manifest from this that choice is other than opinion and will: will and opinion are above all of the end but choice is not. That choice, therefore, is neither simply will nor opinion nor supposition is plain.

What Choice Is. *Choice is (a) about things whose coming to be is up to us, but not all of them; (b) it is not opinion and will but comes from opinion and will; (c) it is deliberative not about the end but of what is for the end, and in order to bring the beginning of action back to us; and hence it is deliberative appetite; (d) everything choosable is voluntary but not everything voluntary is choosable; (e) choice is opinion and appetite as brought together in a conclusion of deliberation.*

1226a18   But in what does it differ from these things and how is it related to the voluntary (what choice is will be plain at the same time)? So, of things that can both be and not be, some are such that it is possible to deliberate about them but about others it is not possible. For some things can both be and not be, but their coming to be is not up to us, but some of them come about

a25   through nature and others through other causes. About these no one would even undertake to deliberate unless he was ignorant. But about things where it is possible not only for them to be and not to be but also for men to deliberate about them, these are all the things that it is up to us to do or not to do. Hence we do not deliberate about things in India[3] nor about how the

a30   circle might be squared, for the first of these is not up to us and the other is altogether not doable.

But neither as regards the doable things that are up to us do we deliberate 1226a31 about all of them, whereby it is also plain that choice is not simply opinion either; but choosable things are in fact doables among things that are up to us. That is also why someone might be puzzled as to why ever it is that doctors deliberate about what they have science of but grammarians do not. A reason a35 is that since a mistake can come about in two ways (for we make mistakes either when calculating or in perception when doing it), both ways of making a mistake are possible in medicine, but in grammar mistakes are according to perception and action, and if they examine this they will go on endlessly.[4]

So, since choice is neither opinion nor will, there is a way[5] it is each—but 1226b2 not both, for no one's choice is sudden but opinion to act and willing are; as from both then, for both of them are present in someone choosing. But how it is from them needs to be examined. The thing is in a way made plain even by the name itself, for choice, while it is a taking of something, is not a taking simply but a taking of one thing before another,[6] and this is not possible without examination as well as will. Therefore choice is from deliberative opinion.

No one, then, deliberates about the end (but everyone has this set in 1226b9 place), but about things tending to it, whether this or that does, or, when a decision has been made, how this thing will be. We deliberate wholly about this until we bring back to us what its coming to be starts from. So if no one chooses who has not prepared and deliberated, either in a worse way or a b15 better, and if what he deliberates about is everything up to us among things for the end that can be or not be, plainly choice is deliberative appetite of what is up to us. For we do all deliberate[7] about what we in fact choose, but all that we deliberate about we do not choose. I call appetite deliberative if its principle and cause is deliberation and the appetite arises because of the act of deliberation.

That is why choice does not exist in the other animals, nor at every age; nor 1226b21 when every man has the age, for the act of deliberation is not there either, nor a supposition[8] of the "why." But nothing prevents an opinion whether to do or not do being found in many of them—though that it be through reasoning no longer holds. For the soul's deliberative part is the part that studies a sort b25 of cause, for the cause "for the sake of which" is one of them; for a cause is the "why," but what something is or comes to be for the sake of, that we say is a cause, as that fetching the merchandise is cause of walking (if that is what one is walking for); hence those who have no posited aim are not deliberative.

Consequently, since what it is up to oneself either to do or not do is 1226b30 something one voluntarily does or does not do (provided one is acting or not acting through oneself and not through ignorance), and since we do many such things without having deliberated or thought ahead, it must be that the choosable is all voluntary but not the voluntary choosable, and that b35 what accords with choice is all voluntary but that the voluntary is not all that accords with choice.

1226b36   It is manifest from this also at the same time that they are making a noble division who legislate that some of the passions are voluntary, some involuntary, and some with forethought. For even if they are not precise, they do at

a1   any rate in a way get hold of the truth (but we will speak about these matters in our examination of things just).[9] But that choice is neither will nor opinion simply is plain; but it is both opinion and appetite when these are brought together in a conclusion from an act of deliberation.

Virtue and Choice

In the Definition of Virtue. *Deliberation begins from the end and is about what is for the end. The end is by nature good but by distortion the apparent good, for some things can be used against as well as for what they are naturally for. But distortion is to the contraries and the contraries of the mean are the more or less, to which we incline because of pleasure and pain. Hence again virtue is shown to be about pleasures and pains. Virtue is a habit that chooses the mean relative to us in those pleasures and pains by which we are said to have a certain character.*

1227a5   Since he who deliberates always deliberates for the sake of something, and he always has some target that he is seeking useful means to, no one deliberates about the end but this is a principle and supposition, like suppositions in the theoretical sciences (in our discussion at the beginning something was

a10   said briefly about these matters, though with accuracy in the *Analytics*).[10] Everyone's investigation, whether with art or without art, is about what is for the end, for example in the case of those deliberating whether to have this war or not. But prior to that will be the "because of what," that is, the "that

a15   for the sake of which," as wealth or pleasure or some other such thing that happens to be that for the sake of which. For one who deliberates, provided[11] the examination from the end has been made, deliberates what contributes to it (so as to bring it to himself) or what he himself can do toward the end.

1227a18   The end, on the one hand, is by nature always a good and is what in a particular case they deliberate about, as that a doctor would deliberate if he should give a drug and a general where he should set up camp (for whom the end, the simply best thing, is good); on the other hand, contrary to nature and by distortion it is not the good but the apparent good. Reason is that as regard some entities it is not possible to use them for other than what they are naturally for, as sight, for it is not possible to see what there is not sight of,

a25   nor to hear what there is not hearing of; but from a science it is possible also to do what it is not the science of, for the same science is not equally of health and disease but is by nature of the one and contrary to nature of the other.

1227a28   Likewise will too is by nature of the good but against nature of the bad as well, and by nature it wants the good but against nature and by distortion it wants the bad too. But further the destruction and distortion of each thing is at any rate not toward some chance thing but to opposites and things in between. For it is not possible to get outside these, since deception is in fact not to chance things but to the opposites in all cases where there are opposites, that is, to those opposites that are opposites according to the science.

So the deception too and the choice must be from the mean to the oppo- 1227a36 sites, and opposites to the mean are the more and the less. The pleasant and painful are cause, for things are such that to the soul the pleasant appears good and the more pleasant better, and the painful bad and the more pain- a40 ful worse. Consequently it is plain from this too that virtue and vice concern pleasures and pains. For they happen to be about things choosable, but choice concerns the good and bad and the things that appear so, and pleasure and pain are by nature such.

So, since moral virtue is both itself a mean and is about pleasures and 1227b5 pains in every case, and since vice is found in excess and deficiency and is about the same things as virtue is, it must be that moral virtue is a habit that chooses the mean relative to us in all those pleasant and painful things in accord with which one is said, by feeling joy or pain, to be of a certain sort in one's character (for a lover of sweet things or a lover of bitter things is not b10 said to be of a certain sort in his character).

Notes

1. Possibly a reference to Alexander the Great.
2. Reading *doxazei* (he thinks or has opinion) at 1226a14, rather than the *doxazein* (to think or have opinion) of the MSS.
3. India was the furthest reach of Alexander's conquests.
4. An implicit reference to *GE* 1.17.1189b19–25, where the spelling of the name Archicles is given as example. There can be no mistake in how to spell this name (spelling is determined by the rules of Greek orthography), but one could make a mistake in writing it out, and there is no end to the ways one could make a mistake doing so. Doctors, by contrast, can make mistakes when calculating the amount of a certain medicine to give a patient (about which they must deliberate) and also when actually measuring and giving it.
5. Reading *estin hōs* at 1226b3 with the accent on the "e" of *estin*, thus giving the phrase the meaning it has in the translation.
6. The Greek for choice is *prohairesis*, which is literally a taking (*hairesis*) of one thing before (*pro*) another.
7. Reading at 1226b18–19 *bouleuometha* (deliberate) with some MSS for both occurrences of the verb rather than *boulometha* (wish) found in other MSS and preferred by Bekker.
8. The Greek is *hypolēpsis* (1226b23), which means a grasp or conception or assumption of something.
9. Book 4.8.1135a15–36a9.
10. A reference perhaps to 1.2 or perhaps better to this chapter at 1226a7ff., b10–12; or also 2.6.1222b15ff.; *Posterior Analytics* 1.2, 4.
11. Reading *ei* (if, provided) at 1227a16 with some MSS rather than *ē* (or) with others and Bekker.

Chapter 11

In Rightness. *Virtue makes choice and the end right and not reason right, for reason is right in the case of continence, and continence is different from virtue. Error is possible in the aim and in what is for the aim and in both. Virtue makes the aim right, for calculation and argument are not applicable to it, for other arts and sciences do not examine the end but what is for the end and argue from the end. The end is the beginning of thinking, and the end of thinking is the beginning of action. Choice is for the sake of the mean of virtue, but it is of things that are for the sake of the mean. Getting these things belongs to other powers, but getting the end right belongs to choice. That is why we judge people's character from their choice, that is, from what they do things for rather than from what they do. That is also why things done involuntarily are not praised or blamed, why praise refers more to the choice than to the deeds, why people who do something base under compulsion are not choosing it, and why it is only because choice is not easy to see that we judge from the deeds. Activity is more to be preferred but choice is more to be praised.*

1227b12   Having determined these things let us say whether virtue makes choice to be without error and the end right, such that one chooses for the sake of what one should; or whether, as some think, it makes reason to be so. But continence is this, for it does not destroy reason, and virtue and continence are different. We must speak about them later,[1] since all those who think that virtue renders reason right do so for this cause, that continence is, on the one hand, such a thing and that it belongs, on the other, to things praised.

1227b19   Our discussion begins with first setting out the puzzles. For it is possible that the aim is right but that there is mistake in what is for the aim; and it is possible that the aim is mistaken but that the things tending toward it are right; and that neither is right. Does virtue make the aim right or what is for the aim? We lay down, then, that it is the aim, because there is of this neither

b25   calculation[2] nor argument. But let this in fact be laid down as a principle, for neither does a doctor examine whether one should be healthy or not, but whether one should take walks or not; nor does the gymnastic expert examine whether one should have a good condition or not, but whether one should wrestle or not. Likewise neither is any other art about the end. For as in the sciences of theory the hypotheses are principles, so also in the sciences of

b30   doing the end is principle and hypothesis: since this thing needs to be healthy this here must be present if it is going to be so, just as, in the former, if the triangle has two right angles this here must be so. Of thought, then, the end is beginning, but the ending of thought is beginning of action.

1227b34   If then either reason or virtue is cause of complete rightness, if it is not reason, it would be virtue that is why the end is right, but not why what is for

46

the end is. An end is the "that for the sake of which." For every choice is of something and for the sake of something. What it is for the sake of, then, is the mean (what virtue is cause of is choosing for the sake of which), but choice is not of this but of what is for the sake of this. Now hitting on everything that one must do for the sake of the end belongs to another power, but hitting on b40 the end being right, of which virtue is cause, belongs to choice.

It is for this reason, in fact, that we judge someone's character from his 1228a2 choice, and this is the "what does he do it for the sake of?" but not "what is he doing?" Likewise vice too makes choice to be for the sake of the opposite things. So if someone, when it is up to him to do noble things and not to do a5 base ones, does the opposite, plainly this man is not virtuous. Consequently, both vice and virtue must be voluntary, for there is no necessity to do wicked things. That in fact is why vice is to be blamed and virtue to be praised. For shameful and bad things that are involuntary are not to be blamed, nor are a10 good things that are involuntary to be praised, but only the voluntary ones. Further, we praise and blame everyone looking more to their choice than to their deeds; and yet the activity is more to be preferred than the virtue. Again, people do base things also under compulsion but none of them is choosing to. Also, because it is not easy to see what his choice is like, that is why we a15 are compelled to judge what someone is like from his deeds. Therefore the activity is more to be preferred but the choice is more to be praised. These things therefore follow from what is laid down, and they agree, moreover, with the phenomena.

Notes

1. Book Six.
2. Reading at 1227b24 *logismos* (calculation) with some MSS rather than *sullogismos* (syllogism) with others.

Book Three: Particular Virtues

Chapter 1

In Particular

Bravery

What It Is a Mean State About. *Bravery is about fear and daring. The coward fears more than he should and dares less than he should and the rash man the opposite. Bravery and the brave are a mean between these and best.*

That mean states, therefore, belong with the virtues, that they are states of choice, that their opposite are vices, and what these are, has all been stated in universal terms. Let us next take each in particular and speak of them one by one, and first let us talk about bravery. `1228a23`

More or less everyone, then, holds that the brave man has to do with fears and that bravery is one of the virtues. We distinguished in the table[1] whether daring and fear are opposites, for they are indeed in a way opposed to each other. So it is clear that people who are referred to by these habits will likewise be opposed to each other, for example the coward (he is the one referred to as fearing more than he should and daring less than he should) and the rash man, for this latter too is referred to as being the sort to fear less than he should and to dare more than he should (that is also why he gets his name from the term, for the rash or daring man is so called by derivation from dare[2]). `1228a26` `a30`

Consequently, since bravery is the habit that is best about fears and daring, and since one should not be as the rash are (for they are deficient in one respect and excessive in the other), nor as cowards are (for these too do the same, only not about the same things but contrariwise, for they are deficient in daring but excessive in fearing), plainly the mean disposition between rashness and cowardice is bravery, for this is best. `1228a36` `b1`

What It Is of and Why. *The brave man is fearless and faces fears and the coward the opposite. But fearful things are divided, like pleasant and good things, into what is simply so and what is so for this or that person. The brave man faces things simply fearful (things fearful for most men or for human nature), which he fears insofar as he is a man but not insofar as he is brave. He is like the healthy and strong who are not much affected by what affects most men. He will fear and dare for the sake of the noble and as reason bids, but the coward fears against reason and the rash dares against reason. Five*

49

kinds of bravery are spoken of by a sort of likeness (political, military, ignorant, of hope, of irrational passion), but none is truly brave.

1228b4　The brave seems to be for the most part fearless while the coward fearful; and the latter seems to fear much and little, and great and small, and to fear greatly and quickly, while the former seems the opposite and either not to fear at all or slightly and with difficulty and seldom and about great things. He also faces up to strong fears, but the other not even to slight ones.

1228b9　What sort of fearful things first, therefore, does the brave man face, whether things fearful to himself or to someone else? If things fearful, then, to someone else, one would deny there was anything grand to it; but if things fearful to himself his fearful things would be great ones, and things fearful are causative of fear in those they are fearful to (for example, if they are very fearful, the fear would be a strong one, if slightly so, a weak one), so that the

b15　brave man turns out to be causing many and great fears for himself. But it seems to the contrary that bravery makes one fearless, and that this means to fear no or few things and slightly or with difficulty.

1228b18　But perhaps the fearful, like the pleasant and the good, is said in two ways. For some things are simply pleasant and good, and others, while pleasant and good for someone, are not simply so but, on the contrary, base and not pleasant—whatever is beneficial to the depraved and whatever is pleasant to children qua children. Likewise fearful things too are in some cases simply so and in others for someone. What a coward qua coward fears, then, are fearful in some cases for no one and in others slightly so. But things fearful

b25　for most people and all things fearful for human nature—those we say are simply fearful. The brave man is fearless toward these and faces these sorts of fearful things, which are in a way fearful for him and in a way not, being fearful insofar as he is a man, and not fearful but either slightly or not at all insofar as he is brave. Yet they are fearful things, for they are fearful for most people.

1228b30　That is why, in fact, the habit is praised, because it is disposed the way the strong and healthy are. For they too are what they are, not because nothing wears them down (no toil the former and no excess the latter), but because they are not affected, either simply or very much, by the things that affect the many and the majority.

1228b35　Now the sickly and weak and cowardly are affected both by common sufferings (though quicker and more than the many are) and, in addition, what the many are affected by they are not at all affected by or slightly. But a puzzle arises, that if there is nothing fearful to the brave then he would not

a1　fear. Or does nothing prevent him fearing in the way stated? For bravery is a following of reason and reason bids one choose the noble. Hence he who faces fearful things not on this account is either beside himself[3] or rash. Only he in fact is brave who is fearless because of the noble.

1229a4　The coward, then, fears even what he should not and the rash dares even what he should not. But the brave does both as he should, and in this way he is a mean, for he fears and dares what reason bids. But reason does not bid the facing of great painful and destructive things unless they are noble. So the rash dares things even if reason does not bid, and the coward does not even if it does, while only the brave does so if it does.

There are five kinds of bravery spoken of by likeness. For they all face the same things but not for the same reasons. One is citizen bravery, and this is the one based on shame. A second is military bravery, and this is based on experience and on knowing, not terrible things, as Socrates said,[4] but that there are helps for terrible things.[5] A third is that based on inexperience and ignorance, which makes children and madmen either, in the one case, face things coming at them or, in the other, pick up snakes. Another is that based on hope, by which those who have often been lucky face dangers, and those who are drunk (for wine fills people with good hope). 1229a11 a15

Another bravery is that based on irrational passion, as love, for example, and spirit. For if one is in love, one is more rash than cowardly and faces many dangers, like the man in Metapontium when he killed the tyrant and the man in Crete whom stories are told about.[6] It is just the same with anger and spirit; for spirit sets people beside themselves. Hence also wild beasts seem to be brave, although they are not; for when they are beside themselves that is what they are like, but otherwise their behavior is uneven, like rash people's. Nevertheless spirit's bravery is most natural of all. For spirit is a thing undefeated, wherefore children too fight very well (law is cause in the case of political bravery). But in truth none of them is bravery, although all of them are useful for encouragement in danger. 1229a20 a25 a30

What Power Fearful Things Have. *Fearful things are cause of destructive pain, and not of other sorts of pain. He who is indifferent to cold and heat but fears death seems a coward. The fearful things that the brave man is about are those that cause destructive pain and are near at hand and commensurate with human nature. Cowards and the rash are deceived by their habits about what is and is not fearful, but the brave man holds what is true. So those are not brave who face fearful things through ignorance, or spirit, or pleasure, or through flight from pain or toil, or through experience of danger and knowledge of helps against it, or through shame. True bravery is the virtue of choosing to face fearful things for the sake of the noble.*

Up to now we have spoken about fearful things in simple terms, but it is better to define them more. Fearful things, then, are said on the whole to be things that cause fear. Such things are whatever appears to cause destructive pain. For it is perhaps a different pain and a different passion that people anticipating some other pain would get, but it will not be fear; I mean, if someone foresaw he was going to feel the pain that the envious feel or the sort that the jealous do or the ashamed. But fear only arises where the sorts of pains whose nature it is to take 1229a32 a35 a40

51

away life appear about to happen. Hence some people who are in certain things even very soft are brave, and others who are hard and enduring are also cowards.

1229b2 It seems, then, in fact that having a certain attitude about death and the pain of it is pretty much proper to bravery. For if someone were of the sort
b5 to do as reason says in facing heat and cold and suchlike pains, which are without danger, but was soft and full of fear toward death, not for any other passion but the destruction itself, while someone else was soft toward the first pains but impassive toward death, the former would seem to be a coward
b10 and the latter brave. For danger is only in fact said of the sort of fearful things where what is close by is cause of the sort of destruction mentioned (danger appears when it appears close by).

1229b13 That the fearful things, then, which we say the brave man is about, are the things that appear cause of destructive pain we have stated. These, however, are things both that appear close by and not far off and also that are or appear to be of such a size as fits human measure. For some things must appear fearful to and alarm every man. For, just as heat and cold and some other powers are beyond us and the conditions of our human body, so nothing stops it being thus also with some of the passions in the soul.

1229b21 Cowards[7] and the rash are deceived through their habits. For the coward deems things not fearful to be fearful and things slightly fearful to be severely so, but the rash man the opposite, deeming things fearful encouraging and
b25 things severe slight, while the brave man above all deems what is true. Hence it is that someone is not brave either if he faces fearful things out of ignorance, for example if someone were out of madness to face thunderbolts coming at him, or if he faces a danger, knowing how great it is, out of spirit as the Celts do when they take up arms and front the waves.

1229b29 In fact barbaric bravery goes on the whole with spirit. There are some also who face things out of other pleasures—for spirit too has a certain pleasure in it, for it is with hope of revenge. But still, neither if someone faces death for this or for another pleasure, nor if he does so through flight from greater
b35 pains, would any of these justly be called brave. For if dying were pleasant the licentious would be constantly dying from incontinence, just as indeed now, while dying itself is not pleasant but the things that cause it are, many knowingly meet it from incontinence, none of whom, even if very ready to
b40 die, would seem to be brave. Nor if they do it, as many do, while fleeing toil, are any of this sort brave either, as Agathon[8] indeed says:

> For base mortals, by their toilings o'ercome,
> Are with death in love.

And as in the myth told about Chiron[9] by the poets, that, though being immortal, he prayed for death from the anguish of his wound.

1230a4 Very close to these also are all who face dangers because of experience, which is the way, pretty much, that the majority of soldiering men do. For it is the opposite of what Socrates thought, who thought that bravery was knowledge. For neither is it because they have knowledge of what is fearful that those are bold who know how to mount the masts, but because they know the helps for terrible things; nor is that bravery that makes people contend more boldly. For then, according to Theognis,[10] strength and wealth would be bravery, "for every man by penury subdued." Some who are manifestly cowards nevertheless face things through experience. The reason is that they do not think there is danger, for they know what the helps are. A sign is that whenever they think they do not have help, but what is terrible is already close by, they do not face it. a10

But as regards all these causes, those who face them because of shame would most seem to be brave, in the way that Homer says in fact that Hector faced danger against Achilles: 1230a16

> . . . On Hector seizèd shame:
> "Poulydamus would 'gainst me first heap blame."[11]

And this is what citizen bravery is.

True bravery is neither this nor any of them, but it is similar to them, just as is also the bravery of beasts, when, because of spirit, they rush to meet the blow. For one should face things, though afraid, not because one will be ill-famed, nor because of anger, nor because one does not think one will die, nor because of having powers of defense (for thus one will not think that there is anything to fear). But since every virtue is a choosing (how we mean this was said earlier,[12] that it makes one choose everything for the sake of something, and this, the "for the sake of," is the noble), plainly bravery, being a certain virtue, will make one face fearful things for the sake of something, so that it makes one do so neither through ignorance (for rather it makes one judge rightly), nor through pleasure, but because it is a noble thing, since, if it is not a noble thing but mad, one will not face it, for it is ugly. 1230a21 a25 a30

What sort of things, then, bravery is a mean state about, and what it is of and why, and what power fearful things have, has been pretty much stated sufficiently in accord with our present procedure. 1230a33

Notes

1. Above, 2.3.1220b38–21a12.
2. The Greek at 1228a34–37 for the rash or daring man is *thrasus* and for dare and to dare *thrasos* and *tharrein*.
3. The Greek root of the word at 1229a3 here (*exhestēken*) gives us our word "ecstatic."
4. Plato *Protagoras* 360d, *Republic* 429b–30b; but cf. *Laches* 193a.
5. There is no need to alter the MSS at 1229a15 here. The Greek can be construed as an accusative and infinitive clause (*einai* understood) with pleonastic *hoti* (*LSJ s.v.* II.2), the *hoti* (that) serving, in this case, to show that the accusatives are not objects of *eidenai* but an indirect statement dependent on it.

6. Nothing much is known of either of these persons or events, though Kenny (1978: 221–22) plausibly identifies the man at Metapontium with the Antileon mentioned in Plutarch *Moralia* 760c.
7. Starting a new sentence at 1229b21 here with most scholars and not, with Bekker, taking it as belonging to the previous clause.
8. Fr. 7 Nauck. Agathon was a tragic poet of the fifth and fourth centuries BC. He appears as a character in Plato's *Symposium*.
9. A centaur reputed for his learning and teacher of Achilles (among others) who, when accidentally wounded by a poisoned arrow from Heracles, gave away his immortality to Prometheus.
10. Theognis 177.
11. *Iliad* 22.100. The first line of the quote is not in our texts of Homer, and it cannot have immediately preceded the second line, for its scansion does not fit. It is perhaps a Vergilian pathetic half line.
12. Above 2.11.

Chapter 2

Temperance. *The licentious are those who have not been corrected or cannot be corrected. They are about certain pleasures and pains, and the insensible, who are a rare breed, are those who are unfeeling about such pleasures and pains. The pleasures are of taste and touch (though really touch), and not those of sight or hearing or smell. These pleasures are also enjoyed by the beasts, which do not get pleasure from sight or hearing, nor from smell, save incidentally (because of expectation or memory of food and drink, and do not enjoy them for themselves, as say the scent of flowers), nor from taste, but rather from the touch of the food in the gullet. All the kinds of license are about the pleasures of touch, for no one is licentious who goes to excess in pleasures of sight or smell or hearing. The insensible are deficient in these pleasures, which everyone else, without license, naturally enjoys. Since these pleasures have excess and deficiency, they also have a mean, and temperance the best habit would be the mean state.*

1230a37   Next we must try to draw distinctions about temperance and license. The licentious is said in many ways. For he is both one who has not been

b1   corrected[1] or cured in some way (as the uncut is one who has not been cut) and, among these, one capable of correction and one not capable. For what cannot be cut and what can be but has not been are both uncut. What is licentious is the same way, for it is both what does not have the nature to be

b5   corrected and what does have the nature but, in the case of faults where the temperate man acts rightly, has not been corrected, like children, for they are called licentious by reason of this lack of correction. And further, they in another way are called so who are hard to cure or totally impossible to cure through correction.

Although there are many ways in which license is said, it is clear that the licentious concern certain pleasures and pains and that they differ, both among themselves and from other things, by the way they are disposed toward these (we gave a diagram earlier about how we are using the name "license" in a transferred sense).[2] 1230b9

For they who, because of insensibility, remain unmoved in the presence of these same pleasures are called insensible by some and are addressed by others with other sorts of names. But the passion is not much recognized nor lies open to view, because everyone errs more on the other side, and because the yielding to, and sensing of, such pleasures is inborn in everyone. The sort are mainly the country boorish type who are brought on stage by comedy teachers and who will not even approach what is measured and necessary in pleasant things. 1230b13 b15

Since the temperate man is about pleasures, he must be about certain desires too. So we must grasp which they are. For the temperate is not temperate about all pleasures and not even about all pleasant things, but, as it seems, about two of the objects of sense, those of taste and touch, though, in truth, about those of touch. For as to pleasure from seeing beautiful things without desire for sex, or pain from seeing ugly ones, and as to that from hearing what is well tuned or out of tune and, further, as to those from smelling what is fragrant or stinks, the temperate man is not about these. For no one too is said to be licentious by feeling or not feeling them. At any rate if, while gazing at a beautiful statue or a horse or a man or hearing someone sing, one were not to wish either to eat or drink or have sex but to gaze at the beautiful objects or hear the singers, one would not be held licentious, just as neither would they be held to be so who are beguiled in the presence of the Sirens. 1230b21 b25 b30

But licentiousness is about the two objects of sense that beasts also happen to be sensitive to when they rejoice or are pained, those of taste and touch. About the objects of pleasure of the other senses beasts all manifestly have pretty much the like insensitive disposition that they have as regards what is well tuned or what is beautiful. For they manifestly sense nothing worth speaking of in the seeing by itself of beautiful things or in the hearing by itself of well-tuned things, unless something prodigious has happened somewhere. 1230b36 a1

But neither are they so as regards fragrances or stinks, and yet they have senses at any rate that are all sharper. In fact, though, they do rejoice in all smells that they are incidentally glad at, but not for the smells by themselves. I say "by themselves" meaning smells that we do not rejoice in by expecting or remembering something, as meats or drinks (for we rejoice in those smells because of a different pleasure, that of eating or drinking), but smells by themselves are the sort that flowers have. Hence Stratonicus[3] hit the right note when he said that the latter were beautiful to smell but the former 1231a4 a10 pleasant—since it is not even about all the pleasures of taste that the beasts are set aflutter, nor even about those that are perceived by the tip of the tongue, but those perceived by the throat, and their passion is more like touch than a15 taste. That is why gourmands do not pray to have their tongue long but to have the throat of a crane, as Philoxenos[4] son of Eryxis did. So, speaking simply, licentiousness must be set down as being about things of touch.

1231a18 In like manner the licentious man is also about such pleasures. For wine bibbing and gluttony and lechery and gourmandizing and all such things a20 are about the senses mentioned, and into these parts is licentiousness divided. But as to the pleasures of sight or hearing or smelling, if anyone is excessive about them, he is not called licentious, but we blame these faults without reproaching them, as we do, on the whole, with everything that people are not said to be continent in (the incontinent are neither licentious nor temperate).[5]

1231a26 Insensible, or however he should be called, is he whose state is such that he is deficient in all the things that everyone, for the most part, needs to share in and enjoy; but he who tends to excess is licentious. For everyone by nature a30 enjoys these things and gets desires for them and is not licentious nor said to be (for they do not go to excess in rejoicing more than they should when they get them, nor in being pained more than they should when not getting them; nor are they without feelings of pain, for they are not deficient in rejoicing or in being pained, but tend rather toward excess).

1231a34 Since there is excess and deficiency in them, plainly there is a mean state as well, and this habit is best and opposite to both. Consequently, temperance the best habit about what the licentious man is about would be temperance the mean state about the pleasures of sense mentioned, being a mean state between license and insensibility. The excess is license and the deficiency b1 is either nameless or addressed by the names mentioned. A more accurate division of the class of pleasures must be made in our later discussion of continence and incontinence.[6]

Notes

1. Aristotle is engaging in etymology at 1230a39 here, for the Greek for licentious is *akolastos* and the Greek for having been corrected or punished is *kekolasmenos*, so that the *a-kolastos* is he who is without correction or punishment.
2. The diagram (table) was given in 2.3, where at 1221a2, *akolasia* , though literally meaning uncorrectedness, is pressed into service as the contrasting term to insensibility and temperance.
3. A musician, contemporary with Aristotle.
4. A famous gourmand and possibly also a poet.
5. An alternative translation would be: "And on the whole where people are not said to be continent or incontinent there they are not licentious or temperate" (Dirlmeier 1962: 53, 327).
6. Book Six.

Chapter 3

Mildness. *Mildness is about the pain that comes from spirit. Opposite the angry and difficult and wild in the diagram are the slavish and thoughtless. The latter do not get angry as they should and are easily abused. Opposite to sluggish spirit is quick spirit, to little spirit vehement spirit, to being a long time pained being a short time pained. So there is someone who is a mean between these and his state must be decent since these others are mistaken. Mildness as the best habit is the mean state.*

We must grasp mildness and harsh temper too in the same way. For we see 1231b5 that the mild man is also about pain, the pain that comes from spirit, by his being disposed in some way with respect to it. We marked on the diagram and set as opposite to the angry and the difficult and the wild (for all this sort belongs to the same disposition) the slavish and the mindless.[1] For these b10 names are pretty much the ones people use most for those whose spirit is not moved even against what it should be but who take insults readily and are abject in the face of contempt. For opposite to being quick of spirit is being sluggish of spirit, to having a quiet spirit having a vehement one, and to feeling the pain we call spirit a long time feeling it a short time.

Since here too, just as we said in the other cases, there is excess and defi- 1231b15 ciency (for the harsh man is the sort who feels the passion quicker and more and for a longer time and when he should not and with the sort of people he should not and with many people, while the slavish man is the opposite), plainly b20 there is a mean of the inequality as well. Since, therefore, the former habits are both in error, it is manifest that the mean habit between them is decent. For it does not start either too early or too late, nor does it get angry with whom it should not, nor not angry with whom it should. Consequently, since mild- ness is in fact the best habit in these passions, mildness would be a mean state b25 too, and the mild man a mean between the harsh man and the slavish man.

Note

1.   2.3.1220b38, 1221a15–17, where the words *analgēsia* and *analgētos* are used, both of which mean dullness to pain and so connote a certain sense- less and servile disposition.

Chapter 4

Liberality. *Liberality is about getting and spending money. The illiberal man feels more joy than he should in getting and more pain than he should in spending; the prodigal is opposite; the liberal man does both as he should.*

Liberality is the mean state between the two and is best. Property has a per se and a per accidens use: the money-lover loves mere coin, the illiberal man pursues per se property, the prodigal lacks necessities, the liberal man gives of his surplus. There are sub-kinds too according to more and less.

1231b27 Magnanimity and magnificence and liberality are also mean states. Liberality is about the getting and spending of things monetary.[1] He who

b30 rejoices more than he should in any case of getting and is pained more than he should in any case of spending is illiberal; he who does both of these less than he should is prodigal; he who does both as he should is liberal (what I mean by "as he should," both in these and in the other cases, is "as right reason says"). But since the former are in excess and deficiency and where

b35 there are extremes there is also a mean and this is best, and since the best is single as regards each kind of thing, liberality too must be a mean state between profligacy and illiberality in getting and spending things monetary.

1231b38 We speak of things monetary and of business in two ways. There is the using of a piece of property per se, as of a cloak or a shoe, and there is a using of it per accidens, not however in the way one might use a shoe for a weight, but as selling and lending do, for shoes are what they provide.[2] The money-

a5 lover is someone eager about current coin, but his current coin is a thing of property instead of a thing of per accidens use. The illiberal man might even be a profligate about the per accidens way of business, for in fact he pursues increase in natural business. The prodigal lacks what he needs. The liberal man gives what he has left over.

1232a10 Kinds of these very things are spoken of as differing by more and less in respect of their parts, for example a tight-fist and a niggard and a profit-scrounger are illiberal: a tight-fist by his not letting go, a profit-scrounger by his accepting anything, a niggard as one who strains much over small things,

a15 a false reckoner and a thief as one whose injustice is in being illiberal. In the same way too the profligate includes a waster by his disorderly expense, and a reckless man by his not facing the pain of calculation.

Notes

1. The Greek at 1231b28–29 is *chrēmata*, which are the things that business, *chrēmatistikē*, deals with, and so the word covers both commodities and money, or in short anything of monetary value. In the *NE* (4.1,1119b26–27) *chrēmata* are defined as "all things whose worth is valued in money."

2. Keeping at 1232a2–3 the MSS reading *chrētai hypodēmata* (literally: "shoes [i.e., and not weights] are provided" sc. by buying and lending shoes), rather than Bekker's emendation to *chrētai hypodēmati* ("it [sc. buying or lending] uses a shoe"). Aristotle is playing on the double meaning of the verb *chraō*: to provide and (in the middle) to use. The point is that in selling and lending one is using shoes as a medium of exchange and not for wearing (so that the use is per accidens), but one is nevertheless providing people

with shoes and not with weights. Thus, as regards the remarks Aristotle makes next, the money-lover treats actual coinage, which is properly silver in its per accidens use as a medium of exchange for property, as if it were by itself property, and the illiberal man cares little for coinage provided he can with it accumulate property for himself.

Chapter 5

Magnanimity. The magnanimous man is someone great in soul and power and seems to accompany all the virtues and they him. He looks down on things, as each virtue does on things great against reason, and prefers and enjoys honor from worthy men and for great things. But magnanimity is nevertheless a virtue distinct from all the others. There are four possibilities: those who are and think themselves worthy of great things; those who are and think themselves worthy of small things; those worthy of small things thinking themselves worthy of great; those worthy of great things thinking themselves worthy of small. The third and fourth are to be blamed. The first is to be praised and is the mean of magnanimity between the third, which is vanity, and the fourth, which is smallness of soul. The second is not magnanimity nor is it to be blamed for it is not opposite or blamed but as reason commands; it would become magnanimity in the right conditions. The small-souled man, if worthy of small things, would think himself worthy of even smaller things. The resident alien is not small-souled if he submits to being ruled but only someone wellborn is who thinks rule a great thing.

About magnanimity we must determine its cause from what is attributed 1232a19 to magnanimous men. For as has happened also with other things—that their closeness and likeness up to a point makes their growing further apart escape notice—so the same with magnanimity. Hence it is that men on opposite sides sometimes lay claim to the same thing, as the prodigal to the same as the liberal man and the disagreeable man as the man of dignity and the rash man as the brave. For up to a point they are indeed about the same a25 things and share the same borders, as that the brave and the rash man face dangers, but the one does it this way and the other that, and these ways are very different.

We speak of the magnanimous man according to the title of his name, as 1232a28 existing in a certain greatness of soul and power, so that he is deemed like both the man of dignity and the magnificent man when in fact all the virtues a30 are what he appears to follow. For in fact it is praiseworthy to judge rightly the great and small among goods; but those goods are deemed great that he pursues who has the best habit with respect to such things (even if they

59

a35 are pleasant);[1] and magnanimity is best. But the virtue in each case judges rightly the greater thing and the lesser (which is just what the prudent man would command as well as the virtue), so that all the virtues follow on it or it on all the virtues.

1232a38 Further, it seems a feature of the magnanimous man to look down on things. Each virtue makes people look down on things great that are against reason, as bravery in respect of dangers (for it thinks that even a great host of the shameful dangers is not in every case fearful)[2] and as the temperate man in respect of great and many pleasures, and the liberal man in respect

b5 of things monetary. But the magnanimous man seems to have this feature because he is serious about few things, and these great things, and not because someone else deems them so. Also, a magnanimous man would more care what one virtuous man thinks than many chance people, as Antiphon said to Agathon[3] after being voted guilty when the latter praised his defense. In fact disdain is especially deemed a passion proper to the magnanimous

b10 man. Again, as for honor and life and wealth, which men seem to take seriously, he seems to care nothing for any of them save honor, and he would be pained if he was dishonored and ruled by an unworthy man, and he rejoices most when he gets honor.

1232b14 He would thus seem, then, to be in opposed states, for that he is mainly concerned with honor and that he looks down on the many and on fame do not seem to agree. But we need to talk about this by making distinctions. For honor is great and little in two ways: it is so either by being from many who are chance fellows, or by being from those who are worthy of account. Again honor differs by the ground on which it is given. For it is not great merely

b20 by the number of those who do the honoring or by their quality, but also by its being honorable. And, in truth, as to rule and the other goods, only those that are great are truly honorable and worth taking seriously. So, as a result, no virtue is without greatness, which is why, as we said,[4] the virtues each seem to make people magnanimous as regards what each of them is about.

1232b25 But nevertheless there is a certain single magnanimity alongside the other virtues, just as too he must be said to be properly magnanimous who has it. Since there are certain goods of which some are honorable and some as before distinguished,[5] and of this sort of goods some in truth are great and some small, and since there are people who are worthy of these and think themselves worthy of them, the magnanimous man must be looked for among these.

1232b31 There must be a fourfold division. For it is possible to be worthy of great things and think oneself worthy of them, and there can be small things and someone worthy of such small things and thinking himself worthy of them, and there is the reverse of each of these, for one of them would be of such

b35 sort as, being worthy of small things, to think himself worthy of great things (goods held in honor), and the other, being worthy of great things, would think himself worthy of small ones.

60

Now he who is worthy of small things but thinks himself worthy of great 1232b37
is to be blamed, for it is mindless and not noble to get things against one's
worth. Also to be blamed is he who, though being worthy of such things when
present to him, does not think that he is worthy to share in them. There is left a1
now opposite to both of these he who, being worthy of great things, thinks
himself worthy of them and is such as to think himself worthy. This man is
to be praised and is a mean between those. Since, therefore, magnanimity is
best disposition about preferring and using honor and the other goods held in a5
honor, and we grant this and that the magnanimous man is not about useful
things, and since too the mean state in question is most to be praised at the
same time, plainly magnanimity too must be a mean state.

Of the opposite states, as we put them in the diagram,[6] that for the one who 1233a9
thinks himself worthy of great goods while being unworthy is vanity (for we
call all such people vain who think themselves worthy of great things when
they are not), but that about not thinking oneself worthy of great things while
one is worthy is smallness of soul (for he seems typical of a small-souled man
who does not think himself worthy of anything great, although he possesses
things because of which he might justly be thought worthy). Consequently,
it is necessary also that magnanimity be a mean state between vanity and
smallness of soul.

The fourth among the divisions made is neither to be blamed at all nor is 1233a16
he magnanimous, having greatness in nothing. For he is neither worthy of nor
thinks himself worthy of great things, hence he is not opposite. Yet it would seem
that opposite to thinking oneself worthy of great things when worthy of great a20
things is being worthy of small things and thinking oneself so. But he is not opposite; nor to not[7] being blamable, for his state is as reason commands; and he
is the same in nature with the magnanimous, for what they are worthy of, that
both think themselves worthy of. He might in fact become magnanimous, for
he will think himself worthy of that of which he is worthy. But the small-souled a25
man, who, when goods great in honor are present to him, does not think himself
worthy of them, what would he do[8] if he was worthy of small things? Would that[9]
he was vain thinking himself worthy of great things than of yet smaller ones!

Hence no one would say someone was small-souled if, being a resident 1233a28
alien, he does not think himself worthy to rule and instead submits, but if he
does so being wellborn and thinking rule to be a great thing.[10]

Notes

1. Emending at 32a34 the MSS reading *einai hēdea* (to be pleasant), which
   hardly makes sense, to *ei kai hēdea* (even if pleasant); other scholars choose
   to delete the words altogether.
2. The Greek at 32b1–2 is not entirely clear and an alternative translation
   would be: "it thinks great matter is in shameful things [sc. it thinks only
   shame, not mere wounds or death, great enough to be avoided] and that
   not every host is fearful."

3. Agathon was the tragic poet. Antiphon was an Athenian politician condemned to death for his part in the revolution of the four hundred in 411 BC.
4. Above at 1232a37–38.
5. Just above at 1232b17–23.
6. 2.3.1221a10, 31–33.
7. The MSS at 1233a21 have "not" (*mē*) before "blamable" (*memptos*), but Bekker leaves it out, both in the text and in the *apparatus criticus*. The sense is that the man in question is not opposite to the state of not being blamable because he himself also is not blamable.
8. The Greek MSS and Bekker have "say" (*eipoi*) at 1233a26, but a Medieval Latin translation must have read "do" (*epoiei*) for it translates as *faceret*. In the parallel passage of *NE*, 4.3.1123b12–13, *epoiei* is found.
9. Reading *ei gar* (would that) at 1233a27 with some MSS rather than *ē gar* (for either) with others and with Bekker. If the latter reading is kept the sense will be: "for either, thinking himself worthy of great things, he would be vain, or [he would think himself worthy] of yet lesser things."
10. Aristotle himself was a resident alien in Athens, and Plato, his teacher, who was wellborn and an Athenian citizen, did not think rule in the city to be something great. Neither of them held political office there.

Chapter 6

Magnificence. *The magnificent man is about great expenses wherein he chooses the fitting magnitude. He who goes beyond this is extravagant. For example, to expend on a marriage feast as for a dinner party is to be shabby, but to do the reverse is extravagant. The magnificent man expends according to worth, both as befits the occasion and himself (unlike Themistocles at the Olympic Games). He who is as it chances has neither the virtue nor the vices.*

1233a31   The magnificent man is also not about any chance deed or choice, but about expense (unless perhaps we are speaking in a transferred sense).[1] Without expense there is no magnificence. For the fitting exists in decorum, and decorum[2]

a35   is not made from any chance outlays but in an excess beyond necessities. He who is chooser of fitting magnitude in great expense and has an appetite for this sort of mean state and for this sort of pleasure is magnificent.

1233a38   He who aims at what is greater and out of tune is nameless, but he is in some way close to those they call tasteless and swaggering. For example, if someone who is rich and is laying out expenses on a marriage for one he cherishes thinks that the sort of arrangement that fits his case is what fits someone throwing a dinner for drinkers to the god of good luck,[3] he is shabby;

b5   but he who receives such drinkers in the former way, not for the sake of glory nor even on account of power, he is like the swaggerer.

But he who does what is according to worth and as reason says, he is 1233b6
magnificent (for the fitting accords with worth; for nothing is fitting that is
contrary to worth). But it must be fitting, for as indeed the fitting is in accord
with worth,[4] there must in fact be a fit both as regards what (for example, one
thing fits the marriage of a servant and another the marriage of a beloved) b10
and for him, if he is really up to so much or such; for example the thinking
was that the embassage Themistocles made to Olympia was not fitting for
him (on account of his former low condition), but it was for Cimon.[5]

He who is disposed to worth as chance has it is the nobody among these. 1233b13
Things are the same way too with liberality, that there is someone who is as
a liberal man is—when he is free to be.[6]

Notes

1. Cf. *GE* 1.26.1192b13ff where the same point is made and an example of a
    transferred sense is given: someone striding along in a magnificent way.
2. The word for decorum at 1233a34 is *kosmos* or ordered adornment (as in
    the cosmic array of the heavens).
3. Such diners would have only one drink at the end of the meal in honor of
    the god of good luck.
4. Giving to *tou prepontos* at 1233b8–9 a verbal force and treating it as a
    compressed genitive absolute.
5. Themistocles, a famous Athenian politician of lowly stock, vied with Cimon,
    a famous Athenian politician of wealthy stock, in the display he made at
    the Olympic Games; Plutarch, *Life of Themistocles* 5.
6. The Greek at 1233b15, and indeed in the two preceding lines, is obscure
    and possibly corrupt, but if it has a sense, the sense is that someone might
    be disposed as the liberal man is but only able to behave so when the condi-
    tions are met, namely when he is free of restraints (financial or physical).
    Similarly in the case of magnificence: one could be disposed as the mag-
    nificent man is but unable to behave so because of lack of preconditions,
    as Themistocles who, though he had, like Cimon, the resources to put on a
    splendid display, did not have the right family status, and so, when he tried
    to be magnificent, only succeeded in being a swaggerer. He should have
    refrained because he was out of his league, or a nobody, in the context.

Chapter 7

Means of Passion
Righteous Indignation. *Righteous indignation is a mean state of envy and joy
at ill; it is pain at good and bad when these happen against worth, and joy
when they happen according to worth.*

Of the remaining things that are praised and blamed in the case of character, 1233b16
they are each pretty much either excesses or deficiencies or mean states in the

passions—such as the envious and he who rejoices at ill; for, as to the habits b20 by which they are spoken of, envy is being pained at those who are deservedly doing well, and the passion of the one rejoicing at ill in the same matter is nameless but he who has it is plain from his rejoicing at cases of undeserved doing badly. Their mean is the righteously indignant man and what the ancients called righteous indignation, which is being pained at cases of doing badly and b25 well that are undeserved and rejoicing at cases that are deserved. That is also why they suppose righteous indignation to be a god.

Shame. *Shame is a mean state of shamelessness and shamed shyness with respect to opinion.*

1233b26   Shame is a mean state between shamelessness and shamed shyness. For he who cares not for any opinion is shameless; he who cares for every opinion equally is shamed shy; and he who cares for the opinion of the manifestly decent has shame.

Friendliness. *Friendliness is a mean state of hostility and flattery with respect to pleasure among company.*

1233b29   Friendliness is a mean state between hostility and flattery. For he who readily accepts the desires in everything of those he associates with is a flatterer; he who resists them all is hostile; he who follows and resists, not with a view to every pleasure but to what is manifestly best, is friendly.

Dignity. *Dignity is a mean state of disagreeableness and fawning in living with others.*

1233b34   Dignity is a mean state between disagreeableness and fawning. For the despiser, living in no way with regard to another is disagreeable; he who lives with regard to someone else in every respect, or even lives as inferior to all, is a fawner; he who shows regard in some cases and not in others and to the deserving is dignified.

Truth. *Truth is a mean state of self-deprecation and boasting about what one says about oneself.*

1233b38   The true and simple man, whom they call straightforward, is a mean between the self-deprecator[1] and the boaster. For he who is knowingly deceptive a1 about himself on the side of what is worse is self-deprecating; he who does it on the side of what is better is a boaster; he who tells things as they are is true and, as Homer says,[2] sagacious. And on the whole he is a lover of truth, but the other a lover of lies.

Wit. *Wit is the mean state between boorishness and buffoonery. It has two forms: taking a joke and telling a joke, and both should be pleasing to him who is in the mean state.*

Wit is also a mean state, and the witty man is a mean between the boor or 1234a4 the dull wit and the buffoon. For just as the squeamish in respect of food differs from the omnivorous in that the one accepts nothing or little and with reluctance while the other readily accepts everything, so too is the boor related to the vulgar man and buffoon. For the first accepts nothing funny save with difficulty, the other everything readily and with pleasure. One should a10 do neither but accept some things and not others and in accord with reason; this is the witty man. The proof is the same, for this sort of wittiness (and not the one we speak of in some transferred sense) is a most decent habit, and the mean state is praised and the extremes blamed.

Since there are two forms of wit—for one lies in enjoying a funny joke, 1234a14 even against oneself (provided it belongs to the sort of thing of which a jest is an instance),[3] and the other in being able to come up with jokes—they are different from each other although both are mean states. For indeed as regards him who is able to come up with the sort of joke that a good judge would be pleased by, even were the joke on him—he will be a mean between a20 the vulgar man and the cold man. This definition is better than the thing said being painful[4] to him who is the butt of the jest, whoever he is; for rather it should be pleasing to him who is in the mean state, for he judges well.

Some General Comments. *These means are praiseworthy but are not virtues because they are without choice; they contribute to the natural virtues, but virtues require prudence. The mean is more opposed to the extremes than they are to each other, since both can even be found together in the same person. Not all extremes are equally opposed to the mean, for reasons already stated.*

All these means are praiseworthy, but they are not virtues nor their op- 1234a23 posites vices, for they are without choice. They are all of them in divisions of the passions,[5] for each of them is a passion, and because they are natural things they contribute to the natural virtues. For, as will be said in later discussions,[6] each is somehow a virtue, natural ones too in another way,[7] when with prudence. So envy contributes to injustice (for actions out of envy are a30 directed at another) and righteous indignation to justice; shame to temperance (which is why they also define temperance in this genus);[8] and the true man is sensible and the false man, by contrast, senseless.

The mean is more opposed to the extremes than they are to each other, 1234a34 because with neither of them does it come to be but they often come to be with each other; and sometimes the same people are rash-cowards, or prodigal in some things and illiberal in others, or are on the whole uneven in a bad way. For whenever they are uneven in a noble way, they become means; for the extremes are in a way in the mean.

1234b6   But the oppositions to the mean do not seem to be both present in the extremes in a like way, but sometimes they accord with the excess and sometimes with the deficiency. Reasons are the two facts mentioned before,[9] both rarity (as of those insensitive to pleasures), and that what we err more toward

b10   appears more opposed; but the third is that what is more similar appears less opposed, as has happened with boldness[10] in respect of rashness, and prodigality in respect of liberality.

1234b13   We have, then, pretty much spoken about the other virtues, the praiseworthy ones; now we must speak about justice.

Notes

1.   The Greek word is *eirōn*, the origin of our word irony.
2.   *Odyssey* 3.20.
3.   The construal of the Greek followed at 1234a16 here is from Von Fragstein (1978: 156). An alternative translation would be: "provided it is of that sort [sc. funny], one instance of which is a jest."
4.   Some scholars wish to insert at 1234a21 a "not" before "painful," but unnecessarily because the Greek MSS have no "not." The sense would be the same in any case: a good joke should not be judged by whether the butt of the joke is pained by it (or not)—it being judged bad if he is pained and good otherwise—but by whether the witty man is pleased by it (Von Fragstein again, ibid.). The witty man is the proper measure not the target of the joke, whoever he is and however he reacts.
5.   2.3.1221a1, 3, 6–8, 23–28, 38–b3.
6.   5.13.
7.   The MSS at 1234a29 have *kai physikai allōs* (natural ones too in another way), but a widely accepted suggestion of Spengel's would emend to *kai physei kai allōs* (both by nature and in another way), thus giving the overall sense: "each virtue in a way exists both by nature and in another way with prudence." The MSS reading, even without emendation, can fit what is said in 5.13.
8.   A likely reference to *VV* 4.1250b6ff., 6.1251a16ff.; also perhaps to Plato *Charmides* 160e4, *Phaidros* 253d6, *Laws* 710a5–8 (Dirlmeier 1962: 358).
9.   3.2.1230b15–20; also 2.5.1222a22–b4.
10.   There is no need at 1234b12 to emend "boldness" or "rashness" to "bravery," as some scholars wish, following Bonitz. The likeness, and contrast, is between the boldness of the brave and that of the rash (Dirlmeier 1962: 361).

Book Four: Particular Virtues: Justice

Chapter 1

Nature of Justice

Legal Justice. *Justice is the habit whereby we do just things and injustice the habit whereby we do unjust things, for habits are not of opposites as the sciences are. Habits are recognized from their subject matter and their opposites, and if one of them has two meanings so does the other, and the unjust man is both the lawbreaker and the grasper for more. The latter is about the goods of fortune, the former about the law, which gives commands about all the virtues with a view to happiness. Legal justice is the whole of virtue and is more wonderful than evening and morning star, being virtue in relation to others and not merely to oneself. Its opposite is worst and the whole of vice.*

We must examine justice and injustice, what sort of actions they happen   1129a3
to be about, what sort of mean state justice is, and between what things the
just is a mean. Let our examination follow the same method as what was
said before.[1] So we see that everyone wants to call justice that sort of habit
by which people are doers of what is just and by which they do just deeds
and want what is just; and the same way about injustice, that it is the habit by
which people act unjustly and want what is unjust. Hence let these things be   a10
laid down first for us in outline. For things are not the same way in respect
of the sciences and powers as in respect of the habits. For in the case of a
power and a science there seems to be the same one for opposite things, but
in the case of a habit the opposite is not of the opposites, I mean that it is not   a15
the opposites but only healthy things that are done by health, for we say that
healthy walking is when one walks as he who is healthy walks.

Now often the opposite habit is recognized from its opposite, and again   1129a17
often the habits are recognized from their underlying subjects. For if good
condition is clear, bad condition also becomes clear, and from things in good
condition good condition is clear, and from this things in good condition. For
if good condition is firmness of flesh, then bad condition must be flabbiness of
flesh, and what makes for good condition is what makes for firmness in flesh.

The consequence holds for the most part that if one or other of two things   1129a23
is said in more than one way, then the other of them is said in more than
one way also, as that if the just is said in more than one way so is the unjust.
Justice and injustice do seem to be said in more than one way, but because
they are close together in their homonymy they escape notice and are not, as
with things further apart, comparatively plain (for there is plenty of difference

a30 with visible form, as that the collarbone of animals as well as what people lock their doors with have the equivocal name of *kleis*[2]). So let us take up how many ways the unjust man is said.

1129a32 Both he who breaks the law and he who grasps more for himself and is unequal seem to be unjust, so that it is plain that the just man will be both he who is law-abiding and he who is equal. The just then is the lawful and the equal, and the unjust is the unlawful and the unequal. Since the unjust man is a grasper for more, he will be about goods—not all of them but those that good and bad fortune are about, and these are always good simply but not always for this or that person. Men pray for and pursue these things,

b5 though they should not; instead they should pray that the things simply good be also good for themselves, but they should choose things good for themselves. The unjust man does not always choose the more but also, in the case of things simply bad, the less. But because the lesser bad seems also in a way a good, and grasping for more is a grasping of the good, this is why he seems to be a grasper for more; and he is unequal, for this includes and is common to both.

1129b11 Since the lawbreaker was unjust and the law-keeper was just, plainly everything lawful is in a way just. For things determined by the lawgiver are lawful, and each of them we say is just. Laws make proclamations about everything

b15 and aim at the common advantage, either of all or of the best or of those in control, according to virtue or in some other way. Thus in one way we say that just things are things that make and protect happiness and its parts for the political community. The law bids one do the deeds of the brave man, as

b20 not to leave the battle line nor to run away nor to throw aside one's weapons; and the deeds of the temperate man, as not to commit adultery or wanton violence;[3] and those of the mild man, as not to hit people or insult them; and likewise too with the other virtues and sorts of wickedness commanding the one and forbidding the other, and doing so rightly when laid down rightly and in a worse way when laid down offhandedly.

1129b25 Now this justice is complete virtue, not simply, however, but in relation to another. And for this reason justice seems often greatest of the virtues, and neither evening nor morning star to be its like in wonder. Also we say

b30 proverbially "in justice is all virtue entire." It is in fact complete virtue above all, because it is use of complete virtue. And it is complete because he who has it can use virtue toward another too and not only by himself. For many can use virtue in private matters but are unable to do so in what relates to

a1 another. And for this reason the remark of Bias[4] seems well said, that rule will show the man. For the ruler exists precisely in relation to another and in a community. For this same reason justice seems, alone of the virtues, also to be another's good, because it is in relation to another, for it does what is

a5 useful for another, whether to a ruler or a partner in community. He then is worst who uses wickedness both in relation to himself and his friends, but he best who uses virtue, not in relation to himself, but in relation to another. For this is a difficult job.

Now this justice is not part of virtue but the whole of virtue; and the op- posing injustice is not part of vice but the whole of it. How virtue and this justice differ is plain from what has been said. For it is the same as justice but its "to be" is not the same, for qua related to another it is justice, but qua this sort of habit it is virtue simply.   1130a8

Notes

1. Perhaps a reference in particular to what was said about magnanimity at 3.5.1232a19–28, to describe the virtue by describing first the man with the virtue, and to distinguish between different things that nevertheless seem the same.
2. Namely "key." An example in English would be "bank," which means both a green, grassy slope and a financial institution.
3. The Greek at 1129b22 is *hubris*, which can mean also rape.
4. Bias of Priene, sixth century BC, one of the traditional Seven Wise Men.

Chapter 2

Particular Justice
That and What It Is. *That there is another and particular justice is shown by there being a particular injustice that is the grasping for more, and that to commit a wrong for the sake of gain, as adultery, is to be unjust rather than licentious, and that to no other vice but injustice is reference made back when someone grasps for more. So, particular justice and particular injustice are about honor and money and security in relation to another, and the unjust is both the unlawful and the unequal, and the just is both the lawful and the equal, each being related as whole to part. The former, which concerns the commands of law about practicing every virtue and avoiding every vice and about education, is not the topic here but rather the latter.*

We, however, are seeking the justice that is part of virtue, for there is one,   1130a14
as we say, and likewise in the case of the injustice that is a part. Here is a sign of the fact. For he who is active in the other sorts of wickedness, as he who has thrown away his shield through cowardice or has spoken ill through harsh temper or has not helped out with his money through miserliness, is not grasping more profit for himself. But when he does grasp more, it is   a20
often not through any such wickedness—no, not even from all of them; yet it is at least through some depravity (for we blame it) and through some injustice. So there is some other injustice, at any rate, that is as a part of the whole, and some unjust that is a part of the whole unjust of breaking the law.

1130a24   Further, if one person commits adultery for the sake of profit and gains by it while another pays for it and suffers loss because of desire, the latter would seem more licentious than grasping and the former to be unjust but not licentious; plainly, then, it was because he made a profit. Further, in the case of all other unjust deeds a reference back to some wickedness is always a30   made, as that, if he committed adultery, reference is to license, if he deserted the comrade beside him in the battle line, to cowardice, if he struck someone, to anger. But if he made a profit, reference is made back to no wickedness but to injustice.

1130a32   It is clear as a result that there is another injustice besides injustice as a whole, a partial one the same with it in name, because the definition is in the same genus. For both have their power in being in relation to another, but the one is about honor or money or security (or whatever single name we might have to cover all these things) and is for the pleasure got from b5   profit, while the other is about everything that the virtuous man is about. That there is more than one justice, then, and that there is also some other besides the whole of virtue, is plain, and what it is and what it is like needs to be understood.

1130b8   So the unjust is divided as the unlawful and the unequal, and the just as the lawful and the equal. Now the injustice first spoken of was injustice in accord with the unlawful. But since the unequal and the unlawful[1] are not the same but different as part to whole (for everything unequal is unlawful, but not everything unlawful is unequal), the unjust and injustice are not the same but different from those, these latter as part and those as whole. For b15   the injustice here is part of total injustice, and likewise the justice part of total justice. We must, as a result, speak about the justice that is in part and the injustice that is in part, and about the just and the unjust in the same way.

1130b18   As for the justice and injustice ranked according to total virtue, the first being use of total virtue and the second of total vice toward another, let them be dismissed. The just and the unjust too that accord with them, it is clear how they are to be defined. For most of the lawful things are pretty much the things total virtue prescribes. For the law prescribes living in accord with b25   every virtue and forbids living in accord with any vice. The things productive of total virtue are all the things of law that have been legislated as to education for what is common. But as to the education of each singly, by which a man is simply good, it must be determined later whether it belongs to politics or some other study. For perhaps it is not the same thing for a man to be good and also for each citizen to be so.[2]

Its Kinds. Of particular justice, one sort distributes the goods of a community, and the other sets exchanges right. Exchanges are either voluntary, as selling and buying and the like, or involuntary, as burglary and assault and the like.

Of justice in part, and of the just in accord with it, one sort is that which 1130b30
is found in the distributions of honor or money or the other things that are
divisible among sharers in the regime (for in these things one person can
have an inequality or an equality with another), and one sort is that which
sets exchanges right. Of this latter there are two parts. For of exchanges a1
some are voluntary and some involuntary, the voluntary being such things
as selling, buying, lending, pledging, using, depositing, hiring (they are
called voluntary because the principle of these exchanges is voluntary), a5
and the involuntary being in some cases by stealth, as burglary, adultery,
poisoning, seduction, alienating of slaves, assassination, slander, and in
other cases by force, as assault, restraint, death, plunder, mutilation, insult
in words, insult in deeds.

Notes

1.   For "unlawful" here at 1130b11 and in the next lines, some MSS have "more,"
     giving the sense "the unequal and the more are not the same . . ." etc.
2.   A reference to the *Politics*, and in particular to 3.4, 4(7).1–2, 5(8).1.

Chapter 3

Distributive Justice. *The equal is the mean of the more and the less, and the
just is the equal and thus a mean. As a mean it is between certain things; as
equal it is between two things; as just it is for certain persons. It is therefore in
four things at a minimum, which must be equal with each other, and if they
are not, fights and complaints arise. But about the principle of worth there is
dispute, whether it is freedom or wealth or virtue. An equality of four terms
(whether discrete or continuous) is a proportion: as A is to B, so B (or C) is to D.
Justice is such a proportion, a geometrical proportion as it is called. Injustice
is against this proportion.*

Since the unjust man is the unequal man and the unjust thing the unequal 1131a9
thing, clearly there is also a mean of the unequal. This is what the equal is.
For the equal is found in any action whatever that the more and the less are
found in. So if the unjust is the unequal the just is the equal, which is something that all think even without argument. But since the equal is a mean,
the just would be some sort of mean. The equal is found in two things at a
minimum. The just, then, must be both a mean and an equal, and be so in a15
relation to something and for certain persons. And insofar as it is a mean, it
must be between certain things (which are the more and the less), and insofar
as it is equal it must be between two things, and insofar as it is just it must be
for certain persons. The just therefore must be at a minimum in four things,

for those between whom the just happens to be are two, and that in which it happens to be, the things, are two.

1131a20 And there will be the same equality for the whom as for the things in which. For as the latter are (the things in which), so the former are. For if they are not equals they will not have what is equal, but this is how fights and accusations arise, when equals have or are allotted what is not equal and not

a25 equals what is equal. Further, this is plain from the matter of worth. For all agree that the just in distributions must be according to some sort of worth, though the worth that they all say it is is not the same, but democrats say it is freedom, oligarchs wealth, others good birth, aristocrats virtue.

1131a29 The just then is something proportional; for proportion is not only a feature of numbers taken as units but of number as a whole. For proportion is equality of ratios and exists in a minimum of four terms. That discrete proportion has four terms is obvious. But so does continuous proportion as well; for it uses one term as two and says it twice, as in the case, for instance, of A being to B as B is to C. So the B is said twice and consequently, if the B is set down twice, the terms of the proportion will be four.

1131b3 The just too is in a minimum of four terms, and the account is the same. For the for whom and the what are divided in like way. So the A term will be to the B term as the C term is to the D term, and then, by alternation, the A term will be to the C term as the B term is to the D term, and consequently the whole, which the distribution couples together, to the whole. And if it puts them together in this way, it couples them justly. The junction then of

b10 the A term to the C term and of the B term to the D term is justice in distribution, and the just is a mean, that is, of what is against proportion,[1] for proportion is a mean and the just is a proportion. Mathematicians call such a proportion geometrical; for in geometry too, the whole happens to be to the whole what each of the two terms happens to be to each. This proportion is not continuous, for the for whom and the what do not become a single numerical term.

1131b16 Now the just is this proportion, but the unjust is what is against proportion. The one term, then, becomes more and the other less; which is what in fact actually happens, for the one who wrongs has more of the good and

b20 the one who is wronged less. It is contrariwise in the case of the bad, for the lesser bad is reckoned a good in comparison with the greater bad; for the lesser bad is more to be preferred than the greater, and what is to be preferred is good and what is more to be preferred a greater good. One form, then, of the just is this.

Note

1. At 1131b11 instead of *tou* (of [what . . .]) a Latin translation read *to de adikon to* (the unjust is [what . . .]). Either reading may stand, the second obviously and the first in the sense that the mean that is proportion is "of" things that are against proportion because it is between them.

Chapter 4

Commutative Justice

What It Is. *Justice that sets things right is not according to geometrical proportion but numerical, for here what makes the difference is not who did the wrong or the harm but what the harm or wrong was that was done. The wrong or harm is a gain to the one doing it and a loss to the one suffering it, and justice is a matter of taking away the gain and repairing the loss, and so it is a mean of gain and loss. This mean is what the judge must find, by determining how much to take away and how much to restore, so as to produce the numerically equal. Hence that by which he who has more exceeds the mean must be taken from him, and that by which he who has less is exceeded by the mean must be added to him. The terms loss and gain come from voluntary exchange, but they are applied also to involuntary exchanges.*

The remaining form is the rectifying one, which happens in exchanges 1131b25 both voluntary and involuntary. This justice has a different form from the previous one. For the justice that distributes the common things is always in accord with the proportion mentioned. For if there is going to be a distribution from common monies, it will be in accord with the same ratio that the b30 amounts brought in have to each other; and the injustice that is counterpart to this justice is the injustice against proportion.

The just in exchanges is something equal and the unjust unequal, only it 1131b32 does not follow the former proportion but the numerical one. For it makes no difference if a decent man has despoiled a base one, or a base man a decent one—not even if it is adultery that the decent or base man has committed. But the law looks only to the difference of the harm and uses both as equals, whether the former is doing wrong and the latter being wronged, or whether he did the harm and the other has suffered harm.

So it is this injustice that, being an inequality, the judge tries to equalize. 1132a6 For whenever indeed one is struck and another strike or also kill and the other die, the suffering and the doing are divided in unequal parts. But he tries to make things equal by imposing a loss, taking it away from the gain. For that is what, speaking simply, is said in such cases, even though it is not a10 a name that fits some things, as gain for him who strikes and loss for him who suffers; but when the suffering is measured at least it is called loss here and gain there. Consequently the equal is a mean of the more and the less, a15 and gain and loss are more and less in reverse ways—more of good and less of bad being gain, and the reverse loss. Of these the equal, which we say is just, was a mean. So rectifying justice would be the mean of loss and gain.

That is why, when people are in dispute, they have recourse to the judge; 1132a19 and to go to the judge is to go to the just, for to be a judge means to be, as it were, the just made alive. In fact people seek a judge who is a mean, and some call judges mediators, on the grounds that if they get the mean they will be getting what is just. The just then is a mean, if indeed the judge is too. The judge does the equalizing and, as if from a line cut into unequal parts, takes off that by which the greater part exceeds the halfway point and adds it to the lesser part. When the whole has been cut in half, they then say, when they get the equal, that they have their own. The equal is a mean of the greater and the less in accord with numerical proportion.

For this reason indeed they name it *just*, because it is *ad-justed*, as if one were to say it was *ad-just* and as if the judge were an *ad-judge*.[1] For when something is taken away from one of two equals and is added to the other, the other exceeds it by this twofold amount. For if there were a taking away but no adding, it would exceed by one amount only. It exceeds the mean, then, by one, and the mean exceeds what had something taken away from it by one. So this is how we will know what we are to take away from what has more and what to add to what has less. For that by which the mean exceeds, this we must add to what has less, and that by which it is exceeded we must take away from the largest. Let the lines *AA* and *BB* and *CC* be equal to each other. From *AA* let the length *AE* be taken, and let it be added to the line *CC* (the length marked *DC*), so that the whole line *DCC* exceeds the line *EA* by the lengths *DC* and *CF*, therefore exceeding the line *BB* by the length *DC*.[2] (This point holds of the other arts too, for they would be destroyed if what the maker did and how much and of what sort was not what and how much and what sort the thing that was being worked on received.)[3]

These names loss and gain have come from voluntary exchange, for having more than what is one's own is called gaining and having less than at the beginning is called losing, as in the case of buying and selling and all other things that the law has left aside. And people say, whenever it happens that things are neither more nor less but are theirs, that they have what is their own and are neither losing nor gaining. Consequently, the just in the case of things that are contrary to what is voluntary is a mean between a certain gain and loss, the having of what is equal both before and after.

Notes

1. The italicized words are an attempt to capture in English Aristotle's etymological pun at 1132a30–32, which makes use of the Greek word *dicha* (in two, half) to derive *dikaion* (just) from an imaginary word *dichaion* and *dikastēs* (judge, juror) from an imaginary word *dichastēs*.
2. The diagram would look something like this:

	A	E	A
	B		B
D	C	F	C

3. The words at 1132b9–11 (in the parenthesis) are repeated at 1133a14–16 and are deleted by some scholars from the text here. They may be retained, however, in both places for they make the same point but relative to different contexts: here relative to equality in taking away and adding, there relative to reciprocity of exchange.

Chapter 5

How It Is and Is Not Reciprocity. *Being done to as one did, in the way the Pythagoreans said, is not justice, for if someone strikes an office holder he should not only be struck back but punished in addition. Reciprocity does, however, hold communities together when it is according to proportion and people give as they have received. The proportion is diagonal conjunction, as when the work of the cobbler is equalized by proportion to that of the builder and each receives equal in the exchange. The measure for equalizing is money (or currency by convention), as reflective of need. Without differences in work done and without need there will be no exchange. Money also varies in value but it is more stable, and by its means community and equalization of goods and exchange are effected.*

Some think that being done to as one did is just simply, as the Pythagoreans said. For the just they defined simply as the other having done to him what he did. But being done to as one did does not fit either distributive or rectifying justice; and yet this is what they at any rate want even the just of Rhadamanthus[1] to mean: 1132b21 b25

Get he what he did, straight would justice be.

For it often fails to agree. For example, if someone in office has struck a blow he should not be struck in return, and if someone has struck an office holder he should not only be struck but punished as well. Further, the voluntary differs greatly from the involuntary.

But this sort of justice, being done to as one did, when it follows proportion and not equality, does hold communities of exchange together. For by proportional doing in return the city stays together. For people seek either to return evil (otherwise, if there is no doing in return, they deem it slavery), or to return good. If not, there is no giving and giving back; but it is by giving back that they stay together. That is why they make a temple to the Graces in prominent places for themselves, to ensure there is giving back. For this is peculiar to grace, that one should give a service back to the doer of a grace, and be the first to do a grace next time. 1132b31 a1 a5

1133a5   What makes for proportional return giving is diagonal conjunction.[2] Let *A* be a builder, *B* a cobbler, *C* a house, *D* a shoe. So the builder must take the cobbler's work from the cobbler and give to him his own work back. If, then,

a10   there is first proportional equality, and next there is being done to as one did, there will be what was said; otherwise there is no equality nor staying together. For nothing stops it being the case that the work of one of them is greater than the other's, so there has to be an equalizing. This point holds

a15   of the other arts too, for they would be destroyed if what the maker did and how much and of what sort was not what and how much and what sort the thing that was being worked on received. For no community exists made up of two doctors, but of a doctor and a farmer and, on the whole, of those who are different and not equal.

1133a18   Still, they must be equalized. So everything exchangeable must be commensurable, which is what money came in for, becoming a sort of mean. For it measures everything, so that it measures excess and deficiency too; it measures, then, exactly how many shoes equal a house or food. What a builder is to a cobbler, therefore, this many shoes must be to a house or food. For if this is not the case there will be neither exchange nor community. But

a25   this will not be the case if the things are not somehow equal. Everything must be measured, then, as was said before, by some one thing. This one thing is, in truth, need, which holds everything together (for if people needed nothing, or not in a like way, there will be either no exchange or not the same exchange). But as a substitute for need currency has, by convention, come about. That is why it has the name "currency," because it does not exist by nature but by current law,[3] and we have it in our power to change it or make it useless.

1133a31   So being done to as one did will exist whenever there is an equalization such that what a farmer is to a cobbler the cobbler's work is to the farmer's.

b1   But one must not draw them into a figure of proportion when they are exchanging; otherwise the one extreme will have both excesses.[4] But when they have what is their own they are in this way equal and sharers, because the equality in question can in their case be made: let *A* be a farmer, *C* food, *B* a cobbler, and *D* his work as equalized. If being done to as one did was not in this way possible there would have been no sharing.

1133b6   That need, as being some one thing, does the holding together is plain from the fact that whenever people are not in need of each other, whether on both sides or on one, they do not exchange in the way they do when someone needs what he himself has, as need of wine when they are giving export of

b10   corn. This, then, must be equalized, and as for future exchange, if nothing is needed now, our guarantee that exchange will be possible if need arise is currency, for he who brings this has to be able to get things.

1133b13   Now currency too suffers the same, that it does not always have equal value. Still it does tend to be more stable. That is why a price has to have

been put on everything, for in this way there will always be exchange, and b15
if exchange, community. So currency is like a measure making things commensurate and equalizing them. For if there was no exchange there would be no community, nor exchange if there was no equality, nor equality if there was no common measure.

Now things so different cannot in truth be commensurate, but it is pos- 1133b18
sible enough in relation to need. So there must be some one thing, and that by supposition; hence it is called currency. For this makes everything commensurate, for everything is measured by currency. Let A be a house, B ten minas,[5] C a bed. Let A be half of B, if the house is worth or equal to five minas. Let the bed, C, be a tenth part of B. So it is plain how many beds equal one b25
house, namely five. That this is how exchange was before there was currency is plain, for it makes no difference whether five beds are exchanged for one house or how much five beds are worth is.

Justice as a Mean State. *Just action is intermediate between wronging and being wronged, and justice is a mean state because it is of a mean. It is the virtue whereby the just man does the just thing and distributes the equal to himself and others. Injustice is distributing more of the beneficial to oneself and less to others and the reverse in the case of the harmful, so it is both an excess and deficiency. The more in the case of an unjust deed is to do wrong and the less is to be wronged.*

What the unjust is, then, and what the just, has been stated. With 1133b29
these things marked off, it is plain that just action is a mean between wronging and being wronged; for the one is a having more and the other a having less. Justice is a certain mean state, not in the same way as the other virtues, but because it is of a mean; injustice by contrast is of the extremes.

Justice is the virtue by which the just man is said to be a doer, by choice, of 1134a1
what is just, and a distributor, both to himself in relation to someone else and to another in relation to another—not of the preferable, so as to give more to himself and less to his neighbor, nor of the harmful, so as to do the reverse, a5
but of the equal, the equal that follows proportion—and to do likewise for another in relation to another. Injustice, on the contrary, is of the unjust. This is excess and deficiency, against proportion, of the beneficial and harmful. That is why injustice is an excess and a deficiency, because it is of excess and deficiency—excess of the simply beneficial as well as deficiency of the harmful a10
as regards oneself, and in like manner as regard others, on the whole, save against proportion whichever way it happens. In the case of an unjust deed, the less is to be wronged and the more is to wrong.

About justice, then, and injustice, what the nature of each is, let our state- 1134a14
ment be like this, and likewise in general about the just and unjust.

Notes

1. One of the judges in the Underworld. The quotation is attributed to Hesiod.
2. The diagram would look something like this, where A gets B's product D, and B gets A's product C:

A   B

C   D

3. The Greek for currency or coin at1133a30 is *nomisma* and is derived from *nomos*, which is the Greek for law.
4. These remarks at 1133a33–b1–2 are obscure. Perhaps the sense is that if a cobbler and a builder start calculating the exchange value of their products in the middle of a transaction, they will calculate on the basis of the products and not on the basis of the relation that the products bear to the producer. Suppose (to mix Aristotle's examples) that the costs and demands of making one hundred pairs of shoes are to a cobbler what the costs and demands of making one house are to a builder. Then, in relation to their producers, one hundred pairs of shoes equal one house. But abstracted from this relation one hundred pairs of shoes are to a house as one number to another number, so that, in an exchange on this basis, the cobbler should get one for one, or one hundred houses for one hundred pairs of shoes (for only thus would he receive the same number as he gave). He would gain much and pay little, while the builder would gain little and pay much, and both excesses would end up on the side of one extreme.
5. A mina was equivalent to one hundred drachmas, and one drachma was an average daily wage.

Chapter 6

Relation of Justice to the Just Thing
That Doing the Thing and Being Just or Unjust Are Different. *Being unjust is not a matter of which things one does, for one can do any unjust thing without being unjust.*

1134a17   Since[1] one can do wrong and not yet be an unjust man, what sorts of wrong acts are those by doing which one is, in the case of each injustice, unjust in fact, as for example a thief or an adulterer or a brigand? Or will there be no difference when the question is taken in this way? For if one had intercourse

a20   with a woman knowing who she was but doing it from passion and not from a principle of choice, then one does do something wrong but without being unjust—one is not a thief, for example, though one did steal, nor an adulterer though one did commit it. And so likewise in the other cases.[2]

Why and How They Are Different
Kinds of Just and Unjust Thing
In General. *The just thing is to be understood in accordance with all the senses of justice: the reciprocal, the simple, the political, and the domestic. The political just is what belongs to those who share self-sufficient existence together, who have law among themselves, and where each gets what is equal and not more (except proportionally). The just of master and slaves and of father and sons is like the political just but not properly, because sons and property are like parts and do not have a share in ruling and being ruled. Wives do thus have a share and domestic justice exists with them.*

Now the way that being done to as one did is related to the just thing was   1134a23
said before, but one must not forget that what we are looking for is both the simply just and the political just.[3] The latter exists in the case of those who share together a way of life aimed at self-sufficiency, who are free and equal, whether in proportion or number. So, all those who do not have this do not have the political just with respect to each other, but rather the just in a certain respect and by way of likeness. For those have justice who also have law   a30
in relation to each other, and those among whom there is injustice have law, for right is judgment of the just and the unjust. And in those in whom there is injustice there is also doing wrong, but not in all those in whom there is doing wrong is there injustice.

Doing wrong is distributing more to oneself of the simply good things and   1134a33
less of the simply bad things. That is why we let reason rule and not man, because man does this for himself and becomes a tyrant. But the ruler is a guardian of the just, and if of the just then of the equal; and since, if he really is just, it seems he makes no gain (for he does not distribute to himself more of what is simply good, unless it is proportional to him; hence he toils for another, and that is why they say justice is another's good, as was also   b5
remarked earlier),[4] so some wage should be given him, and honor and privilege are this. But he for whom this is not enough—these become tyrants.

The just in the case of master and of father are not the same as these but like   1134b8
them. For injustice toward what is simply one's own is impossible, and property and the child (until of a certain age and independent) are as if a part of oneself, but no one deliberately chooses to harm himself. That is why there is no injustice toward oneself, and so not the political unjust and just either. For that was in accord with law and for those in whom law naturally existed, and they were those for whom there is equality in ruling and being ruled. That is why it   b15
is rather toward a wife that the just can exist than toward children or property. For the just in the household is this, and it is different from the political just.

Notes

1. If this paragraph is read as introducing the question of the difference between doing the just or unjust thing, on the one hand, and being just or unjust, on the other (a question that requires first a discussion of just and unjust things in chapters 6 and 7 before being resolved thereafter), it need not be considered out of place, as some scholars suppose (e.g., Ostwald [1981: 129n40], Broadie and Rowe [2002: 346], Kenny [2011:165]).
2. Cf. above 4.2.1130a24–32.
3. The simply just is particular justice, the topic of chapters 2 to 5, and the political just is general or legal justice, the topic of chapter 1.
4. Above at 4.1.1130a3–4.

Chapter 7

The Political Just in Particular. *The political just is both natural and legal, the former being what has the same force everywhere and the latter being indifferent at first and only making a difference by convention. With us (though not with the gods) the natural is variable, and yet some things for us are natural and some not so but by contract. The same distinction holds of hands, where the right hand is naturally stronger but we could all be dexterous with both. Things just by contract are like measures, which are not the same for buying as for selling. So the just human things that are not natural differ, as also do regimes, though only one regime is naturally the best everywhere.*

1134b18   Of the political just there is the natural and the legal: natural being what has everywhere the same force and not because it is thought so or not thought so; legal being what makes no difference this way or that at the start but does after people lay it down, as to charge a mina for a ransom, or to sacrifice a goat and not two sheep, and also what people legislate for particular cases, as to sacrifice to Brasidas,[1] and things passed by decree.

1134b24   Some think everything is of this sort because what is by nature is unchangeable and has everywhere the same force, as that fire burns both here and among Persians, but they see just things changing. This is not how it is, except in a way, though at any rate with the gods perhaps it is not so at all. With us there is something that is by nature. Everything may be changeable but yet one thing is by nature and another not by nature. Which sort is by nature, given that things can also be otherwise, and which sort is not but is by law and contract, if indeed both are changeable, is likewise plain. In fact, the same definition will fit the other cases. For by nature the right hand is stronger, yet there are some who could become dexterous with both. What is by contract and what is of advantage in things just are like measures. For

b30

b35

measures of wine and grain are not everywhere equal but greater for buying and less for selling. And likewise the just things that are nonnatural but human are not everywhere the same, since not even regimes are, though one alone is everywhere according to nature the best.

All the Kinds Together. The kinds of just things are related to their instances as universals to particulars. The thing and the deed are different in each case, for the just and unjust thing exist by nature and order and only become a just and an unjust deed when actually done. An examination of the particulars must await a later occasion.

Of the just and legal things each is as universals are to particulars, for things 1135a5
that are done are many but each of them is one, because it is universal. The unjust deed and the unjust thing are different as well as the just deed and the just thing. For an unjust thing exists by nature or order. But this same thing, when done, is an unjust deed, and before it is done it is not yet so, though it is a10
an unjust thing. The like holds of a just deed, though the general term is called rather just action and a just deed is the setting right of the unjust deed.[2] As regards each particular among them, what their kinds are, how many, what sort of things they are about—that must be examined later.[3] a15

Notes

1. A Spartan general at the time of the Peloponnesian War who, because of his great deeds in battle in Northern Greece (whence Aristotle himself hailed), was much honored there by the people.
2. Aristotle is giving technical precision here to certain cognate Greek terms: *adikēma* is unjust deed, *adikon* unjust thing, *dikaiōma* just deed, *dikaion* just thing, *dikaiopragma* just action.
3. Possibly a reference to the *Politics*, and in particular 8(6).8.

Chapter 8

Kinds of Doing the Just and Unjust Thing. One does wrong or does right when one does a just or unjust thing voluntarily, and then also one is just or unjust but otherwise not. The voluntary is what is up to oneself and is done knowing the relevant facts, not by force or accidentally. Voluntary things are chosen when they are deliberated over, otherwise not. There are several sorts of harms that arise in communities: a mistake is what is done through ignorance but is not unexpected; a misfortune is when it is unexpected; a wrong is when it is done knowingly but not deliberately, and one is unjust when one does it by choice and not through passion. Rightly then is what is done in anger judged not to be done by forethought. Anger is also directed against apparent injustice. If the wrong or the right is done deliberately or by choice the doer is unjust or just. Wrongs done involuntarily are pardonable if done in and because of ignorance, but not pardonable if done in ignorance but because of some unnatural or inhuman passion.

1135a15   Since the just and unjust things are as stated, whenever someone does these things voluntarily he does wrong or does right, but whenever involuntarily he neither does wrong nor does right, except incidentally—for he does things that happen to be just or unjust. But an unjust deed and just action

a20   are defined by the voluntary and involuntary, for whenever it is voluntary it is blamed, and it is then at once also an unjust deed. So there will be a thing that is unjust but that is not yet an unjust deed, unless the voluntary is added to it.

1135a23   I mean by voluntary, as was indeed stated earlier,[1] that which among things up to him someone does knowingly and not in ignorance of the whom or the with what or the for which—as his striking a certain person with a

a25   certain thing and for a certain end and none of these being accidental or by force (for example it would not be voluntary if someone took one's hand and struck another, for it was not up to oneself). It could be that the one struck is his father and he recognizes that he is a man or one of those present but does not know that he is his father.[2] Likewise this sort of distinction must be made about the end for the sake of which and about the action as a whole.

1135a31   So that which is not known, or, though not unknown, is not up to oneself, or is by force, is involuntary. For many things there are even among what exists by nature that we do and undergo knowingly none of which is either voluntary or involuntary, as getting old or dying. The like holds also of the accidental in the case of unjust and just things. For if someone were to give

b5   back a deposit involuntarily and through fear, it should not be said that he is either doing the just thing or acting justly except accidentally. In like manner it should be said that someone who under compulsion and involuntarily does not give back a deposit is by accident acting wrongly and doing wrong things. In the case of voluntary things some we choose to do and others we do without choosing, all the things we deliberate over being things we choose and all the things we do not deliberate over not being things we choose.

1135b11   There are then three harms within communities. Those done through ignorance are mistakes when what he did or against whom or with what or what for are not what he supposed, for he thought he was not hitting or not

b15   with this or not this man or not for this end, but it turned out not to be for the end he supposed (as that he thought not to wound but to prick) or not to be whom or not with what. So when the harm comes about unexpectedly, it is a misfortune, but when it is not unexpected, though it is without vice, it is a mistake (for it is a mistake when the beginning of the cause is in oneself but a misfortune when it is from outside). When, however, it happens knowingly b20 but not deliberately, it is a wrong, as is everything done in anger or in other passions that necessarily or naturally befall men. For when people are causing these harms and doing these mistakes they are doing wrong and what they do are wrongs, but they are not yet for this reason unjust nor are they depraved, for the harm is not done through wickedness. But when one acts from choice one is unjust and wicked.

That is why the judgment that what is done in anger is not done by fore- 1135b25 thought is a noble one. For the one who acts in anger is not the origin but the one who made him angry. Also, the dispute is not about its happening or not, but about its justice. For anger is directed against seeming injustice. For the dispute is not about whether it happened (as it is in contracts where, b30 unless they are acting in ignorance, one party must be wicked), but the deed is agreed, and the dispute is about its justice (though he who planned ahead is not ignorant), so that the one thinks he was wronged and the other does not. If the harm was deliberate he does wrong, and it is in these sorts of a1 wrongs—where the deed is contrary to proportion or equality—that he who does the wrong is unjust. And likewise he who does the just thing by choice is just (he acts justly provided only he does it voluntarily).

Of involuntary things some are forgivable and some are not. What is done 1136a5 not only in ignorance but because of ignorance is forgivable, but what is done in ignorance though not because of ignorance but because of a passion neither natural nor human[3] is not forgivable.

Notes

1. 2.9.1225b1–10.
2. Possibly a reference to the story of Oedipus, who thus unknowingly struck, and killed, his own father.
3. As, for instance, the passion of a cruel tyrant.

Chapter 9

Kinds of Suffering the Just and Unjust Thing
Statement of Puzzles. *First: is it possible to be wronged voluntarily or is it all involuntary? Likewise with being treated justly. Are both all one way or the other, or not? But not all just treatment is voluntary, for some people are involuntarily treated justly. Second: is everyone who suffers wrong wronged or can both be accidental, for a just exchange can be accidental on both sides and doing a wrong thing is not the same as wrongdoing, nor is suffering wrong the same as being wronged (for an agent who wrongs or treats justly is needed in the one case but not in the other)? Third, if wronging is harming someone*

voluntarily and the incontinent harms himself voluntarily, then he is voluntarily wronged, and he also wrongs himself. But, fourth, it is a puzzle whether one can wrong oneself. Fifth, the incontinent might be voluntarily wronged by someone who voluntarily wronged him.

1136a10   One might raise the puzzle, if sufficient distinction has been made about being wronged and wronging, first whether things are as Euripides said in his strange remark:

> "My mother, brief the tale, is by me slain."
> "But willing or unwilling were ye twain?"[1]

a15   For is it truly possible for someone to be wronged voluntarily, or is it not but all of it is involuntary just as all wrong doing is voluntary? And is it all this way or all that way (as all wrong doing is voluntary), or is one side voluntary and the other involuntary? Likewise too with being treated justly (for all just action is voluntary). So the result would be the reasonable one that the

a25 opposites are similar on each side, being wronged and being treated justly being either both voluntary or both involuntary. But it would seem an odd thing, indeed, in the case of being justly treated, that all of it is voluntary, for some people are involuntarily treated justly.[2]

1136a23   Next, one might raise the puzzle whether everyone who suffers wrong is wronged, or whether it is with the suffering as it is with the doing, for a just exchange can be accidental on both sides. Plainly it is similar in the case of wrongs too. For doing the wrong thing is not the same as wrongdoing, nor is suffering wrong the same as being wronged. The like holds of treating justly and being justly treated, for being wronged without someone wronging or being treated justly without someone treating justly are impossible.

1134a31   But if wrongdoing is simply harming someone voluntarily, and if the voluntary is knowing the whom and the with what and the how, and if he who is incontinent harms himself voluntarily, then he would be wronged voluntarily. Also it would be possible for one to wrong oneself. This is in fact one of the

b1 things that are puzzled over, whether it is possible to wrong oneself. Further, someone might, through incontinence, be voluntarily harmed by someone acting voluntarily, so that he would be wronged voluntarily.

Solution to Puzzles

Being Harmed and Being Wronged. *The puzzles are answered by noting that to the definition of wrong must be added that it be against the will of the one harmed. So while being harmed and suffering wrong things can be voluntary, being wronged cannot be; for no one wants to be wronged, not even the incontinent. Even voluntarily giving away a greater gift for a lesser is not a case of being wronged, for being wronged requires that there be someone doing the wrong.*

Or is the definition not right and to "doing harm when one knows the   1136b3
whom and the with what and the how" there must be further added "against
the will of the one harmed?" So one can be voluntarily harmed and voluntarily
suffer wrong things, but no one is wronged voluntarily. For no one wants to
be wronged, not even he who is incontinent, though he does act against his
will. For the fact is both that no one wants what he does not think is good
and that he who is incontinent does not do what he thinks he should. He
who gives away what is his own, as Homer says Glaucon gave to Diomedes   b10

'Gold for bronze, a hundred oxen for nine,'[3]

is not wronged. For while it was up to him to give, it was not up to him to
be wronged, but there needs to be someone present who does the wronging.
So about being wronged, that it is not voluntary, is plain.

Wrong in Distributions. *If he who awards more than is deserved but not he
who receives it does wrong, then someone who voluntarily awards less to himself wrongs himself—as seems to be true of the equitable man. But this is to
simplify, for the equitable man gets more of a different good, as of reputation
or the noble, and he is, if at all, only harmed and not wronged. The wrong in
the award is in him who awards, for the deed originates with him; also instruments do wrong in one sense but not in another; also making a wrong award
in ignorance is not against the justice of law; also the awarder, if he does not
make the award in ignorance, does anyway get some share in the wrong, not
of the thing awarded but of something else (favor or revenge or money).*

Of the things we chose to speak of there are two left, whether the one who   1136b15
distributes more against desert or the one who has it does the wrong, and
whether one can wrong oneself.[4] For if the first thing mentioned is possible
and the distributor of more, but not the one who has more, does wrong, then
if someone knowingly and voluntarily distributes to another more than to
himself, he himself wrongs himself—which is what in fact moderated people   b20
seem to do, for the equitable man is a taker of less.[5] Or is this not a simplifica-
tion? For he takes more, if it chances, of a different good, as of reputation or
the simply noble. Further, the solution comes from the definition of doing
wrong. For he does nothing against his own will, so he is not, for this reason
at any rate, wronged but only, if at all, harmed.

It is also evident that it is the distributor who does wrong and not always he   1136b25
who has more. For it is not he with whom the unjust thing is who does wrong,
but he with whom is the voluntary doing of it; this is where the beginning of
the deed starts, and it is in the distributor not the receiver. Further, since doing
is said in many ways and since there is a sense in which lifeless things and the   b30
hand and the servant of the one who commands do the killing,[6] they are not
committing the wrong, but they are doing wrong things. Further, if someone

passed judgment in ignorance, he does not do wrong according to legal justice, nor is his judgment unjust, though it is in a way (for the legally just is different from the primary kind).[7] But if he knowingly made a wrong judgment, he does in fact himself take more, whether of favor or revenge. It is as if, then, he had divided up the wrong, and he who judges in this way does unjustly have more, for in fact, in making judgment of land for that man, he took, not land, but money.

a1

Being Just and Unjust

Toward Others. *To be a wrongdoer or just is not easy, contrary to what people think, but requires the habit. Also, to know the just and unjust things is not to know the what (as the things the law talks about) but the how, as is also true of health where the doctor is not he who knows the particular healthy things but he who knows how to apply them. Likewise, the just man and the courageous man are physically able to do unjust and cowardly things, yet injustice and cowardice are not in doing these things but in doing them with the relevant habit. Justice is about things that are simply good for those who can have too much or too little of them. So it is not for the gods, who cannot have them too much, nor for the incurably wicked, who cannot have them too little. Justice is thus a human thing.*

1137a4   People think that doing wrong is up to them themselves; hence they also think it easy to be just. But it is not so. To lie with one's neighbor's wife and to strike a bystander and to slip someone money are easy and up to them, but to do these things with such and such a habit is neither easy nor up to them.

a10   Likewise they think it no smart thing to know what is just and what is unjust, because it is not hard to grasp what the laws talk about. But these things are not what is just, except incidentally, but the how of doing and of distributing just things is; and that needs more work than knowing what things are

a15   healthy. For there too it is easy to know about honey and wine and hellebore and cautery and surgery, but to know how to distribute these with a view to health, and for whom and when, that takes as much work as being a doctor.

1137a17   For that very reason, in fact, they think wrongdoing is no less a feature of the just, because the just is no less able to do each of these things but even

a20   more; for he is no less able to lie with a woman or to strike someone. Indeed the brave is no less able to throw away his shield and, turning tail, run off no matter where. But being a coward or a wrongdoer is not in doing these things, except incidentally, but in doing them when disposed thus, just as to cure and heal too are not in cutting or in not cutting, or giving or not giving drugs, but in doing them thus.

1137a26   Things just are found in those for whom there is a sharing in things simply good and who have excess and deficiency in them. For there are some for whom it is not possible to have an excess of them, as the gods perhaps, and others, the incurably bad, for whom no share can be of any benefit but it all harms them, and others for whom sharing up to a point is beneficial. That is why it is a human thing.[8]   a30

Notes

1. Euripides, *Alcmaeon*.
2. Such as criminals, when justly punished.
3. *Iliad* 6.236.
4. The first of these two questions refers back to the Glaucon and Diomedes case just mentioned, and the second was stated with the others at the beginning of the chapter. It is also, however, implicated in the Glaucon case, since perhaps Glaucon could be said to have wronged himself in giving so much and receiving so little.
5. Equity is discussed in the next chapter.
6. One is to imagine a servant carrying out a killing at the behest of his master and doing the killing with a weapon carried in his hand.
7. The primary kind is perhaps the natural just, 7.1134b–35a5. Or it is the respective proportions of distributive and corrective justice, and what a particular city lays down as law is the legal just, which may or may not accord with just proportion (for example, in a city with a deviant regime rule is given by law to those to whom it is not by proportion due).
8. Sc. and not a divine or demonic thing.

Chapter 10

A Clarification about Equity. *Equity is praised as better and yet, if it is other than the just, it should not be. The answer is that equity is better as being more just than the legal just. For law is universal, but doable things cannot rightly be spoken of in universal terms. So the law takes what is for the most part and omits the particular exceptions, leaving these to be corrected by equity. Not everything can be decided by law but decrees are needed, being adapted as indefinite to indefinite (like the lead measure used in building in Lesbos). Equity is the just that is better than the legal just, and the equitable or decent man and the virtue of equity are just by mitigating the strictness of the law.*

Equity and the equitable, how equity relates to justice and the equitable to   1137a31
the just, are the next thing to speak about. For it appears, as one examines it, to be neither simply the same thing nor different in kind. In fact sometimes we praise the equitable thing and the man who is such, so that we transfer   a35
the term in place of "good" to other things too when praising them, making plain that what is more equitable is better. But at other times, as one follows the argument, it appears odd if the equitable, being something other than the just, is to be praised. For either the just is not virtuous, or the equitable, if it is different, is not just; or if both are virtuous then they are the same.

1137b6   The puzzle about the equitable, then, arises pretty much for these reasons. But these reasons are all in a way right and not in conflict with each other, for the equitable, being better than justice of a sort, is a better just and is not better than the just by being some other kind of thing. Just and equitable, then, are the same and, though both are virtuous, the equitable is better. What produces the puzzle is that the equitable is just indeed, only not the just by law but what sets right the just by law.

1137b13   Reason is that all law is universal but there are things that cannot rightly be spoken of in universal terms. So where the law must speak universally but cannot speak rightly, it takes, without ignoring the fault, what is for the most part and is no less right. For the fault is not in the law nor in the lawgiver but in the nature of the thing, for the stuff of doable things is that way from the

b20   start. So when the law speaks universally but the thing in this case turns out contrary to the universal, then, where the lawgiver leaves something aside and, because of speaking simply, made a mistake, it is correct to set right what is deficient; and this is what the lawgiver would in fact have said were he there, and, had he known, would have made a law for. That is why it is

b25   just and better than some just—not than the just simply but than the mistake caused by speaking simply; and this is the nature of equity, a setting right of law where it is deficient because of being universal.

1137b27   For this is reason also that not everything is by law, because some things cannot have a law made for them, so that a decree is needed. For of the indefinite the measure is also indefinite, like the leaden measure, indeed, of house-building in Lesbos. For the measure bends to fit the shape of the stone and is not rigid; the decree too bends to fit the facts.

1137b33   What the equitable is, then, and that it is just and better than some just, is plain. Also clear from this is who the equitable man is. For he who is a chooser and doer of this kind of thing and does not tend to the worse by

a1   strictness for justice but settles for less, even though he has the law on his side, is equitable, and this habit is equity, which is a sort of justice and not some other habit.

Chapter 11

Toward Oneself. *The law gives commands in accord with every virtue, as not to kill oneself; but to do harm contrary to the law is to do wrong: so that the suicide suffers harm but wrongs the city and not himself. Injustice in the particular sense, not the universal one, cannot be committed against oneself but only against another. A harm against another seems unjust because it is done first and voluntarily, but wronging oneself would be to suffer and do at the same time; it would also be a case of being wronged voluntarily. No one can commit adultery against his own wife or steal his own things; and by definition no one is wronged voluntarily. To do wrong is to be vicious but to suffer wrong is not, though it may, incidentally, involve a greater harm. Justice in an extended sense taken from domestic justice is possible toward oneself as between the parts of one's soul.*

Whether one can wrong oneself or not is clear from what has been said.   1138a4
For some just things are those the law commands in accord with the whole of virtue, as that the law does not bid one to kill oneself (and the law dissuades from what it does not bid); also, when someone voluntarily harms someone contrary to the law, not by way of returning harm, he does wrong—acting voluntarily when he knows whom and with what; but he who voluntarily slays himself through anger does this against right reason, which the law does not allow. He does wrong then.

But against whom? Is it against the city and not himself? For he suffers   1138a11
voluntarily but no one is wronged voluntarily. That is in fact why the city inflicts punishment, and why a loss of honor falls to one who does away with himself, because he wrongs the city.

Further, when the wrongdoer is merely unjust, and not base in every re-   1138a14
spect, he cannot wrong himself in that way. (For this case is different from the former; for the unjust man can be depraved in the way the coward is, by not having the whole of depravity, so that his wrongdoing does not accord with it.) For it would be possible for the same thing to be taken from and to belong to the same person. This, however, is impossible, but just and unjust must always involve more than one person. Again, it was voluntary and by   a20
choice and prior, for it is because of having suffered and doing the same thing back that one seems not to be doing wrong. But to wrong oneself is to suffer and to do the same thing at the same time. Again, it would be a case of being wronged voluntarily. In addition, no one does wrong except by way of one of the particular wrongs, and no one commits adultery with his own wife or breaks in through his own wall or steals his own things. But, on the   a25
whole, the case of wronging of oneself can also be solved in accord with the definition about being voluntarily wronged.

Clear too is that both things, being wronged as well as wronging, are base   1138a28
(for the one exists in having less and the other in having more than the mean, and than as the healthy is in medicine and good condition in bodily training). But, still, doing wrong is worse. For doing wrong involves vice and is blamable, and either complete vice and simply blamable or close (for not every voluntary doing wrong involves injustice). But being wronged is without vice or injustice. So being wronged is in itself less base, though nothing stops it   a35
being incidentally a greater evil. Art, though, takes no thought of this, but says that fever is a greater sickness than tripping up, and yet the other could

sometimes be greater incidentally, if someone who trips up happens, because of falling down, to be caught by his enemies and killed.

1138b5   By transference and likeness there is a justice, not of oneself to oneself, but among certain parts of oneself—not, however, in every sense of justice, but that of master and household. For in these discussions[1] the part of the soul with reason is separated from the part without reason. So those who

b10   look at these parts think there can in fact be injustice toward oneself, because among these it is possible for something to happen against their own desires. So they think that as ruler and ruled have a certain justice between them so also do these parts.

1138b13   About justice, then, and the other virtues, the moral ones, let this be our way of determining them.

Note

1.   For example, Plato's *Republic*, Books Three and Four.

Book Five: Prudence[1]

Chapter 1

Prudence
Thought in General
Its Several Virtues
Parts of Thought. *Virtue is of the mean, and the mean is as right reason says, so there is need to say what right reason is and what its mark. The soul has intellectual virtues belonging to its rational part, as well as moral virtues belonging to its nonrational part. The rational part is itself divided into two, the scientific part that studies things that cannot be otherwise and the calculative that studies things that can. Each part has virtues related to the work of each.*

Since we happen to have said before that one should choose the mean, 1138b18 not the excess or deficiency, and that the mean is as right reason says,[2] let us decide this. For in all the habits mentioned, just as there is in other things some target with a view to which anyone who possesses reason exerts effort and slackens, so also is there a mark for the mean states that, being in b25 accord with right reason, we say are between excess and deficiency. But to speak thus, while true, is not at all clear. For in other matters of care too, all those there is a science about, while it is true to say that one should neither toil nor relax either more or less but the mean amount and in the way right reason says, yet, with only this fact in hand, one would not have any greater b30 knowledge, as one would not know what sort of things should be used for the body if someone were to say that they were whatever the medical art bids and as he does who has it. Hence there is need too with respect to the habits of the soul not only that this be said truly[3] but that it also be determined what right reason is and what its mark.

When we divided up the virtues of the soul, we said that some of them 1138b35 were virtues of character and others virtues of thought.[4] The moral virtues we have gone through; the others let us speak about as follows, talking first of the soul. It was said earlier that there are two parts of the soul, the part that has reason and the part that does not.[5] But now a division must be a5 made in the same way about the part that has reason. In fact, let two parts be laid down that have reason, one by which we study all such beings as have principles that cannot be otherwise, and one by which we study those that can be otherwise (for to things other in kind the parts of the soul naturally related to each are other in kind, if it is indeed by some likeness and affinity a10 that knowledge exists in them). Let one of these be called the scientific part and the other the calculative. For deliberating and calculating are the same, and no one deliberates about what cannot be otherwise. So the calculative is one part of the part that has reason. One must grasp, then, what is the best habit of each of these two, for this is the virtue of each, and the virtue has relation to the proper work.

Notes

1. That this book should have the title of "Prudence" in the *EE* is plausibly deduced from Aristotle's own remarks at 1.1.1214a30–b6, 4.1215a32–b14, and 5.1216a27–b25, where he lists prudence, virtue, and pleasure as the three preferred candidates for the happy life. Books Two through Four are clearly about virtue, and this book, while it discusses all the intellectual virtues, is focused on prudence. Suitably then might it receive this title (and suitably too might the next book receive the title of "Pleasure"; see the note there). This book could perhaps also have the same title in the context of the *NE* since in it, at 1.5.1095b14–96a5, the same division into three of the candidates for happiness occurs. A difference, however, is that there the three are introduced, not as pleasure, virtue, and prudence, but as the indulgent life (which concerns pleasure), the political life (which concerns honor or virtue as true ground of honor), and the theoretical life (which is not further specified until Book Ten). The thematic division that guides the *NE* seems rather to be that of moral virtue and intellectual virtue, as at 1.13.1103a1–10 and 2.1.1103a14–18. The same distinction is also found in the *EE*, at 2.1.1220a4–15 (and here below at 1138b35–39a3), but the division in the first book into prudence, virtue, and pleasure seems to take thematic prominence within the treatise as a whole. In the context of the *NE*, however, a better title for this book might be "Intellectual Virtues." The content is the same, but the context of theme differs.
2. 2.5.1222a6–12, b6–8; 3.4.1231b32–33.
3. Reading at 1138b33 *alēthōs* (truly) with some MSS rather than *alēthes* (true) with other MSS and Bekker.
4. 1.2.1220a4–5.
5. 1.2.1219b27–31, 4.1221b27–31.

Chapter 2

Work of Thought. *Perception, intellect, and appetite are that in the soul that control action and truth. Perception is not cause of acting; and as thought asserts and denies, so appetite pursues and flees. Moral virtue is a habit of choice, and choice is right when reason is true and appetite pursues what reason says. This thinking is practical and its truth is the agreement of thought with right appetite. Choice, which begins action in man, itself begins in appetite and in a reason "for the sake of," so it needs both thought and moral virtue. Thought as such does not move but only thought that is for the sake of something and practical. Hence choice is appetitive intellect or thinking appetite (though what is chosen is not anything in the past). Truth is the work of thinking, so its virtues are what most make it to assert truth.*

There are three things in the soul that are in control of action and truth: 1139a17 perception, intellect, appetite. Of these perception is not a cause of acting. The fact is clear from beasts, which have perception but no share in action. And a20 what assertion and denial are in thought, pursuit and flight are in appetite. So, since moral virtue is a habit of choice, and since choice is deliberative appetite,[1] then, for this cause, if choice is to be virtuous, reason has to be true and appetite right and the latter has to pursue the same thing as the former a25 says. Now this is what practical thought and practical truth are, but in the case of thought, which is theoretical and does not act or make, the good and bad are truth and falsehood (for this is the job of everything that thinks), but in the case of what acts and thinks, truth is being in agreement with right appetite.

Now choice is the beginning of action (beginning as where a motion starts 1139a31 from not as what it is for the sake of), and of choice the beginning is appetite and reason for the sake of something. That is why choice is neither without intellect and thought nor without moral virtue. For there is no doing well in action, or the reverse, without thought and character. Thought itself does a35 not move anything, but thought that moves is the one that is for the sake of something and practical. For this is also beginning of the thought that makes things; for every maker makes for the sake of something, and the thing made is not simply goal (rather it is relative to something and of something), but the thing to be done is; for doing well is goal, and his appetite is for this. That is why choice is either appetitive intellect or thinking appetite, and such a beginning a man is.

The choosable is not anything in the past; no one, for example, chooses 1139b5 to have sacked Troy. For no one deliberates about what is in the past but about what is to come and can be, and the past cannot not be. So rightly Agathon:

From god is taken even this alone,
To now undo what is already done.[2]

Of both intellectual parts the job is truth. Thus the habits by which each 1139b12 of them most says what is true, these are the virtues of both.

Notes

1. Book 2.10–11.
2. Agathon, fr. 5.

Chapter 3

Virtues of Thought

Science. *Science is of things that cannot be otherwise and so are necessary and eternal. It can be taught and teaching is from things already known, by syllogism or induction. Induction is beginning of the universal and science begins from the universal, so the beginnings of syllogism are from induction and not from syllogism. Science is a habit of proof from known beginnings.*

1139b14 So let us talk about them again beginning from a higher level. Let the things, then, whereby the soul is true in affirmation and denial be five in number. They are: art, science, prudence, wisdom, intellect. For supposition and opinion are things the soul can err by.

1139b18 So, if we are to speak accurately and not follow semblances, it is clear as follows what science is. For everyone supposes that things we know cannot be otherwise. As for what can be otherwise, these escape our notice whether they are or not when they are out of view. The object of science, then, must be by necessity. It is eternal, then. For things that are by necessity are simply all eternal, and eternal things neither come to be nor cease to be.

1139b25 Further, every science seems able to be taught and the object of science able to be learnt. All teaching starts from things already known, as we said in the *Analytics*,[1] from induction in one case, by syllogism in another. Induction, then, is the beginning of the universal, but syllogism begins from the

b30 universal.[2] So there are beginnings for syllogism of which there is no syllogism. There is induction of them, then. So science is a habit of demonstration together with all the other features we also marked off in the *Analytics*.[3] For when one believes in a certain way and the beginnings are known, one has science. For if they are not more known than the conclusion one will have the

b35 science accidentally. So about science let our determination be on this wise.

Notes

1. *Posterior Analytics* 1.1.
2. *Posterior Analytics* 2.19.
3. *Posterior Analytics* 1.2.

Chapter 4

Art. *What can be otherwise is makeable and doable, and doing and making differ so the habits of each differ. Art is a habit of making with true reasoning and concerns what can come to be and has its beginning in the maker. It is about things of chance and its opposite is a habit of making with false reason.*

Of things that can be otherwise there is something makeable and something doable, but making and doing are different. (We rely for this point also on external discussions.)[1] So also the rational habit of doing is different from the rational habit of making. That is why the one is not contained in the other; for neither is doing a making nor is making a doing.   1140a1

Since building is an art and is what a rational habit of making is, and since neither is anything an art that is not a rational habit of making, nor is anything such a habit that is not an art, an art and a habit of making with true reasoning would be the same thing.   1140a6

Every art deals with coming to be, that is, with devising and studying how something that can both be and not be, and that has its beginning in the maker and not in the thing made, may come to be. For art is not about what is or comes to be of necessity nor about what is by nature, for these things have their beginning in themselves. And since making and doing are different, art must belong to making and not doing.   1140a10

Art is in a way about the same things that chance is,[2] as indeed Agathon said: 1140a17

Of chance was art fond and fond of art chance.[3]

So while art, as was said,[4] is a habit of making with true reasoning, lack of art is its contrary, a habit of making with false reasoning about what can be otherwise.

Notes

1.   See *GE* 1.34.1196b37–7a13.
2.   Cf. *Physics* 2.5–6.
3.   Agathon, fr. 6.
4.   Just above at 1140a10.

Chapter 5

Prudence. The prudent man is he who deliberates well about what is for overall living well. Prudence is not a science for it is not of what exists of necessity, nor an art because doing is not making. It is a true rational habit active about human goods and bads. The end of doing is not other than doing but is doing well itself, and prudence preserves the supposition about this end from the corruptions of pleasure and pain and vice. Art has a virtue but prudence does not; and he who makes a voluntary mistake in art is preferable but not he who does so in prudence and virtue; and prudence is in the part of the soul that opines but is not a rational habit merely.

1140a24 Of prudence we might get a grasp in this way, by studying who those are we call prudent.[1] So it seems a feature of the prudent man to be able to deliberate nobly about things good and useful for himself, not in some partial way, as about what is good for health or strength, but about what is good for living well overall. A sign is that we call those prudent about a thing when they calculate well in view of an end of which there is no art. So, overall, he who has ability to deliberate would be prudent.

1140a31 No one deliberates about what cannot be otherwise or about what he himself cannot do. So if science goes along with proof, and if of things whose beginnings can be otherwise there is no proof (for it can all be otherwise), and

b1 there can be no deliberating about what exists of necessity, then prudence would not be a science or an art: not a science because what is doable can be otherwise, and not an art because doing and making belong to different classes of things. What is left then is that it be a true, rational habit that is active about human goods and bads.

1140b6 The goal of making is something other than the making, but not so would the goal of doing be, for doing well is itself the end. That is why we think Pericles[2] and people like him are prudent, because they are able to work out what is good for themselves and for men. We take household managers and politicians to be of this sort.

1140b11 We also trace the name of temperance from prudence, because it "saves" prudence.[3] And what it saves is the above sort of supposition. For it is not every

b15 supposition that is destroyed or distorted by pleasure and pain, as not one about triangles having angles equal to two right angles, but those about what is to be done. For in the case of things to be done the beginnings are that for whose sake they are done. But he who has been destroyed by pleasure and pain at once stops seeing the beginning, and that he should choose and do everything for its sake or on its account. For vice is destructive of the beginning. So prudence must be a habit that is rational, true, about human goods, concerned with action.

1140b21 Further, there can be a virtue of art but not of prudence; and in an art the one who makes a voluntary mistake is more to be preferred, but in prudence

b25 less so, as also in the virtues. That prudence is a virtue, then, and not an art is clear. And, of the two parts of the soul that have reason, it would be the virtue of the second of them, the part that opines. For opinion is about what can be otherwise, and prudence is too. But prudence is not merely a rational habit, and

b30 a sign is that there can be forgetfulness of such a habit but not of prudence.[4]

Notes

1. Cf. 3.5.1232a19–20.
2. The famous politician of Athens in the fifth century BC.

3. At 1140b11–12 Aristotle is playing on the Greek words for temperance *sōphrosunē* and prudence *phronēsis*, and deducing the former from a combination of *sōzein* (to save) and *phronēsis*.
4. Prudence can be lost, but not by way of being forgotten; rather, as stated at 1140b17–20, by way of being destroyed through pleasure and pain, for these destroy the end, which is the principle of action. Hence prudence is not merely a rational habit, for it cannot exist without the moral virtues that give it its end; see chapters 12 and 13 below.

Chapter 6

Intellect. *Intellect is the habit of grasping the beginnings of science.*

Since science is a grasp of universals and of what is by necessity, and since 1140b31 there are beginnings of demonstrations and of any science (for science goes along with reason), there would not be science of the beginning of scientific knowledge; nor would there be art or prudence, for scientific knowledge is a b35 matter of demonstration, but these are about things that can be otherwise. So neither is there wisdom of them. For it is a feature of the wise man that in the case of some things he has demonstration. So if that whereby we speak truth and never err about things that cannot be otherwise, or also that can be otherwise, are science and prudence[1] and wisdom and intellect, and if none a5 of the three can be of the beginnings (I mean the three of prudence, science, wisdom), then what is left is that intellect is.

Note

1. Prudence is perhaps meant here as a sort of shorthand to include art as well (both being kinds of knowing that deal with things that can be otherwise).

Chapter 7

Wisdom. *Wisdom in art is exactness in the art. Wisdom simply is exactness in science, which is knowledge of the beginnings and of what rests on them, or intellect and science together about the worthiest things.*

Wisdom in the arts we allow to those who are most exact in their art, as 1141a9 that Pheidias was a wise stonemason and Polycleitus a wise sculptor, meaning by wisdom here nothing else than that it is virtue of art. But we think there are some who are wise as a whole and not wise partially nor wise in some other respect, as Homer says in the *Margites*:

> Him the gods made not for to dig nor plough,
> Nor in aught else wise ...[1]

Thus it is clear that wisdom would be of sciences the most exact.

1141a17 So then the wise must know not just what rests on the beginnings but must have the truth of the beginnings too. Thus wisdom would be intellect and science, science crowned, as it were, about the worthiest things.

Prudence as Compared with the Other Virtues of Thought
Prudence and Wisdom

Prudence. *Politics or prudence is not the best, for man is not the best; and the good varies but things white and straight do not, so that being wise is one thing but being prudent is different for different things. There are beings better than man, and wisdom is intelligence and science about these better beings; and those who consider these are held to be wise but not prudent as not considering their own good. Prudence is about human things subject to deliberation, and it deliberates well about things that can be otherwise and that are doable. He who simply deliberates well calculates with a view to the best of human goods. Prudence is not only about universals, but more so about particulars, for doing concerns particulars, which is why those who have experience can be more practical than those who have knowledge.*

1141a20 For it is absurd to think politics or prudence to be the most virtuous thing if man is not the best thing in the world. So if what is healthy and good is different for men and for fish, but the white and straight are always the same, then everyone would say being a wise man was the same thing but being a prudent one was different. For everyone would say that what studies all particulars well in respect of itself was prudent, and would hand the particulars over to it.[2] That is why people say that some beasts (all those that appear to have a power of foresight about their way of life) are prudent.

1141a28 It is clear also that wisdom would not be the same as politics. For if people are going to say that wisdom concerns one's own advantage then there will be many wisdoms. For there is not a single science of the good for all animals but a different one for each, unless there is also a single science of health for all the

b1 things that are. And if man is the best possible of all animals, it matters not. For there are things much more like god in their nature than man, as most obviously the things that the cosmos is made of. So it is plain from what has been said that wisdom is science and intellect of things most worthy in their nature.

1141b3 That is why people say Anaxagoras and Thales and those like them are wise but deny, when they see them ignorant of their own advantage, that they are prudent. They say, in fact, that they know things strange and wondrous and hard and supernatural yet useless, because what they are seeking is not human goods. Prudence is about human things and things that can be deliberated about. For this we say is above all the job of those who are prudent, to delib- b10 erate well. But no one deliberates about what cannot be otherwise, or what there is no goal of and this a doable good. The simply good deliberator is he who is able, with calculation, to aim at the best of human goods.

But prudence is not only about universals; it must also recognize par- 1141b14 ticulars, for it is about doing and doing concerns particulars. That is why some who do not know are more able to act, and especially those who are experienced, than others who do know. For if one knows that light foods are meats easy to digest and healthy but does not know which foods are light, one will not produce health; but one will produce it more if one knows that b20 the meat of poultry is light and healthy. Prudence is practical, so one needs knowledge of both, or more so of the latter. But here too there would be a certain ruling art.³

Notes

1.   The *Margites* was a mock-heroic poem ascribed to Homer. It has not survived.
2.   Alternative MS readings at 1141a25–26 (as those printed in the *OCT*) would give more the sense: "for each thing says that that is prudent which studies well what concerns itself and will hand itself [or what concerns itself] over to that."
3.   Sc. the art of politics, which is talked about next.

Chapter 8

Political Prudence. *Politics and prudence are one in habit but not one in being. Prudence about the city is legislative when it is the ruling art, but it has the common name of politics when it is dealing with particulars. Prudence about oneself has the common name of prudence. There is prudence of the household, of law-giving, and of politics; and of the latter there is deliberative and judicial prudence. Prudence about oneself is considered especially to be prudence, while politicians are considered to be busybodies. One's own affairs need a household and a regime. A sign is that the young can be skilled at mathematics but are not prudent, for the first needs only abstraction but the latter experience and knowledge of particulars.*

Politics and prudence are the same habit but their being is not the same. 1141b23 Of prudence about the city, the one that acts as ruling art is law-giving prudence, but the one that deals with particulars has the common name of politics. This is practical and deliberative, for a decree is something to be done, as what comes last. That is why they say that these people alone are engaged in politics, for these alone are acting in the way of hands-on artisans.

b35 In fact, however, prudence seems most to be what concerns oneself and the individual. Indeed it has the common name of prudence. But of the former, one is prudence in household management, another in law-giving, and another in politics, and of this last there is deliberative prudence on the one hand and judicial on the other.

1141b33 Now knowing one's own advantage is no doubt a form of comprehension, but it differs a great deal.[1] In fact he who knows and spends time on what concerns himself seems to be prudent, but politicians seem to be busy bodies. Hence Euripides:

How were prudent I, who without a care,
One count of many, might an equal share
a5 Amidst the host have ta'en . . .?
For those outstanding and in deeds the more . . .[2]

For they seek their own good and think it to be what they should do. From this opinion, then, has come the view that these are prudent. Yet it is perhaps impossible for one's own affairs to be in a good state without household management and without a regime. Further, how one should manage one's own affairs is unclear and needs investigating.[3]

1142a11 A sign of what has been said[4] is that young people become geometers and mathematicians and wise in such things but do not, it seems, become prudent. The reason is that prudence concerns particulars, which are recog-
a15 nized by experience, but a young man has no experience. For experience is made by much time. Since one might investigate this too, why it is that a boy might become a mathematician but not wise or a natural philosopher. Or is it because the former comes through abstraction, but experience gives the
a20 principles for the latter, and the young do not believe these but merely say them, while the "what is" in the case of the former is not unclear? Further, a mistake in deliberation is either about the universal or the particular, for it is either about all heavy waters being bad or about these waters being heavy.

Prudence and Science
In General. *Prudence is not science but counterpart to intellect as being of what comes last in doing and a sort of direct perceiving.*

1142a23 That prudence is not science is manifest, for it is of what comes last, as was said,[5] for that is what the doable is. So it is counterpart to intellect. For intellect is of the definitions, of which there is no account, while prudence is of what comes last, of which there is not science but perception—not the perception of the proper sensibles, but the sort by which we perceive that the ultimate figure in mathematics is the triangle, for here is where a stand will in fact be made. But this is perception rather than prudence, although perception of another kind.   a30

Notes

1. The Greek at 1141b34 is *echei pollēn diaphoran*, which could also be rendered "there is much dispute about it."
2. Euripides, *Philoctetes* fr. 787, 782.
3. *Politics* Book One.
4. A reference to the preceding remarks, that how to manage one's own affairs is not obvious and depends on subordination to rule in household and regime.
5. Above at 8.1141b25–29.

Chapter 9

Investigation and Deliberation. *Deliberating is a sort of seeking. Good deliberation is not science because science knows and does not seek. Nor is it guesswork, which is quick, but deliberation can be long. Nor is it opinion, which can, as quick wits, also be quick. Bad deliberation is a going wrong and good deliberation is a sort of rightness, so it is not the rightness of science, which cannot be wrong, nor of opinion, which is about an already determinate truth. But it is not without reason, so it must be part of thought, for thought is not yet assertion. Good deliberation is not just successfully getting the end, which even the bad might do, but getting a good end. Yet even getting the good end can be done by false reasoning and can take much time. Its rightness is in accord with what is beneficial and is of what is needed and how and when, and if good deliberation belongs to the prudent it is of the end grasped by prudence.*

Seeking differs from deliberating. For deliberating is a certain sort of seeking. We must grasp what good deliberation is as well, whether it is science or opinion or good guesswork or some other sort. So, first, it is not science, for people do not seek for what they know; but good deliberation is a deliberating, and someone deliberating is seeking and calculating.   1142a31

But neither is it good guesswork. For good guesswork is without reasoning and is something quick, but people take a lot of time deliberating and say that, while one should do quickly what one has deliberated about, one should deliberate slowly. Further, quick wits are different from good deliberation, but quick wits are a sort of good guesswork. Good deliberation, then, is not any opinion.   1142b2 b5

1142b7   But since he who deliberates badly goes wrong, but he who deliberates well deliberates rightly, it is clear that good deliberation is a sort of rightness. But it is not a rightness of science, nor of opinion. For of science there is no rightness, for there is no wrongness either; and in the case of opinion rightness is truth, and everything that is believed is at the same time already determinate.

1142b12   Yet good deliberation is not without reason either. So what is left is that it is part of thought. For thought is not yet assertion. For opinion is in fact not seeking but already a sort of assertion; while someone deliberating, whether he is doing it well or badly, is looking for something and calculating.

1142b16   But good deliberation is some rightness of deliberation. So we must look first for what deliberation is and what it is about. But since rightness is manifold, clearly it is not every rightness. For the incontinent and the base will, by calculation, hit what he proposes he should,[1] so that he will have deliberated rightly but will have got a great evil. But to have deliberated well seems to be a good thing. For this sort of rightness of deliberation, hitting the good, is good deliberation.

1142b22   But it is also possible to hit this by false syllogism, and to hit what one must do but not through what means one should, and for the middle term to be false. So not even is that yet good deliberation by which one can hit what one should but not through what means one should.

1142b26   Further, one can hit it after deliberating a long time, but another can do it quickly. Therefore not even that is yet good deliberation; but it is rightness in accord with what is beneficial and of what is due and of how and when it is. Further, it is possible both to have deliberated well simply and to have done so in relation to a particular end. So deliberating simply is that which goes right in relation to the end simply, and particular deliberating is that which goes right in relation to a particular end.

1142b31   So if having deliberated well belongs to those who are prudent, good deliberation would be rightness in accord with utility for an end that prudence is the true grasp of.

Note

1.   Reading at 1142b19 *ho protithetai dein* (what he proposes he should) with some MSS rather than *ho protithetai idein* (what he proposes to see) with other MSS and Bekker.

Chapter 10

Understanding. *Understanding and good understanding are not science or opinion, but are about what can be deliberated over. Understanding is about the same things as prudence, but prudence commands while understanding passes judgment. Understanding, like learning in the case of knowledge, comes through using opinion to pass judgment on what prudence deals with when another is speaking.*

Understanding and also good understanding, by which we say people are 1142b34 understanding or of good understanding, are not wholly the same as science or opinion (for then everyone would have understanding), nor are they one of the partial sciences, for example medicine, about matters of health, and geometry, about length. For understanding is not about beings that exist always and are unchangeable, nor about just anything that comes to be, but a5 about what one might puzzle and deliberate over. That is why it is about the same things as prudence. But understanding is not the same thing as prudence, for prudence gives orders, since what is to be done or not done is its end, and understanding only passes judgment. For understanding and good understanding, and those of understanding and of good understanding, are the same.

Understanding is neither having nor getting prudence, but, as learning is 1143a11 said to be understanding when one uses knowledge, so is it also said to be, in the case of using opinion for passing judgment on the things that prudence deals with when someone else is speaking, passing judgment well. For "well" a15 is the same as "nobly." For this is where understanding, by which people are good at understanding, gets its name, from the understanding that occurs in the case of learning. For we often say that to learn is to understand.

Chapter 11

Judgment. *Judgment and good judgment are the right judgment of equity, as is indicated by the fact the equitable man is forgiving. All these habits, judgment and understanding and prudence and intellect, tend to the same thing, for we refer them to the same people in the same respect. For all these powers deal with what comes last, and people have these powers in dealing with what prudence deals with; but doables come last, and prudence deals with what comes last, and understanding and judgment deal with doables that come last.*

Judgment so called, by which we say people are good at judgment and have 1143a19 judgment, is right adjudication of what is equitable. A sign is that we say the equitable man above all is forgiving[1] and that it is equitable to be forgiving in some cases. For forgiveness is correct adjudicative judgment of the equitable; and correct judgment is judgment of what is true.

1143a25   Reasonably do all the habits tend to the same thing. For judgment and understanding and prudence and intellect we speak of in referring to the same people, that they have precisely judgment and intellect and are prudent and understanding. For all these powers deal with what comes last and with

a30   particulars; and while it is in judging what prudence deals with that someone is understanding and has good judgment and is forgiving (for things equitable are common to everything that is good in what concerns another), yet it is among particulars and what come last that all things doable are found; for in fact the prudent man must recognize them, and understanding and judgment deal with doable things, and ones that come last.

     Prudence and Intellect. *Intellect is of things that come last, at both ends, but reason is of the demonstrations; and in doable things intellect deals with things that come last and with the principles of the end. Intellect here is perception and, like judgment and understanding, seems to be by nature and to follow people's ages. Hence intellect is the beginning and end, and from and about these are demonstrations; so what must be held onto is the opinions of the experienced and wise and prudent, for they see rightly.*

1143a35   Intellect too is of things that come last, at both ends. For intellect and not reason is of first definitions and what comes last. It is in fact, in the case of demonstrations, of unchangeable and primary definitions, but, in the case of practical habits, it is of things that come last and are possible and with the second premise; for these are principles of the "for the sake of which," since

b5   the universal is from the particulars.[2] So there is need of perception in the case of these things, and perception here is intellect. That is also why it seems that these things are natural, and that while no one seems wise by nature, yet they do seem by nature to have judgment and understanding and intellect.

1143b7   A sign is that we think these follow people's ages, and that "this age has intellect and judgment," supposing nature to be cause. That is why intellect is beginning and end, for demonstrations are from these and about these. So we must cling to the undemonstrated sayings and opinions of the experienced and the old and the prudent no less than to those of demonstration.[3] For because they have the eye of experience, they see rightly.

1143b14   We have spoken, then, about what prudence is and what wisdom, and about what each happens to be about, and that each of them is the virtue of a different part of the soul.

Notes

1.   The Greek for judgment at 1143a19–24 here is *gnōmē* and for forgiveness *sungnōmē*, so that forgiveness, in Greek, is a sort of "judging with." The point is hard to capture in English.
2.   The second premise is the premise about the details of the situation in which one is to act (the first premise would be some general one about pursuing

this or that good, as wealth, say, or power). These details will determine how the "for the sake of which," the end or goal, is to be pursued here and now. The goal as a universal (wealth or power) is said to be "from" the particulars, either because it is reached by induction from particulars or instead, or also, because it consists in the particulars (wealth, say, is not an actual goal of pursuit, as opposed to a general wish, until it is particularized in the details of what can be done here and now).

3. The undemonstrated opinions and sayings of the experienced and old and prudent have the same status as the conclusions of demonstration. For since intellect sees both the beginning and the end of demonstration, what our intellect sees with demonstration, their intellect, because of their experience, can see without it.

Chapter 12

Thought in Action
Prudence and Wisdom. *Wisdom and prudence seem to be of no use, for wisdom does not study the sources of happiness, and while prudence does study them its knowledge is not needed. For, first, the habits are enough without knowledge and if, second, its job is to make habits present then: (a) it is not needed after it has done so; (b) is not needed at all by those who can listen to others; (c) ends up being in control of what is better than it, namely wisdom. But, first, each of these, being the virtue of a part of the soul, is preferable for this reason alone. Second, wisdom contributes to happiness as health does to health, not by making it but by being part of it. Third, prudence contributes to virtuous work by making what is for the aim right as virtue makes the aim itself right.*

A puzzle one might raise about them is what use they are. For wisdom 1143b18
does not study the sources of human happiness (for it is not about any coming to be), and while prudence does have this feature, what do we need it for? Since prudence deals with things just and noble and good for man, and since the good man's job is to do these things, we will not, if the virtues are habits, be better at doing them by knowing them any more than at doing fit and healthy things (all those called so not by making, but by coming from, b25 the habit); for we are not more able to do these things because we know medicine and physical training.

But if we must lay down that a prudent man is not for this purpose but for 1143b28
growing into them, then for those already virtuous he would not be of use; also, not for those who do not have them either, for there will be no difference b30 whether one has them oneself or listens to others who have them; it would be enough too for us, as it is also in the case of health; for although we wish to be healthy, yet we do not learn medicine. Moreover, it would seem an odd

thing that what is worse than wisdom should have more control than it (for the virtue that is maker is what rules and gives orders in each case).

1143b35 We must, then, say something about these matters, for we have so far only been raising puzzles about them. First then we say that each of the two, being, as they are, virtues of each of the two parts,[1] must be preferable for themselves, even if neither of them does anything. Next, they do in fact do something, not in the way medicine makes health but in the way health

a5 does—wisdom in this way making happiness; for as it is a part of the whole of virtue, it makes one happy by way of being a habit and being exercised. Further, work is completed in accord with prudence and moral virtue. For virtue makes the aim right and prudence makes right what leads to it (of the

a10 fourth part[2] of the soul, the nutritive part, there is no virtue of the sort, for in its case there is nothing that acts or does not act).

Prudence and Right Reason
How Moral Virtue Makes Prudence Right. *It is possible to do good things without being good and without choice of the good. Moral virtue makes choice right but does not do what is for the sake of virtue, which belongs to another power. This power is a combination of cleverness, or the ability to hit the aim, and nobility of aim, which comes from moral virtue. So prudence is not without moral virtue, which gives it its principles.*

1144a11 But as to our not being better at doing noble and just things because of prudence, we must go back a little and start from this fact, that as we say that

a15 some who do just things are not yet just—for instance, those who do what is laid down by law either involuntarily or through ignorance or for some other reason (even though they are doing what they should and what the virtuous man must do)—so, as is likely, it is possible to do each thing when one's condition is of such a sort that one is good, I mean, for instance, by choice and for the sake of the things done themselves. Virtue makes the choice right, then, but it is not its job to do what is naturally for virtue's sake; that belongs to some other power.[3]

1144a22 But we should pause and speak more clearly about them. There is a power that they call cleverness. It is the sort of thing that is able to do what leads to the aim set up and to hit it. So it is something to be praised if the aim is noble, but if base, it is an unscrupulous capacity for anything. That is why we even say the prudent are clever and unscrupulous. But the power is not prudence,

a30 though prudence cannot be without it. The habit in the eye of the soul does not come into being without virtue, as has been said[4] and as is plain. For syllogisms in things to be done are in possession of a starting point, since that is what the end and the best is—whatever that happens to be (so, for the sake of

a35 argument, let it be whatever one likes). But it does not show itself except to the good man. For wickedness distorts people and makes them err about the practical principles. So it is clear that one cannot be prudent without being good.

Notes

1. Sc. of the soul, the scientific part and the calculating part, as distinguished earlier at 2.1139a6–15.
2. The third unnamed part, after the two parts of the scientific and the calculating part, is where the virtues of character are found, namely desire or appetite.
3. Cf. 2.11.1227b38–28a2.
4. Just above at 11.1143b2–5 and earlier at 5.1140b16–25.

Chapter 13

How Prudence Makes Moral Virtue Right. Moral virtue is similar. Natural character is a tendency from nature to do virtuous things, but it lacks, as such, the direction of sight or intellect. Such sight is prudence and is what produces moral virtue in the proper sense. But moral virtue, contrary to Socrates' view, is not prudence by itself, nor is it a habit in accord with prudence; rather it is habit along with prudence. Moral virtue is not possible without prudence, nor prudence without moral virtue. Natural virtues can exist separately from each other, but moral virtues must all be present together in prudence. Prudence does not command wisdom but gives commands for its sake.

So we must examine virtue once again. For virtue too is in a like condition: as prudence is related to cleverness (not the same, but similar) so also is natural virtue related to virtue proper. For everyone thinks each character exists in some way by nature, for as soon as we come to be we are just and controlled and brave and the rest. But still we are looking for something else, for being good in the proper sense and for these sorts of things existing in another way. For in fact natural habits belong to children too and beasts, but they are manifestly harmful without intellect, save that so much looks to be visible: that as a mighty body moving about without sight is like to be mightily tripped up because it lacks sight, so here too. But if it gets hold of intellect it behaves differently; and the habit that was like virtue proper will now be it. Consequently, as there are two forms in the case of the part that opines, cleverness and prudence, so there will also be two in the moral part: the one natural virtue and the other virtue proper. Of these the one that is proper does not come about without prudence. 1144b1 b5 b10 b15

Hence some say all the virtues are prudences. Socrates in fact was right in his search in one way but went wrong in another. In thinking the virtues were all prudences he went wrong; in thinking them not to be without prudence he spoke nobly. A sign is that even now when people define virtue they 1144b17 add on, besides what it is about, that it is also the habit in accord with right reason. Reason in accord with prudence is right. So it seems everyone is in some way divining that the sort of habit that is virtue is the one in accord with prudence. But a slight change is needed. It is not merely the habit that accords with right reason that is virtue, but the habit that is with right reason. Right reason about such things is prudence. Socrates thought the virtues were reason (for he thought they were all knowledges), but we say they are with reason. So it is clear from what has been said that one cannot be good properly without prudence, nor prudent without moral virtue.

However, this is also the way to solve the reasoning by which one might dialectically argue that the virtues are separate from each other, for the same person is not naturally best fitted for all of them; consequently he has already got hold of one but not yet of another. For this can happen with the natural virtues, but not with those by which he is called simply good, for, since prudence is one, all the virtues are at the same time found in it. But it is plain that, even if one does not act on it, it would, as being a virtue of the part, still be needed; and also because choice will not be right without prudence, nor without virtue. The latter makes the end right, the former what leads to it.

Further, prudence is not in control of wisdom nor of the better part, just as medicine is not in charge of health. For it does not use it but sees to its coming to be. It gives commands for its sake, then, but not to it. Further, it would be as if one were to say politics rules the gods, because it gives commands about everything in the city.[1]

Note

1.   Cf. 8.3.1249b12–16.

Book Six: Pleasure[1]

Chapter 1

Pleasure in Contrast with Virtue and Prudence
Extremes and Intermediates of Virtue and Vice
Things to Examine and Method to Follow. *Taking another beginning, we must say that the things in morals to be avoided are three: vice, incontinence, brutishness. Opposite to vice is virtue, to incontinence continence, to brutishness heroic or divine virtue. The last two are rare, but brutishness is found mainly among barbarians or the sick and deformed or extremely vicious. The things to talk about now are continence and incontinence as being neither the same as nor different in kind from vice and virtue. The phenomena must first be set down and examined and, if possible, proved.*

Making, after this, another beginning,[2] we must say that there are three 1145a15 kinds of things to be avoided in matters of character: vice, incontinence, brutishness. The opposites of two of these are clear, one we call virtue and the other continence. But in opposition to brutishness one might most fittingly speak of the virtue that goes beyond us, a sort of heroic and divine one, such as Homer made Priam say about Hector, because he was exceeding good,   a20

> . . . nor seemèd he
> Of mortal man but god the child to be.[3]

So if, as we say, gods come from men through excess of virtue, such virtue would clearly be the habit opposed to brutishness (for as in fact there is no vice or virtue in a beast, so neither is there in a god, but his state is more honorable than virtue while the beast's is a kind different from vice).

But since it is a rare thing indeed for there to be a divine man (as the 1145a27 Spartans are wont to call him when they greatly admire someone—"a godly man" they say), so the brutish among men too is rare. He is found mainly among barbarians, but there are also some cases brought about by sickness and deformity. And those who exceed men in vice we also speak thus ill of. But about this sort of condition some mention must be made later,[4] while vice was spoken of earlier.[5] Incontinence and softness and luxury are what a35 must be talked about, as well as continence and endurance. For none of these must be supposed either to be the same habit as virtue and wickedness or as different in kind.

1145b2   We must, as elsewhere, set down the phenomena and, having first raised puzzles about them, prove in this way all the views, if possible, that are held about these experienced states or, if not, most of them or those with most authority. For if the hard points may be solved and the views held left in place, the thing shown would be enough.[6]

Continence and Incontinence
Statement of Phenomena and Puzzles
The Phenomena. *The continent man seems to be virtuous and praiseworthy and the incontinent man not, since the former stands by his conclusion against his desires but the latter fails to; the former is said both to be and not to be self-controlled and the latter both to be and not to be intemperate; the prudent man is said both to be and not to be capable of incontinence; some are also said to be incontinent in honor and anger and gain.*

1145b8   It is held, then, that continence and endurance belong to things virtuous and praiseworthy, but incontinence and softness to things base and blameworthy; that he who is continent is the same as he who stands by his calculation, or that he who is incontinent is the same as he who leaves his calculation; that the incontinent man does, because of passion, what he knows to be base, while the continent man, knowing his desires to be base, does not, because of his reason, follow them. People say that the temperate
b15 man is continent and enduring, but some say that everyone of this latter sort is temperate but others not; some say the licentious man is incontinent and the incontinent man licentious without distinction, but others say the two are different; sometimes they say that the prudent man cannot be incontinent, and at other times that some who are prudent and clever are incontinent;
b20 further, people are said to be incontinent even in anger and honor and gain. These then are the things said.

Notes

1.   This book might suitably have the title of "Pleasure" in the context of *EE*, since it answers to that topic as broached in Book One (see the next note). The book, of course, deals mainly with continence and incontinence, and within the *NE* it would more properly have this title, for there it serves to complete the treatment of all the phenomena to do with virtue (again see the next note). It also serves the same purpose in the *EE* but as subordinate to the more general theme of pleasure.

2.   This beginning in the context of *EE* refers back to 1.5.1216a29–37 where two questions about pleasure are raised: whether bodily pleasure contributes to happiness and whether there are other pleasures that belong to the happy life to make it pleasant (the reference at 2.11.1227b15–17 is subordinate to the larger theme announced in Book One, as is confirmed by the later reference at 3.2.1231b2–4). Both questions were there postponed and are answered here: the first in chapters 1 to 10 (about continence and

incontinence), and the second in chapters 11 to 14 (about all pleasure generally). Within the *NE* this beginning refers back to the end of Book Four (5.1128b33–35) where continence, in an aside, is referred to as a sort of mixed state, not a virtue, and something to be dealt with later. So this book, despite the identity of content, has the theme in *NE* of such mixed states (continence and its opposite, incontinence), with pleasure introduced as subordinate to them (the treatment of pleasure proper is given in *NE* 10.1–5), and not the theme of bodily and other pleasures, as it does in *EE*. Hence a division of this book in the context of *NE* would start with the second subtitle given here at the head of the first chapter (Extremes and Intermediates of Virtue and Vice), and not with the first (Pleasure in Contrast with Virtue and Prudence).

3.   *Iliad* 24.258–59.
4.   Chapter 5 below.
5.   Especially in Book Three, on the particular virtues and vices.
6.   Cf. also 1.6.1216b26–17a17, 2.1.1220a15–22, 7.2.1235b13–18.

Chapter 2

Puzzles Arising from the Phenomena. *A first puzzle (i) is that of Socrates, that no one acts against what he knows to be right, which view is opposed to the facts and prompts one to ask about the "how" of knowing. Hence (ii) some say the incontinent man goes against opinion and not knowledge, but this view makes weakness something forgivable and not blameworthy. To suppose (iii) that he goes against prudence is odd because (a) no one is both prudent and does base things, and (b) the prudent man acts on his prudence. Also, (iv) if the continent man has strong desires he will not be temperate nor the temperate man continent (for the temperate man does not have strong or base desires), but (v) he should because, if his desires are not base, his habit of resisting them will be bad, and, if his desires are weak, there is nothing grand in resisting them. Again, (vi) if continence makes one follow any opinion, it will be base in making one follow a false opinion, and (vii) if incontinence makes one oppose any opinion, it will be virtuous when it makes one oppose a false opinion (as with Neoptolemus). There is (viii) the sophism that a continent man standing by a false opinion is base. Also (ix) he who does the pleasant thing by choice seems better than he who does so by incontinence, for the former would be easily cured if he changed his mind, but not the latter. Finally (x) if one can be incontinent about anything, who is the incontinent man simply (for no one has all the kinds of incontinence)?*

A puzzle one might raise is: what sort of correct supposition does one act incontinently with?[1] Now if one has knowledge some deny one can do it.   1145b21

111

For it would be a strange thing, as Socrates thought, if, when one has knowledge within, something else can get control and drag one about like a slave.[2] For Socrates fought altogether against the argument, on the ground incontinence was nonexistent. For, he said, no one acts against the best when supposing so but when ignorant. Now this reasoning is in open dispute with the phenomena, and one must investigate what it is that happens: if it is through ignorance, what is the manner of the ignorance? For, that he who acts incontinently does, before the thing happens to him, at least not think he should, is clear.

1145b31   There are some who go along with parts of this but not with others. For they agree that nothing is greater than knowledge but do not agree that no one acts against what seems better. And on that account they say that the incontinent man is overcome by pleasures, not when he has knowledge, but when he has opinion. But if it is indeed opinion and not knowledge, nor a strong supposition but a mild one, which does the resisting, as in those who doubt not standing by these against strong desires is something to forgive. But wickedness is not something to forgive, nor anything else blamable.

1146a4   Is it when prudence does the resisting, then, for this is a very strong thing? But that is odd, for the same man will be prudent and incontinent at the same time, but no one would say that doing the basest things voluntarily was the mark of a prudent man. In addition, it has been shown before that the prudent man is one who does at least act, for he is one who concerns what comes last and he has the other virtues.[3]

1146a9   Further, if the continent man is in a state of strong and base desires, the temperate man will not be continent nor the continent man temperate, for it is not a mark of a temperate man to have too great desires or base ones. But at least he should; for if, on the one hand, his desires are honest ones, the habit that prevents him following them is base, so that continence is not wholly virtuous; while if, on the other, his desires are weak and not base, there is nothing grand about him, and if they are base and weak nothing great.

1146a16   Again, if continence makes one stand by any opinion, it is base, as when it makes one stand by a false opinion. And if incontinence makes one abandon any opinion, there will be an incontinence that is virtuous, as with Sophocles' Neoptolemus in the *Philoctetes*, for he is praiseworthy for not standing by what he was persuaded of by Odysseus, because of the pain he felt in telling lies.[4]

1146a21   Further, the deceptive argument of the sophists is a puzzle. For because they want paradoxical refutations (so as to be clever when they succeed), the syllogism they make is a puzzle when it comes about. For thought is bound down when, on the one hand, it does not want to stay where it is because it does not like the conclusion, but, on the other, it cannot go forward because it does not have a solution to the argument. There is, then, a certain argument the result of which is that folly with incontinence is a virtue: incontinence makes one do the opposite of what one supposes, but one supposes that what is good is bad and not to be done, so one does the good and not the bad.

Further, someone who acts by persuasion, pursuing and choosing the 1146a31 pleasant, would seem better than someone not acting by calculation but with incontinence. For he is easier to cure, because he might be persuaded otherwise; whereas the incontinent man falls foul of what we say in the proverb: "when water chokes you, what should you drink for it?" For if he had a35 been persuaded to do what he is doing, he would stop if he were persuaded otherwise, but now, though persuaded, he none the less does something else.

Further, if one can be incontinent and continent about anything, who is 1146b2 the man simply incontinent? For no one has all the kinds of incontinence, yet we do say some people are incontinent simply.

Notes

1. Following at 1145b21–22 the construal of the Greek proposed by Broadie and Rowe (2002: 190, 385–87). The alternative construal would be: "how does one do things incontinently when one has correct supposition?"
2. Plato, *Protagoras* 352b–c.
3. 5.5.1140b20–21, 7.1141b14–22, 8.1142a23–27, 10.1143a6–10, 11.1143a25–35, 12.1144a34–b1, 13.1144b30–45a6.
4. Sophocles, *Philoctetes* 54–122, 895–916.

Chapter 3

Solution to the Puzzles and Saving of the Phenomena
Order of the Examination. *Solving the puzzles must begin with the question of knowledge; then of what incontinence and continence are about; then of whether the continent man has endurance; then of the rest. First to be examined is whether incontinence and continence differ in the what or the how, and then whether they concern everything or not; for incontinence is in fact about what indulgence is about and differs from it in not pursuing pleasure by choice.*

The puzzles, then, turn out to be of some such sort, and we must take away 1146b6 some of these things and leave others, for to solve a puzzle is to find things out.[1] First, then, we must examine whether they know or not, and how they know; next must be set down what things the incontinent and continent man b10 are about; I mean whether about every pleasure and pain or about some in particular and whether the continent man is the same as the man of endurance or not; likewise too about all the other puzzles germane to this study.

The examination's beginning is whether the continent and the incontinent 1146b14 man are different in the about what or the how, I mean whether it is by being about these things that the incontinent man is incontinent, or not but by how he is so, or not but by both. Next, whether incontinence and continence are about everything or not; for neither is the simply incontinent man about everything but about what the licentious man is about, nor is he related simply to these things (for that would be the same thing as license), but related in this way. For the one is carried off choosing to be so, believing he should always pursue the present pleasure; but the other thinks he should not and yet does so.

The Puzzles about Knowledge. *As to (i) the claim that the incontinent goes against opinion and not knowledge, this makes no difference, for some have belief in the way others have knowledge. But (ii) knowledge can be had without being exercised and there is nothing strange in going against possessed but un-exercised knowledge; (iii) if, of the two premises, the universal is exercised but not the particular, there is nothing strange in going against the particular; (iv) the universal ranges over two particulars, the thing and the person, and if the particular premise about the thing is not exercised, there is nothing strange in going against it; (v) knowledge can be had as the drunk or asleep or mad have it, and that way is how the passions affect the incontinent (their words are no sign of knowledge, since words can be spoken without knowledge); (vi) the universal and particular premises must be combined in two ways by the soul, in a conclusion and an act, but passion can move to action and so, incidentally, change the reasoning too (hence beasts are not incontinent because they do not grasp universals); (vii) people recover from incontinence as they recover from being drunk or drowsy (and so the thing is subject for natural science), for the particular premise is had in the way the drunk have it; (viii) what Socrates said, that no one acts against knowledge, seems to happen because it is sense knowledge and not knowledge proper that is dragged about.*

Now about its being true opinion and not knowledge that people act incontinently against, that makes no difference to the argument. For some who have opinion do not doubt, but think they know for certain. So if it is because belief is weak that those with opinion rather than those with knowledge act against what they think, knowledge will differ in nothing from opinion; for the belief some have in their opinion is not less than what others have in their knowledge, as Heracleitus[2] shows.

But since we speak of knowing in two ways (for both he who has knowledge but is not using it and he who is using it are said to know), there will be a difference between having knowledge of what one should not do but not considering it, and having it and considering it; for the latter seems strange, but there is nothing strange if he is not considering.

Further, since there are two styles of premises, nothing prevents acting against knowledge when one has both of them but is using the universal and not the particular. For things to be done are particulars.

114

There is a difference too in the universal premise, for part is for oneself and part for the thing, as for example, that dry foods are good for every man, and that he is a man or that such and such is dry. But whether this here is such and such he either does not have or is not exercising. So it is incalculable how much difference these ways will make, so that there seems nothing odd his knowing like this but amazing his knowing like that.[3] 1147a4

Further, the way men have knowledge is different from what is now said. For we see that when one has it but is not using it there is a difference in the habit, so that in a way one has it and does not have it, as when one is asleep or mad or drunk. But that is how people are when in a state of passion. For anger and desires for sex and other suchlike things plainly change the body's condition and in some cases make people mad. So it is plain that the incontinent must be said to be in a like state with theirs. 1147a10 a15

That they speak arguments that come from knowledge shows nothing. For people in these states of passion speak the demonstrations and verses of Empedocles, and those who have just learnt string the arguments together but do not yet know them; for they have to grow into them, and for this there is need of time. So one must suppose that the incontinent speak the way actors do. 1147a18

Further, one can look at the cause in a physical way like this: for one opinion is universal and the other about particulars (which is precisely what perception has control over), and the soul, when a single opinion arises out of them, must, on the one hand, here assert the conclusion, but must, on the other, in things to be done at once act. For instance, if everything sweet is to be tasted, and if this here, as one of the particulars, is sweet, then he who can and is not held back must also at the same time act. 1147a24

So when there is one universal opinion present stopping one tasting and another that everything sweet is pleasant, and this here is sweet (and this last opinion is active), and desire happens to be present, then the universal tells one to flee it but desire pulls one toward it; for each of the parts can cause motion.[4] Consequently, one acts incontinently by reason and opinion in a way, but not by an opinion that is in itself contrary to right reason but incidentally, for it is desire that is contrary and not opinion. Consequently, for this reason too beasts are not incontinent, because they do not have grasp of universals, but imagination and memory of particulars. 1147a31 a35

As to how ignorance is let go and the incontinent man again becomes knowing, the account is the same as for the drunk and the drowsy and is not peculiar to his experience, and must be got from listening to the natural scientists. But since the final premise is an opinion about something sensed, and it has control over what is doable, either the man in the grip of passion does not have this, or he has it in such a way that the having is not a knowing but a speaking, in the way the drunk speak the words of Empedocles. 1147b6 b10

Also, because the term that comes last is not the universal, nor does it seem scientific as the universal is, then what Socrates was seeking for looks 1147b13 in fact to happen.[5] For the experiences arises, not when what seems to be knowledge proper is present,[6] nor is this what the passion drags about, but when sense knowledge is.

1147b17   Let so much, then, be said about knowing and not knowing, and about what way of knowing one can be incontinent with.

Notes

1.   Or alternatively the Greek at 1146b7–8 could be construed: "the solution is a finding out of the puzzle."
2.   The famous Pre-Socratic philosopher from Miletus, who claimed to believe contradictory statements.
3.   The universal premise contains two universal terms, "dry foods" and "every man," so there will be two particular premises subsumed under it, "this food here is dry food" and "I am a man." Failure to subsume either premise under the universal would result in failure to draw the conclusion, "I should eat this food here"; but of course one could hardly fail to know one is a man, so it is the other premise one fails to subsume under the universal, either because one does not have it or because one does not exercise it. Acting against knowledge if one has the universal but does not have, or does not exercise, the particular is not strange, but it would be if one did have the particular and was exercising it too.
4.   Or alternatively, at 1147a35, "it [sc. desire] can move each of the parts." On this alternative the sense is that desire can move each part of the body (or possibly each part of the animal, by moving the universal out of the way and then moving the body to act); on the other, the sense is that each of the parts of the soul, desire and (practical) reason, can move one to act.
5.   Sc. that no one acts against knowledge.
6.   Present in the sense of being exercised. There is thus no compelling reason to change, at 1147b16, *parousēs ginetai* (arises . . . is present) to *periginetai* (overcomes) with Broadie and Rowe (2002: 194, 393; following Stewart), to give the sense: "it is not what seems to be knowledge proper that the passion overcomes." On either reading, the point is the same, that incontinence happens when sense knowledge, and not knowledge proper, is dragged about.

Chapter 4

The Puzzles about Subject Matter
The Normal Case. *Incontinence and continence have to do with certain pleasures and pains. But some pleasures are necessary, the bodily ones, while others, like victory and honor and money, can be had to excess but are in themselves preferable. Those incontinent in the latter are not incontinent simply (for they are not blamed as vicious), but incontinent in victory or honor or gain. Those who are incontinent in the former are simply incontinent, for only in these*

indulgences are people called soft; the licentious belong here too, for they are all about the same things but in different ways. Some desires and pleasures are noble and virtuous (for pleasant things are by nature preferable), or the opposite, or in between (things like victory and honor), and all are blamed if pursued to excess, so that pursuing noble and virtuous things to excess is also blamed, as with Niobe and Satyrus. But there is no wickedness here, nor incontinence either, because these are naturally preferable things, while incontinence is something to be blamed as well as avoided. Continence and incontinence are only said of other things by addition and by likeness.

Whether anyone is simply incontinent, or everyone is so in part, and, if 1147b20 there is, what things he is about, must be stated next. Now, that the continent and enduring, the incontinent and soft, deal with pleasures and pains is clear. But since some things that cause pleasure are necessary and others, while in themselves preferable, involve excess, and since the bodily ones are necessary b25 (I mean the sort of things to do with food and the use of sex and all the sorts of bodily things we set down license and moderation as being about), but the others, while not necessary, are in themselves preferable (I mean, for instance, victory, honor, wealth, and such goods and pleasures as this), those people b30 then, who are excessive in the latter against the right reason they possess,[1] we do not say are incontinent simply but incontinent with the addition of "in money" or "in gain" or "in honor" or "in spirit" and not simply so, as being different and referred to by way of likeness, like Man who was victor at the b35 Olympic Games (for his common account was little different from his personal one, but still it did differ).[2] A sign is that incontinence is blamed not as a fault only but as a vice, whether simply so or in part, but none of these people is.

But among those having to do with bodily indulgences, which we say the 1148a4 temperate and licentious man are about, he who does not pursue by choice excesses of pleasures and avoid excesses of pains (hunger, thirst, heat, cold, and all things that concern touch and taste), but does so against choice and thought, he is said to be incontinent, not with any addition that he is so in a10 things like anger, but just simply. A sign is that people are called soft in these latter but not in any of the former. And that is why the incontinent and the licentious, but none of the former, we place together with the continent and the temperate, because they have to do with the same pleasures and pains. a15 But while they are all about the same things, they are not about them in the same way, but the one choose and the others do not. Hence we would call him licentious who pursues excesses when he has no or weak desire and avoids pains that are moderate, rather than him who does so because of intense desire. For what would the former do if he had a young man's desire in addition and his pain at lack of things necessary was strong?

But since some desires and pleasures are, of their kind, among things noble 1148a22 and virtuous, for some pleasant things are by nature preferable, and some are a25 the opposite of these, and some are in between[3] (the way we distinguished them before),[4] as money and gain and victory and honor, and with respect to all of them, both those of the preferable sort and those in between, people are not blamed because they feel and desire and love them, but by going to excess in some way, hence it is that all those are blamed who are overcome by or pursue, contrary to reason, one of the naturally fine and good things,

a30 as for instance those who are more earnest about honor than they should be, or about children and parents. For these things too are among goods, and people are praised who are earnest about them, but yet there can be excess even in these things, if someone were to fight, like Niobe, even against the gods, or like Satyrus about his father, the one surnamed Philopator (father-lover), for he seemed to be excessively foolish.[5]

1148b2 Now there is in these things, on account of what was said, no wickedness, because each is of itself among things naturally preferable. But it is the excess that is base and to be avoided. Likewise there is no incontinence here

b5 either. For incontinence is not only something to avoid but is of blameworthy things.[6] But people add, by a likeness to the passion, something to the word and say there is incontinence in each of them, the way they say that someone is a bad doctor or a bad actor whom they would not call bad simply. So just as they would not say it in this case, because none of these sorts of badness

b10 is a vice but is like it by analogy, so it is plain that in that case too one must suppose that incontinence and continence without addition are what have to do with the same things that temperance and licentiousness have to do with. Of spirit we say it by way of likeness. Hence too we add on that someone is incontinent or continent in spirit, as we do also in the case of honor and gain.

Notes

1. At 1147b32 *autois* (they [possess]) is technically ambiguous and could refer to the right reason in the people, which they use or fail to use, or the right reason in the things, which determines, in the case of these things, what the right amount is.

2. A man called Man (*Anthrōpos*) won in boxing at the Olympic Games in 456 BC. As the term "man" is the general name for human beings, so too "incontinence" is the general name for all the kinds of incontinence. But incontinence when it means incontinence proper (incontinence in bodily pleasures) is that particular case of incontinence that is given the name "incontinence" simply. Hence it is like Man who won the Olympic Games: he is a particular man, and so falls under the general name, but he has Man also as his own personal name. In the same way we might call the simply incontinent man Mr. Incontinent, while the others we would have to call Mr. Money-Incontinent or Mr. Anger-Incontinent.

3. This distinction into three kinds of pleasant thing is not entirely clear, but the kinds would seem to be things like virtue and prudence as regard what are in themselves preferable, things like bodily needs as the opposite (for they are not preferable but merely necessary), and thinks like honor and

wealth as those in between (for they are naturally preferable, but only for the virtuous who can use them well, and not for the vicious who cannot). The first and the last, but not the second, would be among things noble and virtuous.

4. Above at 1147b29–31.
5. Niobe claimed, because of her many children, to be equal to the goddess Leto, who was only mother of two children, Apollo and Artemis. The two gods slew Niobe's children as punishment and turned her into stone. Not much is known of Satyrus but he may have been a king's son who (again in despite of the gods?) sought to deify his father.
6. It is of blameworthy things because it is about the bodily pleasures, or has them for its object, and these, being merely necessary and not in themselves preferable, have an element of blame attached to them; cf. *GE* 2.6.1202b4–9.

Chapter 5

Extreme Cases. *Besides habits that are natural because related to things pleasant by nature, so are there brutish ones and ones of disease and of madness. Where nature is to blame, there is no incontinence properly speaking, nor where disease from custom is, but these are beyond the limits of vice. And as there is a wickedness that accords with man, as well as a kind that is brutish or diseased, so is it also with incontinence.*

Since some things are pleasant by nature, and of these some are simply 1148b15 so and others according to kinds of animals and men, and since other things are not so but some come to be because of deformities and others because of customs and others because of wicked natures, then in the case of each of these too similar habits can be seen. I mean the brutish ones, as in the case of the human female who they say ripped open pregnant women and ate b20 their babies, or in the case of the sort of things they say some of the wild men about Pontus delight in, some in raw meat, some in human flesh, and some in sharing out babies for mutual feasting, or in the case of the story of Phalaris.[1]

These are the brutish ones, but others come about because of disease and, 1148b24 in some cases, madness, as with the man who sacrificed his mother and ate her, and the man who ate his fellow slave's liver. Those because of disease or custom are, for instance, pulling out one's hair or chewing fingernails or coal or earth, and the habit of sex among men. They happen to some people by nature and to others by custom, as with those who were wantonly abused[2] from childhood.

All those where nature is to blame no one would say were incontinent, just 1148b31 as no one would say women were because in sexual intercourse they are acted on and not acting. The like holds too of those diseased through custom. So each of these states is beyond the limits of vice, as brutishness is too. Having these states and overcoming or being overcome by them is not incontinence simply but by a certain likeness (just as someone who is this way disposed as to spirit should be called "incontinent in the passion" and not "incontinent"). For all extremes of folly and cowardice and license and harsh temper are some brutish and others diseased. For he who is by nature such as to fear everything, even the noise of a mouse, is a coward with a brutish cowardice, but he who was afraid of weasels was so by disease. As for the foolish, those who from nature lack reason and are living by sense alone are brutish, like some of the far off tribes of barbarians. Those by sickness, as the epileptic, or by madness are diseased.

In the case of some of these things it is possible just to have them but not to be overcome by them; I mean for instance if Phalaris had held in check his desire to eat babies or for outlandish sexual pleasures. It is possible also to be overcome by them and not just to have them. As with wickedness too, therefore, the one in accord with man is called wickedness simply but the other with an addition, that it is brutish or diseased and not simply, plainly there is also in the same way an incontinence that is brutish and one that is diseased, but only the one in accord with human license is simply so.

That incontinence and continence have to do only with what license and temperance have to do with, and that what has to do with other things is incontinence of another sort, called so in a transferred sense and not simply, is clear.

Notes

1. Phalaris was a tyrant in Sicily in the sixth century BC; he was notorious for roasting his victims alive in a bronze bull.
2. The word at 1148b30 is *hubrizomenous*, which also carries the connotation of rape.

Chapter 6

The Other Puzzles

Spirit. *Incontinence in spirit is less disgraceful, because (i) it obeys reason in a way though too quickly, while desire does not follow reason at all; (ii) forgiveness belongs to natural appetites, and spirit is more natural than is desire for excess and for things unnecessary; (iii) those who plot more wrong more, and spirit does not plot while desire does; (iv) anger is with pain but wanton violence is with pleasure, so that incontinence because of desire is more unjust. But some desires are natural and human while others are brutish or diseased, and it is only the first that incontinence concerns (hence beasts are not said to be licentious or temperate except in a transferred sense). Brutishness is more frightening but less vicious for in it the principle was not destroyed but never possessed; so it causes more destruction, yet vice does more evil.*

Let us take note of the fact that incontinence of spirit is also less disgraceful 1149a24 than that of desire. For spirit seems to hear something of reason but mishears, like hasty servants who rush off before they have heard all that is being said and then mistake the instruction, or like dogs that, before looking to see if it is a friend, bark as soon as they hear a sound. Thus spirit, because of the heat a30 and haste of its nature, does hear, to be sure, but not what is ordered, and rushes to vengeance. For reason or imagination showed there was wanton outrage or slight, and spirit, syllogizing, as it were, that war must be waged on this sort of ground,[1] flares into anger at once.

Desire, on the other hand rushes to enjoyment provided only reason or 1149a34 perception says the thing is pleasant. Thus spirit follows reason in a way, but desire does not. It is more disgraceful, therefore. For he who is incontinent in spirit is in a way overcome by reason, but the other by desire and not by reason.

Further, forgiveness follows more on natural appetites, since it also follows 1149b4 more on such desires as are common to all and insofar as they are so. But spirit and harsh temper are more natural than desires for excess and unnecessary things, as the man said in defense of hitting his father, "yes, for he too hit his father, and he his father before him, and this fellow," he said pointing to b10 his son, "will hit me when he's a man; for it runs in the family." And the man being dragged out by his son would bid him stop at the door, for he himself, he said, had dragged his father no further.

Also, those who plot more wrong more. Now he who is spirited does not 1149b13 plot, nor does spirit but acts in the open. But desire is like what they say about Aphrodite

of Cyprus born, weaver of wiles[2]

and Homer says of her "embroidered girdle"

enticement, which steals wits e'en of the wise.[3]

So if this incontinence be more wrong and more disgraceful than incontinence of spirit, then it is incontinence simply and, in a way, a vice.

Further, no one commits wanton violence when in pain, but everyone who 1149b20 does something in anger does it in pain; wanton violence, however, is done with pleasure. If, therefore, the things it is most just to get angry about are the things that are more unjust, incontinence because of desire is also more unjust, for in spirit there is no wanton violence.

1149b23   That incontinence about desire, then, is more disgraceful than incontinence about anger, and that continence and incontinence are about bodily desires and pleasures, is plain, but how these latter themselves differ needs to be grasped. For, as was said at the beginning, some are human and natural, both in kind and amount, others are brutish, others a result of deformity and

b30   disease. It is only the first of these that temperance and license have to do with. That in fact is why we call the beasts neither temperate nor licentious, except in a transferred sense or when in some respect one sort of beast differs as a whole from another, in wanton violence and destruction and voracity; for they do not choose or calculate but have departed their nature like madmen.

1150a1   Brutishness is something less than vice, but it is more frightening. For it is not that the best part has been corrupted as in man; rather it is not there. So it is like comparing a lifeless thing with a living one—which is worse? For

a5   the baseness of what has no principle (and intellect is a principle) is always less destructive. It is close, then, to comparing injustice with an unjust man, for there is a way that each of the two is worse.[4] For ten thousand times more bad might be done by a bad man than by a beast.

Notes

1.   Or alternatively, at 1149a33–34, "against this sort of thing."
2.   Author unknown, though Sappho fr. 1 speaks of Aphrodite as "weaver of wiles."
3.   *Iliad* 14. 214, 217.
4.   Injustice is worse because it is the essence or idea; an unjust man is worse because he it is who actually does the unjust things. Hence a beast is worse in its nature (it lacks the reason that men have), but an unjust man is worse in actual doing because he can do far worse things than a beast.

Chapter 7

License, Endurance, Softness

That License Is Worst. *As regard the pleasures and pains that license and temperance are about, it is possible to be stronger or weaker with respect to them than the many are. To be stronger or weaker as regard the pleasures is to be incontinent or continent, and as regard the pains to be soft or enduring. Most people are between these though inclining to the worse. He who by choice and for no other reason pursues to excess the necessary pleasures and flees to excess the contrary pains is licentious; he is unrepentant and incurable. He who is deficient in this respect is opposite, and the mean is temperate. Those who pursue pleasure or flee pain without choosing differ from each other and, because doing so without great passion, are licentious by way of softness. The incontinent is opposed to the continent, and the soft man to the man of endurance, but continence, because it conquers, is preferable to endurance.*

Softness is deficiency in respect of things the many are able to struggle against. So also with continence and incontinence, for being overcome by excessive pleasures and pains is not surprising and is forgivable (as in the Philoctetes' example, as well as others), but not otherwise, except because of inheritance or disease. The lover of play is soft. Some incontinence is impulsive, when passion carries one off before deliberation (as with the melancholic), and some is weakness, when one does not stand by what has been deliberated.

As regard the pleasures and pains of touch and taste and the pursuit and 1150a9
avoidance of them, which license and temperance were before distinguished
about, one can be in a state such as to be overcome even by those of them that
the many are stronger than, and in a state such as to be stronger even than
those of them that the many are overcome by. In the case of pleasures, one
of these is incontinent and the other continent, and in the case of pains one
of them is soft and the other enduring. The habit of most people is between
these, even if they decline more toward the worse.

Since some pleasures, while not others, are necessary, and are so up to a 1150a16
point, but not their excesses or deficiencies, and since the like holds of desires
and pains, he who pursues the excesses of pleasures, or pleasure to excess,
and by choice,[1] for their own sake and in no respect for a different outcome, is a20
licentious, for he must be unrepentant and so incurable (for the unrepentant
is incurable). The one who is deficient is opposite him, and the one who is a
mean is temperate. Likewise too with him who flees bodily pains not because
he is overcome but by choice.

Of those who do it without choosing, one is carried off by pleasure and the 1150a25
other because he is fleeing the pain that is apart from desire;[2] consequently
they differ from each other. But everyone would deem someone worse if he
does something disgraceful when he has no or weak desire than if he does
it when he has intense desire, and if he strikes when not angry than when
angry—for what would he do if he was impassioned? Hence the licentious
man is worse than the incontinent man. So, of those mentioned, the kind is
rather that of softness, but he is licentious.[3]

To the incontinent man the continent man is opposed and to the soft man 1150a32
the man of endurance; for endurance is a matter of holding out, but continence a matter of conquest, and holding out is different from conquering,
and so also not being overcome from winning. Hence continence is more a35
to be preferred than endurance. He who is deficient in relation to what the
many struggle and have power against is soft and indulgent (for indulgence
is a softness of sorts)—who lets his cloak drag so as not to be burdened with
the pain of picking it up, and, while imitating someone ill, does not think
himself wretched, though he is being like him.

The like holds of continence and incontinence. For it is no wonder if someone 1150b5
is overcome by strong and excessive pleasures and pains—rather it is something

to forgive if he is struggling against them, as the Philoctetes of Theodectes
b10 when bitten by the snake, or Cercyon in Carcinus' *Alope*, and as with those
trying to hold in their laughter who guffaw it out all in one go, as happened to
Xenophantus.[4] It is a wonder, however, if someone is overcome by and cannot
struggle against what the many can struggle against—unless it is because of
family nature or disease, in the way softness runs in the family of the Scythian
b15 kings, or in the way the female stands distinct from the male. The lover of play
also seems to be licentious but he is soft, for play is a letting go, since it is rest,[5]
and the lover of play is one of those who go to excess in this regard.

1150b19   Of incontinence part is impulsive and part weakness. For there are some
who, when they have deliberated, do not stand by their deliberations because
of passion, and there are others who, because of not having deliberated, are
carried off by passion. For as people do not feel tickles if they have tickled
others first,[6] so also by perceiving and seeing in advance and waking themselves up and their calculation beforehand they are not overcome by passion,
b25 neither when it is pleasant nor when it is painful.[7] But it is especially the quick
and melancholic who are incontinent with sudden incontinence. For the first
by their hastiness and the second by their intensity do not stand by reason,
because their tendency is to follow imagination.

Notes

1.   Reading at 1150a19–20 *ē kath' hyperbolēn, kai dia prohairesin* (or pleasure
to excess, and by choice) with some MSS rather than *ē kath' hyperbolas ē
dia prohairesin* (either according to their excesses or by choice) with others
and with Bekker.

2.   Treating *apo* (apart from) at a26 as expressing separation, not origin; cf.
8.2.1248a36. The pain "apart from desire" is the pain that does not come
from frustrated desire but is, as it were, simply bothersome, as with the
man, mentioned shortly (1150b3–4), who shuns the pain of picking up his
cloak. The pain does not come from any frustrated desire (as the pain of
not having another drink would be to a recovering alcoholic), but is just
the effort involved in doing something one cannot be bothered with.

3.   That is, the kind of fault of him who flees pains without choosing is softness, because he is failing to resist pain. But he himself is licentious, and not
incontinent, because he is fleeing pains when he has no strong passions to
do so (as with the man who lets his cloak drag). Understood in this way, the
remarks about doing something disgraceful without strong desires can be
taken to be integral to the point being made, and not out of place as some
scholars think (e.g., Broadie and Rowe [2002: 199, 396–97]).

4.   Theodectes was a tragic dramatist and student of Aristotle's. In the play,
Philoctetes, after long suppressing his pain, finally cries out "cut off my
hand!" Carcinus was another tragic dramatist of the same period whose
character Cercyon, upon discovering who had committed adultery with
his daughter Alope, was so overcome by grief he renounced living. Xenophantus was a musician at the court of Alexander the Great. Nothing is
known of the event here recorded about him.

5. Cf. *Politics* 5(8).3.1337b37–38a1.
6. Or reading, at 1251b22, the passive of the verb with some MSS rather than the active with others, to give the sense "as people do not feel tickles if they have already been tickled."
7. An example is given in *GE* 2.6.1203a29–b5 of telling oneself that a beautiful woman is about to walk by so as to get a grip on oneself in advance.

Chapter 8

That it is Incurable. The licentious man is unrepentant but the incontinent man is not, so the latter is curable. Also, incontinence does not escape one's notice but vice does. Of the incontinent, those who are so as being beside themselves are better than those who do not stand by their deliberation. So incontinence is not a vice save in a way, for part of it follows choice and part not. Those who are such as to pursue pleasure against reason but not because of persuasion can be persuaded otherwise, but not those who are not, for virtue saves the principles and wickedness destroys them. Virtue, whether natural or habitual, is of right opinion about the principles, and such is the temperate man but his opposite is licentious. The incontinent man is he who is conquered by passion against reason but he retains the principles so he is better than the licentious man.

The licentious man is, as was said, unrepentant; for he stands by his choice. 1150b29
But everyone who is incontinent is repentant. Hence things are not the way we said in the puzzle, but the former is incurable and the latter curable. For wickedness is like dropsy and consumption but incontinence like epilepsy, for the first is continuous depravity, and the second noncontinuous. And b35
generally, incontinence is in a different class of things from that of vice. For vice escapes one's notice but incontinence does not.

Of these very people those who get to be besides themselves are better than 1151a1
those who have reason but do not stand by it. For the latter are overcome by a lesser passion and are not without deliberation as the former are. For the incontinent man is like those who get drunk quickly and from a little wine and less than the many do.

That incontinence, therefore, is not a vice is clear, though perhaps it is in 1151a5
a way; for part is against choice and part in accord with it. Yet in its actions it is like what Demodocus said against the Milesians:

The Milesians are not a stupid crew,
But they do the things stupid people do.[1]

So the incontinent are not unjust but they do do wrong.

125

1151a11   Since the one sort is such as without being persuaded to pursue bodily pleasures too much and against right reason, but the other is persuaded because he is of the sort to pursue them, the former can easily be persuaded

a15   otherwise, but the latter not. For virtue saves and wickedness destroys the principle, and in doable things the "for the sake of" is principle, like hypotheses in mathematics. So neither in this case nor in that is reason teacher of the principles; rather it is virtue, whether natural or habitual, that has right opinion about the principle.

1151a19   Such a person, then, is temperate, while his opposite is licentious. But there is a sort of person who is beside himself contrary to right reason because of passion, and he is so conquered by the passion that he does not act in accord with right reason, but yet he is not so conquered by it that he is such as to be persuaded he should pursue such pleasures without more ado. He is the incontinent man, better than the licentious man, and not

a25   simply base. For his best part, the principle, is preserved. Opposite to him is another, who stands by reason and is not beside himself because of passion. It is clear then from what has been said that the one habit is virtuous and the other base.

Note

1.   Demodocus, fr. 1. He wrote lampooning verses in the sixth century BC. The translation of these verses given here is adapted from Ostwald (1981: 198).

Chapter 9

Wrong Opinion and Right Desire. *The opinion one stands by or abandons is in itself the true opinion but accidentally it is any opinion. Some stand by their opinion because stubborn, and these have a certain likeness to the continent because it is not easy to make them change their mind. The opinionated and unlearned and boorish are stubborn. The first of these are so because they enjoy winning if they can stand by their views, but they are pained by losing if their opinions get voted down; they are like the incontinent. Some fail to stand by their opinion because of noble pleasure, as Neoptolemus did, and such are not base. The continent man is a mean between the incontinent man, on the one hand, and the man, on the other, who fails to stand by reason bidding him enjoy bodily pleasures as he should; the first is virtuous and the other two both vicious, but the first of these latter is considered to be the opposite for the second is seldom manifest. The temperate man is said to be continent by a certain likeness, but he differs in not having base desires; the licentious man is like the incontinent in pursuing bodily pleasures, but the first thinks he should and the second does not.*

Is he continent who stands by any reason whatever and by any choice 1151a29 whatever or he who stands by the right one, and is he incontinent who does not stand by any choice whatever and by any reason whatever or he who does not stand by false reason and by the choice that is not right, as in the puzzle raised earlier?[1]

Or is it accidental that it is any reason and choice whatever and in itself 1151a33 it is true reason and right choice that the one stands by and the other does not? For if someone chooses or pursues this thing because of that thing, in itself he pursues and chooses the latter but accidentally the former. But we say that the "in itself" is simply so, hence in a sense it is any opinion that the one stands by and the other forsakes but simply speaking it is the true one.[2]

Some of those in fact who stand by their opinion people call stubborn, 1151b4 as those hard to persuade or not easy to dissuade. They have a certain likeness to the continent, just as the profligate to the generous or the bold to the confident, but they differ in many respects. For the one, the continent, is not made to change by passion or desire, since, on occasion, the continent b10 will be easy to persuade; but the others are not made to change by reason, since they get to have desires and many are carried off by the pleasures. The opinionated are stubborn and the unlearned and the boorish, the first being so because of pleasure and pain. For they enjoy winning if they are not dissuaded, and they are pained if their opinions get voted down, like decrees; so they are more like the incontinent than the continent.

There are others who, not because of incontinence, fail to stand by what 1151b17 seems to them, like Neoptolemus in Sophocles' *Philoctetes*, and yet it was pleasure that made him not stand by his opinion, though a noble pleasure. For it was a noble thing for him to speak the truth, but he was persuaded by Odysseus to lie. For not everyone who does something because of pleasure is licentious or base or incontinent, but he who does so because of a shameful one.

Since there is indeed someone who is such as to enjoy bodily things less 1151b23 than he should and to fail to stand by reason, the continent man is the sort to be a mean between him and the incontinent man. For the incontinent fails to stand by reason because of what in some respect is more, and this man because of what in some respect is less. But the continent does stand by it and does not change because of either. If continence is something virtuous, both these opposed habits must be base, as they in fact clearly are. But because b30 the one is clear in few people and rarely, then, as temperance seems alone to be opposite to license, so also continence to incontinence.

Since many things are spoken of according to likeness, so the "continence" 1151b32 of the temperate too has followed along according to likeness. For the b35   continent is such as to do nothing because of bodily pleasures against reason and the temperate too, but the one has and the other does not have base desires, and the one is such as not to be pleased against reason and the other is such as to be pleased but not to be carried off. The incontinent and the licentious are alike, though being something different, and both

a5   pursue bodily pleasures, but the one when also thinking he should and the other when not.

Notes

1.   Above at 6.2.1146a27–31. The construal of the paragraph here follows Von Fragstein (1974: 277) who defends the MSS reading against the scholarly emendations.

2.   The point is that any opinion that one follows one follows thinking it true even if in fact it is false. Hence "in itself" one follows what is true but accidentally any opinion.

Chapter 10

Prudence. The same man cannot be prudent and incontinent for the prudent man is virtuous and a doer, but the incontinent is not a doer. The clever man, however, could be incontinent, for it is by choice, rather than reason, that he differs from the prudent man.

1152a6   Nor is it possible for the same man to be prudent and incontinent at the same time, for a prudent man has been shown to be virtuous in character at the same time.[1] Further, he is not prudent by knowing alone but also by being a doer, and the incontinent man is not a doer. But nothing hinders the

a10   clever man being incontinent; which is why, in fact, some people are held to be prudent but incontinent, because cleverness differs from prudence in the way we said in our original discussion,[2] and because while it is close in respect of reason it is different in respect of choice.

Summary. So the incontinent man: (i) is like someone asleep and not someone knowing; (ii) acts voluntarily; (iii) is not wicked, because (a) his choice is decent, (b) he is not unjust, for he does not plot, (c) he is like a city that votes good laws but does not use them, while the wicked is like a city that has wicked laws and uses them; (iv) he is, along with the continent man, about what exceeds the habits of the many either by more or by less; (v) is more curable if melancholic than if deliberating and not standing by it, and if incontinent by custom than by nature.

So neither is it the case that he[3] is as one who knows and considers, but as one who is asleep or drunk. Also, he acts voluntarily (for he is in a way a knower of what he does and why). But he is not wicked, for his choice is decent, so that he is half wicked. Also, he is not unjust, for he is no plotter; for one sort among them does not stand by what he deliberated, and the melancholic is not a deliberator at all. Also, the incontinent is like the city that votes for everything it should and has virtuous laws but does not use them at all, as in the jibe of Anaxandrides: 1152a14 a20

So willed the city—that cares naught for laws,

while the wicked is like a city that does use its laws, only one that uses wicked laws.

Incontinence and continence concern what exceeds the habit of the many, for the one stands more and the other less than most people can. Of the sorts of incontinence, the one that the melancholic are incontinent by is more easily cured than the incontinence of those who deliberate but do not stand by it; and those incontinent by custom are more easily cured than those naturally so. For custom is easier to change than nature. For that is also why custom is hard, because it is like nature, as Evenus indeed says: 1152a25 a30

Much time it takes to be practiced, my friend,
To make it nature for men in the end.[4]

What continence is, then, and what incontinence, what endurance and what softness, and what state these habits are with respect to each other, has been stated. 1152a34

Notes

1. Book 5.12.1144a20–b1.
2. See the previous note.
3. Sc. the incontinent man.
4. Evenus of Paros was a sophist of the late fifth century BC.

Chapter 11

Pleasure and Happiness[1]
Statement of Puzzles. *Study of pleasure and pain belongs to the philosopher of politics because he studies the end, and vice and virtue have to do with pleasure, and happiness is with pleasure. Some say no pleasure is good, some*

that most are bad, others that no pleasure is the best thing. The first say that pleasure (i) is a sensible coming to be and no coming to be is the goal; (ii) the temperate man flees pleasure; (iii) the prudent man pursues absence of pain, not pleasure; (iv) pleasure impedes thinking; (v) there is no art of pleasure; (vi) children and beasts pursue pleasure. The second say that (i) some pleasures are shameful and reprehensible and (ii) others harmful. The third say that (i) pleasure is not an end but a coming to be.

1152b1   To study pleasure and pain belongs to him who philosophizes on politics. For he is master craftsman of the end that we look to when we say simply of each thing that one is bad and one good. Further, to examine them is also something necessary. For moral virtue and vice we lay down as having to do with pains and pleasures,[2] and most people say happiness is with pleasure, which is also why the name for being "blessed" they have taken from enjoying "bliss."[3]

1152b8   Now some people hold that no pleasure is good, either in itself or incidentally. For, they say, good and pleasure are not the same thing. Others hold that some pleasures are good but that the majority are base. There is further a third among these, that even if all pleasures are good yet the best thing cannot be pleasure.

1152b12   That, therefore, it is altogether not good is because every pleasure is a perceptible coming to be to one's nature, but no coming to be is in the like kind with the ends, as for instance no house-making is in the like kind with

b15   a house. Further, the temperate man flees pleasures. Further, the prudent man pursues the painless not the pleasant. Further, pleasures get in the way of thinking, and the more there is of enjoyment the more there is of getting in the way, as with the pleasure of sex (for no one could think in the middle of it). Further, there is no art of pleasure, yet every good is the work of some art. Further, children and beasts pursue pleasures.

1152b20   That not all pleasures are virtuous is because there are shameful and reprehensible pleasures; and, further, there are harmful ones, for some pleasant things bring disease. That pleasure is not best is because it is not an end but a becoming. These then are pretty much the things that are said.

Notes

1.   The final chapters of this book suitably have the title "Pleasure and Happiness" in *EE* because they answer the part of the question about pleasure, from 1.5.1216a29–37, which concerns the relation of pleasure to the best good of happiness. In the *NE* these chapters serve the same role but as subordinate to the discussion of continence and incontinence, of which they are a sort of appendix (and perhaps the title "Appendix" should, within *NE*, be added to the subtitle). The discussion proper of pleasure and happiness is given in *NE* in Book Ten, chapters 1–5, before the final definition of happiness is itself given there in chapters 6–8.

2.   2.4; also 2.1.1220a34–36, 5.1222a11–16.

3.   Aristotle is playing, at 1152b7–8, with the words for blessed, *makarios*, and for enjoying, *chairein*, as if the first were derived from the second.

Chapter 12

That Pleasure Is Good and Best

In Answer to the Puzzles. *These arguments do not prove their point, for (i) pleasures base in themselves need not be base for everyone, or all the time, or really pleasures; (ii) the good is both activity and habit and those pleasures that restore to a natural habit are only accidentally pleasant (as facts show), but there exist pleasures without pain and desire and these do not come from restoration; (iii) not all pleasures are comings to be, but some are activities and ends and puttings to use, so that pleasure is unimpeded activity in accord with nature, and the error arises from thinking that activity is a coming to be; (iv) base pleasures are not base because they impede other activities, for all pleasures alien to the activity do the same, while pleasures proper to the activity enhance the activity; (v) if pleasure is an activity it is not surprising there is no art of it for art is of the power, yet even so some arts are arts of pleasure, as cooking and perfumery; (vi) the prudent and the temperate have their own pleasures, which are not those of children or brutes or the licentious.*

That these things do not make it the case that pleasure is neither good nor best is plain from the following. First, since the good is twofold (the good simply and the good for someone), natures and habits will follow suit, so that changes and comings to be will too, and the pleasures held to be base will be some base simply but not base to a particular person; rather they will be preferable for this man (and some not even for him, except at some point and for a short time), but they will not be preferable; others will not even be pleasures though they appear to be—all that are with pain and for the sake of cure, I mean the pleasures of the sick. **1152b25** **b30**

Further, since the good is part activity and part habit, those pleasures are incidentally pleasant that restore to a natural habit—the actualization in the desires is of what remains of the habit and of nature (since there are in fact pleasures without pain or desire, as are the activities of contemplation, where nature is not in need). A sign is that people do not delight in the same pleasant thing when their nature is being filled up and after it has been restored, but after it has been restored they delight in things simply pleasant but when it is being filled up they delight in the opposite. For they even delight in sharp and bitter things none of which is pleasant either by nature or simply, so that the pleasures are not either. For as pleasant things stand to each other so also do the pleasures that come from them. **1152b33** **a1** **a5**

Further, there is no necessity that something else be better than pleasure, in the way that some say the end is better than coming to be. For they are not all comings to be nor are they with coming to be but activities and an end; nor do they happen when there is coming to be but when there is using. **1153a7** **a10**

Nor is an end something different in all cases, but in the case of things being led to the completion of their nature. Hence, in fact, it is not a fine thing to say that pleasure is a perceived coming to be, but rather one should say that it is activity of a habit in accord with nature and, instead of "perceived," say "unimpeded." But, because it is a good in the authoritative sense, it seems to be a sort of coming to be, for people think activity is a coming to be. But it is different.

To say pleasures are base because some pleasant things bring disease is the same as saying some healthy things are base for business. So both are base in this respect, but not for this reason base, since in fact contemplation is sometimes harmful for health. But no prudence or habit is impeded by the pleasure that comes from each of them but by a foreign one, since the pleasures that come from contemplation and learning make one contemplate and learn more.

That no pleasure is the job of art is reasonable, for neither is there art of any other activity but of the power. Yet even so the art of perfume making and cooking are held to be arts of pleasure.

That the temperate man flees pleasure, and the prudent man pursues the painless life, and that children and beasts pursue pleasure, are all solved in the same way. For since it was said that all pleasures are in a way simply good and in a way not good,[1] it is the latter sort of pleasures that children and beasts pursue, and it is the absence of pain from these that the prudent man pursues—the pleasures that are with desire and pain and that are bodily (for they are of this sort), as well as the excesses of them that the licentious man is licentious by. That is why the temperate man flees them, since the temperate man too has his pleasures.

Note

1. Above at 1152b26–b7.

Chapter 13

Direct Proofs. *(i) Pain is to be avoided, and the opposite of what is avoided is good, so pleasure is good; (ii) some pleasure can be best even if certain pleasures are base, and some pleasure must be best if pleasure is unimpeded activity and if the activity of some habit is best; (iii) hence everyone says the happy life is pleasant, for no activity is complete if impeded, which is why bodily and external goods are needed for happiness, though only as far as happiness requires; (iv) everything pursues pleasure, which is a sign that it is the best thing, whether the pleasure is different in each case or in some sense the same (the bodily pleasures seem to be the best only because everyone shares them);*

(v) if pleasure is not good then the happy man does not live pleasantly, for he would not need pleasure and could live in pain, for pain would not be bad.

But anyway it is agreed that pain is bad and to be avoided, for one sort 1153b1 is simply bad and the other somehow gets in the way. But to the avoidable, qua avoidable and bad, the opposite is good. Pleasure then must be a good. For the way Speusippus[1] solves it turns out not to be a solution, as that the greater is opposite both to the less and to the equal. For he would not say that pleasure was something essentially bad.[2]

And, if some pleasures are base, nothing prevents a certain pleasure being 1153b7 best, just as also nothing prevents knowledge of some sort being best though some are base. Perhaps indeed, if each habit has unimpeded activities, it is necessary, if either the activity of them all is happiness or of some one among b10 them (provided it is unimpeded), that it be most to be preferred. And this is pleasure. Consequently some pleasure would be the best, though most pleasures, if it so happen, are simply base.

And that is why everyone says the happy life is pleasant, and they tie in 1153b14 pleasure with happiness—reasonably; for no activity is complete when impeded, but happiness is among things complete. Hence the happy man has need of the goods in the body too and of external goods and goods of fortune, so that he not be impeded in respect of them. But those who say a man on the rack, or who has fallen into great misfortunes, is happy, provided he be b20 good, are saying nothing, whether they mean to or not. Indeed, because of the need we have in addition for fortune, some hold that good fortune is the same thing as happiness, though it is not, since this too, when in excess, is an impediment and is perhaps no longer justly called fortune; for the limit of it is by reference to happiness.

The fact that all things, both beasts and men, pursue pleasure is a sign of 1153b25 its being in some way the best thing:

In naught a voice doth altogether die
That many hosts...[3]

But since neither the same nature nor the same habit is best or held to be, everyone does not pursue the same pleasure either, though they do all pursue b30 pleasure. Perhaps indeed they do not pursue the pleasure they think, or the one they say they do, but the same pleasure; for everything by nature possesses something divine. But the bodily pleasures have got inheritance to the name because people both meet with them most often and all share them. So because these alone are notable they think that these alone exist.

It is also clear that if pleasure and its activity are not a good, it will not 1154a1 be the case that the happy man lives pleasantly—for what would he need it for if it was not a good?—but possible even that he lives in pain. For pain is neither good nor bad if pleasure too is not, so why would he flee it? The virtuous man's life, then, is not pleasant either, if his activities also are not.

Notes

1. Nephew to Plato and his successor as head of the Academy.
2. Speusippus argued that if pain is bad and pleasure is the opposite of pain, it does not follow that pleasure is good, because a thing can have two opposites: the contrary extreme and the intermediate (as the greater has both the equal and the less as opposites). Hence it need only follow that the intermediate between pain and pleasure, the neutral state, is good. Aristotle's response is that if the intermediate of the three is good then its extremes must both be bad. But it is absurd to say that pleasure is like pain in being something bad as such; for not all pleasures can reasonably be called bad, but they would all have to be if pleasure was bad as such. Aristotle's point seems to be that, by hypothesis, only an extreme has opposites that are not equally opposed to it (the intermediate and the other extreme) and where, accordingly, one opposite might have the opposite characteristic and not the other. The intermediate, however, is equally opposed to both extremes, so that both must have the opposite characteristic. Hence if the intermediate, the neutral state, is good and if one of the extremes, pain, is bad, as Speusippus allowed, then the other extreme, pleasure, must be bad too. One might also say, further, that if pain is bad and the neutral state good but pleasure neither, then pleasure should be between bad and the neutral state and not, as it plainly is, at the opposite extreme to pain.
3. Hesiod, *Works and Days* 763–64.

Chapter 14

Why Bodily Pleasures Seem to Be but Are Not Best. *Bodily pleasures and their opposite pains can both be bad because the pleasures can be had in excess; but where there is no excess of the best neither is there excess of the pleasure. The necessary pleasures and pains are pursued and avoided to excess and not as they should be. But bodily pleasures appear more desirable, for (i) they cast out pain and people pursue excess of pleasure because of excess of pain, which is why these pleasures seem base though incidentally they are good; (ii) they are pursued because of their force by those who cannot enjoy other pleasures, for these people have nothing else to enjoy and mere absence of pain is painful to the many; (iii) the young are like the drunk and youth is pleasant; (iv) the melancholic need a cure, for their body pains them and they seek the pleasure that drives out pain, though in fact the pleasures that are without pain are pleasant by nature, not by way of cure, and they are cause too that the other pleasures are pleasant; (v) our nature is not simple but has in it something else, and what the one part does is against the nature of the other, whereas the god, being simple, always enjoys a single and simple pleasure in his changeless activity, but things depraved need and enjoy change.*

An examination, then, of the bodily pleasures is required of those who 1154a8
say that some pleasures at least are intensely preferable, as the noble ones,
but not the bodily ones and those that the licentious man has to do with. So a10
why are the opposite pains wicked, since to evil good is opposite? Or are the
necessary pleasures good in the way that what is not bad is good? Or are they
good up to a point? For in the case of all habits and changes where there is
no excess beyond the best, neither is there of the pleasure; but in the case of
those where there is, there is of the pleasure too. There is excess in the case a15
of bodily pleasures, and the base man exists in pursuing the excess not those
that are necessary. For everyone in some way enjoys meats and wines and
sex, but not everyone as they should. The opposite is the case with pain, for
one does not flee the excess of it but it altogether. For pain is not opposed to
excess except for him who pursues excess.

Since one must not only state the truth but also the reason for what is false 1154a22
(for this adds to one's belief, for whenever the "why" of a thing's appearing
true though it is not true appears to be reasonable, it makes one believe the
truth more), one must, as a result, say why the bodily pleasures appear more
to be preferred.

First then because it casts out pain; and because of pain's excesses[1] people 1154a26
pursue, on the grounds of its being a cure, excessive pleasure and bodily pleasure generally. For, because they show up against the opposite, the curative
ones get to be intense, and that is why they are pursued. And pleasure seems a30
not to be virtuous, as was said,[2] for these two reasons, that some are actions
of a base nature, either base in origin, as in the case of a beast, or because of
custom, as those of base men, but the curative ones because they are of what
is lacking, and having is better than coming to be; but they happen when we
are coming to be complete, so they are virtuous incidentally.

Further, because they are intense they are pursued by people unable to 1154b2
enjoy others. At any rate they procure certain sorts of thirsts for themselves;
so when they procure harmless ones, the thing is without reproach, but when
harmful, it is base. For they do not have anything else to take enjoyment in, b5
and what is neutral is painful to the many because of their nature. For the
living creature is always toiling, as the arguments of the naturalists testify
when they say that seeing and hearing are painful (but, they say, we have
long got used to it).

Likewise in youth people are like the drunk because they are growing, 1154b9
and youth is pleasant.

The melancholic always need a cure. For their body, because of its mixture, 1154b11
ends up gnawing them, and they are always in a state of intense appetite. Pleasure drives out pain, whether it is the opposite pleasure or, if it be strong, any

b15   pleasure. And that is why people become licentious and base. But pleasures without pains do not have excess, and these are the ones pleasant by nature and not incidentally. By incidental I mean the pleasant things that are curative, for because one gets to be cured when the remaining healthy part does something, that is why cure seems pleasant. But those pleasant by nature are what produce activity in a healthy nature.[3]

1154b20   But in no case is the same thing always pleasant,[4] because our nature is not simple but has in it, insofar as we are corruptible, something else as well, so that if one or either of them does anything, it is, for the other nature, against nature; but when they are equalized, what is done seems to be neither pain

b25   ful nor pleasant, since if anything had a simple nature the same act would always be most pleasant. Hence the god is always enjoying a single and simple pleasure. For there is activity not only in change but also in changelessness, and pleasure is more in rest than in change. But

Change of everything is sweet

b30   according to the poet,[5] because of some depravity. For as he who is depraved is a man easily changeable, so too is the nature that needs change. For it is not simple and not decent either.

1154b32   We have spoken about continence and incontinence, about pleasure and pain, both what each is and how some are good and some bad. But as for what remains we will also speak about friendship.

Notes

1.   Cf. 1.5.1215b15–22.
2.   Above 5.1148b15–31, 12.1152b26–33.
3.   Or possibly, a nature adapted to the activity in question.
4.   Or alternatively, at 1154b21, "nothing pleasant is always the same."
5.   Euripides, *Orestes* 234.

Book Seven: Completion of Happiness: Complete Life[1]

Chapter 1

Completion of Happiness
Complete Life
Friendship and Life
Reasons for Investigating Friendship. *The nature and kinds of friendship and of friends and their treatment need to be examined because: (a) it is the job of politics to make people friends; (b) the just and unjust have most to do with friends; (c) the same man seems both to be good and a friend; (d) friendship is a moral habit and reconciles people and stops them wronging each other; (e) friends are among the greatest goods; (f) the just in relation to friends is up to us but the just in relation to others is fixed by law.*

About friendship,[2] what it is and what it is like, and who the friend is, and 1234b18 whether friendship is said in one or many ways, and, if in many, how many, and further how the friend is to be treated and what the just is in the case of friendship—these must be examined no less than things noble and preferable in character. For it seems to be especially the job of politics to produce friend ship; also this is why they say virtue is useful, for those wronged by each other b25 cannot be friends with each other; further, we all say that the just and unjust have to do with friends most of all; and the same person seems to be both a good man and a friend; and friendship seems to be a certain moral habit and, if one wants to make people not do wrong but into friends, seems to do it,[3] for true friends do not wrong (although, of course, they will also not wrong if they are just); so justice and friendship are either the same thing or something close.

In addition, we suppose that the friend counts among the greatest of goods 1234b31 and that lack of friends and solitariness is a most terrible thing, because the whole of life and voluntary companionship is with friends; for it is with family or with kinsmen or with colleagues that we pass our days, or with children or a1 parents or wife. Also, only just things in private, those that have to do with our friends, are up to us, but those to do with other people are fixed by law and are not up to us.

Puzzles about Friendship. *The puzzles about friendship are (as extraneous ones): (a) whether it is with the like or (b) with opposites; and (as ones more germane to the topic): (c) that friendship is only with the good; (d) that mothers will love their children regardless; (e) that friendship is only with the useful (which opinion is in conflict with the first two); (f) that friendship is easy;*

(g) that it is hard and requires good fortune; (h) that friends in bad times are acting out of self-interest.

1235a4 But there are many puzzles about friendship, first those raised by people who bring in extrinsic matters and use the term in larger sense. For some hold that like is friend to like, whence the saying "how god always draws like to like," for there is also "jackdaw to jackdaw" and "thief knows thief and wolf

a10 wolf."[4] The natural scientists put even the whole of nature into cosmic order taking as principle that like goes to like, whence Empedocles said that the dog sat on the tile because it was most alike to it.[5]

1235a12 Now that is how some speak about the friend, but others say that the opposite is friend to the opposite. For they say that the thing beloved and desired is dear to all, but the dry does not desire the dry but the wet, whence the saying "earth longs for rain" and "change of everything is sweet"[6] (change is to the opposite). But the like is hostile to the like, for indeed "potter strives with potter"[7] and animals that live on the same food are enemies of each other.

1235a20 These suppositions, then, are greatly at odds, for some say the like is a friend and the opposite an enemy:

Always the less is to the more the foe,
And thence begins the day of hate to grow.[8]

Further opposites are in separate places, but friendship is held to bring things
a25 together. Others say opposites are friends. Heracleitus in fact found fault with the poet's line: "may strife perish from gods and from men!" For he said there would not be harmony without the opposites of high and low, nor animals without those of female and male.

1235a29 There are, then, these two opinions about friendship, and they are too general being too much removed from things; but there are others that are closer to and akin to the phenomena. For some hold that the base cannot be friends but only the good. Others hold it an odd thing if mothers do not love their children (friendship is clearly present even among the beasts, which
a35 is why they choose to die for their offspring). Others hold that the useful alone is dear. A sign is that everyone is in pursuit of these things, and even such of them as are prostitutes[9] throw away what is useless (as Socrates the elder was wont to say, instancing spit and hair and nails), and that we cast off
b1 parts that are useless, even the body in the end when it dies, for the corpse is useless (though those who have a use for it keep it, as in Egypt). All these are held to be opposed to each other, for the useless is opposed to the like, and contrariety is most removed from likeness, and the opposite is most useless to the opposite, for the opposite destroys the opposite.

1235b6 Further, some hold it easy to get a friend, but others that to know a friend is very rare, and cannot be done without good fortune,[10] for everyone wants

to be deemed friends with those who are doing well. But others do not think
they should trust even those who stay close by in misfortune, supposing them   b10
to be deceiving and putting on an act so that, by keeping company with those
who are unfortunate, they may get something when these are doing well again.

Notes

1.   The happy life was said earlier, 1.8.1218b10–28, 2.1.1219a35–39, to be
     complete. The sense of completeness there meant was not specified. The
     specification comes here in this and the next book, both of which show,
     among other things, how the happy life becomes complete through having
     a sufficiency of true and virtuous friends, on the one hand, and through the
     fullness of virtue that is the gentleman, on the other. Suitably, therefore,
     might these final two books be given the title "Completion of Happiness."
2.   The Greek words for friendship (*philia*), to be a friend (*philein*), and friend
     (*philos*) can also variously be translated as love or dear and sometimes need
     to be. The etymological connection in Greek is impossible to preserve in
     English without unwieldy paraphrase; it should nevertheless be kept in mind.
3.   Punctuating the Greek at 1234b28–29 thus: . . . *tis einai hexis kai, ean tis
     boulētai poiēsai hōste mē adikein all' eis philous, poiēsai.* Otherwise un-
     necessary emendations are forced on the text.
4.   The first of these quotations is from *Odyssey* 17.218, the others are tradi-
     tional proverbs.
5.   Empedocles was one of the Pre-Socratic philosophers; the story of the dog
     is told more fully at *GE* 2.11.1208b7ff.
6.   Both quotations are from Euripides, the first from an unknown play and
     the second, just quoted at 6.14.1154b28–29, from *Orestes* 234.
7.   Hesiod, *Works and Days* 25.
8.   Euripides, *Phoenissae* 539–40.
9.   A gap is found in the MSS at 1235b37 after *hai toiautai tōn* . . . (such of the . . .)
     with space for about six letters. Von Fragstein (1978: 301) suggests adding
     pornōn (prostitutes), the sense being that even prostitutes throw away the
     devices of their trade (and also their clients) once they have used them up.
10. Sc. the good fortune to learn the true character of one's friend, not the good
     fortune of wealth (which is rather an impediment to finding true friends, as
     the next remark recalls). There seems, then, no need to change at 1235b8
     the word "good fortune" (*eutychia*) to "misfortune" (*atychia*).

Chapter 2

Nature and Kinds of Friendship
The Three Basic Kinds
In General. *An account must be given that saves the phenomena on both sides.
The key is that the thing loved is either the good or the apparent good, and
that the good and the pleasant are both the good and pleasant simply and the*

good and pleasant for someone; there is also the good as the useful. Things and people can be loved for any of these goods. So friendship is when someone loves and is loved back for the good or pleasant or useful. So there are three kinds of friendship, related to each other not as species of a genus but analogously in view of a first (like "medical"). Most people's friendship is based on utility; that of the young on pleasure; that of the best on virtue.

1235b13   We must adopt an account[1] that will at the same time return us the views most held on these matters as well as solve the puzzles and contradictions. This will happen if the contradictions are shown to be reasonably held, for such an account will most agree with the phenomena; and if what is said is in a way true and in a way not, the opposing sides end up staying in place.

1235b18   But there is also a puzzle whether the pleasant or the good is the thing loved. For if, on the one hand, the thing loved is what we have desire for and if erotic love is especially of this sort (for "none is in love who is not friend for aye"),[2] and if desire is of the pleasant, then, to this extent, the thing loved is the pleasant; but if, on the other hand, it is what we wish for, then it is the good. The pleasant and the good are different.

1235b24   We must try to determine these puzzles and those akin to them by taking the following for our beginning, that the thing we have an appetite for and the thing we wish for is either the good or the apparent good. That in fact is why the pleasant is an object of appetite, that it is something that appears good, for some think it so and to others it appears so even if they do not think it, for appearing and opinion are not in the same part of the soul. That the good and the pleasant are dear, then, is plain.

1235b30   This being determined, we must take up another assumption. For of goods some are good simply while others are good for someone but not simply. Also the same things are simply good and simply pleasant. For we say that the things that benefit the body when healthy are simply good for the body and
b35   not the things that benefit it when ill, like drugs and surgery, and likewise too the things that are pleasant to the body when whole and healthy are simply pleasant for it, like seeing by daylight and not in the dark (though it is the opposite for someone with ophthalmia), and a pleasanter wine is not one that is so to someone with tongue destroyed by wine-bibbing (since neither is it pleasant to them when they pour vinegar in with it),[3] but to a percep-
a1   tion that has not been destroyed. The like is true of the soul, and things are pleasant that are so not to children and beasts but to adults; at any rate while we remember both, we choose the latter. But what a child or a beast is to an adult that the base and senseless man is to the decent and prudent; and to the latter the things that accord with their habits are pleasant, and these are the good and noble things.

1236a7   Since therefore goods are manifold, for we call one thing good because it is such and another because it is beneficial and useful, and since[4] the pleasant is either that which is simply so and simply good or that which is so for someone or an apparent good, and just as in the case of lifeless things we can choose a10 and love something for each of these goods, and just as we can a man too (for we choose and love this sort of man in fact because of his virtue, that one because he is beneficial and useful, that one because he is pleasant and for pleasure)—thus a friend comes to be when, being loved, he loves back and neither of them fails in any way to notice the fact. There must, therefore, be a15 three types of friendship, and not all in accord with one thing, nor as kinds within one genus, nor said altogether homonymously.

For they are spoken of with a view to some one and first friendship. "Medi- 1236a17 cal" is similar, for we say a soul is medical and a body and a tool and a job; but the controlling sense is the primary one, and that is primary whose account is in us, as a medical tool is what a doctor uses but the account of tool is not part of the account of doctor. Now what is everywhere sought for is the first, and because the universal is first they take the first to be universal as well. But this is false. Hence too they cannot give for friendship an account of all the a25 phenomena. For when a single account does not fit they do not think there are other friendships. But there are, though not all in the same way. They, however, when the first does not fit, supposing that if it was first it would be universal, deny that the others are even friendships.

But there are many kinds of friendship; for this was precisely among the 1236a30 things stated, since the determination was that friendship is said in three ways. For one of them is determined on the basis of virtue, one on that of the useful, and one of the pleasant. Among these the one based on the useful is that between[5] most people, for they love each other because and insofar as they are useful, as the proverb has it: "Glaucus, an ally's friends, so long he a35 fight,"[6] and "Athenians no longer acknowledge Megarians." The friendship of the young is the one based on pleasure, for that is what they have percep- tion of. Hence the friendship of the young is unstable, for as their characters change with their ages so does the pleasant. But the friendship based on b1 virtue is that of the best men.

The First Kind. *The first friendship is reciprocal loving and choosing of the good for each other and is found only among human beings. The other friend- ships can be found among beasts too. The base also can be friends of utility and pleasure. They are all friendships but only as related by analogy to the first friendship. The simply good is simply pleasant and so also is the simply good friend. The simply good is simply preferable but preferable for oneself is the good for oneself. Virtue puts these in harmony, and politics is for making this to be so for those for whom it is not yet so. The way is through the pleas- ant, and virtue puts pleasure and nobility in harmony. The first friendship is that of virtue, and first friends will be simply good because they are virtuous and simply pleasant too; but the same is not true of those not simply good.*

For pleasure is taken in things familiar and alike, whether one is complete or incomplete; but the virtuous man is complete. Friendship is a habit and the activity of friendship is an actuality in the lover, but the actuality of being loved is not in the beloved, so that loving is with pleasure but being loved is not. The pleasure that comes from loving the friend qua friend is friendship's proper pleasure, and if it is pleasure in the friend qua good it is the first friendship; otherwise not. An accidental impediment might stop friends living together but not stop them being well disposed to each other.

1236b1   From this it is clear that the first friendship, that of the good, is reciprocal loving and choosing in respect of each other. For dear is the thing loved to him who loves it, but dear is he to the one loved when his loving is also b5 reciprocal. Now this friendship is found only among men (for it alone has perception[7] of choice), but the others are also found among beasts. The useful indeed is clearly found among them to a small extent, both in relation to man (among domestic animals) and in relation to each other, as Herodotus says of the sandpiper and the crocodile,[8] and as the seers say of the flocking together and parting of birds.

1236b10   The base too might be friends with each other on account both of the useful and of the pleasant. Yet some deny that they are friends, because the first friendship is not found in them, for the base will wrong the base and the wronged do not love each other. They do not, however, not[9] love, save it is not b15 with the first friendship (since no one is holding the other friendships from them); for in doing for themselves harm to each other because of pleasure they are suspicious, as if they were incontinent.[10] Yet, they who love each other on account of pleasure, when accurately inquired into, do not seem to be friends either; because their friendship is not the first, for that friendship is stable but this one unstable. It is, however, a friendship, as was said, only not that one but derived from it.

1236b21   To speak of the friend only like that, therefore, is to force the phenomena and necessarily to speak paradoxes. The friendships can, however, all accord with a single account. The way left, then, is this, that in a sense only the first is friendship and in a sense all are, neither as homonymous and related to themselves as chance would have it, nor in accord with one kind, but rather in view of one thing.

1236b26   Since the same thing and at the same time is simply good and simply pleasant (unless someone prevents it), the friend truly and simply is the first, and such a person is he who is preferable because of his very self[11] b30 (and there must be such a person, for as one wishes good things on one's own account to exist so one must prefer that one exist oneself). But the true friend is also pleasant simply. Hence it is held that any friend at all is pleasant. But there needs to be yet more distinction about this (there is a halt to it).[12]

For is it the case that the good for oneself is dear or the good simply? And is 1236b33
it the case that the actual act of loving is accompanied by pleasure, so that the
thing loved is also pleasant, or is it not? For both[13] must be brought together
to the same point. For things not simply good but bad are simply, by fortune,[14]
to be avoided; and what is not good for oneself is nothing to oneself. But the
object of search is this, that things simply good be in this way good. For the
simply good is preferable but preferable for oneself is the good for oneself. a1
These things should be in harmony, and this is what virtue does; politics too
is for this purpose, to make it so for those for whom it is not yet so.

But one is ready and on the way to this if one is a human being (for by na- 1237a3
ture the things simply good are good to him) and likewise too if one is a man
instead of a woman and simple instead of clever.[15] But the way is through the
pleasant (noble things are necessarily pleasant), and when this is discordant
he is not completely virtuous, for incontinence could arise (for incontinence
is the discord of the good with the pleasant in passions).

As a result, since the first friendship accords with virtue, the friends too 1237a9
will themselves be simply good, and this not because they are useful but in
another way (for the good for this man here and the good simply are distinct).
And likewise, as in the case of the beneficial, so in the case of habits, for the
simply beneficial and noble are other (exercising is like this with respect to
being given medicine), so that the habit that is the virtue of a man is so too. a15
For let man be among the naturally good[16] things; for the virtue of what is
naturally good is good simply, but the virtue of what is not is good for it. The
like, then, holds also of the pleasant.

For here we must call a halt[17] and examine whether there is friendship 1237a18
without pleasure, and what difference it makes, and which of the two the
loving is in, and whether it is because he is good even if he is not pleasant
(though not because of that). So since loving has two senses, does the sense
that is actual loving appear to be not without pleasure because it is good?
Plainly, as things freshly studied and learnt in the sciences are most perceptible in their kind, so also is recognition of those alike in habits (the account a25
is the same in fact in both cases). By nature, at any rate, the simply good is
pleasant simply, and to whom it is good to them it is pleasant. Hence things
alike take immediate delight in each other, and man is pleasantest to man, so
that, since this is so even with incomplete things, plainly also with complete
ones. But the virtuous man is complete.

If the activity of loving is a mutual choice, along with pleasure, of knowing 1237a30
each other, it is also plain that on the whole the first friendship is a mutual
choice of things simply good and pleasant because they are good and pleasant.
And this friendship is a habit on which such choosing depends. For its work
is activity, and this not outside but within the lover himself (but it is outside a35
every potentiality,[18] for either it is in another or is other). Hence loving is
enjoying but being loved is not. For being loved is a loved thing's actuality,

but loving is also friendship's actuality; and this latter is in a living thing but the former also in a lifeless one (for lifeless things too are loved).

1237a40   Since loving is the thing loved being in act, which is to use it qua thing loved, and since the friend is something loved and is so for a friend qua being a friend but not qua musical or medical,[19] then the pleasure that is from him qua him, this pleasure is friendship's pleasure; for he loves him not because he is so to someone else. As a result, if he does not enjoy him qua good, it is

b5   not the first friendship, nor indeed does anything accidental hinder him more than the good gladdens him. For why is a man left who smells very badly? Because being kindly disposed toward him is embraced[20] but one would not live together.[21]

The Other Kinds. *The first friendship is firm and requires time. But wanting to be friends and even doing the offices of friendship is not yet to be friends, as the parallel with health and the phenomenon of dividing people by slander show. The base are incapable of the first friendship, because not being trustworthy, not having the things of friends as common, and not preferring friends to things. The first friendship exists only among few, those who are virtuous and have spent time together and have become dear to each other. But someone simply good can be useful to others with whom he is unable to be a first friend. First friends are stable and stand by each other in hard times. Even useful friends take time. Pleasant ones can be quick, but only in the case of the superficial pleasures. Friendships of utility and pleasure can exist among children, beasts, and the base. The base can be pleasant to each other as base or as having some talent or because there is something good in everyone; they can be useful friends too, relative to their particular choices. The virtuous and the base can also be useful and pleasant friends with each other in all these same ways.*

1237b7   Now this is the first friendship, which all agree on, and because of it the other ones are both held to be so and are matter of dispute. For friendship is held to be something firm and only this one is firm. For what has passed judgment is firm, but when things do not happen quickly or easily the judgment is not made rightly, and there is no firm friendship without trust, and there is no trust without time, for one must make trial, as Theognis in fact says:

b15   Thou canst not mind of man or woman tell
Till thou hast tried them, like an ox, full well.[22]

And neither is there a friend without time.

1237b17   But people have a wish to be friends and this sort of habit of theirs is most of all mistaken for friendship. For when they are eager to be friends they think, because they do all the services of friends to each other, that they are not

b20   wishing to be but are friends. But in fact things happen in friendship the way

144

they do in other things, for people are not healthy by wishing to be healthy; so that, even if they wish to be friends, they are not friends already in fact. A sign is that those who are disposed in this way without having made trial are easily slandered. For as regard things they have given trial to each other b25 of they are not easily slandered, but as regard things they have not, they are persuaded when those doing the slandering allege tokens of evidence.[23]

At the same time it is clear that this friendship is not among the base either. 1237b27 For the base is not to be trusted and is bad in character toward everyone, for he measures others by himself. That is why the good are rather easy to trick, unless trial has made them distrustful. But the base choose the natural b30 goods over their friend and none of them loves a man more than things. The result is they are not friends. For "the things of friends" are not in this way made "common,"[24] since the friend is made to belong to his things, not the things to his friends.

The first friendship, then, does not arise among many, because it is hard to 1237b34 make trial of many, for one must live with each of them. So, one should not make a choice about a cloak and a friend in like way either. Yet in all cases it is held to be the part of anyone with intelligence to choose the better of two things, and if he was using the worse a long time and the better never the latter is to be chosen—but not the unknown friend, if he is better,[25] in place of b40 the old friend. For the friend is not without trial nor in a single day, but needs time. Hence "the measure of salt" has become proverbial.[26] But if one must choose[27]at the same time that he be not only good simply but also be good for you, a friend will be dear to you. For a simply good man and friend, when these are both in harmony, is simply good by being good and dear by being good for a5 another.[28] Consequently, what he is simply is a good for the man other than this—yes,[29] even for one not simply virtuous but other he is good—because he is useful. But to be friends to many at the same time is to hinder loving, for it is impossible to be active toward many people at the same time.

So it is clear from this that it is rightly said that friendship is a stable thing, 1238a10 just as that happiness is a self-sufficient thing. It is also rightly said:

For nature is firm, but money is not.[30]

But it is much nobler to say "virtue" than "nature," both because time is said to show the beloved and because misfortunes are said to do so rather than a25 good fortune. For then it is plain that "the things of friends are common." For only they, instead of the natural goods and bads that good and bad fortune are about, choose a man rather than that some of these exist and others not. But misfortune shows those who are friends not really but because of chance utility. Time shows both.

For neither is it the case that the useful man is plain quickly but rather the 1238a21 pleasant one—save that not even the simply pleasant is quick. For men are like wines and foods, for in their case too the pleasant quickly shows itself, but when it continues longer it is unpleasant and not sweet; and likewise with a25 men. For the simply pleasant must be defined by the end and by the time (and even the many would agree), not on the basis of the results only but in the way they call "sweeter" in the case of drink: for this on account of the result is not pleasant, but it deceives because of what is not continuous but is first.[31]

1238a30 The first friendship, then, and the one that the others are said because of, is the one that accords with virtue and is based on the pleasure of virtue, as was said earlier.[32] But the other friendships come to be also among children and beasts and the base. Hence the sayings:

Youth delights youth,

and

Bad joint to bad is in pleasure melded.[33]

a35 In fact it is possible for the base to be pleasant to each other and to be so as base, or as neither but as both singers, for instance, or one as thrifty and one as singer. Also, insofar as there is good in everyone, then they in this way harmonize with each other. Further, they might be useful and beneficial to each other, not simply but relative to their choice, or they might be neither.

1238b1 In fact it is possible for a base man to be friend to a decent man. For in fact he might be useful with respect to choice, the base man to the virtuous man for his present choice, and the latter both to the incontinent man for his b5 present choice and to the base man for the choice he has by nature. And he will wish him goods, things simply good simply but by supposition those good for him, whether it be poverty that is to his advantage or sickness (these for the sake of things simply good; in the way that drinking medicine itself is in fact, for one does not wish this but wishes it for the sake of that). Further, in b10 accord with the ways that even the non-virtuous might be friends with each other.[34] For he would be pleasant not qua base, but qua sharing something of what is common, as for instance if he was musical. Further, insofar as there is something decent in everyone; hence some are gregarious even if they are also virtuous. Or insofar as they harmonize with each, for there is something of good in everyone.

Notes

1. Reading *logos* (account) at 1235b13 with one of the MSS rather than *loipos* (remaining) with the others, or the emendation *tropos* (manner) with Bekker.
2. Euripides, *Troades* 1051.
3. Taking *parengcheousin* (for them pouring in), at 1235b39, not as a finite verb but as a participle, with Von Fragstein (1978: 303n). The sense seems to be that people whose palate is destroyed and who pour vinegar into their

wine are not doing so to make it pleasanter but to make it perceptible to them at all.

4. Reading at 1236a9 *epei de* (and since) with the MSS rather than *epeidē* (since indeed) with Bekker.

5. Retaining the *dia* with *tōn pleistōn* (through/between most people) at 1236a33 and not omitting it with Bekker. If *dia* is omitted the sense will be "... that of most people," which seems to specify a certain group and implicitly to exclude the few virtuous: "... that of most people [sc. but not of the few virtuous]." If *dia* is retained no limitation is implied; and indeed the virtuous may have useful friendships, namely with others than their virtuous friends.

6. The MS readings at 1236a35–36 do not scan nor make much sense as they stand: *Glauk' epikouros anēr ton sophon philon eske machētai* (Glaucus, a helper a man, the wise friend, until he fights). The standard emendation (from Fritzsche) is to replace *ton sophon philon* with *tosson philos*, thus giving the sort of translation in the text (an ally is a friend as long as he fights). Bekker replaces it with *ton son philon* (a man is an ally until he fights your friend).

7. Or "he alone has perception . . ."; the Greek at 1236b6 is ambiguous.

8. Herodotus, *Histories* 2.68.

9. Retaining at 1236b14 the double negative *oud' ou philousin* of the MS (They do not, however, not love . . .), and not changing it with Bekker to *hoi de philousin* (They do love, however . . .).

10. Cf. below 7.7.1241a22–23. Bonitz' emendation at 1236b16 would replace the *hyponooousin* of the MS (they are suspicious) with *hypomenousin* (they abide, put up with), thus giving the sense: "because of pleasure they put up with each other though being harmed, as long as they are incontinent."

11. The MSS at 1236b29 variously say *di'auton auton* (because of his very self), translated here, or *di' hauton hauton* (because of himself himself) or *di' auton autos* (himself because of himself). Bekker splits the differences and prints *di' hauton autos* (himself because of himself).

12. Sc. to drawing distinctions. The reference ahead is to 1237a18–19.

13. The two questions or the two goods, or both.

14. The Greek at 1236b37 is obscure, but the meaning seems to be that bad things are simply to be avoided if possible, that is, if fortune permits. There may be an implicit reference ahead to the chapter about fortune, 8.2.

15. The Greek words at 1237a6 are *a-phyēs* (literally "not with nature") and *eu-phyēs* (literally "with good nature"). The meaning in the context is unclear.

16. The Greek word at 37a16 and a17 is *spoudaios*.

17. A reference back to 1236b30.

18. Taking the genitive *dunameōs de pasēs* (every potentiality) at 1237b36 as dependent on the following *exō* (outside). Other scholars take it as dependent on *ergon* (work), supplied from the previous line, to give the sense: "the work of a potentiality is outside it." A potential qua potential is not actual; so it becomes actual by some addition from without, either from another thing or from itself as other.

19. Reading at 1237b2 *iatrikos* (medical) with one of the MSS rather than *iatros* (doctor) with another and with Bekker.

20. The Greek word at 1237b7 is *agapatai*, which also means love but without necessarily implying affection.

21. A reference, perhaps, to Philoctetes who was "left" (the meaning of *leipetai* at 1237b7) on the island of Lemnos by the other Greeks on the way to Troy, because the wound he received there from a snake bite festered and produced a very foul stench.
22. Theognis, 125.
23. Othello in Shakespeare's play is a classic instance, for he would never have believed Iago's slanders, or his tokens of evidence, had he really made trial of Desdemona's character.
24. A proverbial expression.
25. Or alternatively, at 1237b40: ". . . not the friend not known to be better in place of . . ."
26. The sense is presumably that one cannot be friends with someone until one has shared many meals together (enough to consume a certain measure of salt).
27. Supplying *haireteon* from 1237b39–40 and making the rest an accusative and infinitive dependent on it (as at 1238a18–19).
28. Omitting the colon that Bekker inserts at the end of 1238a5 and reading 1238a4–6 as all belonging to one sentence.
29. Accenting *ē* at 1238a7 so that it means an emphatic assertion and is not the word for "or."
30. Euripides, *Electra* 941.
31. The drink deceives by its initial sweetness, but it is not in fact pleasant, or sweet, in the end. The infinitive *exapatān* (deceives) at 1238a30, may be retained and need not, with Bussemaker, be changed to the indicative *exapatāi*, because the clause is in implicit indirect speech after *kalousi* (call) at 1238a28.
32. 1236a7–20, b23–37b9.
33. Euripides, *Bellerophontes*, fr. 298 Nauck.
34. Those just listed above at 1238b35–b1.

Chapter 3

How These Kinds Can Be Equal and Unequal. *The three kinds of friendship are in accord with equality. But there can be friendships of virtue also in accord with excess, as of god and man and ruler and ruled, where there is equality of proportion and not of number. The friendship of father and son is of benefactor and benefited, that of man and woman of ruler and ruled. Here loving and return of love are not the same, but the ruler is more properly loved, or loves in another way, and the same with the pleasure involved too. Friendships of utility and pleasure can also be according to equality or excess. Complaints arise when friends in the latter way mistake themselves for lovers in the former.*

1238b15   There are three forms of friendship, then, but in all of them friendship is said in a way according to equality. For in fact friends according to virtue are friends with each other in a way by equality of virtue. But another difference in them is that of excess, as god's virtue in relation to a man (for this is a different form of friendship), and on the whole of ruler and ruled; as the just is different too, for it is equal in proportion but not equal in number.

In this class is father to son and benefactor to benefited. But among these themselves there are differences, one of father to son and another of man to woman, the latter as of ruler and ruled and the former as of benefactor to benefited. In these friendships there is not return loving, or not in like manner. For it would be laughable if someone brought a charge against the god that being loved back by him is not for anyone[1] like the way he is loved—or that it is not alike for ruler and ruled. For being loved, not loving, is proper to the ruler, or loving in another way; and pleasure is different and is not one thing[2] in the case of the self-sufficient man over his own property or his child and of the needy man over what comes to him.   1238b22   b25   b30

In the same way also with those who are friends on the basis of use and pleasure, some of them accord with equality and others with excess. Hence too those who think they are friends in the former way complain if their friends are not similarly useful and do them good. The same with pleasure; it is plain in erotic love. For this is the cause of their often fighting with each other, for the lover ignores the fact that their pleasure in eagerness does not have the same account. Hence Aenicus has said,[3] the "beloved, but no lover, would say such things." But they are supposing there is the same account.   1238b32   b35

Notes

1.   Taking *tōi* at 1238b27 in the sense of *tini* (for anyone). The meaning is that it would be laughable to complain that god does not love anyone in return the way he is loved (by worship, say, and thanks). God and rulers generally love in another way, by conferring benefits not by receiving them.

2.   Reading at 1238b30 *oud' hen* (and is not one thing) with Jackson rather than *ouden* ([differs in] nothing) with Bekker and the MSS.

3.   Accepting at 1238b38 Jackson's emendation of *eurēkenai neikos* (to have found strife) to *eirēken Ainikos* (Aenicus has said). Aenicus, or Eunicus, was a dramatic poet of Attic Old Comedy. The word *ho* (the) at 1238a38 may perhaps be kept, not as part of the quotation (it does not fit the scansion), but as introducing it. The sense of the MSS reading without emendation will be something like: "the beloved would say, not loving such things, that he has found strife."

Chapter 4

Equality and Loving Are More Proper to Friendship. *While these friendships can be either among equals or unequals, one is friends with equals and not inferiors (whether in age or virtue or family or the like). The superior supposes he should be loved and not love. Friends are equals but loving back is possible without being friends. Men prefer friendships of excess because they get love and excess at the same time (hence they hold flatterers more in honor than friends). Thus some are lovers of honor and excess but others are love-inclined and enjoy the pleasure of loving (which pleasure must be present when they are actively loving). The latter is more in accord with friendship than the former, since a friend would chose rather to know or to do a good than to be known and to receive a good.*

1239a1 So, as has been said, since there are three kinds of friendship (in accord with virtue, in accord with the useful, and in accord with the pleasant), these are again divided into two, for some accord with the equal and others with excess. Now both are friendships, but friends are those in accord with equality,

a5 for it would be odd if a man were friends with a child, though he does at any rate love and is loved. Sometimes, while the one who excels must be loved, he is reproached if he loves, as loving one unworthy, for he is measured by the worth of his friends and by a sort of equality. Now some things are unworthy to be loved in like manner because of lack of age, but others in relation to virtue or family or other such excess.

1239a11 The one who excels, they say,[1] always thinks he deserves to love less or not at all, both in the useful and in the pleasant and in relation to virtue. Now disputes are reasonable where the excesses are small (for in some cases the small has no force, as in a weight of wood, though it does in a

a15 piece of gold; but people judge the small badly, for one's own good appears great because it is close by but another's small because it is distant); but when it is extreme not even do they themselves seek that they should in addition either be loved back or be in like manner loved back, for example if someone were to claim it of the god. So it is manifest that people are friends when they are on an equality, but that loving back is possible without being friends.

1239a21 It is also plain why men seek friendship of excess more than friendship of equality, for thus they get to be loved and to have excess at the same time; hence the flatterer is more in honor among some people than the friend, for

a25 he makes it appear that the one flattered has both. But those who love honor are most like this, for being admired exists in excess. Some are by nature love-inclined and others lovers of honor. He is love-inclined who enjoys loving more than being loved; the other, however, is more honor loving. So he,

a30 enjoying being admired and loved, loves excess; but the first, the love-inclined, loves the pleasure of loving—for it is necessarily present in him when he is active,[2] for that he loves someone is accidental (for it can escape the notice of the one loved) but his being a lover is not.[3]

1239a33 Also loving accords more with friendship than being loved does; being loved accords more with the loved object. A sign is that the friend, if he cannot have both, would choose rather to know than to be known, as women do in putting up children for adoption,[4] and Antiphon's Andromache.[5] For it seems indeed that one wishes to be known for one's own sake (that is, for receiving something good but not for doing it), but to know for the sake of doing and loving. That is why we praise those who keep to their love for the dead. For they know but are not known. a40

That there are, then, several modes of friendship, and how many they are 1239b2 (namely three), and that being loved and being loved back and friends differ, some by equality and some by excess, has been stated.

Notes

1. The sentence at 1239a11–12 is in implicit indirect speech hence the "they say." Alternatively, following Susemihl and Cook Wilson, one could change *aei* (always) at a11 to *dei* (must), giving the sense: "The one who excels must think. . . ."

2. Reading at 1239a31 Richards' emendation *anangkēi* (necessarily) rather than *anangkē* (necessity) with the MSS, but keeping the *energounta* (when he is active) at 1239a32 as an accusative absolute. Pleasure is necessarily present when activity is unimpeded.

3. At 1239a32 *to philein* (that he loves someone) may be retained and not replaced by *to phileisthai* (that he is loved). An act of love has an object that it loves (it loves someone) and a subject that does the loving (which is actively a lover). The object is accidental to the act because the object may not know it is the object, but the subject is not because the act exists in the subject. The position of the particles *men . . . de* at 1239a32–33 requires that *philounta* (his active loving) be paired and contrasted with *philein* (having a love), and not with the intervening *lanthanein philoumenon* (escape the notice of the one loved).

4. Reading at 1239a37 Victorius' emendation *tais hypobolais* (putting up for adoption) rather than the MSS *tais hyperbolais* (excesses).

5. Antiphon was a tragic poet in Syracuse at the court of Dionysius I (c. 430–367 BC), by whom he was put to death. Andromache, widow of Hector of Troy, is said to have given her son Molossus (whom she had by her Greek captor Neoptolemus) to others to bring up.

Chapter 5

Like and Unlike Friendships. *The like and unlike are friends to each other. The like is so on the basis of the good and pleasant (for the good are stable but the bad not). Also the like (including the base) find pleasure in the same things. Opposites are dear as being useful (the like is useless to the like) and for reaching the end but not being in it. Thus they are of the good because they want the opposite for the sake of the mean, and are of the mean per se but of the opposite per accidens (it takes them out of their natural condition). This love of the unlike exists in nonliving things but in living ones it becomes friendship, though per accidens and because of the good.*

1239b6 Since "friend," as was in fact said at the beginning,[1] is spoken of in a more universal way too by those who take in extrinsic matters as well (for some say the like is friends, others that the opposed is), we must also say how these stand in relation to the friendships stated.

1239b10 The like is referred both to the pleasant and to the good. For it is both the case that the good is simple while the bad takes on many forms, and that the good man is always alike and his character does not change while the base and the senseless are not alike at dawn as at dusk. Hence, if the base do not come to agreement, they are not friends with each other but separate. But the friendship that is not firm is not friendship.

1239b16 In this way, then, the like is dear, because like is good. But there is a way it also accords with the pleasant, for to the like the same things are pleasant and each thing is by nature pleasant itself to itself. That is why voices and habits and spending days together are most pleasant to those of the same sort as each other, even among the several animals. In this way in fact even the base can love each other:

Bad joint to bad is in pleasure melded.

1239b23 But the opposite is dear to the opposite as useful, for the like is itself useless to itself. Hence a master needs a slave and a slave a master, and woman and man need each other. In fact, the opposite is pleasant and desired as useful, that is, not as in the end but as for the end. For when one gets what one desires one is in the end and does not desire the opposite, the way the hot desires the cold and the dry the wet.

1239b29 But friendship of the opposite can in a way also be of the good. For opposites have an appetite for each other through the mean; for they have an appetite for each other as matching tallies. Hence they are a mean not by a single thing coming to be out of both;[2] further, they are per accidens of the opposite but per se of the mean. For the opposites do not have an appetite for each other but for the mean; for people are set in the mean if, being overly

b35 cold, they are warmed and if, being overly hot, they are cooled. Similarly in the case of other things too. Otherwise they are always desiring and not in the mean. But he who is in the mean rejoices, without desiring, in things naturally pleasant, and they rejoice in everything that takes them out of their natural habit.

1239b39 Now this kind exists even in lifeless things, but it becomes love of friendship when it is in living things. Hence sometimes people rejoice in those who are unlike them, as the austere in the witty and the hasty in the sluggish, for they are set in the mean by each other. So opposites are per accidens friends, and because of the good.

How many kinds of friendship there are, then, and what are the differences 1240a4
in accord with which people are said to be friends and lovers and beloveds,
and in such a way as to be friends and not to be so, has been stated.

Notes

1. 7.1.1235a4–28.
2. Retaining at 1239b31–32 the MSS reading *dio ou tōi ginesthai* (Hence . . .
    not by [a single thing] coming to be) rather than changing it, with Spengel,
    to *dia to houtō ginesthai* (because in this way there comes to be [a single
    mean out of both]). The sense (as indicated by the tally example and by the
    others which follow) is that the extremes, when they come together, do not
    cease to be extremes but just have their defects supplied by each other.

Chapter 6

Friendship with Oneself. *Friendship with oneself is friendship by analogy,
for friendship is between two things. Hence the continent and incontinent are
more properly said to be friends because the parts of their soul are in a certain
relation to each other. If the soul has parts, then, it can have the properties
of friendship but otherwise not. Still, the habit one has to oneself is a way to
define the modes of friendship, since a friend wishes good things and existence
for his friend for his sake and to live with him, as well as to feel his pain and
joy. It is said further that equality is amity and true friends are one friendship.
All these are referred to the individual's relation to himself. The good man also
has them toward himself, but not the bad man who can even be an enemy
to himself and is different from one moment to the next and unstable. Hence
friendship with oneself is reduced to the friendship of the good and is like the
unity that subsists between Coriscus and good Coriscus. The good man has in
himself two things that are naturally friends and impossible to separate, which
is not true of animals or children who are not a two as not having choice as
well as desire. Such friendship with oneself is like friendship of relatives and
is not something up to oneself to change but endures through life.*

About being oneself a friend to oneself or not there is much to investigate. 1240a8
For some hold that each is himself most a friend to himself and they judge
friendship toward other friends using this as a standard. But, according to the
arguments and the properties held to be those of friends, it seems in some
respects contrary and in others clearly alike, for friendship is by analogy this
in a way but simply it is not. For loving and being loved are in two distinct
things, because of which it is more in the case of the incontinent[1] and con- a15
tinent that he is said to be himself a friend to himself (voluntarily in a way

or involuntarily), because the parts of his soul are in some relation to each other. In fact all such things are alike—if one is oneself a friend to oneself or an enemy and if any self wrongs itself. For all these are in two things and by way of division. If the soul also is in a way two, these in a way belong to it; but if there are not distinct parts, they do not.

1240a21 But from the habit toward oneself is how[2] the other modes of friendship are defined, the modes by which we are wont to investigate it in our discourses.[3] For a friend is held to be he who wishes good things (or such things as he thinks good) to someone, not on his own account but for that person's sake, and, in another way, to whom he wishes existence on that person's ac-

a25 count and not his own (even if, not bestowing goods, he does not seem to be, by wishing[4] him existence, particularly a friend), and in another way with whom he chooses to live for company's sake and not for some other reason,

a30 as fathers wish existence to their children but live together with others. So these are all in conflict with each other, for the one does not think he is loved without the "for themselves," another without the "existence," others the "living together."

1240a33 Further, we will lay down as love to feel pain with someone in pain—not for some other reason, as slaves do with their masters, because when in pain

a35 they are harsh, but not on their account in the way mothers do for their children and birds grieving together. For the friend most wishes to feel not only pain with his friend but also the same pain, as to thirst with him when thirsty (if he took it upon himself[5] because he was not very near at hand). The same argument holds of rejoicing: not to do it on any other account but on his, that he is rejoicing, is proper to a friend.

1240b1 Further, the following sorts of things are said about friendship, as "equality is amity" and further[6] that those truly friends are one friendship[7]—all these are referred back to the individual. For the individual does in fact want good

b5 things in this way for himself (for no one does good to himself on some other account, not even on account of some favor,[8] nor does he say he did so qua one individual, for he who makes a show that he loves wishes to seem[9] to love but not to love). Also he wants existence above all, and living together, and being glad together, and in pain together, and so being one soul, and being unable without each other even to live but to die together. For this is how the individual is disposed. Perhaps too he is company for himself.

1240b11 All these things the good man has toward himself. But in the depraved there is dissonance, as in the incontinent, and for this reason it seems possible for a self even to be an enemy to itself. But qua one and undivided a self is desirable to itself. Such the good man is, and the friend on the basis of virtue, since the wicked at least is not one but many and is contrary during the same day and unstable.

1240b17 Consequently the friendship of oneself to oneself is reduced to the friendship of the good. For because he is in a way like himself and one

154

with himself and good to himself, in this way he is a friend and desirable
to himself. Such a one is by nature, while the depraved is against nature. b20
The good man does not at the same time curse himself as the incontinent
does, nor does his later self curse his earlier self, as the man who gets a grip
on himself[10] does, nor his earlier his later, as the liar does. And generally,
if one must make distinctions as the sophists do, he is as "Coriscus" and b25
"virtuous Coriscus," for it is plain that he himself is virtuous to the same
extent (since when people bring a charge against themselves it is themselves
they are slaying).[11]

But every self is held to be good to itself, and he who is simply good seeks 1240b27
also to be, as was said, himself a friend to himself, because he has two things
in himself that naturally want to be friends and it is impossible to split them
apart. Hence in the human case each self seems a *friend* to itself, while in
the case of the other animals, as a horse, it seems a *self* to itself, so it is not a
friend.[12] But children are not either, except when they already have choice,
for then the child[13] is precisely in discord with desire. Friendship to oneself b35
is like friendship among relatives, for it is not up to people themselves to
dissolve either of them but, even if they fall out, nevertheless the latter are
still relatives and the former still one, as long as life lasts.

In how many ways loving is said, then, and that all friendships are reduced 1240b37
to the first, is plain from what has been said.

Notes

1. Treating the whole of 1240a14–17 as a single sentence and not marking a
   separate sentence at a15 with *di' ha* (because of which) or at a16 with *epi
   tou akratous* (in the case of the incontinent . . .). These emendations would
   give the sense: "Therefore one is a friend to oneself rather in the way that
   being voluntary and involuntary are said in the case of the incontinent and
   incontinent, because the parts. . . ."
2. Keeping at 1240a22 the *hōs* (how) of the MSS and not deleting it with Bekker.
3. Likely a reference to *GE* 2.11.1210b32–11a36.
4. Supplying after *tōi* (by) at 1240a27 the verb for "wishing" (*boulesthai*) from
   its appearance (*bouletai*) in the previous line. The sense is that to wish
   someone existence is, to this extent, to be his friend even if, because one
   does not also share one's goods with him, one does not seem to be much
   of a friend. The Greek is obscure in any event and scholars offer a variety
   of emendations.
5. Taking *enedecheto* at 40a38 in its personal sense (he took it upon himself)
   and not its impersonal one (it was possible). The sense is that a friend would,
   in solidarity, take it upon himself to suffer as his friend is suffering if he is
   too far away to give direct assistance.
6. Reading at 1240b2–3 *kai mēn mian* (and further . . . one . . .) instead of the
   MSS *kai mē mian* (and not . . . one . . .), which in the context makes little
   sense and seems just a scribal error (the same scribal error of *mē* for *mēn*
   is made at 1245a15).

7. The MSS at 1240b3 read *philian* (friendship), but scholars generally accept Casaubon's emendation of it to *psychēn* (soul), partly in view of 40b9 where the fact of friends being one soul is mentioned, and partly because friends being one soul was a known saying. But that true friends are one friendship covers, and so explains, all the features Aristotle mentions in the next lines, while true friends being one soul repeats one of them. Further, true friends being one friendship would seem to be a saying that lies behind the discussion (at 10.1243b15–37) of those friends who are not true because they are not one but several and conflicting friendships.

8. Retaining at 1240b6 the MSS *charitos* (favor) but understanding it with *dia ti* (on account of some . . .) from the previous phrase.

9. Reading at 1240b6 *dokei* (he seems) with some MSS rather than *dokein* (to seem) with others, and keeping at 1240b7 *bouletai* (he wishes) and not changing it with Bekker to *boulesthai* (to wish).

10. Retaining at 1240b23, with most MSS, the reading *metalēptikos* (getting a grip on himself [i.e., stopping his previous behavior]) rather than the other MSS reading of *metamelētikos* (repentant).

11. Reading at 1240b27 Fritzsche's emendation *hautous* (themselves) for *autous* (them) and *hautous* (themselves) for *autois* (for them) of the MSS. The sense is that since Coriscus and virtuous Coriscus differ in name only, so also to blame oneself as bad is to blame oneself simply (i.e., to this extent to slay oneself or oneself qua bad).

12. An animal, unlike a man, is not a "two" in its soul and so cannot be a friend with itself. Like the child mentioned next, these have desire but no choice and so do not have parts that can either conflict or be brought into friendship with each other.

13. The MSS reading *pais* (child) at 1240b34 can stand and does not need to be changed, with Fritzsche, to *nous* (intellect) or the like. The sense is that when the child is old enough to have choice it can be in conflict with itself as regards desire. (It judges and chooses one thing as better but is drawn by desire to something else.)

Chapter 7

Kindly Disposition and Oneness of Mind. *Kindly disposition is close to but is not friendship. It does not exist in useful or pleasant friendships but only in those of character. Kindliness wishes good but friendship does good, so kindliness is only the beginning of friendship. But friends are of one mind and those of one mind are friends. Oneness of mind is about things friends do, and it contributes to living together. It is in thought and appetite together and not in one alone, and concerns good things. Oneness of mind in this sense is first, and is naturally virtuous. But the base can be of one mind in a secondary sense, if they choose and desire the same things and these things they can both possess; otherwise they fight, and those of one mind do not fight. There is oneness of mind when people agree who should rule and be ruled. Political friendship is of this sort.*

Proper also to our investigation is the study of oneness of mind and kindly 1241a1 disposition, for some hold that they are the same and others that they do not exist without each other. Kindliness is not wholly other than nor the same as friendship for, friendship being divided in three ways, it does not exist in useful friendship nor in the friendship of pleasure. For if one wish a man a5 good things because of utility, one would be wishing them not for his sake but for one's own. And it seems as if[1] also kindly disposition is not his who is kindly but his to whom he is kindly.[2] If the friendship is in one of pleasure, there would also be kindly disposition for lifeless things. Consequently it is plain that kindliness concerns friendship of character.

But it is a feature of him who is kindly to wish merely, whereas of the 1241a10 friend also to do what he wishes, for kindliness is friendship's beginning. For every friend is kindly but not everyone kindly is a friend; for one who is kindly is only like a beginner, therefore he is friendship's start but not friendship.

For it seems both that friends are of one mind and that those of one mind 1241a15 are friends. But the one-mindedness of friendship is not about everything but about what is to be done by those of one mind and about everything that contributes to living together. Neither is it only in thought or appetite, for the moving element can have opposite desires[3] (in the way that in the incontinent this element, which he needs to be of one mind in choice and in desire, is in discord).[4]

Being of one mind concerns good things (the base at any rate, when they 1241a21 are choosing and desiring the same things, are harming each other). It also seems that being of one mind is not said simply, as neither is friendship, but one way is first and by nature virtuous (hence it is not possible for the base to be of one mind), and the other is that by which the base are of one mind a25 whenever they have choice and desire for the same things. But their appetite must be of the same things in a way that they can both possess what their appetite is of, for if their appetite is of such a thing as they cannot both possess they fight; but those of one mind do not fight.

There is oneness of mind when choice about ruling and being ruled is the 1241a30 same—not about each ruling but about the same person ruling. Also, oneness of mind is political friendship.

About oneness of mind, then, and kindly disposition let so much 1241a32 be said.

Notes

1. The *hōsper* (as if) at 1241a7 is used like *hōsper* at 1241b23 below, q.v.
2. Kindliness is focused on the other and not on oneself (otherwise it could hardly be called kindliness).

3.   Treating at 1241a19 *tānantia* (opposite) as adverbial with *epithumein* (desire), and taking *epithumein* itself with *to kinoun* (the moving element) as an accusative and infinitive after *esti* (it is possible), contra Dirlmeier (1962: 432).

4.   Reading at 1241a20 *hou dei* (which he needs) with Bekker and not *ou dei* (there is no need) with the MSS.

Chapter 8

Love of Benefactors and Benefited. *Benefactors are lovers more than the benefited are, although the opposite seems to be just. Reason is that to give is also helpful to the giver and activity is naturally preferable and the receiver is as it were the work of the giver. Hence parents love offspring more than offspring love parents, and mothers love more than fathers since the pain of childbirth makes offspring seem more their work.*

1241a35   A puzzle arises as to why they are more loving[1] who do good to receivers than they who receive good from doers. The opposite seems to be just.

1241a37   Someone might suppose that this is because of what happens to be useful or helpful to him, for the one must receive help and the other give it away.[2] Yet not only is this the case but it is natural too, for activity is more to be preferred. Work and activity have, indeed, the same account, and he who receives good is as it were the work of him who does good.

1241b2   Hence animals too are zealous about offspring and of generating and preserving what has been generated. And so fathers, and mothers more than

b5   fathers, love their children more than they are loved. And these again love their children rather than their parents, because activity is best. And mothers love more than fathers because they think that their children are more their own work. For people define work by the difficult and a mother suffers more pain in childbirth.

1241b10   So about friendship with oneself and about friendship within a group, let this be the way of defining them.

Notes

1.   Reading at 1241a35 *philountes* (loving) with the MSS rather than Bekker's emendation to *philousin* ([those who do good] love [those who receive it . . .]).

2.   The sense is perhaps that it is useful and helpful to have people to give things to (cf. 7.12.1245b7–9), say, because it displays one's goodness or brings one praise and honor. Alternatively one could accept at 1241a38–39 Fritzsche's likely emendation of the MSS from *ton . . . ōpheleisthai* (the one [must] receive help) to *tōi . . . opheleitai* (to one a debt is owed), with the sense: "for to one a debt is owed and the other should pay it."

Chapter 9

The Justice of Friendship
Summary Statement. *The just is the equal and friendship is in the equal, and regime and community are based on justice, so that forms of friendship are forms of justice and community. But there is only community and the common good where there is a two, and so not between artisan and tools and between master and slave. All communities are parts of the city, and regimes are present in family relations, as kingship between father and son, aristocracy between man and wife, polity between brothers (and the deviations too). Justice is numerical and proportional, and so are friendships and communities; as those of companions are numerical, while aristocratic and kingly ones are proportional as well as those where someone exceeds and another is exceeded.*

The just seems to be something equal and friendship to exist in equality (unless "amity is equality" is vainly said) and all regimes to be a form of justice. For they are a community and everything common is established on the basis of justice. So that what are forms[1] of friendship are also forms of justice and of community.   1241b12

In fact all these border on each other and have differences close to each other. Since soul is related to body as artisan to tool and master to slave, no community exists among these things, for they are not two but the first is one and the other is *of* the one and not one.[2] The good is not divisible between each of the two either, but the good of both is of the one for whose sake it is. For the body is a naturally conjoined tool, and a slave is a part and, as it were, separable tool of the master, and the tool is, as it were, a lifeless slave.[3] But other communities are either a part of the city's communities (as for example the community of clans or of sacred rites), or those that are business communities still are regimes.[4]   1241b16   b20   b25

All regimes are present together in household affairs, both the correct and the deviant ones (for it is with things in regimes the same as it is with harmonies).[5] Kingly is that of the one who begets, aristocratic that of man and woman, polity that of brothers, but deviation from these is tyranny, oligarchy, the populace; and so there are that many sorts of justice.   1241b27

Since the equal is on the one hand numerical and on the other proportional, these will also be forms of justice and of friendship and of community. For the community and friendship of companions is numerical (for it is measured by the same limit), but the best aristocratic community[6] and kingly community are proportional. For justice is not the same but proportional for one who exceeds and one who is exceeded. The friendship also of father and son is similar, and in communities it is the same way.   1241b32   b40

159

Notes

1. The MSS at 1241b15 have *hostis aei dē* or *dia* (whoever always indeed ... *or* on the basis of...), which makes little sense in the context. Bonitz' plausible emendation of it to *hōste hosa eidē* (so that all the forms ...) might more simply be to *hōste ha eidē* (so that what are forms ...).
2. Reading at 1241b20 Jackson's emendation *ou d' hen* (and not one) instead of *ouden* (nothing) with the MSS.
3. Cf. *Politics* 1.4.1254a12–17.
4. The meaning of the Greek at 1241b26 is obscure and scholars not unreasonably accept Fritzsche's proposal that *eti politeiai* (still regimes) be deleted as dittography from the *hai politeiai* ([All] regimes ...) that immediately follows in b27. If the MSS reading is kept, Aristotle is presumably presenting an argument, by *reductio*, that one must say either that communities are part of the larger community of cities or, absurdly, that what is still or merely a business community could by itself be a regime or an ordering of life in a city (something he argues against in *Politics* 3.9.1280a25–81a4).
5. *Politics* 5(8).7, also 6(4).3.
6. As opposed to lesser or so-called aristocracies, which are not the simply best aristocracy; cf. *Politics* 6/4.7.

Chapter 10

Particular Discussion

In the Household. *Friendships exist in different communities in different ways. In families they exist by equality and by proportion. Political friendship is based on utility and equality, and the just here, as being the political just, is the one that is most just (there is no justice between artisans and tools and masters and slaves). All justice is in relation to a friend or sharer in something common, which if it is not the city is the household. The household is a sort of friendship where justice is by proportion (as between superiors and inferiors or benefactors and benefited and rulers and ruled), or by equality (as between equals). The three kinds of friendships are divided also into those of equality and of excess and the just in each case differs, being by proportion in the case of excess, save that the superior gets honor in exchange for the service of ruling.*

1242a1   Friendships are said to be of relatives, of companions, of community (the one called political). Friendship of family has several forms, that of brothers on the one hand and that of father and sons on the other; for it is both by

a5   proportion, as that of a father, and numerical, as that of brothers. For the latter is close to friendship of companions (for there too they assume ranks of seniority). Political friendship is founded on utility even most of all, for people seem to come together because of lack of self-sufficiency (since they would have come together at any rate even for the sake of joint survival). It is only with political friendship (and with the deviation against it) that there is not merely friendship but also sharing in common as friends (the others accord with superiority).

The just in the friendship of those who are useful is most of all just, because 1242a11 the political just is this. For the coming together of saw and art was not for the sake of something common (for soul and tool form a whole) but for the sake of the user. This fact occurs too, that an instrument gets the care that is a15 just in view of its work (for that is what it is for the sake of). Existence for a gimlet is double too, of which the more controlling is activity, the act of bor-ing; and in this form are body and slave, as was said before.[1] So to seek how one should associate with one's friend is to seek for what is just.

For in fact generally all justice is in relation to a friend. For the just is for 1242a20 certain people, that is, for sharers, and a friend is a sharer, one in family and another in way of life. For he who is friend of a man alone does not belong to a city[2] though he is in fact a household animal and does not, like the other animals, couple together by occasion and with any chance male or female. a25 But man is in private not a solitary[3] animal but a sharer with those for whom he has a natural kinship, and therefore community and a certain justice, even if no city.

A house is a certain kind of friendship. Between master and slave, then, 1242a27 there is what there is between art and tools and soul and body, and such are not friendships nor are they justice, save by analogy, as also the healthy is not just save by analogy.[4] But of woman and man there is friendship as a thing useful, as well as community; and of father and son there is the same friend-ship as of a god toward a man and of the one who does good toward the one who receives it, and on the whole of the one who is by nature ruler toward the one who is by nature ruled. But the companionship of brothers in relation a35 to each other is above all the one in accord with equality:

Bastardy in nothing was by him shown;
Sire to us twain my ruler Zeus I own.[5]

For these things are said as of those seeking equality. Hence it is in the house-hold that beginnings and springs of friendship and of regime and of justice are first found.

But since there are three friendships—according to virtue, according to util- 1242b2 ity, according to the pleasant—and of each of these there are two differences (for each of them is either according to excess or according to equality), and since what is just with respect to them is plain from the debates held about b5 them, then the claim of proportion in friendship according to excess is not made in the same way but he who exceeds claims by inverse proportion: as he is to the lesser so what comes from the lesser is to what comes from him, his disposition being[6] like that of ruler to ruled. But where that is not the case, he would nevertheless claim what is numerically equal.

1242b11   For such indeed is also what happens in the case of the other communities, that they share what is equal sometimes in number and sometimes in ratio. For if he has brought in a numerically equal amount of silver then they make an equal division also by numerical equality, but if it was not equal then by proportion, and he who is exceeded returns what is inversely proportional and their union is diagonal.[7]

1242b16   But in this way he who exceeds would seem to come off worse, and friendship and community to be a burden of service. It is necessary then to equalize and bring about proportion by something else, and this is honor, which belongs to the ruler by nature and to god in relation to the ruled. The profit must be equalized with the honor.

In the City. Political friendship is according to equality and utility. Ruling and being ruled are here carried out by turns, so as to preserve the equality. Useful friendships are legal or moral. Political friendship focuses on equality of deed and is by law when it follows contract and moral otherwise. The latter gives rise to complaints because it seeks unnaturally to combine utility with virtue, and useful friendships are most liable to complaints, unless they take the legal form, where separation is by financial terms. In the moral form it is by choice and not by law and each side clothes itself in its own complaints, either about the value of the thing or of its value to giver and receiver. Political friendship is by law and more useful, and moral friendship by choice and more noble, but people complain for they profess the latter but care about the former. In moral friendship what matters is equality of choice; in legal the utility of the contract; in doubtful cases let a just man decide the issue. Where friendships are not in a straight line but one is friend for pleasure and another for utility, or each is friend for different utilities, complaints arise that are difficult to adjudicate. The measure here must instead be that of proportion, as when cobblers and farmers exchange their respective products, or a teacher exchanges learning with a student for gold.

1242b21   Friendship according to equality is political friendship, and political friendship accords with utility, and the way cities are friends to each other is the way in fact that citizens in like manner also are.

b25   Athenians acknowledge Megarians no longer . . .

nor do citizens when they are not useful to each other but their friendship is from hand to hand. But there is here a ruling and ruled element, not the natural or kingly one, but by turns; nor is it for the sake of doing benefit, as the b30 god does, but so that there might be equality of the good and of the burden. Political friendship, then, is meant to be in accord with equality.

There are two kinds of friendship of utility: legal and moral. Political friend- 1242b31 ship looks to what is equal and to the deed, as do sellers and buyers. Hence the saying: "wages for a man that is a friend."[8] So whenever this political friend- ship follows a contract it is by law, but whenever they rest it on their trust the friendship is meant to be that which is moral and is between companions.

That is why complaint arises most in this friendship, reason being that it is 1242b37 against nature. For the friendship of utility and that of virtue are different, but they want to have both things at once, and while they associate for utility's sake, they make it one of character, as though they were decent men. So, as basing a1 themselves on trust, they make it not to be one of law. For most complaints on the whole are in the useful one among the three friendships. For virtue is beyond complaint, and pleasant friends part after getting and giving, but useful friends do not immediately break off if their dealings are in a nonlegal and comradely way.

Nevertheless the legal form of useful friendship is without complaint. 1243a6 Separation in the case of the legal is in terms of money, for by it the equal is measured, but separation in the case of that of character is voluntary. Hence there is in some places a law that those associating as friends are not to have lawsuits over contracts that are voluntary—rightly, since it is not naturally just for the good, even when they have contracts, and they are by supposition good.

In this friendship the complaints that clothe them—how each will complain 1243a12 when their trust is one of character and not law—are on both sides.[9] And so there is a puzzle how the just man should judge, whether in relation to the thing done, looking to how much and what sort the service was, or by the recipient. The matter can be what Theognis says:

'Tis small for thee, goddess, but great to me.[10]   a20

For it can also be the opposite, as in the saying:

This is sport to you, but it's death to me.

Thence are complaints lodged. For the first thinks he should be repaid as one who did a great service because he did it for someone in need (or saying some other such thing as regards how much was the help that it was able to do the other but not what it was to himself). But the second says the opposite, how little it was to the other but not how much it was to himself. Sometimes indeed he clothes himself in complaints even when he is getting his share. a25 For he says how little he got out of it, but the other how great a thing it was able to do him; for instance, if he ran risks to give a drachma's worth of help, he talks of the amount of risk but the other of the amount of silver, as in the giving back of currency. For that is what the dispute in these cases in fact is about; for, unless they made an express statement,[11] the one wants its value to be the way it then was, but the other the way it now is.   a30

1243a31   Now political friendship looks to the contract and the thing done but friendship of character to the choice, so that the latter is more a thing of justice and a justice that is of friends. But a reason for fighting is that friendship of

a35   character is more noble but useful friendship more necessary, and they are coming together as friends in character and on account of virtue, but, when they come up against a matter of private interest, they make it plain that they were something other. For it is as a superfluous extra that the many pursue the noble and hence also the more noble friendship.

1243b1   Consequently it is manifest how to draw the distinction in these matters. For, if they are friends of character, they must look to see if their choice was equal and nothing else must be claimed by either from the other but, if they are friends as useful and political, how making a contract would have been

b5   to their advantage. But if one of them says it was this way and the other that, then it is not a noble thing to be speaking noble words when what is due back is deeds; and likewise in the other case too. But since they did not make an express statement of it as a matter of character, someone should be judge and neither of them should deceive in giving answers. Consequently they should be content with what chances.

1243b9   That friendship of character is by choice is plain, since even if after receiving much one does not make a return, through inability, save as one can, it is nobly done. The god too puts up with the sacrifices he can get. But it will not be enough for a seller if one says one cannot give him more, nor for a lender.

1243b14   Many complaints arise in friendships for those not in a straight line even to see the just, for to measure a difficult thing by a single thing is not easy for him who is not in a straight line,[12] as happens in love affairs. For the one pursues as after someone pleasant to live with, and the other after him as sometimes useful. But when he stops being in love, the other becomes different because

b20   he has become different. It is then that they count up the what in return for what[13] and fall out as Pytho and Pammenes did or as teacher and learner on the whole (for knowledge and money do not have a single measure), and as Herodicus the doctor and the one who gave him little for his wage, and as the harpist and the king.[14] For the king held the former for a pleasant companion

b25   and the former held him for a useful one. But when he should have paid in return, the king made as though he was pleasant, saying that as the other had given pleasure by singing so had he by making promises.

1243b27   Nevertheless it is clear even here how to find the thing out. For here too there must be one measure, but one in ratio and not in definition. For one

b30   must measure the proportion the way the political community is measured (for how will a cobbler associate with a farmer if their products are not made equal by way of proportion?). And for those who are not friends in a straight line proportion is measure, as that if he claims he gave wisdom and the other claims he returned silver, the proportion is in wisdom to wealthiness. Next

b35   there is what has been given to each, for if he gave half of the smaller amount but the other not a fraction of the greater, it is clear the latter is in the wrong. But there is here too an initial dispute, if the one says[15] they came together as useful but the other denies it and says instead it was some other friendship.

Notes

1. Above, 7.9.1241b17–24.
2. Retaining at 1242a22–23 the MSS *ho gar anthrōpou monon ou politikos* (For he [sc. who is friend] of a man alone does not belong to a city . . .) and not Casaubon's emendation, adopted by Bekker, of *ho gar anthrōpos ou monon politikon* (For man is not only a political [animal but also . . .]). The emendation tends to disrupt the argument, which is that even if one is not part of a city one is always part of some other community.
3. Reading at 1242a25 Spengel's emendation *alla idiāi ou monaulikon* (but . . . in private not a solitary . . .). The *all' hai dia dumon aulikon* of the MSS makes no sense.
4. An implicit reference, perhaps, to Plato's *Republic* where justice is said to be the health of the soul, for it has the same analogy to the soul as health has to the body.
5. Sophocles, fr. 684 Nauck.
6. Reading at 1242b9 Bonitz' emendation of the accusative *diakeimenon* of the MSS to the nominative *diakeimenos* (his disposition being . . .).
7. Book 4.5.
8. Hesiod, *Works and Days* 371.
9. The Greek at 1243a12–14 is obscure. The sense seems to be what is said shortly at 1243a25 (where the same word *amphiballō*, to "deck out in" or "clothe with," is used), that in these friendships, which are supposedly based on character and not law, either party will have equal grounds of character to complain against the other.
10. Theognis 14.
11. Reading at 1243a31 *dieipōntai* (made an express statement) with some MSS (the word occurs again at 1243b7), rather than *dihepōntai* (managed it, sorted it out) with others and Bekker.
12. The sense is that a just exchange in friendship is a difficult thing, and to measure it by the single thing of equality is not easy if one is not looking at the same equality in the first place, but one party is looking at one equality (pleasure) and the other at another (utility).
13. Reading at 1243b20 Jackson's emendation *ti anti tinos* (what in return for what) in place of the MSS *panti tinos* (to all of something), which makes no sense in the context.
14. A discussion of these historical references can be found in Kenny (1978: 222–223). Pammenes was a Theban general and Pytho presumably his student in strategy; Herodicus (the MSS say Prodicus who, if he is the famous sophist of that name, was not a doctor) taught the more famous Hippocrates. The story of the king and the harpist is told of the tyrant Dionysius of Syracuse in Plutarch *De Fortuna Alexandri* 2.1. Also *NE* 1164a16.
15. Reading, with Bekker, at 1243b37 *an phēi ho men* (if one says . . .) rather than the *an phēsomen* (if we say . . .) of the MSS.

Chapter 11

In Multiple and Changing Friendships. Is one to do well by one's friend or by the virtuous man? If the two are the same the answer is not hard; but if they were or will be but are not, or contrariwise, the problems are many. So give deeds for deeds and words for words. Also, different things are due to a father and to a mother, and to a useful friend and to a virtuous or pleasant one; and different accounts hold of different friendships, as that to some belongs existence, to others living together, to others feeling pain and joy together. Some love their friend's things, as his wine or wealth, rather than the friend, and complaints arise when they seek to find in their friend a good man having first sought in him someone useful or pleasant.

1244a1   As for the friend good and according to virtue, we must examine whether it is to him one is to give assistance and help in things useful or to him who does or can pay back. This problem is the same as whether one is to do well

a5   rather by one's friend than by the virtuous man. For it is not too difficult if he is equally a friend and virtuous (unless one magnifies the one fact and minimizes the other, making much of him as friend and little as decent). But if he is not, the problems that arise are many, as that if the one was but is not going to be and the other is going to be but is not yet, or if he was becoming so but

a10   is not, hence he is but was not and will not be. However that is rather wearisome. For maybe Euripides is onto something when he composed the lines:

> A word may'st thou take as a word's just wage;
> A deed for them that had a deed as gage.[1]

1244a12   Not everything in fact is due to one's father but there are other things that are due[2] to one's mother (even though the father is better). For not everything is sacrificed to Zeus, nor does he get all the honors, but some. So perhaps

a15   some things are due to the useful and others to the good. For instance, it is not the case that if he[3] gives food and necessaries he is owed living together as well. Nor is he who is owed living together[4] owed the thing that not he but the useful friend gives. But those who do this for him are giving everything to the one they are in love with when it is not due.

1244a19   Nor even do the marks of friendship in the dialogues[5] possess worth. All are marks of friendship in a way but not of the same friendship. For to the useful friend belongs wishing him good things, as also to the benefactor and he who is of the sort he should be (for this mark of friendship is not distinctive), and to another belongs wishing existence and to another living together. And to

a25   the friend of pleasure belongs feeling pain and joy together. All these marks accord with some friendship, but none with just one. Hence they are many and each seems to be but is not of one friendship, as the choice of existence for instance—for in fact the superior and benefactor wishes that his own work have it; and to him who gives existence is existence to be given back again; yet living together is not with him but with the pleasant friend.

Some friends wrong each other, for it is rather the things but not the pos- 1244a30 sessors of them they love; hence they are even friends to the things, as that he took his wine because it was pleasant and took his wealth because it was useful. For it was more useful; hence indeed he gets annoyed,[6] the way he would if he were taking more in place of less. And complaints start, for now they are a35 seeking in him the good man, having first sought the pleasant or the useful one.

Notes

1. Euripides fr. 882 Nauck. The MSS at 1244a11–12 do not give lines that scan. Scholarly emendations are several. An alternative (translated here) is to move the errant *eis* of *eispherois* (may'st thou take) in the first line to before *parescheto* (was gage) in the second line but change it to *hois* (that . . .) and the preceding *erga* (deeds) to *ergon* (deed), thus giving: *ergon d' ekeinois ergon hois parescheto.*
2. Reading at 1244a13 *all' ha dei* (other things that are due) with Susemihl rather than the *alla de* (but others) of the MSS or *alla estin ha* (but there are those which) with Bekker.
3. Reading at 1244a16 *ouk ei* (not . . . if) with one set of MSS rather than *ouchi* (not) with others and Bekker.
4. Reading at 1244a17 *suzēn* (living together) with one set of MSS rather than *eu zēn* (living well) with others and with Bekker.
5. Possibly a reference to Plato's *Lysis* and *Symposium*, where ambiguities in the meaning of "friend" and "love" are much exploited and played with.
6. Reading at 1244a34 *dio dē aganaktei* (hence indeed he gets annoyed) with one of the MSS rather than *dio dei aganaktein* (hence he should get annoyed) with others and with Bekker. The sense is that if one prefers a friend's things to the friend, the friend will be as annoyed as he would be if one took from him and did not give, or gave less, in return.

Chapter 12

Friendship and Self-sufficiency
Need of Friends. *Does the self-sufficient and good man need friends or is his self-sufficiency and virtue enough for happiness? God is not in need of friends or of anything else, so neither should the happy man be, as far as possible. But in that case his friends should not be useful ones but virtuous ones, for indulging with and giving benefits to. To solve the puzzle one must note that life in actuality and as end is knowing and perceiving, and living together is perceiving together. But this knowing is us living and knowing, not a separated knowing,*

which is like someone else knowing instead. Living is both preferable and the good, and the first must be seen to fall under the second if the good life is to be available to us. The known and the preferable are something determinate, and wanting to know is wanting oneself to be determinate, which only happens in acts of perceiving and knowing whereby we become ourselves known; hence wanting to live is wanting to know and to be oneself the known. Living together is in part trivial if it is a sharing in trivial or lesser things, but sharing together the best we are capable of, bodily pleasure or music or philosophy, is pleasanter and makes us want to be close to friends. Properly, however, a friend is another self, but no other is like oneself in all respects, so different friends are enjoyed for different things. It is better to share the diviner pleasures, to see oneself in a better good, and so it is better to contemplate together and feast, but not in food and necessities. Everyone needs, therefore, to live together and have friends, and the best man most of all. The comparison with the god was misleading, for he has well-being in himself but we only in relation with others.

1244b1   We need to examine how self-sufficiency and friendship are disposed to each other in respect of their powers. For one might be puzzled whether, if someone were self-sufficient in everything, he will have a friend[1] (supposing it is in need that a friend is sought for) or not,[2] or whether a good man will

b5   be most self-sufficient (supposing the man with virtue is happy, what need would he have of a friend?). For it does not belong to the self-sufficient man[3] to need useful friends, nor ones to cheer him,[4] nor society, for he is enough for himself to be with.

1244b7   The thing is particularly evident in the case of god. For it is clear that as he is in no further need of anything, neither will he be in need of a friend, nor will he have one, who also has nothing characteristic of master.[5] Conse-

b10   quently the happiest man too will least need a friend, except insofar as it is impossible for him to be self-sufficient. The man, then, who lives best must have fewest friends, and they must get fewer, and he must not be eager to have friends but must think little, not only of useful friends, but also of those to be preferred for living with.

1244b15   But then in fact it would seem clear that his friend is not for the sake of use or help but that he who accords with virtue alone is friend. For when we are in need of nothing then everyone seeks people to indulge with, and more those who will be benefited than will benefit. And we have better judgment being self-sufficient than in need, and we most need friends worth living with.

1244b21   About this puzzle we must examine lest possibly it be that something is in one respect nobly said but in another escapes notice because of the comparison.[6] The thing is plain if we take what living as actuality and as end

b25   is. Clearly, then, it is perceiving and knowing. Consequently living together is perceiving together and knowing together. But it is the very perceiving and the very knowing that to each are most preferable, and for this reason the appetite for life is inborn in everyone. For to live is to handle[7] some sort of knowledge. So if one were to cut off and put the knowing itself by itself, as well as not[8] do so (but this escapes notice as it has been written in the b30 argument,[9] though in the thing one can notice it), one would make nothing different[10] than another knowing instead of oneself, and that is like another living instead of oneself. But it is reasonably one's own perceiving and knowing that is more to be preferred.

For there is need, at the same time, to put two things together in the 1244b34 argument, that living is indeed a thing to be preferred and that it is the good, and need, from these (because the A is under the B),[11] for this sort of nature to be available.[12] If then always in this sort of ordered series[13] one of a1 two things is in the division of the other of them,[14] and if the thing known and the thing to be preferred[15] are, speaking on the whole, the sharing of determinate nature,[16] consequently wanting to perceive oneself is wanting to be of this sort oneself.

Since, then, we are not each of these[17] by ourselves but by sharing in our 1245a5 powers in the act of perceiving and of knowing (for when one is perceiving one becomes perceived to the extent and in the respect one is first perceiving, and in the way and what one is perceiving, and in knowing one becomes known), consequently, on this account, one also wants always to live, because one wants always to know—and that because one wishes oneself to be the known.

Choosing, then, to live together would seem, on examination, to be in a 1245a11 way simple-minded—to start with as regard being companions also with the other animals, as eating or drinking together. For what difference is there, if you remove speech, whether these things take place among those nearby or apart? But even to share casual speech is another case of like sort. At the same a15 time, too, neither teaching nor learning is possible for self-sufficient friends, for if he is learning he himself is not as he should be, and if he is teaching his[18] friend is not. Likeness is friendship.

But still the appearance is there at least, and we all partake of good things 1245a18 more pleasantly with friends, to the extent these fall to each,[19] and the best that each is capable of. But among these it falls to one person to share bodily pleasure, to another musical study, to another philosophy; and so he is bold to be with his friend. That is why he says "a burden friends far away," supposing they should not be separate from each other when this is happening.[20] Hence erotic love too seems something like friendship; for the lover has an appetite for living together, though not particularly in the way he ought, but to feel it.

The argument, then, is saying those things by way of puzzle; but the fact 1245a26 is so clearly the case that it is clear its puzzle-raising is somehow leading us astray. The truth must be examined from this, that "friend" means, as the proverb has it, "another Heracles," "another self."[21] However, things are split and a30 it is hard for them to come to be in one individual, but while in nature he is what is most akin, in body another like him is so, another in soul, and another in one part of these and another in another part. Nevertheless "friend" means to be as it were a separate self. Therefore the perceiving of one's friend must in a way be the perceiving of oneself and in a way the knowing of oneself. Consequently, even enjoying the vulgar things and living together with one's friend is understandably pleasant (for there is always perception of him at the same time), but the diviner pleasures more so. Reason is that it is always pleasanter to contemplate oneself in the better good. And this is sometimes a feeling, sometimes a doing, sometimes something else (provided one can live well, and one's friend in this way too), and it exists in working together at living together or at a community of things included in the end, and[22] particularly so. Hence it is to contemplate together and feast together, not in matters of food and things necessary (such do not seem to be associations but indulgences). Everyone, however, wants to live in the end that he is able to attain. Otherwise they choose mainly to do and receive good turns from their friends.

1245b9   That there is in fact need, then, to live together, that everyone most wants this, and that the happiest and best man is most of all such, is clear. But that it was not clear in the argument, though it was speaking truth, was reasonable too. For the solution is how the comparison, though true, was put together,[23] that it is because the god is not that sort of thing, for example to need a friend and a friend worthy in respect of his like. However, according to the argument in question, the virtuous man will not even think,[24] for it is not thus the god has well-being but in a way better than to think something else besides self-thinking himself; reason is that for us well-being is by relation to another, but for him he is himself his own well-being.

Number and Treatment of Friends. *To want many friends and to think many friends are no friend are both right. Many would be better if it were possible, but it is too hard, because: (i) trial is required to obtain them and one must use them all when possessed; (ii) sometimes we want friends to be absent if we cannot at the same time be together and prosper (as with Heracles and his mother and the Spartan's quip about the Disocuri); (iii) it is the mark of a friend to want and not to want to share troubles with his friend, for (a) friends should be pleasant to their friends, (b) they should not choose their own inter-est over his, though a lesser good together is better than a greater good apart, (c) the matter is disputed but sometimes being apart is better, (d) the same holds of misfortunes, (e) bad men are motivated by these considerations to kill their beloveds along with themselves.*

1245b19   And as for our seeking and praying for many friends and our saying at the same time that he who has many friends has no friend—both statements are right. For were it possible to live together with many people at the same time and perceive with them together, having as many as possible would be most to be preferred. But since that is very hard, actualizing of joint perception must be among fewer. Consequently, not only is it hard to obtain many (for there is need of trial) but also to use them when they are there.

Also, sometimes we want the loved one to be absent when he is doing 1245b26 well, and sometimes, by contrast, to share the same things. In fact to wish to be together is a mark of friendship, for when it is possible to be and do well together, that everyone chooses. When it is not possible, however, we do not, but choose the way perhaps his mother would have chosen for Heracles, that b30 he be a god rather than, being with her, serve Eurystheus. For she[25] would perhaps say something like the quip the Spartan made when someone bade him call on the Dioscuri during a storm.[26]

It seems to be a mark of the one who loves to keep his friend from sharing 1245b33 together in his troubles, and of the one who is loved to want to share together in them; and both these views are reasonable. For the friend should not be to his friend a thing as painful as pleasant, and it seems he should not choose his own interest. Hence friends keep friends from sharing with them (for they are enough themselves for their sufferings) so as not to appear, by focusing on what is their own, to be preferring the enjoyment (although their friend a1 is being pained), and preferring, moreover, to be less burdened because they are not bearing their ills alone.

But since both well being and being together are preferable, it is plain that 1246a2 in fact being with a lesser good together is somehow preferable to being with a greater one apart. Since indeed it is not plain how much being together can achieve, at this point they differ. In fact they think[27] that sharing everything a5 together is a mark of friendship and, as with dining together, they say it is pleasanter to have everything the same together. The others, however, would not want to. But when someone posits extremes at any rate, they would agree on their doing very badly together than on very well apart.

It is very similar in misfortunes too. Sometimes we want our friends to 1246a10 exist but not to pain them when they are not going to be able to do anything further. Sometimes we want those who are pleasantest to be present. But the fact of this opposition stands also very much to reason. For it happens because of what was said before,[28] and because while we simply flee contemplating a15 our friend being in pain or in a bad way, as we also flee it in our own case, yet seeing one's friend is pleasant, as is seeing any other very pleasant thing, for the reason stated, and seeing him not ailing if one is oneself.

Consequently, whichever of these is more pleasant, it puts the weight 1246a18 on wanting him to be present or not. In fact it then puts the weight on its happening with worse people, and doing so for the same reason. For they are most ambitious that their friends not do well, and would be ambitious for them not even to be if[29] it was also going badly with themselves. Hence sometimes they kill off their beloveds along with themselves. For it is a mark of the one who is akin to feel an evil more, the way he who also remembered a25   that he was once doing well would feel it more than if he thought he was always doing badly.[30]

Notes

1.   The MSS show a gap of several letters at 1244b3. A likely supplement might be to add a word for something like "need," as ". . . he will have *any need* for a friend."

2.   Reading at 1244b4 *ē ou* (Von Fragstein's [1978: 344] emendation of the MSS *ē ho*) instead of deleting it with Bekker.

3.   Reading at 1244b6 *autarkous* ([belongs to] a self-sufficient man) with one of the MSS rather than *autarkōs* (self-sufficiently) with others and with Bekker.

4.   Reading at 1244b6 Spengel's emendation *euphranountōn* (ones to cheer him) rather than the MSS *eu phronoutōn* (ones thinking well).

5.   The Greek at 1244b 9–10, *oute mēthen* (neither nothing), is ungrammatical and needs emendation, and the easiest emendation of it would be to *hou* (or possibly *hōi*) *te mēthen* (of whom also ... nothing . . .), which is the translation given here (note that *ou* needs to be replaced by *hou* at 1245a20) The sense is that neither a friend nor anyone else is needed by god, whose rule over the cosmos is not that of a master (a master needs someone to be master of), but is, as it were, an overflow of his goodness and not a need of his nature.

6.   The comparison of man with god just mentioned.

7.   Bonitz' emendation at 1244b28 of *diatithenai* (to handle) to *dei tithenai* (one must set down [living as a sort of knowing]) may be philologically plausible but is repetitious and destroys the sense. Aristotle has just said, at 1244b23–25, that living is knowing and hardly needs to say the same thing again so soon. What he is now saying (as his next remarks indicate) is that living is someone's actual conducting or handling knowledge.

8.   Placing a comma at 1233b30 after *kath' hauto* (by itself) and before *kai mē* (as well as not), and taking the *mē* as negating the whole phrase from the previous line and not just the last part of it.

9.   The argument here being given, whose point is best seen if one considers the actual facts and does not rest merely with the words, cf. below 1245a26–29, b12–14.

10.   Taking at 1244b *diapheroi* (make . . . different) transitively rather than intransitively.

11.   The MSS at 1244b36 have *to auto tois* (the same as the), which does not make sense. Several emendations have been suggested. The emendation proposed and translated here is *to A hypo to B* (which, in early Greek MSS, would look very like *to auto tois*: TOAΥΠOTOB instead of TOAΥTOTOIΣ), meaning that "the A is under the B," or that the first ("[living as] to be preferred") is under the second ("[living as] the good"). Phrases like *to A hypo to B* are found in the *Prior Analytics* (e.g., 1.9.30a40, 30b13, 11.31a30, a37, b17, b20, as well as elsewhere).

12.   The phrase "this sort of nature" refers to life as the good, and such life being "available" is its being a life that is to be preferred for us because the life to be preferred for us (the life we can live as our own) falls under it.

13. The Greek word at 1245a1 is *sustoichia*, which means an ordering of one thing under another (as of A under B).
14. A variant in the MSS at 1245a1–2 has "to be preferred" (*hairetou*) instead of "the other of them" (*heterou*).
15. A variant in the MSS at 1245a2 has "perceptible" (*aisthēton*) in place of "to be preferred" (*haireton*).
16. Sc. nature as determinately actualized and not as still indefinitely potential, cf. 1244b23–24.
17. The "these" refers to the three of: the known, the to be preferred, and the determinate.
18. Reading at 1245a18 Bonitz' emendation of the MSS *ou* (not) to *ho* (his).
19. Reading at 1245a20 Ross' emendation of the MSS *hekaston* (each) to *hekastōi* (to each).
20. Reading at 1245a24 Fritzsche's emendation of the MSS *ginomenon* (happening) to *ginomenou* (when . . . happening).
21. Accepting at 1245a30 the Latin translation's emendation *autos* (self) of the MSS *houtos* (this [man]).
22. Retaining at 1245b4 the *te* (and) of the MSS rather than changing it to *ge* (at least) with Bekker.
23. The solution is found by distinguishing what the comparison put together, namely happiness and its attainment. The happy man attains happiness but not the way the god does, for what the god has by his very nature the happy man has only through friends.
24. A reference to the argument stated at 1244b7–15, for in reducing the happy man to himself alone it deprived him of all friends with whom to think, and indeed of anything at all to think.
25. The MSS at 1245b32 say either *eipoie* or *eipoien*. The first is incorrect and needs to be changed either, with Bekker, to *eipeie* (she would say) or to the other reading of *eipoien* ([all] would say).
26. The Spartan's quip was that he would rather the Dioscuri (the twin stars Castor and Pollux, who were especially honored at Sparta) stay safe where they are in the sky than come down and share his troubles here.
27. Reading at 1246a6 Casaubon's emendation *oiontai* (they think) for the MSS *hoion kai* (as for example and).
28. Above at 1245b36–46a10.
29. The Greek at 1246b22 reads *mēd' einai anangkai autois kakōs* (not even to be necessities for them badly), which does not make sense. The *anangkai* needs changing. Smith's suggestion of *an kai autoi* ([not even to be,] if they themselves were also doing badly) seems on the right lines but can perhaps be improved to *an ei kai hautois*, which (with "[would be] ambitious" supplied from the previous line), is what is translated here.
30. This last sentence in the Greek at 1246a23–25 is elliptical and ambiguous. An alternative translation would run: "for they suppose themselves to perceive their proper evil more [sc. should their beloved survive], the way one who also remembered that he was once doing well would feel it more than if he thought he was always doing badly."

Book Eight: Completion of Happiness: Complete Virtue[1]

Chapter 1

Complete Virtue
Using Virtue: Supremacy of Prudence. *Is it possible to use things dear both properly and accidentally, as an eye is used for seeing or mis-seeing and also for selling or eating? Likewise, knowledge can be used both as itself and like ignorance, to make mistakes, and if virtues are cases of knowledge it will be possible to use justice, say, as injustice. But justice cannot be used in this way. Knowledge too cannot be used as ignorance but only to imitate ignorance by doing ignorant things knowingly. Prudence is a sort of knowledge so it should be possible to use prudence to do imprudent things, or to do imprudent things prudently. Now in the case of knowledge some higher knowledge uses it to do ignorant things, but the thing that uses the highest knowledge cannot be knowledge, nor can it be virtue (for prudence uses virtue). This highest thing cannot be passion either, after the model of incontinence where passion distorts intellect to do the opposite of what it wants. For then it would be possible to use justice unjustly and to be thinking imprudently, as well as the opposites, to use injustice justly and imprudence or ignorance prudently. The like is not found in other cases of knowledge, that passion makes ignorance knowledgeable as it makes knowledge ignorant (the incapacity is included in the capacity but not vice versa). Prudence, therefore, is supreme and cannot be knowledge but some other kind of knowing.*

One might raise the puzzle whether it is possible to use each thing that is dear[2] on the basis[3] natural to it and otherwise, namely[4] this, insofar[5] as it is pleasant incidentally.[6] For example: either[7] an eye is to see or also in another way to mis-see, when distorting it so that one thing appears two (so both these uses are, on the one hand, that it was an eye, and, on the other, that it was with an eye); but the other use is incidental, as for instance if it was to sell or eat. 1246a26

Likewise, then, with knowledge too, for it also exists in a true way as well as in making mistakes; for instance, when one voluntarily writes incorrectly one will now be using[8] it indeed as ignorance, as if contorting the hand (the foot is sometimes in fact used by dancing girls like the hand and the hand like the foot). So if all[9] the virtues were knowledges, it would be possible[10] to use justice also as injustice. One will, then, in doing wrong, do wrong[11] from justice, just like doing ignorant things from knowledge.[12] But if this is impossible, it is clear that virtues would not be knowledges. 1246a31 a35

1246b1   Nor, if it is impossible to be ignorant from knowledge but only to make mistakes and to do the same as is done from ignorance, will one do anything from justice at any rate as one does from injustice. But since prudence is

b5   knowledge and is something true, it too will do the same thing, for it would be possible to be imprudent from prudence and to make the same mistakes as the imprudent man does. But if the use of each thing, insofar as it is such, is simple,[13] then those acting in this way would be acting prudently.

1246b8   Now, in the case of the other knowledges, a different controlling knowledge does the distorting.[14] But what is in control[15] of it, of the one that controls all knowledges? For it would not at any rate be knowledge any longer, nor intellect. But it is not virtue either, for it uses it; for the virtue of what rules uses the virtue of what is ruled.[16] What is it, then?

1246b12   Is it the way incontinence is said to be a vice of the irrational part of the soul and the incontinent man a sort of licentious man possessed of intellect? But if then it is the case[17] that, should desire be strong it will produce

b15   distortion and draw conclusions opposite to what intellect loves,[18] it is plain that, if in this part[19] there is virtue and in reason folly, the two are reversed. Consequently justice will have a just and a bad use[20] and one will be thinking[21] imprudently.

1246b18   Consequently there will be the opposites[22] too. For it is odd if, on the one hand, wickedness will distort virtue in the calculating part (when this at any

b20   time comes to be present in reason)[23] and make one ignorant, but, on the other hand, virtue, when it comes to be present in the unreasoning part, will, when folly is present, not distort this and make one judge prudently and as one should, and again, odd if prudence in the calculating part would not make correction[24] in the unreasoning part act temperately (which is what endurance seems to do). Consequently it will in fact be possible for the virtue that comes from ignorance to act prudently.

1246b25   But these things are[25] odd, especially behaving prudently from ignorance. For we do not at all see this in the case of other things—in the way license distorts medicine or the art of grammar but not yet[26] ignorance, if it is opposed, because there is nothing excellent in ignorance. But we see virtue

b30   to be on the whole more related toward vice in this way. For in fact it is the just man who can do everything that[27] an unjust man can and, in general, the incapacity is included in the capacity.

1246b32   Consequently it is clear that they are prudent at the same time, and that someone else's habits are those good ones,[28] and the Socratic remark is correct, that nothing is stronger than prudence. But that he said prudence

b35   was knowledge was not correct. For it is a virtue and not a knowledge but a comprehending of another kind.[29]

Notes

1.   See note at the beginning of the previous book.
2.   At 1246a26 some MSS omit the word for "dear" (or "friend").

3. Retaining at 1246a27 the *eph' hōi* (on the basis) of some MSS rather than the *eph' ha* (for the things which) preferred by others and by Bekker. An eye, for instance, is used on the basis natural to it when it is used for seeing (whether correctly or incorrectly), and not when it is used for something other than seeing.

4. Taking at 1246a27 the *kai* before *touto* as epexegetic for "that is" and not as "and."

5. Reading at 1236a27 Jackson's emendation *hēi* (as) for the *ē* (either) of the MSS.

6. If the term for "dear" is retained at 1246a26 there is no need to follow Jackson and emend the MSS *hēdu* (pleasant) to *ē au* (or). The puzzle in question here is a continuation of what was said at the end of the previous chapter, about using a friend badly, by killing him along with oneself, because one judges it pleasanter, or less painful, that way.

7. Keeping at 1236a28 the *ē* (either) of the MSS and not Jackson's emendation of it to *hēi* (as).

8. Reading at 1246a33 Moraux's emendation of the MSS *chrēstai* or *chrēsthai* (to use) to *chrēsetai* (one will be using).

9. Reading at 1246a35 Spengel's emendation *ei dē* (so if) for the *ēdē* (already) or *eidē* (kinds) of the MSS.

10. Reading at 1246a36 Spengel's emendation *eiē an* (it would be possible) for the *eipan* (they said) of the MSS.

11. Reading at 1246a37 Spengel's emendation *adikēsei* (one will do wrong) for the *ei dikēs ei* (if of right if) of the MSS.

12. Doing wrong from justice and ignorant things from knowledge will be cases of incidental use (like eating an eye), for they are not uses, nor even misuses, of justice qua justice or knowledge qua knowledge.

13. Simple as in the case of the eye, for seeing or even mis-seeing (which is also a seeing). Eating an eye, by contrast, is not using it simply as an eye but incidentally, as something pleasant to eat.

14. Reading at 1246b9 *strophēn* (distorting), which seems in fact to be what the MSS say, and not the (impossible) *trophēn* (food) doubtfully printed by Bekker.

15. The word for "controls" at 1246b10 can be supplied from the context, though the sense, in view of the previous clause, must be "controls it so as to distort it."

16. Sc. whatever controls knowledge must control virtue and not be controlled by it, if virtue is itself controlled by knowledge or if, as 1248a29 says, virtue is an instrument of intellect.

17. Reading at 1246b14 Spengel's emendation *ei dē* (if then it is . . .) for the MSS *ēdē* (already, precisely).

18. At 1246b15 the MSS show a gap of several letters and preserve only *hē . . . sphi . . .* The reading adopted here is *ē ho nous philei* (than what intellect loves), which is a combination of Apelt's and Von Fragstein's (1978: 360–61) suggestions. Apelt suggested *ē ho logos philei* (than what reason loves) and Von Fragstein *ē ho nous phronei* (than what intellect thinks).

19. Sc. the irrational part of the soul, mentioned at 1246b13.

20. Something said just above, at 1246a38, to be impossible. At 1246b17, if *estai dikaiosunēi* is translated as "justice will have . . ." rather than as "it will be possible for justice . . ." then the following *to dikaiōs chrēsthai* (just [and bad] use) of the MSS can be kept and translated as a regular verbal

noun phrase. There is no compelling reason to change it, with Bekker, to *kai dikaiōs chrēsthai* (to use both justly [and . . .]) or, with Jackson, to *t' ou dikaiōs chrēsthai* (to use both not justly [and . . .]).

21. Following at 1246b18 Von Fragstein's suggestion (1978: 361) to treat *phronēsei* as a verb (one will be thinking) and not as a noun (with prudence).

22. Sc. the opposites of where, instead of the vice distorting the virtue, the virtue distorts the vice.

23. The Greek at 1246b19–20 hardly makes sense as it stands. It seems necessary to accept at b19 the accusative *tēn men en tōi logistikōi aretēn* (virtue in the calculating part [from a Renaissance Latin translation]), making it object of the verb "distort," rather than the genitive *tēs . . . aretēs* of the MSS. The further emendation at b20 (from Spengel and Susemihl) of *engenomenē men tōi logōi* ([wickedness] when it comes to be present on the one hand for reason) to *engenomenē en tōi alogōi* ([wickedness] when it comes to be present in the irrational part), while possible, could, on philological grounds, be more easily changed to *engenomenēn en tōi logōi* ([virtue] when it comes to be present in reason), and the latter is what is translated here.

24. At 1246b24 the "not" is supplied from the context. Scholars also change *kolasin an* (would . . . correction) to *akolasian* (license) to give the sense: ". . . not make license act temperately." The emendation is plausible and attractive but not strictly necessary. Endurance makes licentious desires behave temperately by correcting or disciplining them.

25. Reading at 1246b25 Spengel's emendation *esti de* (But . . . are) for the MSS *epi te* (And upon).

26. At 1246b28 the MSS have *oun ho* (therefore he), which does not fit the context. Rackham's change to just *ou* (not) or Jackson's to *oun ou* (therefore not) seem on the right lines, but a change to *oupō* (not yet) might be philologically easier.

27. Adapting Jackson at 1246b31 and changing *ho adikos* (the unjust man) to *ha adikos* (everything that an unjust man).

28. Sc. the habits when good in one part of the soul distorts bad in the other, which will be habits of such as the continent and enduring and not of the prudent.

29. At 1246b36 the MSS have *gnōs* followed by a gap of several letters. Spengel's emendation to *gnōseōs* (of knowing) seems certainly correct.

Chapter 2

Acquiring Virtue: Good Fortune
What It Is
Discussion of Puzzles. *Since not only prudence but also good fortune produces well doing, we must consider whether good fortune is by nature or not. Some people, though foolish, do get things right; are they so by habit or nature?*

Some people have a certain character from nature, and the fortunate are like that, since they do not go right by prudence (being unable, as they are, to give a reason for their actions). Even if they are clever in other things, they are fortunate where they are foolish, like being loved by god or moved by something external—though it is odd for such a man and not the best to be helped by the god. So if they do not go right by reason or by divine guidance, the cause must be nature. Nature, however, causes things always or for the most part but luck does not, so good fortune would not seem to be by nature. If, however, the fortunate succeed always, nature must be cause and they will not after all be fortunate, for luck is cause of fortune. So is luck cause or not? If it is not, then luck is just a name for a cause we do not see or understand. If there is a cause and the same cause always causes the same things, then the same things should always result and luck will not then be a cause; nor is it a thing we can learn from experience (else people would have learnt to be fortunate). Why then do strings of luck not happen to people continuously? However, there are impulses in the soul from calculation and others, which are prior, from irrational appetite. So if some people are well endowed by nature (like natural singers who do not need training) and are impelled to desire what they should, they will go right even if foolish, and they will be fortunate by nature.

Since not only does prudence produce well-doing and virtue,[1] but we also 1246b37
say that the fortunate do well, supposing that good fortune imparts[2] well-doing just as that knowledge does the same, we must then consider whether it is by nature that one person is fortunate and another unfortunate or not, and how things stand in these matters.

For that there are some people who are fortunate is a fact we see, for they 1247a3
get many things right, despite being foolish, which luck has control over. And although[3] there are things where art has control, nevertheless there is much of luck involved in them too, as in generalship and navigation. Are these people fortunate, then, from some habit? Or is it not because of any character in themselves that they are doers of fortunate things? For that is what people now think, supposing there to be some who are of this sort by nature.

Nature does make some people to have a certain character, and they differ 1247a9
as soon as they come to be, as that some are gray-eyed and some dark-eyed (because they have a necessity of being such),[4] and that is how the fortunate and unfortunate are. For it is plain they do not go right by prudence. For prudence is not without reason, but it has a reason because of which it so acts, whereas they could not say why they are right (for if so it would be art).

They, however, are clearly foolish—not that they are so in other matters 1247a15
(for this is not strange, for example Hippocrates was clearly a geometrician but in other matters he seemed stupid and foolish and while on a sea voyage[5] lost much gold coin, because of his simplicity so they say, to the collectors of the 2 percent customs duty at Byzantium), but that they are foolish even in a20

some of the things where they are fortunate. For in helmsmanship it is not the most clever who are fortunate, but it is as in throwing dice where one man throws nothing and another makes a throw that accords with his being naturally fortunate, or by being loved, as they say, by the god and being put right by something from outside.

1247a25   For example, a ship badly made often sails better, not, however, because of itself but because it has a good helmsman. He, however, being fortunate, has the divine spirit[6] for good helmsman; though it is odd for god or a spirit to be friends with a man of this sort and not with the best man and the most prudent. If, then, it must be either by nature or intellect or some guardianship that they do the right thing, and two are not possible, then they would be fortunate by nature.

1247a31   Nature though, at any rate, is cause either of what is always the same way or of what is so for the most part, but luck is the opposite. If, therefore, success contrary to reason is held to belong to luck, but a man is fortunate if at all because of luck, it would not seem that the cause was the sort to be

a35   always, or for the most part, of the same thing. Further, if this sort of man does indeed succeed or fail[7] the way a man, because gray-eyed, does not see sharply, luck is not cause but nature. He is not fortunate, then, but is as one having a good nature. Consequently what should be said is this, that those we call fortunate are not so because of luck. They are not fortunate then. For all those are fortunate[8] whose good things have good luck for cause.

1247b1   But if so, will luck be altogether a cause or will it be a cause but no longer altogether (though it must be, and must be a cause)? So it will in fact be a cause of good or bad things for some people. But if it must be altogether

b5   taken away then[9] nothing must be said to come about from luck, but we, when something else is the cause, say, because we do not see it, that luck is a cause (hence too when they define luck they lay it down as a cause irrational[10] to human calculation, supposing it to be nature of some sort). That, then, would be another problem.[11]

1247b9   Since we see that some people are fortunate once, why are they not also fortunate again, because of the same thing setting them right[12] again? For the same thing is cause of the same thing.[13] So this[14] will not be a matter of luck. But when the same result happens, things being infinite and indefinite,[15] there will be the good or bad but knowledge of it will not be knowledge based on experience—since some would have learnt to be fortunate, or all

b15   knowledges would in fact, as Socrates said,[16] be matters of good fortune. What then prevents such things happening to someone often one after the other, not because they somehow must[17] but the way that always throwing high in dice would be?[18]

1247b18   What then? Are there not impulses in the soul, some from calculation and others from irrational appetite, and the latter are prior? For if the impulse that arises from desire of the pleasant and the appetite are by nature, then everything would advance toward the good.[19] So if some people are well endowed in nature (as singers[20] are in this way well[21] endowed in nature who have not learnt singing), and if impulse without reason drives them in the way that[22] nature naturally does, and if their desire too for this thing when and how is as it should be and what it should be and when it should be, these will[23] go right even if they happen to be foolish and irrational, just as they b25 also will sing well who are not[24] capable of teaching it. Such people at any rate are fortunate, who without reason go right most of the time. The fortunate, then, would exist by nature.

Solution of Puzzles. *Good fortune is said in fact in more than one way, and some things are done from impulse and others not, and in both cases people succeed. The former can succeed by natural impulse without reasoning well, but the latter succeed by luck, sometimes succeeding when they reason and sometimes not. Are these two kinds of fortune the same? The cause in the case of those who succeed by natural desire against reason is not open to human reasoning, and in this sense it is luck because luck is against reason. It is not really luck, however, though it seems to be, but rather nature, and what really is luck is a cause but not cause of all it seems to be cause of.*

Or is good fortune said in more than one way? For some things are done 1247b28 from impulse and from people choosing to do them, but other things are not but the opposite. And in the former cases, in which they seem to have reasoned badly, they are led right[25] and we say they are fortunate; again too in the latter cases, if they would have wanted or would have taken the lesser good. So as regards the former it is possible that they are successful through nature, for their impulse and their appetite, being of what it should be, went right, but the reasoning was silly; and as regards the latter, when there would b35 have been[26] a reasoning seemingly right, luck however being here cause and it being right saved[27] them. But sometimes there was, because of desire, again reasoning in this way, and it was unlucky.

So how in the other cases will there be good fortune in accord with a well 1247b38 endowed nature of appetite and desire? But if [28] there is good fortune in this case and luck is double,[29] is the former then the same or are there several kinds of good fortune? Since we see that there are some people who are fortunate against all knowledge and all correct reasoning, it is plain that the cause of their good fortune would be something different. But whether it is a5 good fortune or not which desired the things it should and when it needed to,[30] there would not be human reasoning of the fact. For, to be sure, that of which[31] the desire at least is natural is not altogether without reasoning, but it is damaged by something. It does therefore seem to be good fortune, because luck is cause of things against reason, and this[32] is against reason a10 (for it is against knowledge and the universal). But it is, as is likely, not from luck, though it does seem for this reason to be so.

1248a12   Consequently this argument does not show that good fortune is by nature, but that those who seem to be fortunate do not all go right because of luck rather than nature. Nor does it show that luck is in no way cause of anything, but that it is not cause of everything of which it seems to be cause.

How Luck Is and Is Not a Cause. Does luck cause the desire of what one should desire? If so it would be cause of everything, including thought and deliberation. For since deliberation cannot be caused by a previous deliberation and so on ad infinitum, luck would be the cause. But there is a principle that has no principle beyond it, and as god moves all things so the divine thing in the soul moves everything in the soul. It is stronger than reason and intellect and can only be god. The fortunate, therefore, are thus impelled without reason to go right, having something greater than deliberation to guide them. Others lack this guidance and they when without reason fail. Their power of divination through reason is almost the same as the other kind (some of them have it through experience and some through familiarity). Both use the divine element but the first kind do so when their reason is disengaged for then it acts more strongly in them. There are, then, two kinds of good fortune: the one divine where people go right through impulse and the other where they go right against impulse. Both are irrational but the first is continuous and the second not.

1248a15   One might, however, raise this puzzle, is luck cause of this very fact, desiring what one should and when one should? Or will it rather in this way be cause of everything? For it will be cause of thinking too and deliberating. For there was indeed no deliberating preceded by a deliberating and a deliberating of that, but there is a beginning. Neither was there a thinking preceded by a

a20   thinking first to think, and so on to infinity. Thought[33] then is not beginning of thinking, nor deliberation beginning of deliberating. What else then is it except luck? Consequently everything will be from luck.

1248a22   Or[34] is there a principle that has no principle outside it and, because[35] it is such in its being, such is what it can do?[36] The thing we are looking for is this, what the beginning is of motion in the soul. Plainly, then, as god is in the whole so is he in that, for the divine in us in a way moves all things. Reason's beginning is not reason but something greater. What then might one say was stronger even than knowledge and intellect[37] except god? For

a30   virtue is instrument of the intellect. In fact that is why, as[38] I said before, they are called fortunate who, though irrational, have an impulse to go right. Also they get no advantage from deliberating, for they have a principle that is of a kind greater than intellect and deliberation.

1248a33   Others have reason but do not have that, nor inspiration;[39] they are incapable of it. For when they are without reason they fail.[40] Also, one must suppose[41] that the divination of these prudent and wise is swift and is almost the divination that is apart from[42] reason; but some have the use of it in their speculation[43] through experience and others through familiarity. These divinations use the god, and this sees well both what will be and what is—even in the case of those whose reason is thus[44] disengaged. That is why the melancholic also have correct dreams. For the principle seems to be stronger when the   a40 rational element is disengaged,[45] just as the blind remember more because disengaged from having their memory attached to visible things.[46]

It is manifest that there are two kinds of good fortune. The one is divine, 1248b3 which is why the fortunate man seems to go right because of god. He it is who is set right in accord with his impulse. The other is set right against his   b5 impulse. Both are without reason, and the one is a more continuous good fortune, but this other is not continuous.

Notes

1.   Or if, at 1246b38, the alternative MSS reading *aretē* (nominative) is taken instead of *aretēn* (accusative), the sense will be: "Since not only do prudence and virtue produce. . . ."
2.   Reading at 1247a1 Fritzsche's emendation *empoiousēs* (introduce, impart in) instead of the MSS *eu poiousēs* (do well).
3.   Retaining at 1247a5 the MSS *ei de kai* (And although) rather than Bekker's emendation *hoi de kai* (And those) or Spengel's *eti de kai* (Further too).
4.   At 1247a11–12 the Medieval Latin translation expands this phrase to: "because they must be such in accord with their being disposed to be such."
5.   Reading at 1247a19 *pleōn* (while on a sea voyage) because of the Medieval Latin translation rather than *pleon* (more) with the Greek MSS.
6.   The Greek at 1247a27 is *daimōn*.
7.   Retaining at 1247a36 *toios dē* (this sort of man does indeed) and *ē apotungchanei* (or fails) with the MSS rather than changing the first to *toiosdi* (this sort of man) and deleting the second with Bekker.
8.   Reading at 1247a39–b1 *eutucheis* (fortunate) with the Medieval Latin translation rather than *tuchēs* (of luck) with the Greek MSS and Bekker.
9.   Treating *kai* at 1247b4 as apodotic (cf. Denniston, *Greek Particles*: 308–309).
10.   Reading at 1247b7 *alogon* (irrational) with the Medieval Latin translation rather than *analogon* (analogous) with the Greek MSS and Bekker.
11.   This problem is picked up and answered at 1248a15ff.
12.   Reading at 1247b10 with the Medieval Latin translation, *dia to auto katorthōsai* (because of the same thing setting right), rather *dia to apokatorthōsai* (because of resetting right) with the Greek MSS and Bekker.
13.   Again reading at 1247b11 with the Medieval Latin translation *tou gar autou to auto aition*. The Greek MSS say *to gar auto touto aition* (for the same thing, this, is cause).
14.   Again reading at 1274b11 with the Medieval Latin translation *touto* (this) and not the *ou to* (not the) of the Greek MSS.
15.   Or, with the Medieval Latin translation, "happens from things both infinite and indefinite."
16.   Plato, *Euthydemus* 279d.
17.   At 1247b17 the Greek MSS have the senseless *tois dei* (to the it must), and the Medieval Latin translation perhaps read *tous dei* (it says *hos oportet*,

"they must"). Neither is correct Greek. A variety of emendations has been offered. Perhaps the easiest emendation, however, would be to read *pōs dei*, which is the translation offered here.

18. Reading at 1247b17 Sylburg's emendation *eiē* (would be) with the Medieval Latin translation, rather than *eien* (they would be) of the Greek MSS.

19. Following at 1247b20–21 Kenny's rendition of the Greek (1992: 164; 2011:144).

20. Reading at 1247b22 Sylburg's emendation *ōidikoi* (singers) for the MSS *adikoi* (unjust).

21. Reading at 1247b23 with the Medieval Latin *eu* (well) rather than *ou* (not) with the Greek MSS.

22. Reading at 1247b23 *hēi* (in the way that) with Jackson and the Medieval Latin instead of *hē* (the) with the Greek MSS.

23. Reading at 1247b25 the future tense of the verb, *katorthōsousi*, with the Medieval Latin rather than the present tense, *katorthousi*, with the Greek MSS.

24. Reading at 1247b26 Sylburg's *āisontai* (will sing) for the *esontai* (will be) of the MSS, and *ou didaskalikoi* (not capable of teaching) with the Medieval Latin rather than *eu didaskalikoi* (capable of teaching well) of the Greek MSS.

25. Adding at 1247b31 *en hois* (in which) after *ekeinois* (those cases) with the Medieval Latin and retaining *katorthountai* (they are led right) also with the Latin and one family of Greek MSS rather than the emendation *katorthountes* (when they go right) with Bekker.

26. The Greek at 1247b36 is obscure and somehow corrupt. The translation given here replaces *mē* (not) with *ēn* (there would have been [the same construction of a tense of the indicative with *an* to express a past condition as at 1247b32; cf. Goodwin 1421³]). This emendation does not have the support of the Medieval Latin, but it does produce something grammatically as well as philosophically intelligible. The sense is that in these cases people seem to be calculating well but events are contrary and they only escape failure because they do by chance other than they planned. For example, their plan to travel to town by a first road seemed reasonable, but because of some chance they chose a different road and so avoided the thieves lying in wait, unbeknownst to them, on the first.

27. Reading at 1247b37 *esōsen* (saved) with the Medieval Latin rather than the grammatically dubious *exōsen* of the Greek MSS. The Latin also has the word for "desire" in the previous phrase, which would perhaps give the sense: "luck . . . cause and being itself with right desire." The meaning would be that luck saves in this case because the desire happens to be correct but not the reasoning (they plan on taking the unlucky road but some chance desire makes them choose the lucky one instead).

28. Reading at 1248a1 *ei* (if) with the Latin rather than *hē* (the) with the Greek MSS.

29. Sc. sometimes luck saves from disaster and sometimes not.

30. Reading at 1248a6 *edeito* (it needed to) with one family of Greek MSS rather than *edei to* (it should the) with others and with Bekker.

31. Reading at 1248a7 Jackson's emendation *hou ge* (of which at least) rather than *oute* (neither) of the MSS.

32. Reading at 1248a10 *touto* (this) with the Medieval Latin rather than *toutou* (of this) with the Greek MSS and Bekker.

33. The Greek word is *nous* elsewhere translated as intellect.
34. Reading at 1248a22 *ē* (or) with the Medieval Latin rather than *ei* (if) with the Greek MSS and Bekker.
35. Reading at 1248a23 *dihoti* (because) with the Medieval Latin and Kenny (1992: 159) rather than *dia ti* (why) with the Greek MSS and Bekker.
36. Reading at 1248a24 *toiouto dunatai* (such it can [do]) with the Medieval Latin and Walzer and Dirlmeier instead of *to touto dunasthai* (the being able [to do] this) with the Greek MSS and Bekker.
37. At 1248a28 "and intellect" is supplied by Spengel from the Medieval Latin.
38. Reading at 1248a29 *ho* (which, as) with the Latin and Jackson instead of the *hoi* (they) of the Greek MSS. The reference is to 1247b30–32, 34–35).
39. Reading at 1248a33 *oud' enthusiasmon* (nor inspiration) with Langerbeck and Spengel following the Medieval Latin, rather than *kai enthusiasmoi* (and divinely inspired) with the Greek MSS and Bekker.
40. Following at 1248a33–34 Von Fragstein's construal of the Greek (1978: 376).
41. Reading at 1248a36 *hupolabein* (suppose) with Ross, following the Medieval Latin, rather than the *apolabein* (take away) of the Greek MSS and Bekker.
42. The Greek is *apo*; cf. above 6.7.1150a26.
43. The Greek at 1248a37 is obscure and something has likely dropped out. A variety of emendations has been suggested. The one translated here is to change the *te en* (and in) to *to en* (the [use of it] in [their speculation]) and supply *echousi* (they have) from the context.
44. Reading at 1248a39 *houtōs* (thus) with the Medieval Latin and Jackson in place of the *houtos* (this) of the Greek MSS.
45. Reading at 1248a40–b1 *apoluomenou tou logou* (when the rational element is disengaged) with the Medieval Latin and Spengel instead of the *apoluomenous tous logous* (the rational elements disengaged) with the Greek MSS.
46. Reading at 1248b2 *tois horōmenois* (visible things) with the Medieval Latin and Ross in place of the *tois eirēmenois* (things said) of the Greek MSS. The Latin would also add a "more strongly." An attractive alternative, suggested by Von Fragstein (1978: 377), would be to keep *eirēmenois*, change *tou* to *tōi*, and translate: ". . . the blind, being disengaged, remember more because their memory is attached to things said."

Chapter 3

The Quality of the Gentleman
What it is. *The virtue of the gentleman is that which is composed of all the individual virtues. To be good is one thing, to be a gentleman another. Those goods are ends that are preferred for their own sake, and those ends are noble that are praiseworthy, both they and their deeds (but health and the deeds of health, while they are good, are not to be praised). The good man is he for whom naturally good things, as honor and wealth and good fortune, are good and not harmful (as they are for the foolish and unjust and licentious). The*

gentleman is he who possesses and does the noble things for their own sake, that is, virtues and their deeds. Those who pursue the virtues for the sake of natural goods, like the Spartans, are wild and not gentlemen because not having the noble things for their own sake. Those who do have them for their own sake choose both them and the naturally good things, which are noble for them. For these are noble when chosen for noble ends, for the just is noble and the fitting is noble, and natural goods are deserving and fitting for the noble. Hence even advantageous things are noble for the gentleman. In the case of the many there is dissonance, for the simply good things are not good for them; and he who does noble things for the sake of external goods does noble things incidentally. Things simply pleasant are also noble and things simply good are pleasant. But pleasure comes about in action. Hence the happy man will live pleasantly.

1248b8   We spoke earlier about each particular virtue.[1] But since we divided up the power of them separately, we must also articulate the virtue composed of

b10   them, which we were already calling that of the noble and good, the gentleman.[2] Now it is manifest that he who is truly to get this appellation must have the particular virtues. For it cannot be otherwise in anything else either, for no one has his whole body healthy and yet not any part of it, but all the parts or most of them and the most controlling must be disposed the same way the whole is.

1248b16   Being good, then, and being a gentleman are different not only in their names but in themselves. For in all goods those are ends that are themselves preferable for their own sake. But among these all those are noble that, ex-

b20   isting on their own account, are praiseworthy. For they are those where the deeds as well as they themselves are praiseworthy—justice itself and its deeds, the temperate too, for temperance is also praiseworthy. But health is not a praiseworthy thing, for neither is its work; nor is strong action praiseworthy, for neither is strength; but while they are good they are not praiseworthy. The like is clear by induction in the case of the rest as well.

1248b26   Now a good man is he for whom the things naturally good are good. For the things that are fought over and seem to be the greatest goods—honor and wealth and virtues of body and good fortune and capacities—are by nature

b30   good but can, for certain people because of their habits, be a source of harm. For neither a fool nor someone who is unjust or licentious would get any benefit from using them, just as neither would the sick man from using the food of the healthy, nor the weak and maimed man from using the adornments of the

b35   sound and whole. But a gentleman is so because, among the goods, he has the noble ones on their own account, and because he does noble things for their own sake. Things noble are the virtues and the deeds resulting from virtue.

1248b37   There is a certain political habit that is the sort the Spartans have or that other such types might have. This is a habit of the following sort: that there are people who think it necessary to have virtue but for the sake of natural

a1   goods. Hence they are wild[3] men, for while they have the natural goods they do not have the quality of gentlemen; for they do not have noble things for their own sake.

But those who do have them for their own sake[4] in fact choose what is noble 1249a3 and good;[5] and not these things only, but also things that are not naturally noble but that, being naturally good, are noble for them. For they are noble a5 when what people do and choose them for is[6] noble things, because to the gentleman the naturally good things are noble. For what is just is noble, and the just is what accords with worth, and this man is worthy of these things. The fitting too is noble, and these things, wealth, good birth, power, are fitting for this man. As a result even very useful things themselves are, for the gentleman, noble too.

For the many, however, there is here dissonance, for the simply good things 1249a11 are not good in fact for them, though they are good to the good man. They are also noble to the good man, for he carries out many and noble actions through them. But the one who thinks he should have the virtues for the sake a15 of external goods does noble things incidentally. The quality of the gentleman, then, is complete virtue.

About pleasure, too, it has been said what sort of thing it is and how it 1249a17 is good, and that it is both the case that the simply pleasant things are also noble and that the simply good things too are pleasant.[7] But pleasure does not come about except in action. That is why the truly happy man will also a20 live most pleasantly, and it is not in vain that people make this claim.

What Its Target Is. The doctor has a mark by which to judge what is healthy. So also should the virtuous man for his actions, choices, and possession of natural goods. To say he should live as reason says is true but unclear. He should live by reference to the ruling element, as a slave does to his master and each thing to its principle, since a man too has a ruling and ruled element. The ruling element is either that which rules or the end it rules for, and thus it is with the contemplative part of the soul. God is ruler in the second way, and prudence gives orders for his sake, not for his benefit (god needs nothing) but for him as end. The choice and possession of natural goods, therefore, that most brings about contemplation of god, this is best and this mark is noble. What hinders the worship and service of god is base. So the soul's best condition and mark is to perceive least the other part of the soul.

Since the doctor too has a mark by reference to which he judges the healthy 1249a21 and non-healthy body, and by which he judges how far each thing should be done and is good for health (but if it is less or more, no longer so), thus also the virtuous man needs to have, as regards actions and choices of things that are naturally good but not praiseworthy, some mark both for habit and for a25 his choice, and as regards avoiding abundance and paucity of money and of the things of fortune.

1249b3   Now in the earlier arguments[8] the mark was said to be "as reason says." But this is as if someone were to say in matters of food "as medicine and medical reason say." This is true but not clear. So one should live, as in the case also of other things, by reference to the ruling element, that is, to the habit in actuality of the ruling element, as a slave does by reference to his master and each does to the principle appropriate to each.

1249b9   Since[9] man is in fact made up of a ruling and ruled element, and so each element should live by reference to its own principle—but this is double, for the medical art is a principle in one way and health in another, and the former is for the latter; and so it is with the contemplative part, for god is not ruler by giving orders but is he for whose sake prudence gives orders;[10] but "for the

b15   sake of" is double (the distinction has been made elsewhere,[11] since god at any rate does not need anything)—therefore whatever choice and possession of things good by nature, whether of body or money or friends or the other goods, will most bring about the contemplation of god, this is best and this mark most noble. But whatever choice and possession prevents by deficiency or by excess the worship and contemplation of god, this is base.

1249b21   And for the soul this holds and the soul's best mark is this: let it least perceive[12] the soul's other part insofar as it is such. About what gentlemanly quality's mark is, then, and what its target for things simply good, let this be

b25   our statement.

Notes

1. Book Three.
2. The Greek for the quality of a gentleman is *kalokagathia*, which means literally a combination of beauty or nobility and goodness.
3. The MSS at 1249a1 say *agrioi* (wild) but scholars, including Bekker, universally change it to *agathoi* (good). The change is unwarranted. Aristotle does think the Spartans were like wild beasts, and because they pursued virtue only for the sake of gain (*Politics* 2.9.1271a41–b17, 4(7).15.1334a40–b3, 5(8).4). The brutality of the Spartans when in possession of rule over others was notorious.
4. This phrase at 1249a3 does not appear in the Greek MSS and is supplied by scholars from the Medieval Latin.
5. Reading at 1249a4 *kalokagathon* (what is noble and good) with the Latin rather than *kaloi kagathoi* (gentlemen) with the Greek MSS and Bekker.
6. Reading at 1249a6 Fritzsche's emendation *ēi* (is) rather than *ē* (or) with the MSS and Bekker.
7. Book 6.11–14.
8. Book 5.1–5.
9. The way the Greek has been construed in translating this paragraph owes much to Verdenius (in Moraux and Harlfinger [1971: 285–94]).
10. Book 5.13.1145a6–11.
11. *Ibid.*, and *Metaphysics* 1072b2, *Physics* 194a32–36, *De Anima* 415b2. The distinction of "for the sake of" is between "for whose benefit" on the one hand and "for which end" on the other.
12. Reading *aisthanētai* (let it perceive) with some MSS rather than *aisthanesthai* (to perceive) with others and with Bekker.

Translation of *On Virtues and Vices*

Chapter 1

Virtues and Vices
General Classification

Praise is due to things noble; blame to things disgraceful. Among things noble $\quad$ 1249a26
the virtues lead the way; among things disgraceful the vices. Praise too is due
to the causes of the virtues, to what comes along with the virtues, to what
results from them, and to their deeds; blame to the contraries.

$\qquad$ The soul, to follow Plato, having three parts, of its calculating part pru- $\quad$ 1249a30
dence is virtue, of its spirited part mildness and courage, of its desiring part
temperance and continence, and of the whole soul justice and generosity and
magnanimity. Of its calculating part folly is vice, of its spirited part angriness $\quad$ b30
and cowardice, of its desiring part license and incontinence, of the whole soul
injustice and illiberality and smallness of soul.

Chapter 2

Definitions of Virtues

Prudence is a virtue of the calculating part that puts together what tends $\quad$ 1250a3
toward happiness. Mildness is a virtue of the spirited part that makes people
slow to get angry. Courage is a virtue of the spirited part that makes them hard
to panic in face of the fears of death. Temperance is a virtue of the desiring
part that takes away their appetite for enjoying base pleasures. Continence
is a virtue of the desiring part that makes them, through calculation, hold $\quad$ a10
back desire's drive for base pleasures. Justice is a virtue of soul that metes
out what is deserved. Liberality is a virtue of soul that spends well on things
fine. Magnanimity is a virtue of soul that makes people fit to bear good and
bad luck, honor and dishonor.

Chapter 3

Definitions of Vices

1250a16 Folly, a vice of the calculating part, is cause of living badly. Angriness is a vice of the spirited part that makes people quick to get angry. Cowardice is a vice

a20 of the spirited part that makes them panic in face of fears and those of death most of all. License is a vice of the spirited part that makes them prefer joy in base pleasures. Incontinence is a vice of the desiring part that makes them

a25 prefer base pleasures even though calculation forbids.[1] Injustice is a vice of soul that makes them grasp for more contrary to desert. Illiberality is a vice of soul that gives them appetite for everywhere making gain. Smallness of soul is a vice of soul that unfits them to bear good and bad luck, honor and dishonor.

Note

1.   An alternative MSS reading for this sentence at 1250a23–25, printed by Bekker, would give: "Incontinence is a vice of the desiring part whereby they hurry on by unreason the desire that is pushing them to enjoyments of base pleasures."

Chapter 4

Accompaniments, Consequences, and Deeds of Virtues and Vices
Of Virtues
Prudence, Mildness, Courage, Temperance

1250a30 It belongs to prudence to deliberate, to judge things good and bad and all that in life one should prefer and avoid, to make noble use of all the good that comes to hand, to hold right converse, to take full view of occasions, to be quick witted in use both of word and of deed, to be experienced in all things

a35 useful. Memory and experience and quick wit are each of them either from prudence or go along with prudence. Or some of them are like joint causes of prudence, as are experience and memory, and others are like parts of it, like good deliberation and quick wit.

1250a39 It belongs to mildness to be able to bear complaints and slights in a measured way, and not to be quickly driven to revenge nor easily moved to anger, not bitter in character and not a lover of strife, having peace and steadiness in one's soul.

190

It belongs to courage to be hard to panic under the fears of death, and to 1250a44 be bold readily in terrible things, and to dare dangers well, and to take rather noble death than disgraceful safety, and to be cause of victory. Further, it also belongs to courage to toil and to be steadfast and to act the man's part. Along with courage come daring and good cheer and boldness, love of toil too and steadfast endurance.

It belongs to temperance not to marvel at enjoyments of bodily plea- 1250b6 sures, and to have no appetite for any pleasure of shameful enjoying, and to fear disorder,[1] and to live an orderly life in things both small and great. b10 Along with moderation come good order, decorum, a sense of shame, caution.

Note
1.   Other MSS would read: "a just ill repute."

Chapter 5

Continence, Justice, Liberality, Magnanimity

It belongs to continence to be able to hold back desire by calculation when 1250b12 it drives toward base enjoyments and pleasures, and to be steadfast, and to withstand the need and pain of nature.

It belongs to justice to mete out what is deserved, and to keep ancestral 1250b15 customs and norms, to keep the written laws, and to speak truth in things that matter, and to guard agreements. First among claims of right are those to the gods, next to spirits,[1] next to fatherland and parents, next to the departed; b20 among these claims is also piety, being either a part of justice or coming along with it. With justice there also come holiness and truth and faith and hatred of wickedness.

It belongs to liberality to be openhanded with money for things praise- 1250b24 worthy, and lavish in spending on anything needful, and to be helpful in things that matter,[2] and not to take from where one should not. The liberal man is also clean in his dress and his dwelling, and is fond of getting for himself things out of the ordinary and beautiful and that afford pleasant and cultivated leisure b30 without bringing profit, and he is a nurturer of animals that have something out of the way or wondrous to them. Along with liberality come easiness of character and a winning way and love of mankind and being merciful and a lover of friends and a lover of strangers and a lover of beauty.

It belongs to magnanimity to bear nobly luck both good and bad and honor 1250b34 and dishonor, and to marvel not at luxury or attention or power or victories in games, but to have a certain depth and largeness of soul. Also magnanimous is not he who sets much store by being alive or is fond of being alive, but is simple in character and genuine, able to bear wrong, and not spiteful. Along with magnanimity come simplicity and truth.

b40

Notes

1.   The Greek is *daimones*.
2.   Or alternatively at 1250b27, "matters of dispute"; the Greek is ambiguous.

Chapter 6

Of Vices
Folly, Anger, Cowardice, License, Incontinence

1250b43   It belongs to folly to judge things badly, to be bad in deliberation, to hold bad converse, to use badly the goods that come to hand, to have false opinions about what is noble and good for life. Along with folly come inexperience, poor learning, incontinence, ham-fistedness, forgetfulness.

1251a3   There are three kinds of angriness: belligerence, bitterness, sullenness. It belongs to the angry man not to be able to bear small slights or put downs, and to retaliate and take revenge, and to be moved to anger easily at any chance deed and word. Along with angriness come being prickly of character and fickle and bitter of speech, and being irked at trifles, and feeling these things quickly and on slight occasion.

1251a10   It belongs to cowardice to be easily moved by any chance fear and by fears of death and bodily maiming above all, and to suppose that it is better to win safety by any means than to die nobly. Along with cowardice come softness, unmanliness, shirking of toil,[1] love of life. There is also under it a certain cautiousness and submissiveness of character.

1251a16   It belongs to license to take enjoyment in harmful and disgraceful pleasures, and to suppose that they are most of all happy who live in such pleasures, and to be fond of laughter and mockery and witticisms, and to be reckless in words and deeds. Along with license come disorder, shamelessness, lack of decorum, luxury, slackness, carelessness, contempt, looseness.

1251a23   It belongs to incontinence to take enjoyment in pleasures when calculation forbids it, and though supposing it better not to take part in them, to take part in them nevertheless, and to think one ought to do what is noble and of advantage but to turn away through pleasure. Along with incontinence come softness and carelessness and most of the same things that also come along with license.

Note

1.   Or at 1251a15, instead of *aponia* (shirking of toil) some MSS read *aponoia* (unbalance of mind).

Chapter 7

Injustice, Illiberality, Smallness of Soul

There are three kinds of injustice: impiety, greed, wanton violence. Impiety   1251a30
is trespass with respect to gods and spirits and the departed and parents
and fatherland. Greed is trespass with respect to contracts, taking what is in
dispute[1] contrary to desert. Wanton violence is that by which they procure
pleasures for themselves while leading others into things of reproach, hence   a35
Evenus says about it "she that getting no gain yet does wrong." It belongs to
injustice to transgress ancestral customs and norms, and to disobey the laws
and the rulers, to lie, to commit perjury, to transgress agreements and pledges.   b1
Along with injustice come slander, imposture, pretense of philanthropy, evil
character, unscrupulous behavior.

Of illiberality there are three kinds: love of base gain, penny pinching, and   1251b4
cheapness. Love of base gain is what makes people seek gain everywhere and
put more stock by the gain than by the shame. Penny pinching makes them
not spend money on what is needful. Cheapness is what makes them spend
indeed but a little and badly, and suffer greater loss by not doing what matters[2]
at the right time. It belongs to illiberality to put most store by money, and   b10
to think nothing matter of reproach that makes profit—a menial and servile
and sordid way of life, foreign to honor and liberality. Along with illiberality
come petty speech, sullenness, smallness of soul, lowness, lack of measure,
no breeding, hatred of mankind.

It belongs to smallness of soul to be able to bear neither honor nor dishonor   1251b16
nor good luck nor bad, but when in honor to be conceited and when lucky in
trifles to put on airs, to be unable to put up with even the least dishonor, to
judge any chance mishap a great misfortune, to be grieved at all things and to   b20
take everything badly. Further, the man small of soul is like to call any slight
a wanton violence and a dishonor, even those that happen out of ignorance
or forgetfulness. Along with smallness of soul come petty speech, readiness
to blame, despair, lowness.   b25

Notes

1.   Or at 1251a34 *to diaphoron* could be rendered "the superior part."
2.   Or if at 1251b10 instead of *poieisthai* (doing) one reads the emendation *prohesthai*, the sense will be "not letting go the difference at the right time."

Chapter 8

In General

1251b26   In general it belongs to virtue to make one's disposition of soul virtuous, with use of emotions peaceful and ordered, in harmony in all its parts. That is why a virtuous disposition of soul seems to be also model of a good regime. It

b30   belongs to virtue both to benefit those who deserve it, and to love those who are good and hate those who are base, not to be inclined to punish nor to take revenge, but to be gracious and kind and forgiving. Along with virtue come

b35   usefulness, decency, kindliness, optimism, and further such things as love of home and of friends and of comrades and of strangers and of mankind and of beauty—which indeed are all among things praised.

1251b37   Of vice are things opposite and what comes along with it are things opposite. All that belongs to vice and comes along with it is among things blamed.

Book One: The Science of Happiness

Chapter 1

Introduction to the Science
Worth, Nature, and Questions of This Science
The *Eudemian Ethics* begins and ends with god, but with the popular god 1214a1
(referred to by his popular genealogy) and a poet at the beginning,[1] and with
a philosophical and cosmic god and the gentleman, the man of "nobility and
goodness," at the end. The latter is also preferred to the former, for what the
poet says in the presence of the popular god is stated only to be at once rejected, and what it is rejected for, as the long argument in the intervening books
makes plain, is what the gentleman does in the presence of the philosophical
and cosmic god at the end. We are entitled to presume that this fact about
the treatise's composition is not to be taken lightly. As confirmation we may
adduce the opening chapters of this first book, which are as much marked by
their style[2] as by their rejection of popular opinions and their replacement of
them with the opinions of a man, the philosopher Anaxagoras, noted for fleeing
Athens on a charge of impiety. The *Eudemian Ethics* is an extended defense of
the life and the god of Anaxagoras, or the life and god of philosophy. It is a work
for and of philosophers. Were Aristotle so minded, and should the populace
consent, it might be what he would set up before the god in Delos. It would
be the *apologia pro vita sua* that he would offer to replace that of the poet.

If so, the god should be pleased. For the poet, who says that the pleasant
and the good are not the same as the noble and just, is encouraging people to
commit injustice, including the injustice of impiety, to get the pleasure and
goodness they want. The philosopher who says that the best and noblest thing
is also the pleasantest is doing the reverse. He is saying that that which is in
itself best, the noble, is also best for us. (Aristotle merely assumes the thesis
here, but the rest of the treatise is an extended defense of it, with the final
Book Eight as a sort of crowning summary.)[3] The contrary assumption of the
poet, as of most men, that the best or pleasantest for us is not necessarily the
best in itself or the noblest and justest, together with the unspoken inference
that it is sometimes best for us to do what is unjust, is here simply repudiated
by Aristotle. The philosopher, not the poet, is pious.

So much is already hinted at by Aristotle in his opening lines. Philosophers 1214a8
will note the hint if the poets and the populace do not. But philosophers want
argument, not poetry, especially not poetry that is impious. So Aristotle gives
them argument, and straightaway, from the remarks just made. For if what

is best and pleasantest and noblest is disputed, and if the best and pleasantest and noblest is what we want so as to live well, then the dispute must be examined. But examinations, which are as such theoretical exercises, are not all the same, for some are simply theoretical and aim at knowledge alone while others aim beyond it to getting and doing. Clearly, as even the poet knows, the best and noblest and pleasantest is something to get and do. So the necessary conclusion is that merely theoretical philosophizing must here be set aside, for living well is a getting of something and not just a knowing of it.

Aristotle seems nowhere to return to simply theoretical philosophizing in this treatise. Such philosophizing looks rather to be what the "good and noble" gentleman will undertake at the end through worship and contemplation of the god. One should perhaps, therefore, not judge the reference to theorizing that aims at knowledge and theorizing that aims at practice as indicative of any division of parts, whether specific or general, within this treatise.[4] A division into specific parts does, however, immediately follow.

1214a14 The division is into the questions of what living well is found in and of how it is acquired, which are both, as subsequent remarks confirm, cases of theorizing that aims at practice. The two questions are, anyway, the necessary questions to ask if the aim is to live well, for no aim can be attained if we do not know, first, what the aim is and, second, how to get it. These questions can be used to divide suitably the whole of the treatise that follows, though Aristotle largely leaves us to do it for ourselves. What he himself immediately does is run through the prevailing opinions about the questions. He does so, as is not seldom his wont, in reverse order, beginning first with opinions about the how and second with those about the what.

Happiness, then, is said to be acquired by nature, or by learning, or by exercise and habituation, or by divine possession (a "charmed life" as we might say), or by chance. No other options are anyway available, adds Aristotle, for everything that comes to be (and happiness is clearly something that comes to be) comes to be in one or other of these ways. Even thoughts, which also come to be when we contemplate, fall somehow under the coming to be that is learning. Desire and wish, we might add, will fall under nature or habituation or both (depending on whether the desire is natural or acquired), and force will fall under some one or more of the listed headings since forced things are forced by some other thing and that other thing, if it is itself not forced by another, must be acting in some one of the ways mentioned.[5]

1214a30 As for the what of happiness or what it is found in, the prevailing opinions are three: that it is found in prudence or in virtue or in pleasure, though there are also disputes about which of these contributes more to happiness and whether happiness comes from all three or just two or one of them. We might immediately wonder why other candidates are not mentioned, such as money or fame or power. But such things are in fact mentioned next, and with requisite nuance.

Notes

1. Von Fragstein (1974: 13), Buddensiek (1999: 44).
2. As in particular the absence of hiatus; Dirlmeier (1962: 144).
3. Contra Woods (1992: 43–44). There is no parallel to Book Eight of *EE* in *EN*. A likely reason is that *EN*, being directed primarily to legislators, adopts the aim of legislators, and this aim is the best for man (legislation takes that best for its object) and not also the best in itself. That the best in itself is also, in fact, the best for man is not denied in *NE* (nor in the *Politics*, which is its complement), but it is not there thematized. It is however, in its form as the noble, perhaps the main theme of *EE*.
4. Contra Dirlmeier (1962: 146–47), Rowe (1971: 15n4, 70–71) in Moraux and Harlfinger (1971: 87 and n67). Kenny (1978: 191–2).
5. Gigon (1969: 205, 210–11) sees this passage about causes as ironic, but unnecessarily.

Chapter 2

Review of Others' Opinions
Reasons for Disputed Opinions about Happiness

The Greek of the opening sentence here as given in the manuscripts is dubious in its grammatical form but not impossible of the construal that, following Dirlmeier,[1] is given in the translation. The question concerns rather the resulting sense, for it seems implausible to say that everyone *does* in fact set up some target to aim at in life. Hence some editors suggest adding a "should"[2] to produce the sense that everyone *should* set up such a target, even if many do not. The original sense can, however, be preserved if the point is stressed that the people who do in fact set up a target are described as those who can live by their own deliberate choice (1214b6–7). Since one cannot live by one's own deliberate choice if one does not have leisure from necessities but is forced to be a slave or to work for one's living,[3] the sense will be that those with the requisite leisure who do not set up some target for their life are not, after all, living by their own choice. They may, indeed, do particular acts by choice (as even a slave might), but they are not living by choice. Rather their life is a series of disconnected decisions that do not constitute a deliberately chosen whole. They are living haphazardly, as it were, or without thought, which is what Aristotle adds by saying that it is a sign of much folly not to order one's life in view of a goal. It is a sign of much folly because although, *ex hypothesi*, one has the leisure to live one's life by deliberate choice, one is not doing so but following the chances and changes of the moment. One is thus throwing away command over one's life and, whether one admits it or not, living like a slave in dependence on external necessities.

If, however, there are people who choose to make choices as the occasion determines, who choose as it were to live haphazardly, then they are setting up a goal of life, namely the goal to live haphazardly. Such people, even if their choice is a poor one, have at least embraced the idea of organizing their life in view of some target. They are, therefore, in principle open to the sort of discussion Aristotle now embarks on, about what the target should be. Since they consider the question relevant (for they have an answer to it), they cannot dismiss out of hand discussion of what the answer really should be, whether the choice they have already made or a different one. On the other hand, people who live haphazardly, without choosing to do so but just going along with the flow, as we say, are no fit audience for the present treatise. For those who care not to plan their lives can care naught for finding answers to the questions of what happiness is and how it is to be achieved.[4]

Confining attention, then, to those who live by some sort of deliberate choice, Aristotle mentions things like honor and repute and wealth and education as targets set up for choice, or precisely things he did not mention at the end of the previous chapter where he listed only prudence, virtue, and pleasure. An explanation of the difference can be found in Aristotle's argument here, since living by deliberate choice means setting up some target of noble living; therefore we must define with care which of "the things that are ours" and that we therefore have some choice over is what living well consists in.

The things that are ours are, however, more than the constituents that such living consists in and include also the conditions that such living cannot exist without. The distinction is evident from health, where what constitutes health (as good state of body) and what are necessary conditions for health (as food and exercise) are not the same. The implication (confirmed by what follows in the next chapters) is that some at least among the listed targets, honor and repute and wealth and education, cannot count as constituents of happiness but only as conditions. The three listed in the previous chapter, prudence and virtue and pleasure, can, by contrast, all count as constituents and do all end up, after suitable qualifications, as actually being constituents.

1214b17   The point about constituents and conditions and its importance is illustrated by a distinction between things common and things private or special. Breathing, waking, and moving are common to all our habits and actions and not just to the habit of health or to the action of life; eating meat and walks after meals are special to a good bodily habit. The importance of this distinction between the common and the special would seem to be that common conditions could not easily be confused with constituents, although the special conditions could. For constituents are proper to the thing of which they are the constituents, so that common conditions, not being proper, will be seen at once not to be constituents; but special conditions, by contrast, since they are proper, may thus more easily, but still falsely, be seen to be constituents. The disputes about happiness, therefore, will concern confusions about constituents and special conditions and not about constituents and common conditions.[5]

There is, however, a further confusion to notice, which Aristotle does not so much mention as gesture to. For what, in the examples he gives, is to be taken as a condition for what? Are eating meat and walking after meals to be taken as conditions for a good bodily state? Or is a good bodily state to be taken as a condition for eating meat and walking after meals? To use the broader example, is health to be taken as a condition for life or life as a condition for health? Both ways of taking the examples seem legitimate and serve the purpose. So which way does Aristotle intend? Or does he intend both ways indifferently and is he thus further intending that we should notice the ambiguity? If so, then the problem of confusing constituents and conditions in the case of happiness is not just a matter of special conditions looking like constituents but also of constituents becoming special conditions and special conditions becoming constituents depending on which we take as prior. For if we take good bodily state as prior, eating meat will become a condition; but if we take eating meat as prior, good bodily state will become a condition. Perhaps it is obvious to most of us that eating is generally for the sake of health and not heath for the sake of eating, but some think otherwise, as gluttons perhaps. So another source of confusion and of dispute about happiness seems to be lurking here as well.

Perhaps it is too much to suppose Aristotle could intend so much in so few words, but it is a feature of *EE*, in contrast with *NE*, to pack a lot into a little[6] (such is what a philosophical audience will, after all, both expect and enjoy). Indeed the compact density of its reasoning is not a little responsible (as will be noted at relevant points) for the textual problems under which it has long been known to labor. What we may notice here, though, is that if Aristotle does intend so much to be noticed from so little, it will help explain why he thinks that disputes about happiness arise from confusing conditions and constituents. For we might think, on the contrary, that these disputes have other causes too.[7] But if the confusion is not only about thinking a condition is a constituent but also, since a constituent taken in one way is a condition taken in another, about which way to take each alleged constituent or condition, then the claim that confusion about constituents and conditions is at the bottom of disputes about happiness does indeed seem plausible. In Aristotle's understanding, those people, for instance, who think thought is for the sake of action and therefore deny that thinking could be happiness and say that something else must be (as pleasure or fame or power), will be guilty of confusing conditions and constituents because they are guilty of looking at thinking under its aspect as a condition (for thinking is a condition for successful pursuit of power or fame or pleasure) and not under its aspect as a constituent (the way that Anaxagoras, for instance, looked at it).

Notes

1. Dirlmeier (1962: 155).
2. Woods (1992: 185–86).
3. Dirlmeier ibid.
4. See also Buddensiek (1999: 50–54) for a similar interpretation.
5. The point is made by Dirlmeier (1962: 157), whose interpretation is, to this extent, to be preferred to Wood's (1992: 48–49).
6. Dirlmeier (1962: 363, also cf. 199) speaks, in this regard, of Aristotle's "Brachylogie" in *EE*; also Von Fragstein (1974: 397), Jost (2001: 208, 213), Kenny (1992: 115, 141), Lieberg (1958: 120), Mingay (1987: 27, 29, 31), Mueller-Goldingen (in Steinmetz [1990: 19]), Natali (2007: 368–75).
7. As Woods, ibid.

Chapter 3

Which Opinions to Consider

1214b28   Differences of opinion, then, arise for the above stated reason, but not all opinions are worth considering. Those who do not bother even to set up a target for living well lack, as we have seen, a relevant opinion to begin with. The same goes for those who may give voice to some opinion about happiness but whose opinion cannot be taken seriously, such as children and the ill and the insane. Such people do not need argument and discussion, for they are incapable of the relevant degree of it. Rather they need either to grow up or to be punished, whether medically to get rid of the disease or politically to get rid of the folly. For by folly Aristotle must mean, not the folly that is the result of disease (which would require a medical cure), but the folly that is the result of wickedness, since it is to wickedness that political punishment is directed. All men may by nature be reasoning animals but not all are by nature in a fit state to reason with.

Thus too the opinions to be examined cannot be those of the many alone, for their opinions are stated at random and without serious thought. The many therefore should not be reasoned with (for they, like criminals, need to suffer so as first to be brought to a saner mind), but their opinions nevertheless deserve examination, for even what is said at random may, despite itself, happen to have some sense to it, especially if it is said often and by many. But they should not be the only ones examined. The opinions of those who do not speak at random should be examined too, and more so.

1215a3   These other opinions Aristotle mentions now in effect by mentioning that every undertaking has puzzles proper to it. For those who engage seriously in the undertaking, as the sane of mind must certainly do in the case of the best life, will not fail to notice such puzzles or to express opinions about them. So we should put these opinions to the test, since, as a matter of logic, the refutation of an opinion is a proof of its contradictory and thus a way to establish what the truth is. The truth will determine our hope. The whole investigation is aimed, as is evident, not merely at knowing what living nobly is, but at the sources of being able to share in it, and so at our hope of getting each of the decent things relevant to it.

The opinions and the things to examine are twofold: what living nobly is 1215a12 and how it comes about, which, as suggested before, is the division that drives the whole treatise. The answer to the first question will determine the answer to the second, and the answer to the second will determine our hope. For if living nobly is a thing that depends on what is not up to us or in our care, as chance or nature, then most of us will have no hope of it because there will be nothing we ourselves can do to get it. Those who have it will have it by chance or nature regardless of what anyone does. On the other hand, if it depends on our character and our deeds, then it will be something we can hope for, because it will be "more common and more divine" (1215a16–17). It will be more common because it is open also to those who lack the advantages of nature or chance (regardless of how many actually make use of the opportunity thus offered),[1] and it will be more divine because happiness will belong to those who give themselves and their deeds a certain character (1215a19). Aristotle does not state but implies the reason for this last remark. What is in our control, and not what is in the control of nature or chance, makes us divine. For the divine is divine by its goodness, but most of us are not good by nature or by chance; we are good by the character and deeds that we ourselves make. Hence happiness must be more divine if it is a question of character and deeds, for only thus, for most of us, could it be something good like the deity. That it will thereby also be something we can hope for shows that, in the case of happiness, our hope is in becoming like god.

Note

1. Woods doubts happiness will be more common if it is in our control (1992: 50). Aristotle's point would seem to be that it will be more common in opportunity if not also in achievement.

Chapter 4

Summary of Opinions

So far Aristotle has given reasons for examining opinions and outlined which 1215a20 sort of opinions alone deserve to be examined. He has not, except incidentally and by way of illustration, listed what these opinions are. So he gives that list now but in a certain order. For, as is evident and as is now expressly said, the disputes and puzzles that are at issue in the rival opinions will be clear if the question about what happiness is, and not the question about how it comes to be, is answered first. Aristotle then adds that getting the definition right turns on whether happiness is a matter only of one's being of a certain sort in one's soul, or whether one must indeed be of a certain sort but, more, one's deeds must be of a certain sort. The first opinion is attributed to certain unnamed sages and elders.

The curiosities here are several. First, if happiness is a matter of the character of the soul or also of the deeds, then the question raised at the end of the previous chapter, about what happiness depends on, is being begged and not answered. For the only options being canvassed for definitions of happiness will be those that do not depend on nature or chance but on us, namely on our character or on our being "of a certain sort in our soul" (1215a22–23). The second curiosity concerns the sages and elders and why they are mentioned and who they are. The third curiosity concerns the discussion of the three lives that next follows and how it is meant to further the investigation into whether happiness is a matter of the character of the soul or also of the deeds.

An approach to unraveling these curiosities may begin with the fact that the opinion attributed to the sages and elders is how one is like "in one's soul" and not how one is like "oneself." There is a view common in the ancient poets, including especially Homer, that the sort of life one has, whether happy or miserable, is determined by the gods and the fates. According to this view, then, the good life of happiness does not depend on oneself or on what one does but on what one is like "in one's soul," that is, in what fate one's soul was allotted at birth by the gods. If so, the first and second curiosities are readily unraveled because the question about what happiness depends on, whether it is or is not something in one's control, is not being begged but rather restated, and because the sages and elders will be the traditional poets of Greek education,[1] who are here rightly introduced as being "the sages and elders" of traditional culture and as teaching that happiness depends on fate and the nature one gets from fate. The other option that Aristotle then sets alongside theirs is the proper and expected alternative that happiness depends, not on what fate or something else does, but on what one oneself does, namely one's deeds and the character one thus forms through one's deeds.

1215a25   The third curiosity, about the division of lives that follows, can be unraveled accordingly. First, however, the division needs to be stated. But here a problem arises, for most editors and commentators want to change the text and to insert a "not,"[2] so that its opening sentence reads "Since ways of life fall into groups, and since some of these do *not* lay claim . . ." (a26). The reason for making the addition is that the lives first listed are all dismissed as not really being about happiness but as for the sake of necessities, and only the three lives listed at the end are regarded as serious competitors for the title. But the addition is unnecessary, for Aristotle can be taken instead as making the point that, although the first listed lives *claim* happiness, their claim cannot be taken seriously because they are not pursued as happy but as necessary.

The lives that make this false claim are said to be three: those devoted to the vulgar arts or to business or to the mechanical arts. The way the first of these is described is peculiar: they are those that people carry on "just for glory." The word for glory (*doxa*) could also mean mere repute or even opinion. The ambiguity seems deliberate. Aristotle is speaking in such a way that the Homeric heroes, in addition to many artisans, can also be numbered among those who carry on these vulgar arts, for what these did was a physical exercise, wielding arms, for the simple sake of glory. Wielding a sword or a spear is, as far as its physical exercise goes, little different from wielding a hammer or a chisel, and since this physical wielding is not for its own sake but for glory in the one case and some useful product in the other, rightly might it be called vulgar. Singers of heroic tales, like Homer himself and his epigones, will be in the same division, for they wield the lyre or kithara for glory—the glory that their poems or their recitals bring them. To the extent, however, poets and singers may also sit "for pay," their life will, unlike that of the heroes they sing of, fall under the mechanical arts too. The third division, into business, seems to stand more apart, since it is about selling, either in the marketplace or by foreign trade. But Homer's heroes engaged in foreign trade, either by sheer brigandage and piracy when they went on raids to get provisions and trophies,[3] or by elaborate exchanging of gifts, which even if they did not give money for, they always measured by monetary value.[4] These raids and exchanges are not conventional selling, but they are not far off either.

Of course Aristotle is not excluding from his divisions those more commonly thought to be engaged in the vulgar and mechanical arts and in business (artisans, mechanics, petty traders, and the like). It should, however, be stressed, as an unraveling of the third curiosity mentioned above, that he is also not excluding from those who live lives devoted to necessities the heroes on the one hand, whose happiness depends on fate, and the "sages and elders" on the other, who celebrate the fact.[5] Such a demoting of the claims about happiness of the likes of Homer and Achilles has, to be sure, more the form of a rebuke than a refutation, but as the next division of lives highlights, it contains the elements of a refutation. (To anticipate, the elements are: (1) the happy life is not a necessary but a leisurely life; (2) the happy life is a divine and human life; (3) therefore, from (2), the happy life depends on us, and, from (1), it is not a matter of necessities, which do not depend on us and are not leisurely.)

Setting aside, then, the necessary lives and their false claim to happiness, Aristotle lists those that, as he says, are drawn up with a view to "a happiness of cultured pursuits." Since Homer's heroes seem to be lurking behind Aristotle's words at this point, we should perhaps be reminded of the cultured pursuits or pastime that these heroes claimed to enjoy, which was not in wielding swords against the foe beneath the lofty walls of Ilium; rather, to quote the words of Odysseus that Aristotle himself quotes in his *Politics*, the best pastime is when "the feasters, seated in order up and down the hall, listen to a bard."[6] It matters not that the bard they listen to is more than likely singing of the deeds of war, for listening to heroic deeds is not the same act as performing them. Rather is it the relaxed enjoyment of them in poetic imitation. It will fall, therefore, under one of the three goods of virtue and prudence and pleasure that Aristotle now mentions, and in particular it will fall under pleasure. True, Aristotle goes on to describe the pleasure in question as bodily, but the pleasures of feasting are bodily and so are those of music insofar as they are delights of the ear. They are cultured pleasures that are bodily.[7] They are also described as being, along with the goods of virtue and prudence, the greatest possible for men and the goods chosen by those who are in power and so who, unlike those from the first division of the necessary lives, are not doing one thing in order to get some other and necessary thing, but who can do at once the very thing they want, whether politics or philosophy or indulgence.

1215b1   The life of philosophy is said to be about prudence and the study of truth (so that "prudence" is here taken in a loose way to mean study of any truth and not just practical truth),[8] the life of politics about noble deeds or the deeds of virtue, and the life of indulgence about bodily pleasure. The mention of the last of the three is followed immediately by remarks from Anaxagoras saying to a questioner that the happiest man is not anyone the questioner is thinking of, and by remarks from Aristotle saying that the questioner was thinking of someone great or rich or noble, but Anaxagoras was thinking of someone living painlessly in justice and divine contemplation. The questioner, then, was thinking of the life of bodily pleasure as best, for bodily pleasures both naturally attend the noble and are always at the command of the great and rich. Anaxagoras was thinking of some life of philosophy but such a life as was not marred by pain or sullied by injustice, and so a life of philosophy that was not lacking in either virtue or pleasure, though different pleasures.[9] The questioner, by contrast, is not said to have included anything about study or justice in his view of the happy life. The philosopher is being pious, unlike the questioner, for on the latter's view the happy man, provided he is noble or rich or great, could well be a fool and a knave. The questioner is thus following Homer and the other sages and elders[10] in placing happiness in things like beauty and greatness and wealth, which, first, are among things necessary; second, could only make up a kind of life if the aim of that life were glory and the supply of bodily pleasures; and third, depend for their presence less on us or our deeds than on our birth or our fortune or the whimsy of the poetic gods. No wonder Aristotle highlights Anaxagoras instead.

Notes

1.   And so not, as Dirlmeier opines (1962: 163), certain members of Plato's Academy.
2.   A notable exception is Von Fragstein (1974: 20), whose larger interpretation, however, is not followed here.

3. It is precisely such a raid that furnishes the occasion for the whole action of the *Iliad*, for Achilles' wrath stems from what happened after the raid to the girl he kidnapped in the raid for his concubine, *Iliad* 1.
4. The Odysseus of the *Odyssey* is the notorious example, but Diomedes in the *Iliad* (quoted later at 4.9.1136b9–11) is almost as notorious.
5. Contra Woods (1992: 51).
6. *Politics* 5(8).3.1338a27–30, quoting *Odyssey* 9.5–6.
7. As in the physical attachment of Achilles to Patroclus.
8. See the discussion in the comments on Book Five and in the Introduction.
9. Again contra Woods (1992: 51, 53).
10. A point rightly noted by Dirlmeier (1962: 168–69) who says the questioner is here functioning as "Vertreter der alten Adelsethik" (representative of the ancient ethic of the nobility).

Chapter 5

Discussion of Opinions
The Different Ways of Life

The opinions have so far been summarized rather than discussed, though   1215b15
enough has been implied to indicate how they should be discussed. Aristotle
starts that discussion now, but he is inevitably led by it beyond the limits of the
introduction he has so far been conducting into starting the science proper,
for the opinions, though important, are only the beginning.

It is a truism that, in the case of many and different things, making a right
and noble judgment is not easy, but strangely, there is one topic that, by
contrast, everyone thinks very easy, the topic of what makes life worth living.
But they are mistaken, for the topic is one of the hardest. People presumably think it is easy (though Aristotle himself gives no explanation), because
everyone has to live and no one can go on living if he does not think life worth
living. So everyone, perforce, must both have and act on an opinion about
what makes life worth living. But if everyone must have such an opinion, then
surely everyone must be naturally equipped to form one, and a correct one
too, since otherwise we will have to swallow the unpalatable consequence that
most people are ignorant of what they cannot afford to be ignorant of and
are living wholly irrational lives. Human folly would thus be almost universal
and almost unavoidable.

One can, of course, swallow this consequence, and Socrates notoriously did
(in saying that he only surpassed others by knowing that he did not know); but
if one does not want to imitate him, one will be forced to say that the opinions
of all or most people about what is good in life are correct. But since people
differ from each other in their opinions, and even indeed from themselves
at different times, their opinions can only be correct if the only standard of

correctness is the opinions themselves or, in other words, if what seems so to someone is so just because it so seems to him. The Protagorean thesis that each man is the measure for himself of good and bad would thus have to be true. What this thesis reduces to in practice is that the good is pleasure. For a person can know at once and without mistake if something pleases him, so he can know at once and without mistake what the good is if the good is pleasure. But, further, the pleasures that most men know at once and without mistake are the bodily pleasures, for these are the obvious pleasures. So the thesis that most men are not ignorant of the good or of what makes life worth living reduces to the thesis that the good is the physically pleasant.

This set of inferences seems clearly at the back of Aristotle's mind, for he now proceeds to make a series of remarks that serve to undermine these inferences by showing that if the good is physical pleasure then life is very far from being worth living.[1] First he mentions kinds of painful disasters that people kill themselves for, as disease, anguish, and storms (or bodily torment, emotional torment, and external torment). So if physical pleasure is the good and if these are the sorts of things that afflict one's life, then one's life was not worth living, and it would have been better not to have been born to begin with.

1215b22   The conclusion can be strengthened by noting that birth is followed by childhood and that childhood is not anything that someone with sense would want to return to. Childhood no doubt has many pleasures, but it has many pains too, as in particular the pain of being subject to and dependent on others, which those who treasure physical pleasure as the good of life would hate to have to endure again. Such dependence means not having the pleasures one wants (parents and guardians forbid them) and having the pains one does not want (as the pains of punishment and enforced learning). It is far better to be an adult and pursue one's own pleasures as one wishes than suffer the restraints of childhood. Further, there are many things even in adulthood that are either neutral as to pleasure or, if pleasant, are base, so that not having them is better than having them or not living is better than living.

Indeed, generally, if one brings together "everything that everyone does or undergoes but not voluntarily because not for its own sake," that is, not for any intrinsic good they have, then even a life indefinitely extended would not be more worth living. At least, such is the calculation one must come to if the intrinsic good of things is physical pleasure. For, generally speaking the things that have this pleasure are outweighed by the things that are either neutral and lack it or are positively painful. So if the balance in life is thus negative, it will remain negative however long life is extended.

1215b30   The calculation is not changed even if we make as an assumption that the pleasures of food and sex, or the pleasures of touch, remain but the pleasures of knowledge and the other senses are taken away. For while we would, on this assumption, escape the pains that come through knowledge and other

206

senses, as in particular anxiety about the future or regret about the past, yet we would, besides losing the contrasting pleasures (as those of thinking, music, painting, perfumery, and the like), also lose everything that makes us human. For animals enjoy the pleasures of food and sex no less than we. Indeed, as Aristotle notes dryly, the ox worshipped in Egypt as the god Apis enjoys more privileges here than many monarchs.

Nor is the calculation changed if, in order to remove all occasions of sorrow and distress, we imagine having only the pleasures of sleep. For this assumption, however long the sleep is supposed to last, reduces us below the level even of oxen to that of plants and children in the womb. 1216a2

All these considerations have been made on the implicit assumption that the goods that make life worth living are predominantly or only those of physical pleasure, especially the pleasures of touch. But if this assumption is the one we make, then the upshot is that what is good in life just escapes us.

Aristotle has thus effectively removed the opinion that what makes life worth living could, at least for most of us, be a matter of physical pleasure. For, despite all the attractions, theoretical and practical, that that opinion initially seems to have, there is, to say nothing of other things, not enough pleasure in most lives to outweigh all the pain and absence of pleasure that is there as well. So not unnaturally Aristotle turns to discuss other opinions. 1216a10

He begins by going back to Anaxagoras who, in answer to the question what makes life worth living, said it was study of the heavens and the cosmos, or a life of knowledge of some kind. This answer (which must not be taken as excluding the elements of purity and painlessness that Aristotle says it had when it was introduced earlier) is the answer that recurs, and is endorsed, at the end of the treatise (8.3). Here it is stated without elaboration. But it is stated first, and so it is privileged as the first plausible answer to what makes life worth living. For since this answer does not turn on physical pleasures, it escapes the objections Aristotle has just raised against that opinion.

The second answer (from people who admire Sardanapalus, Smindyrides, and the like) seems to be a return to the above opinion, as if it had not just been dismissed. But in fact there is an important difference, for the opinion now is not that physical pleasure makes life worth living, but that the life worth living, or the life to "bless," is the life that excels in such pleasures (as in the case of Sardanapalus and Smindyrides). The lives of these two had such excess of the physical pleasures that any pain or absence of pleasure also present would be wholly overbalanced in the scale. Sardanapalus and Smindyrides are the exceptions that prove the rule. The physical pleasures that most men have in life can never make life worth living, but these pleasures could perhaps make life worth living if they abounded to excess. Most men, at any rate, have this view, because they bless Sardanapalus and Smindyrides as happy. The view, then, that physical pleasures make life worth living need not be false if these pleasures are present in abundance. However, such a view does make happiness rare and dependent on chance. For only a few could ever enjoy such abundance and only by chance could they ever manage to keep it for very long. Moreover, only those "of a certain sort in their soul" could enjoy such a life, for the physical pleasures easily cloy and to be always ready to enjoy them, and day after day as well, argues a capacity for psychic as well as physical recovery that is beyond most men. Perhaps oxen can do it and perhaps one needs to be like an ox in one's soul to live like Sardanapalus or Smindyrides. If so, then while such a life would have a surplus of pleasures, it would hardly count as human. Still, it cannot thus be dismissed as a possible candidate for happiness, for perhaps happiness is physical pleasure, and perhaps, therefore, most beasts are happy while most men are miserable. A sad state of affairs, to be sure, but a state of affairs that admirers of Sardanapalus and Smindyrides must think obtains.

1216a19   The third answer, to the question what makes life worth living, is deeds of virtue. In order for this answer to count as a genuine third, however, it must be construed as differing both from the answers of pleasure and prudence associated with Sardanapalus and Anaxagoras and from the practice of most of those who allegedly adopt it. For a life of virtuous or noble deeds must be chosen for its own sake if happiness is to be identified with it. Otherwise happiness is being identified, not with it, but with whatever else it is chosen for, either glory, as in the case of the poetic heroes, or money and empire and the like, as in the case of many politicians and the Spartans (8.3.1248b37–49a2). But the political life, as a distinct life and not as reducible to pleasure or gain or empire, must be devoted to noble deeds for their own sake and not to anything else. Nor, further we might add, must the political life be reducible to the philosophic life of someone like Anaxagoras, for then it would not be a third life. It cannot, therefore, be construed as a political life informed by philosophy nor, indeed, as a philosophical life adorned by political activity. It must be a political life where prudence, however construed, plays no or very little role and where character or breeding plays the whole or greatest role.[2]

1216a27   There are, thus, only three candidates for the happy life: the political, the philosophical, and the indulgent. The other lives that have been discussed either reduce to one of these (as that of the poetic heroes who, when they are feasting and listening to a bard, really lead a life of indulgence), or do not even pretend to be happy (as the lives of necessity, which include, besides that of the several artisans, also that of the poetic heroes when they are fighting for glory).[3]

How They Deserve Examination

1216a29   So much, then, clarifies the precise bearing of the opinions about happiness summarized in the previous chapter. With that clarification in place, it is now possible to determine how and to what extent they deserve examination.

Aristotle's answer is that all three lives that opinion identifies with happiness are to be examined, including the life of indulgence. For this life does have the opinion of the many on its side, and while, to be sure, the opinions of the many are not the only ones to examine, they should nevertheless be examined.[4] The examination will not be about what the pleasures of indulgence are and what their sources, for both these facts are obvious. (Their obviousness is the chief reason that the many, who only consider the obvious, think these pleasures are happiness.) Rather it will be about things that are not obvious. The questions Aristotle lists are two pairs of two: on the one hand, whether these pleasures contribute anything to happiness, and how they do so; and, on the other, whether, if pleasures do contribute, it is these pleasures that do so, or whether, while these pleasures are necessary, it is other pleasures in fact that make the happy life pleasant. He then says these things must be investigated later. This reference forward can only plausibly be to Book Six, which is about pleasure as well as more generally about continence and incontinence with respect to pleasure. In that book, it is decided that pleasures do contribute something to happiness, namely because happiness is activity and pleasure is unimpeded activity. It is also shown there that these pleasures are noble because the activity of happiness is noble, and that the bodily pleasures are only noble to the extent they are disciplined by the virtue of temperance, and not as they exist in the continent, the incontinent, and the intemperate (where they cause pain and baseness).

EE Book Six is also the same as *NE* Book Seven, but if Aristotle is referring to that book here, then it cannot be serving the same role in *EE* as it serves in *NE*. For in *NE* the question about the indulgent life, as also the related question about pleasure having different kinds according to different acts, has been discussed and decided before that book is reached, since it is decided already in Book One (in chapters 5 and 8). Hence the same book, if it belongs to both treatises, must be serving different roles in each. But no surprise need thereby be generated. It is a commonplace that the same statements can prove different conclusions if they are joined to different other statements. That Book Six of *EE* does indeed, for this very reason, serve a different role from Book Seven in *NE* will be further argued later.

Nothing further, then, is going to be said about the indulgent life until we reach that later book. Accordingly Aristotle turns next to the other two lives and to explaining both why they need discussing and why discussion of them must come first and discussion of the indulgent life be postponed. The reason virtue and prudence must be discussed is that we need to know in their case not only what we do not know in the case of the pleasures of indulgence, whether they are parts of the good life or not, but also what we do already know in the case of those pleasures, namely what they are. In addition, we need to know whether it is virtue and prudence that are parts of the good life or the deeds that result from them, for unlike pleasures, from which nothing further results (or nothing further with a view to happiness), virtue and prudence do have deeds resulting from them, and these may be

1216a38

more what happiness is than what they result from. Not everyone, of course, thinks that virtue and prudence and their deeds belong to happiness (the many who praise Sardanapalus do not), but all those worth talking about do, as true politicians and also philosophers like Anaxagoras. Their opinions certainly ought to be examined, and not least if the opinions of the many are also to be examined.

Aristotle's words here are programmatic. We are accordingly entitled to conclude that the following books are about virtue and prudence, about what each is, and whether and to what extent each fits into happiness. That Books Two to Four, after the remaining introductory matter of Book One, are about virtue is clear. But since Book Five (which is the same as *NE* Book Six) is also clearly about prudence, we would seem entitled further to conclude that Books Two to Four are a discussion of the political life and Book Five a discussion of the philosophic life.[5] On the whole, this conclusion can be sustained, but since Book Five draws a distinction between prudence and wisdom that *EE* otherwise ignores (save in passing, as at 1.8.1218b14, 3.7.1234a29–30, 8.1.1246b35–36), we would seem also forced to see Book Five as introducing a lesser prudence that falls under the greater prudence as a specific part of it.[6] This conclusion too can, on the whole, be sustained, but it requires that Book Five in *EE*, like Book Six in the same work, be doing something other than what the identical book in *NE* is doing, because *NE* draws a distinction between prudence and wisdom in its very first book (as at 8.1098b24) and gives it special stress in the last book (10.6–8). This point about Book Five, like the similar one about Book Six, will be taken up and argued later.

1216b2   The paragraphs that next follow about Socrates seem to serve a twofold purpose, first to show that prudence and virtue are not the same but different goals, and second to continue the programmatic remarks just given (distinguishing between the what of virtue and the way it comes to be).[7] On the first point, then, Socrates was of the view that the goal in the case of virtue was knowledge alone, and so he sought for definitions of each of the virtues, as justice and courage and their parts. His view was, to this extent reasonable, that it followed from his conviction that all the virtues were kinds of knowledge, so that, in order to be just, for example, it was enough to know what justice is. Geometry and house-building, for instance, are of the sort that to have learned them is thereby to have become a geometer or an architect of houses. The learning of them is the acquiring of them and there is no need, once one knows them, to ask how to acquire them. Hence Socrates was content to seek for what virtue was and not to seek also for how it came about.

1216b10   This characterization of Socrates is so far accurate to what we otherwise know of him (from both Plato and Xenophon)[8] that it captures his conviction that knowledge is enough for practice. Another thought motivating Socrates' position, of course, was that he who knows what is good cannot fail to choose it, and that to fail to choose it is proof that he did not know it.[9] This thought is discussed extensively later in Book Six on incontinence. Nothing is said about it here, presumably because, first, it adds nothing to the position even if it adds a reason for the position, and because, second, the reason that is given (the analogy with the sciences and arts) explains why the position raises problems that need here to be dealt with. For if virtue is like science, then first, there will be no difference between prudence and virtue, and second, there will be no need to ask, as an additional question, how to acquire virtue. Thus, if Socrates is right, the study of ethics will be much reduced: there will not be two lives to consider, that of virtue and that of prudence, and there will not be two questions to ask, what virtue is and how to get it. Aristotle must, before embarking on the study of ethics, confront Socrates' position, since if it is correct, he must follow it, and if it is false, he must say why it is so and how ethics must be studied instead.

The first thing that Aristotle does, then, is to distinguish the sciences and to say that Socrates' position holds for the theoretical sciences but not for the productive sciences. So astronomy and natural science and geometry (all of which recall Anaxagoras and the philosophic life) have as their job the study of their respective subject matters alone and whatever utility might follow is incidental and secondary. The sciences of making, by contrast, like medicine and politics, have as their goal something beyond the science, namely the production of health or good law.

One is inclined to puzzle at once why Aristotle used the productive science of house-building earlier as an example in support of Socrates' thesis when now he uses the productive sciences of medicine and politics as examples against it. One might also wonder if politics is rightly called a productive science. But, as far as making or producing goes, politics does make or produce something, namely regimes and their laws, and, as far as the productive sciences go, all three examples work in two ways. They show both that knowing a productive science is enough to make one a practitioner of it, and also that knowing the science is not the same as practicing it. Socrates focused on the first point but not on the second. Aristotle focuses on both and uses the second to show the inadequacy of Socrates' inference as based on the first.

Aristotle also distinguishes the productive from the theoretical sciences   1216b19 so that, even if Socrates' inference would be correct as drawn from examples of the latter, what he is talking about, virtue, requires him to draw the inference from examples of the former. For while, to be sure, it is noble to know noble things, and hence noble to know the beauty that is virtue, yet to discern what virtue comes from is more honorable than merely to know it, because it is our wish, as even Socrates would allow, to be virtuous and not just to know virtue. The proof comes from the point about productive sciences that Socrates ignored, namely that knowing a productive science is not yet to produce anything. For what we want from a productive science is not to *know* what it produces but to *have* what it produces, as health in the case of medicine, and we will not get that if we only know the science and do not also put it into practice.

Hence, the science of ethics must concern itself both with the question what virtue is and with the question what it comes from. The two questions will, of course, be related, since what virtue comes from will be learned in large part from learning what it is. But the two questions are different and each needs dealing with.[10] There is no clear indication in *EE* where the second of these questions is dealt with. In *NE*, judging by its last chapter 10.9, the second question is reserved for proper treatment in the *Politics*. But there is a certain vagueness in the way Aristotle states the second question. He says it is about "what virtue is from," and as so phrased, this question has two answers. The first is that virtue comes from habituation; the second is that habituation itself comes from law and politics (the teaching of the last chapter of *NE*). *EE* deals not at all with the second answer (*EE* has no continuation into the *Politics*). It deals with the first answer as it advances in defining and describing the virtues (rather in the way *NE* also deals with it), although it does devote some express attention to it in the chapters on choice and the voluntary in Book Two, as well as in the discussion of friendship and of fortune and gentlemanliness in Books Seven and Eight. Consequently, we may regard those chapters and books as generally concerned with the first answer to the second question.

The silence of *EE* about the second answer to the second question may be taken as an indication that it is intended for those who are, as such, not concerned with law for right habituation, either because, unlike the audience of *NE*, they are not legislators, or also because they are already rightly habituated without law. In this respect *EE* is like the *GE*, which is also directed to people who are already rightly habituated. The difference is that the audience of *GE*, being an audience of decent citizens, thinks it obvious that the political life of virtue is sufficient and best and is unaware, or suspicious, unlike the audiences of *EE* and *NE*, of the question whether the philosophical life of prudence or wisdom might not be better.[11]

Notes

1.	Thus read, these remarks are not at all out of place, contra Rowe (1971: 16–17, 76n) and, in part, Woods (1992: 53–54). Dirlmeier (1962: 170–71) speaks better, though his speculations (ibid. and 1958: 97) that the "pessimism" of the remarks is perhaps a sign they were written when Aristotle was grieving the loss of a dear friend are without much warrant.

2.	Such a view of the political life is assumed by the intended audience of Aristotle's *GE*, and in that work Aristotle has to be very careful how he handles it. The view also seems to be what he describes as the second-best happy life, in *NE* 10.8, and perhaps also the life of those fortunate by nature discussed in 8.2, who lack reason but nevertheless always or often succeed; possibly too it is, in a truncated form, the life of Spartans and those like them, mentioned rather negatively in 8.3.

3.	So, contra Woods (1992: 53), Aristotle's listing of lives is suitably exhaustive, especially if the life of indulgence describes Homer's heroes when they are not fighting, and the life of necessity describes them when they are.
4.	Hence the earlier passage about examining the opinions of the many, at 1.3.1214b34–1215a2, needs to be taken in the sort of way there suggested, since this way allows that the opinions of the many are to be examined, though not the only ones to be examined.
5.	The suggestion that *EE* divides up in this sort of way was maintained by Fritzsche and Walzer and endorsed by Von Fragstein (references in Von Fragstein 1974: 25–26), as well as by Kenny (1978: 53–54, 195–96). It is rejected by Dirlmeier (1962: 177–79). See also Rowe (1971: 19, 65–68) and Woods (1992: 55).
6.	Contra, for example, Rowe (1971: 67).
7.	Dirlmeier (1962: 179–81), Kenny (1978: 196), Rowe (1971: 19), Woods (1992: 56–57).
8.	See the notes in Dirlmeier (1962: 181) and Woods (1974: 55–56).
9.	A point raised by Woods, ibid.
10.	Contra the ruminations of Woods (1992: 56–57).
11.	See the commentary thereon in a separate volume (forthcoming from Transaction Publishers).

Chapter 6

The Science Proper
The Method

So far Aristotle has summarized and briefly discussed opinions about hap-	1216b26
piness and set out, in the light of them, what questions are to be examined and in what order. He now turns to say what method is to be followed, or what arguments are to be used and what evidence must be relied on. That science must use argument to reach certain or trustworthy conclusions is obvious enough, especially where things are disputed, as they are in the case of happiness, for argument is the way to resolve disputes. That the evidence to be relied on must be the phenomena is also obvious enough, because experience or what appears is where we have to begin to know anything. (For even if there is innate knowledge, as some philosophers have thought, it is phenomena that bring this knowledge into act, as these philosophers have themselves admitted.) The phenomena in the case of happiness are the opinions, for happiness is not like color or sound, which are known by eye and ear, but happiness can only be known, if at all, through the exercise of judgment and comparison. For even if happiness is pleasure and so something that can be felt, the fact that pleasure is happiness is not thus felt but must rather be judged by reflection. Judgments come to view in the opinions that men have and express, so that the phenomena in the case of happiness must

be the opinions. Consequently, just as in all other sciences we follow the evidence, so we should do the same in the science of happiness.

Hence, as Aristotle says, "the greatest thing" is if all men are manifestly in agreement with our conclusions. But if not, because men's opinions are in conflict, then the next best is that they should agree in a way, which they will do if their opinions change in the course of discussion. That such change will not destroy the evidence but rather bring it more fully to view follows from what Aristotle next says, that all of us are familiar with the truth to some extent (happiness, we may say, is far too common and intense a concern of all men for any to be wholly ignorant of it). What we lack, then, is not so much truth as clarity about the truth, for what we typically think and say is confused and not carefully thought through. So as we think it through, which is what the following discussion will do for us, we should be able to reach greater clarity by reaching better known and more accurate statements.

1216b35 True to his intention, Aristotle begins by immediately introducing some clarifications about method (for if we can be confused about happiness, doubtless we can also be confused about how to examine it). His clarifications are three: the first about the method and the other two about the parts of the method, for one of them is about argument in relation to the subject matter and the other about phenomena in relation to the argument.

The first, then, is about the fact that the method is philosophical, for philosophy is what we are now doing, and philosophy, as a general name for the pursuit of scientific knowledge, is a matter of knowing things through their causes. Thus philosophical arguments differ from non-philosophical ones (as those, say, of rhetoric or even of sophistry) by being about the why of things. The why of things is also the what, since the what of the subject matter is the why of its properties (as the what of a triangle is the why of its having angles equal to two right angles). But the what is only seen to be the why when, through a demonstrative syllogism, or a series of them, the fact that the subject has the property is seen to be reduced to the what of the subject. So, in the case of a triangle, the reduction is after this fashion: the angles on a straight line are equal to two right angles; the adjacent external and internal angles of a plane figure are angles on a straight line; the external angle of a three-sided plane figure equals the two opposite internal angles; the what of a triangle is to be a three-sided plane figure. Since philosophy is the search for such demonstrations, the search of the present treatise on happiness must be the same. Hence, in the chapters and books that follow, Aristotle looks for the what of happiness, to which he progressively reduces, as to its demonstrative why, the thesis stated at the beginning: happiness is at once the noblest, the best, and the pleasantest.

1216b40 So much for the philosophic method in general, but a caution is now in order, which brings Aristotle to his second clarification. For it can appear, if the philosophic method is to argue and speak with reason about things, that any such arguing or speaking is philosophic. But herein lies a serious error. Not all subject matters are the same, and the philosophic method requires not only argument but argument appropriate to the subject matter.[1] The argument turns on the what and the what is different for different things. One deceives oneself, therefore, if one ignores this fact and gives arguments and reasons foreign to the subject matter (and there are some, Aristotle appositely adds, who are thus deceived culpably, because deceived by their boasting or their wish to appear important and clever). Even people otherwise experienced and able in action (in political action, one presumes) may be thus caught. The reason is twofold: the incapacity of those who deceive them and the incapacity of themselves. Those who deceive them are those who, while presumably clever enough at speaking, are incapable of thinking.[2] They lack the sort of thinking that can act (unlike those they deceive) and that, further, can rule in practical arts. This latter or ruling thought is what those they deceive must lack (for if they did not lack it, they could hardly be deceived), and the lack of such thought comes from lack of education. For it is precisely the mark of education to be able to judge what reasoning is appropriate to what subject matter. Experienced and active men, therefore, need education to avoid being deceived by ignorant boasters. They need philosophers to arm them against sophists.

Philosophy and philosophical argument are about both facts and reasons, though perhaps more about reasons, since the aim of science is to get the why of the facts. Still, the facts have to be got, and sometimes if one has discovered the why, one will discover other facts not hitherto noticed or expected. (The discovery of Pluto would be a case in point for modern astronomical science.) With regard to happiness, as Aristotle has already said, in addition to getting the facts, one must also clarify them, since the opinions, which are the facts in the case of happiness, while not wholly false, are, in most cases, unclear and confused. Finding the what of happiness will do much, no doubt, toward the clarification (a case in point is pleasure, which opinion correctly attributes to happiness, but opinion, as emerges in due course, is wrong in attributing to it only or mainly the bodily pleasures). Here too, however, a caution is in order, which brings Aristotle to his third clarification. The reason may be needed to explain the fact, but the fact has a ground independent of any alleged reason, namely as a given of experience. One should not, therefore, judge the fact by the reason but distinguish the reason from the fact and not allow any alleged reason to overthrow a given of experience.

He gives two reasons for this conclusion. First, what was just said, that making everything depend on the argument exposes even the experienced to ignorant and boastful arguers, requiring them to give up the fact and follow the argument if they cannot refute it, whereas, on the contrary, they should keep to the fact despite the argument. Second, even if the reason supports the fact, the reason can be false and yet the fact remains true, for it is a matter of

1217a10

215

logic that a truth can be deduced from a falsehood. Accordingly, if an alleged reason turns out to be false, we should not thereby give up the fact it was used to prove, for the fact can remain true regardless. In short, we should not give up a fact because we cannot refute the reasons against it, nor should we give up a fact because we can refute the reasons for it. Both are erroneous because both fail to judge the reason separately from the thing proved. A simple enough point, perhaps, but easily forgotten.

Notes

1. Taking Aristotle's point to be that arguments must be appropriate to the subject matter, but Woods (1992: 58) may be right to suggest that he is also saying, if implicitly, that not everything can be established by argument, for what argument begins from must be known without argument.
2. A reference, no doubt, to sophists; see the references in Dirlmeier (1962: 186).

Chapter 7

Subject Matter: Happiness
Happiness Is the Best Thing Doable

1217a18 What Aristotle has so far said is all in a way introductory to the science proper, as he indicates by saying that the remarks he has just given about method are said as preface "too" (*kai*), which presumably means[1] that they are also a preface along with the earlier chapters on the worth, nature, and questions of the science, and on the initial statement and review of opinions. The preface has been artfully and even stylishly written.[2] The discussion that now follows in the remaining chapters and books is no less artfully written but with less surface elegance. In fact, the language and the thought become at times extraordinarily compressed.[3] Aristotle seems to go out of his way, after the preface (and even sometimes within it), to make few or no concessions to his readers in ease of comprehension. His practice contrasts with that in *NE* where his generally more relaxed and diffuse style[4] does make such concessions. The difference may be put down to difference of audience,[5] if we suppose that *NE* is for legislators and *EE* for philosophers, and that as the first is diffuse in order to be an aid for the former in the highest exercise of political prudence, so the second is compressed in order to be an exercise for the latter in the unraveling of densely compact reasoning.

With the preface out of the way, Aristotle follows the method he has outlined and looks first for the what of happiness using the facts or phenomena about happiness, that is, the opinions, as starting point. He also takes first, as the method requires, opinions that are universally agreed upon, even though unclear, aiming thereby to discover something clear. What is universally agreed upon is that happiness is greatest and best of human goods. He does say "human," however, and for two reasons, because of what is better than man and because of what is worse. So, first, some better being, as a god, might perhaps also possess happiness, and second the beings worse than man, the other animals, do not share in happiness. If so, human happiness will indeed be just the human best because it will be too low for the gods and too high for the animals

Aristotle does not say that these opinions about god and the animals are both agreed on, even by himself.[6] Indeed he indicated earlier that some people think some animals are happy, as the ox called Apis (for the many, at least, must think this ox happy). Further, even if most would admit, with Homer and the poets, that the gods have a superhuman happiness, the happiness they attribute to the gods is little short of ox-like pleasures in an endless life. The many, in fact, think divine happiness is animal happiness and they "bless" the animal life of Sardanapalus and Smindyrides, as if it were divine. Aristotle pointedly does not mention the ox in his list of animals that are not happy, but speaks only of horse, bird, fish, and any other being that does not "by its name" share in "anything divine". The ox Apis does, of course, by its name share in something divine, for Apis is the name of a god. To the extent, then, that the many agree that horse and bird and fish are not happy, they should think it strange that the ox, by contrast, could be happy. Conversely, to the extent they agree the ox is happy, they should think it strange that horse and bird and fish, by contrast, could not be happy. The opinions of the many are confused and need clarifying.

Aristotle postpones the clarification until later (he means Book Six where 1217a29 pleasure, and in particular bodily pleasure, is dealt with). Other clarifications, related to opinions that all and not just the many agree on, are of more immediate relevance. For all agree that happiness is the greatest and best of human goods, and while not all agree that divine and animal goods are not human and so not happiness, yet all must agree that goods that do not come within the scope of human action are not human and so not happiness. By humanly doable goods, Aristotle means those that share in change, for human action is a sort of change, and so any good attainable by human action must, to this extent, share in change. But the Greek is ambiguous, and instead of "because some beings do not share in change so neither do they in the (sc. human) goods," it could mean "because some beings do not share in change, so neither do some goods."[7] Perhaps not much hangs on the difference, for the phrase, however translated, must be understood in context, that these beings are perhaps the best and that some of them are doable but only for what is better than us. However, the "some" is again ambiguous and could mean "some goods" or "some of them (the beings just mentioned)." If we adopt the latter we must understand the overall sense to be that some beings do

217

not share in the human goods because they do not share in change, but that some of these beings are the object of doing for what is better than us. The beings in question are perhaps the heavens (which, if they change in place, do not change as men do nor have the goods that men have), or the Platonic Forms (which do not change at all), or the objects of mathematics (which, if not also Platonic Forms, are at least abstracted from change).[8] Those of these beings that are doable for what is better than us will then be the Forms that the Platonic demiurge gazes at when making the world or the heavens whose souls, or whose Aristotelian unmoved movers, spin them in circles.[9] Possibly the cosmos as a whole is meant, which is a doable for the contemplative study of philosophers like Anaxagoras, and such philosophers, if not better than all of us men, must be better than those of us who admire nothing but animal pleasures and the monarchs who enjoy them.[10]

1217a35 This last thought about Anaxagoras is not perhaps so out of the way, or so out of Aristotle's current purview, because he now adds that doable is meant in two ways, both as the thing done and as the thing it is done for, as in the case of health and healthy things, for we do the latter for the sake of the former. Happiness, then, will be the best of things doable by man, at least in the sense of what we do things for the sake of. This conclusion does not, as such, rule out the possibility, left open from earlier, that happiness is a gift of chance or inspiration from some spirit. For we can pray for such things, or try to catch them by means of lucky charms and amulets, so that happiness will, to this extent, be something doable. Besides, even if happiness does come by chance, it will at least be doable for those to whom it comes.[11]

Notes

1. Following Dirlmeier (1962: 190).
2. The striking absence of hiatus in the opening chapters (and the resumption of hiatus thereafter) is remarked on by several commentators, including Dirlmeier (1962: 110–11, 144, 194, with references) and Rowe (1971: 20). The artfulness of their organization (and even of the *EE* as a whole) is rightly stressed by Rowe (ibid.: 17–18), though even he perhaps underestimates how artful it really is.
3. A number of passages in the Greek, noted hereafter, that have puzzled translators seem to arise from this extraordinary compression; cf. Dirlmeier (1962: 111), Von Fragstein (1974: 3–4, 33).
4. See Chapter 2 n6 above.
5. And not necessarily, contra Rowe (1971), to difference of date and order of composition.
6. Contra Woods (1992: 60). Aristotle does argue later (7.12) that animal pleasures are not happiness, but he also argues later that divine pleasures are happiness.
7. The former is the construal of Dirlmeier (1962: 13, 192), followed by Von Fragstein (1974: 30–31), the latter of the translations by Solomon (1927) and Rackham (1961: 223) and Kenny (2011: 10).
8. Dirlmeier (1962: 193).

9. Plato *Timaeus*, Aristotle *Metaphysics* Lambda (12).
10. For somewhat differing interpretations, see Dirlmeier ibid. and Von Fragstein ibid.
11. A distinction unmentioned here, but perhaps implicit (cf. the analogous distinction referred to at 8.3.1249b15–16), is between the end as the object of our action and the end as the action in which we possess the object. The heavens, for instance, are the object of philosophic contemplation and the contemplating is the act in which we possess them. The latter alone is strictly speaking the end as doable, for the heavens as such are not subject to our action, only contemplating them is. A quote Dirlmeier (1962: 207) gives from *Parts of Animals* 1.5.645a23ff. for a later context (in 1.8.1218a21) is apposite here, about the difference between things that exist for the goal being in the world of nature but the goal itself being in the realm of the noble or beautiful.

Chapter 8

What This Best Is Not

Having taken from common opinions, or from the facts, that happiness is 1217b1 the best, and the best of human and doable goods, Aristotle turns, naturally enough, to consider what the best is. Here also he begins, as his method requires, with the opinions, of which there are three. He does not start by summarizing what these are but proceeds to examine them separately one after the other. The three are as follows: what he has just said, that the end, or the "for the sake of," is the best; that the Idea of the Good is the best; that the common or universal good is the best. The Idea of the Good is taken first, not because it is most familiar (most men doubtless know little if anything about it), but because, presumably, it is most familiar to, and popular with, the philosophers who are Aristotle's primary audience.

The doctrine about the Idea of the Good is broken down into the following series of inferences:

(1) the good itself is best;
(2) the good itself is (a) first of goods and (b) the cause, by its presence, of the goodness of other things;
(3) both (a) and (b) belong to the Idea of the Good;
(4) therefore, the Idea of the Good is the good itself;
(5) therefore, from (1), the Idea of the Good is best.

Conclusion (5) is left unstated, as being obvious; conclusion (4) is stated shortly after further argument. For what Aristotle proceeds to show next is that (3a) effectively follows from (3b). The good is "said truly most of" (17b8–9) the Idea (and so, by implication, secondarily of everything else), because (6) other things are good by sharing in it and having its likeness, and the Idea is first of goods because (7) when what is shared in is taken away the things that share in it are taken away (which is how the first relates to the later). Thus, (4) the Idea of the Good is the good itself—because (8) the Idea of the Good is separable, like the other ideas, from what shares in it.

Propositions (6) and (7) repeat or rely on (3b), putting the term "sharing" in place of the term "causing." Proposition (8), which introduces the element of separability, is presented as being an additional argument that the Idea of the Good is the good itself. The reasoning is presumably as follows: what is separable from what shares in it remains as what it is when what shares in it is taken away, which is an implication of proposition (7). But the Idea of the Good, according to the theory, is separable from the goods that share in it. Hence, since it will remain as good even when all other goods are taken away, it must be the good itself.

This series of inferences is unexceptionable enough and also reflects statements about participation or sharing that crop up often enough in Platonic dialogues.[1] The inferences do, of course, assume the doctrine of sharing rather than prove it, but the assumption, once made, does establish the conclusion, as here intended, that the Idea of the Good must be the best.

1217b16   The next thing is to examine it, and following his earlier remarks on method, Aristotle's examination covers two things: the relevance of the thesis to the subject matter and the separability of the truth of the conclusion from the truth of the premises. He deals with the first point first and then, in his criticisms of the inferences, attacks the conclusion separately by itself before attacking the premises.

As to the first point, the consideration of the doctrine of the Ideas will not fall under ethics but under a study of a more logical character, as dialectics, where common arguments destructive of a given position are alone appropriate (other sciences are all distinct in having a distinct subject matter). For, as Aristotle immediately adds, the doctrine is itself logical and empty, that is, empty in the sense of common and not proper to a determinate subject matter,[2] and to criticize such a doctrine is necessarily to engage in counter arguments that are likewise logical and empty.

The doctrine should therefore really be left to one side, but since it does propose an answer about the best good, and the best good is under investigation here, it cannot entirely be ignored but must rather be dealt with, if only to show that we need to get it out of the way.

That the doctrine is logical and empty, which is in fact the first of Aristotle's criticisms against it, is something that, he says, has been examined elsewhere. Accordingly, apart from some incidental remarks in what follows, he refrains from saying more on the matter here. His references to other works are, in the case of philosophical discourses, presumably to the *Metaphysics* (its last two books especially) and *NE* (1.6), and, in the case of exoteric works, most likely to *GE* (1.1.1183a24ff.).[3] In this latter work, he

220

alleges the following against the doctrine: the science of politics does not look into the Idea of the Good but into the good for us; no science says of its good that it is good (it rather assumes it as a given), but it will have to say its good is good if it speaks of the Idea of the Good (for it will affirm the Idea of all goods, for all goods are good by sharing in it, and so it will say of all goods, including its own, that they are good); that sciences proceed from their proper principles, but the Idea of the Good is not proper to any science, for any good can be considered by itself without also having to consider the Idea. Such arguments do indeed seem to show that the Idea of the Good is empty (because it is not proper to any particular science) and logical (because it says things, as about universal predication, that fall only under the common science of logic).

This first criticism, then (culled from *GE*), has been against the relevance of the Idea of the Good to the science of happiness. The next criticisms concern the series of inferences and the claim it concludes that the Idea is best. First, in accordance with the method, Aristotle criticizes the claim by itself, saying that, even if the Idea exists, it is of no use for good life and action. Hence, of course, it cannot be the best, or not the best we are now looking for (because what we are now looking for is precisely something of use to life and action). The criticism rests on an appeal to the doctrine of the categories of being, and that good is said in as many ways as being. The categories are briefly summarized and illustrated (only six of the ten are given), and the conclusion drawn that the good is not one, just as being is not one.   1217b23

From this conclusion the further conclusion is then drawn that, since the goods are not one but many, the sciences of good, as of being, are not one but many.[4] This conclusion is strengthened by the yet further conclusion that there are many sciences even of goods in the same category. The illustration is taken from the categories of when and how much, where the right time and the due measure in food are judged by gymnastics and medicine, where the right time and due measure in military action are judged by generalship, and where there is no one science that studies the good itself. From these examples it is evident that the good useful for life and action, or the doable good, is particular goods studied by particular sciences, and not the Idea of the Good studied by some one science proper to the good itself.   1217b34

Aristotle's criticism here may be thus summarized:

(a)   the good is said in many ways or categories;
(b)   the sciences of the good are not one but many according to the categories (evident from (a) and also from particular instances of sciences in particular categories);
(c)   the goods and sciences useful for life and action are these goods and sciences, which are many according to the categories;
(d)   therefore, the Idea of the Good and the science of it, which are one and not divided according to categories, are not useful for life and action.[5]

The argument relies on facts evident to experience about goods and sciences of good, and since it thus proceeds by a sort of induction (the goods and sciences that are useful are the ones divided according to the categories), it is vulnerable to the possibility of an exception that there is, after all, a good and a science that are useful and not divided according to the categories. But then this good and science, which are the exception, must be identified, and one does not identify them merely by asserting an Idea of the Good. One has to show concretely that this Idea and the science of it are useful. But nothing to this effect has been done, and moreover, the evidence—of the goods and sciences that are useful as a matter of experienced fact—is against it.

1218a1   The next two criticisms attack the existence of the Idea of the Good (which the previous criticism had, for the sake of argument, allowed). They do so by attacking the premises in the original series of inferences for the Idea. The first of them attacks the premise numbered (3) and its elaboration (that the Idea of the Good is both first of goods and cause, by its presence, of the goodness of other things). It runs as follows:

(i)   wherever things have in them a prior and a posterior (and the good will be such if, like being, it is in all the categories), there is not beyond them a common thing that is separate;

(ii)   for then there would be something prior to the first;

(iii) for the common and separate is prior, because

(iv)   once the common is taken away, the first is taken away too.

An example is given for purposes of clarification. Suppose the double is the first of the multiples (that is, suppose the multiples form a series of prior and posterior of which the double is first, the triple second, and so on). Then the common term "multiple," which is predicated of them all (for all are multiples, including the double), cannot be separate. The reason is that the common will then be prior to the double (that is, it will be prior to what was supposed to be the first in the series)—or at least the common will be thus prior if it is posited as an Idea and separate.[6]

Clearly the criticism turns on the claim that the Idea is not only common but also separate (as the repeated mention of the fact stresses). There is, after all, no problem with saying of the double and the triple and the quadruple that they are all multiples, for the common term multiple does properly apply to them. But then the term multiple is not itself a multiple. It will, however, become a multiple if the common term is hypostatized into a separate Idea. For, like all Ideas, the Idea of the multiple must itself be what it says (as the Idea of the Good is itself good), because it is by being such that, according to the theory, an Idea causes what shares in it also to be such. Accordingly, the Idea of the multiple will itself be a multiple. Moreover it will be the first multiple. The reason was stated at the beginning: the Idea is prior because when what is shared in is taken away, the things that share in it are taken away, and the Idea is what the other things share in. Aristotle's criticism now follows straightforwardly: the Idea of the multiple, or the common posited as separate, must be prior (proposition [iii]); because when it is taken away, all the multiples that fall under it must also be taken away (proposition [iv]); thus, the Idea of the multiple will be prior to the first multiple (the double) (proposition [ii]); but this result is clearly absurd; hence, wherever there are things that have in them a prior and posterior, any common term that is predicated of them cannot be a separate Idea, or there is not beyond them a common thing that is separate (proposition [i]). All we need do now is apply the same argument to the Idea of the Good, for goods too have in them a prior and posterior (the prior and the posterior of the categories);[7] hence, by (i), there cannot be a separate Idea of the Good.[8]

So much, then, serves to refute premise (3) and its associated premises in the series of inferences from the beginning. What Aristotle effectively does next is to refute premise (1) of the same series, that the good itself is best.[9] He begins by confirming that the theory of Ideas does posit the common as separate. For the proponents of the Idea say that if there are several things that are good, as justice and courage, then there is some good itself, adding "itself," to the common term. But by the addition of this "itself" the proponents mean that the common term is eternal, that is, separate (it will be separate if eternal because it will not belong with the many particulars that come to be and perish). But if such is the meaning, the good itself is not the best of goods. For, first, an eternal good is not better because eternal, just as a white thing is not whiter because eternal, and consequently, second, as regards separation, the common good is not made to be the good itself or the Idea by being made separate (as the proponents of the theory suppose), for to make it separate is to make it no longer common (the common is what is present to things and not what is separate from them). Thus, for both reasons, the good itself, at least as the proponents of the Idea mean it, is not the best of goods: its eternity does not make it best, and its separation removes it from the goods and so removes it from being the best of them (for, as separate, it is not "of" them at all).

A point worth noting about this criticism and the preceding one is that while they deny that the Idea of the Good could either be or be best by way of common predication, they do not deny that it could be or be best in some other way, as by transcendent exemplar causality (the way the Ideas exist and function for the demiurge in Plato's *Timaeus*). The Ideas as transcendent exemplar causes can survive Aristotle's criticism, and in this guise, indeed, they come to enjoy a long life among Aristotelian-minded Platonists (like Plotinus) and Platonist-minded Aristotelians (like Aquinas) right through the Roman world and into the Middle Ages.

At all events, if the above analyses are correct, Aristotle has attacked premises (1) and (3) of the original series of inferences. He has not, however,

1218a9

1218a15

223

attacked premise (2), nor does he attack it later, for in fact he accepts it, suitably interpreted, and uses it at the end of the chapter (together with (1) now likewise suitably interpreted) to prove his own position about the best. What he does next instead is turn to other arguments against the Idea, criticizing things that were not mentioned earlier but that are nevertheless also used by the proponents to prove the Idea of the Good.

The value of these further criticisms is that they help to show why the proponents of the Idea go wrong. These proponents, contrary to the method stated in chapter 6, do not start with the phenomena as their evidence. For they start with things agreed to *have* the good when they should start with things agreed to *be* good.[10] So they start with numbers and prove that justice and health *are* good because justice and health are orderings and numbers and because the good belongs to numbers and monads, that is, numbers and monads *have* the good; and the reason they have the good is that the One (the principle of order and number) is good itself.[11]

Aristotle says that this argument is used to prove the good itself, and the proof works by a sort of inference to the best explanation.[12] So, first, it says that number explains why justice and health are good because justice and health are order and number, and order and number have the good. But, next, it says, in effect, that if number and order have the good, the explanation must be that the One is the good itself. For it is by having the One, the Unit, as principle that number and order are number and order. Therefore the One is the good itself.

The problem with this argument is that it gets the agreements back to front. Justice and health are not agreed to *be* good because they are order and number, which are agreed to *have* the good. On the contrary, things that have order and number are agreed to *have* the good because the things that are agreed to *be* good are order and number. Or as Aristotle puts it: because it is agreed that health, strength, and moderation *are* good, therefore the noble (the good at its best) exists more in changeless things, or the changeless things *have* the noble more. For health, strength, and moderation are order and rest, and if so then the changeless things are more noble because they have order and rest more.

As so analyzed, Aristotle's argument shows that, had the proponents of the Ideas followed its pattern, they would not have posited an Idea of the Good as best. Rather they would have posited as best that which is supremely ordered and resting, namely the unmoved movers that turn the heavens round in order and number and whose ordering and numbering we, through health and strength and moderation, come to imitate (which is, more or less, the conclusion Aristotle urges at the end of this treatise).[13]

1218a24 The next criticisms are less difficult to unravel. The proof that the One is the good itself because numbers desire it (and, of course, what all things desire is the good), assumes that numbers desire the One. But nothing clear is said about how they desire it (the assertion is just baldly or simply made), and if we take it in the obvious sense of appetite then numbers are being credited, absurdly, with an attribute of living things.[14] Something must be said, therefore, about how numbers desire. Certainly, adds Aristotle dryly, we should not leave without supporting argument what is going to be hard enough to believe even with supporting argument. But if the supporting argument is that all things desire some single good (and so numbers, being among the things, will desire the single good, and the One is this single good), then it is false. All things in fact desire their own proper goods, as the eye sight, the body health, and so on.

Aristotle now says, as a summary, that "such" difficulties show that there is not some good itself. The "such" will refer to all the criticisms onward from the one about the prior and posterior (at 1218a1), for its preceding criticism about the uselessness of the good itself as Idea did not require or entail that the Idea not exist. Aristotle now adds further criticisms that likewise do not entail or require that the Idea not exist (and so are also attacks on the conclusion independent of the premises).   1218a33

The first is in a way a repetition of the uselessness argument only now stated more simply without reference to the categories. The Idea is not useful for politics (which the study of happiness will be part of if happiness is something political), but rather its own proper good is, as is true of the other arts (like gymnastics, which was also mentioned earlier).

The second refers to an argument, given elsewhere in the discourse, that the Idea (or form) of the Good, is useful either for all arts or for no art (so since, as just said, it is not useful for politics, it is not useful for any art). That the Idea must be useful for all arts or none rests presumably on the claim that the Idea is a universal (it is just the common as separate). For then it must apply universally if it applies at all, and hence, if there are cases it does not apply to, there are no cases it applies to. An argument at least implicitly along these lines is found in GE (1.1.1183a38–b8) and NE (1.6.1096b35–7a13), so the discourse referred to is likely to be one or both of these.[15]

The third argument is a bald assertion that the good itself is not doable. It is not doable if it is separate as an Idea, for then it can serve neither as a means we can use nor as an end we can reach, for it will always be beyond us. It might, perhaps, as suggested earlier, be doable as an end in the sense of the object of the end, as the Unmoved Mover can be the object of the end that is contemplation. But then it will not be the Idea in the sense here under examination, for it will not be a common term but a transcendent exemplar. Aristotle's arguments do not strictly rule out the Idea as exemplar, but the exemplar will come into play, if it does, only after the question of happiness as a doable good has been answered in such a way that the exemplar somehow emerges as its object. At all events, it is of no further relevance now.

Aristotle comes now to the second of the opinions about the best mentioned at the beginning of the chapter, that the common good is best.[16] He does not explain why it is held to be best, nor does he need to.[17] For if it is   1218a38

225

one of the opinions, or one of the phenomena, as it is, then, according to the method outlined in chapter 6, it needs examining. True, he did explain why the Idea is held to be best, but only because the reasons for the Idea proved to be crucial to seeing what was wrong with it as a candidate for the best. That the common good is not best can, however, be shown without any reference to its reasons, and Aristotle does so at once. The common good, he says, is neither good nor doable.

To state Aristotle's first point as that the common good is not good is controversial because the Greek could also be translated, and usually is translated, as that the common good is not (the) good itself, that is, it is not some absolute good.[18] The translation is possible but does not allow one to make much compelling sense of the ensuing argument.[19] Aristotle's point can, however, be made compelling if what he is saying is that the common good is not good. For by common good he presumably means, not common as ontologically separate (which would be the Idea), but common as logically universal, that is, as what is common to all goods because predicated of all goods.[20] But if the common good as logical universal is itself good (and not just a universal term), then it will be the good in all goods including little ones, that is, it will be the goodness of the little good. But the common good is also supposed to be the best (for that thesis is the one now under examination). Consequently the common good will be at the same time both little and best, or both small and great, which is absurd. So the common good cannot be good. Therefore it cannot be best, for what is not even good cannot be the best of goods.[21] The presupposition of this argument is, of course, that the common good is ontologically in good things as being precisely the goodness of each good thing. Without this presupposition, the criticism will not work, but also without this presupposition, the common good will be the same as the Idea as being ontologically separate.

Aristotle's second point, that the common good is not doable, can now be explained in a similar way.[22] For we must continue to suppose that the common good is being taken as itself good (for it is being taken as best and only if it is good can it be best). But as thus good the common good is the good in any and every good whatever, and such a good is not a good that anyone or anything *does*. The fact is clear from induction. Medicine, for instance, does not undertake to make present a good that is present in anything whatever, but rather to make the good of health present, and health is not present in anything whatever but only in living bodies. The like holds of all other arts, or of all doings simply, that they too undertake to make present a good that is present only in certain things and not in anything whatever. Thus the common good is not doable. Hence it is not best, since, as chapter 7 showed, the best in question now is the doable best.

The opinion about the common good criticized here, that it is the logical universal but as itself what it says (the common good is good), has been attributed, if controversially, to Socrates and some members of Plato's Academy.[23] It is, in any event, a stage toward the Platonic Idea, because it shares the crucial feature of the Idea (it *is* what it *says*). One gets to the Idea by separating this common good from the particulars so that it exists apart, which, according to Aristotle himself, was the move Plato made. It seems to be the move one must make to avoid the criticisms of the common good here leveled. For, in particular, if the common good is made into a separate Idea, which is not the good of particular goods but is rather that which particular goods are good by sharing in, then it would after all not be small in a small good, nor would it be a good present in anything whatever, for any good whatever, including health, while it would be good by sharing in it, could still be a good realizable only in particular things, as health is only realizable in living bodies. That one thus nevertheless falls foul of other and worse criticisms (those raised against the Idea earlier) suggests that the wiser move is to go back to the beginning and deny that the common good is good. That move is the one Aristotle made.

What This Best Is

Aristotle now turns finally to the third opinion, his own (and that of most people in fact), that the end or the "that for the sake of which" is best.[24] He begins by stating that the good is manifold, but he is not hereby recalling the categories, for the manifoldness he now mentions is that one division of the good is the noble, and therefore he seems to be referring to the division of the good into the noble, the useful, and the pleasant.[25] He then adds that one part is doable and another not doable, which seems to mean that one part of the noble (and not one part of the good) is doable and another not doable.[26] So his next remarks will mean that the part of the noble that is doable is the sort of good that is "that for the sake of which," but this noble is not the noble manifest in changeless things.[27] It is not the noble manifest in changeless things because the noble manifest in changeless things, the Idea (which, as we recall, is separate from the world of change), is not the good we are looking for. Nor, of course, is the common good the good we are looking for, because (as has just been argued) although the Idea is changeless and not doable, the common good, while changeable (it is not separate from the world of change), is not doable. The "that for the sake of which," by contrast, taken as end,[28] is doable (the doable was divided earlier into the end and what we do for the end [1.7.1271a35–39]). It is also best and cause and first. So if the best and cause and first is the good itself, then the end must be the good itself.

That what is best and cause and first must be the good itself is not only obvious (what could be more the good itself than the best good and the good that is cause of other goods and the first good?) but is also, of course, what the proponents of the Idea relied on to argue that the Idea is the good itself. Yet plainly, the end is not going to labor under any of the problems that beset the Idea or the common good. So if we are going to appeal at all to the premise that the good itself is best (numbered [1] above in the argument for the Idea) and to the reasons for it (numbered [2] above), then the end is this good itself.

1218b12 Having just said that the end is best and cause and first, Aristotle now proves each claim in turn—perhaps in reverse order, as is not seldom his wont, or perhaps not. For it is not clear if the first argument that follows is meant to prove that the end is first or that it is best, nor that the argument that follows third is meant to prove that it is best or that it is first. Perhaps both are meant to prove both. So the end is first and best because it falls under the art that is first and best, the art that controls, or is supreme over, all other arts. This art, he says, is politics and household management and prudence, which differ from other arts precisely by being thus in control of them. For household management is in control of all arts in the household, politics of all arts in the city, and prudence of all arts and doings whatsoever. How they differ from each other (that politics embraces household management and prudence politics) is explained later (5.8, 13).

1218b16 Next, that the end is cause is shown from teaching, that we prove from the end the goodness of other things, because the end, the "that for the sake of which," is cause of the other things being good. We first say what health is, for instance, and then we prove about all the things related to health that they are good. So because health is such and such, this other thing, which leads to it, must be what is useful for health. The good as end is cause of the good as useful. Of course, as Aristotle clarifies immediately, the good as useful is also in a way cause of the good as end. But it is only cause as moving or efficient cause, in the way the useful for health makes health to be in this or that living body. It is not cause of the goodness of health; the end is cause of that.

1218b22 Finally, Aristotle proves that the end is best or first from the fact that no one proves that health, or the end, is good. But, as we have seen, everyone does prove from the goodness of health that things related to health are good. So the goodness of the end is first because argument begins with it, or it is best because its goodness is underived while the goodness of other things derives from it. The fact, however, that sophists seek to prove that health or the end is good shows nothing, for sophists do not know, or care, what they are talking about and drag in anything they can from outside to make their sophisms. Those who know and care what they are talking about, as doctors in the case of health, do not prove that their end is good, just as no one proves any other principle. Health, for instance, is a principle in medicine, for medicine is about how to secure health, and so it assumes to begin with, and does not prove, that health is a good worth securing.

One should note, nevertheless, that health and other principles are not arbitrarily assumed. Not only do doctors seek to define health (which is no arbitrary exercise), but the goodness of health is known with a certainty greater than proof, because it is known with the certainty of self-evidence. Or if its goodness can be proved, it will be proved in some higher-order science, and that higher-order science will assume some other good as self-evident. So if one proved that health was good because the happy life is good and because health is part of the happy life,[29] one would prove the goodness of health in a higher-order science (the science of ethics), and this higher-order science would be taking as a self-evident principle that happiness is good.

The end or good, then, will not be proved, but it will, like health, be defined.   1218b24 Hence, because we now know that the end is the best of things doable for man, we must define this end. And since definition proceeds by way of division, we must divide how many ways the end is the best, that is, what things are ends and best and how they are so. Aristotle proceeds, therefore, to this task immediately at the start of the next book, taking, as he says, another beginning, the beginning of the classification of goods (for the best is not going to be found anywhere else).

Such seems to be the meaning of the concluding sentence of this book. There are oddities about it nevertheless, as that the word "best" appears three times, and that the "how many ways" has no "it is said" after it, which, however, we might normally expect. Suggestions are, therefore, made to alter the text, as to delete the third appearance of best ("since this is best" at 1218b26), or to divide the sentence into two, or to change "how many ways" either to a simple "how" or to read it with "it is said" understood.[30] But all of these suggestions face problems. The question how many ways the best is said was posed at the beginning of this chapter and answered in terms of the three of the Idea, the common good, and the end. The rest of the chapter has argued that, of these three, the best is the end, so it would be odd for Aristotle to pose the same question again as if it had not been discussed and answered. Moreover, the final sentence seems to start by taking this answer as established. Changing "how many ways" to "how," besides having no textual warrant, also produces something odd, for to ask how the good for man as end and best of things doable is best of all seems otiose. The good as end and best of things doable is best of all as end and best of things doable.

An alternative suggestion is to keep the text as it is, neither changing "how many ways" to "how" nor adding "it is said," but to press the fact that the "how many ways" refers to how many ways the good as end and best of things doable is best of all, that is, best of all things doable. For we learned much earlier how many ways the best as end is *said*, namely as the three lives of pleasure and virtue and prudence, and while we do now know that the best is end (and not the Idea or the common good), we still do not know which of these lives is that end. This whole treatise about happiness is indeed devoted to answering that question. So since Aristotle is proceeding to the next stage of his argument, it makes sense for him to say how the next stage is a continuation of his search to find the answer.

This next stage cannot, then, be about how many ways the best as end is said, but it could be about how many ways the best as end *is* best of all things doable. For to ask that question is to ask how the three things said to be best, pleasure and virtue and prudence, are best and best of all things doable. It is going to turn out, indeed, as Aristotle's argument proceeds, that all three are best, and best of things doable, but in a certain order or way, namely in relation to act. Acts of prudence are the end as the thing actually done, acts of virtue are integral to the end as done for and through prudence, and pleasure is the act of prudence as the end perfected, as realized to the full without any impediment.

Thus interpreted, this sentence suitably concludes what has already been argued and suitably introduces what comes next. The text, therefore, makes sense as it is and may be left as it is.

Notes

1. Woods (1992: 61–62)
2. As was said earlier in chapter 6 on method, 1217a2–3; but see also Dirlmeier (1962: 197) and Woods (1992: 64).
3. Following Thomas (1860: 23–54) in endorsing here (and elsewhere) a reference to *GE*, against Dirlmeier (1962: 199; 1956: 274–75), also Rowe (1971: 21n5) and Von Fragstein (1974: 34); though there may be reference as well to other and lost works of Aristotle.
4. There can, of course, be a science of being as such, namely metaphysics, and Aristotle should not be read as excluding such a science here, so Von Fragstein (1974: 34) against Dirlmeier (1962: 201), Woods (1992: 66–68), with references. What there could not be is a single science of all the particular beings at once, as of "shoes and ships and sealing wax and cabbages and kings." That way lies confusion.
5. Thus reading everything from 1217b23 to 1218a1 as a single criticism. Other analyses, as Dirlmeier's (1962: 199–202) and Wood's (1992: 64–70), divide up the passage into different criticisms, but only at the cost, as Woods himself complains, of making the argumentation bizarre.
6. This statement of the conditional "if the common happens to be the idea, that is, if one were to make the common separate" at 1218a8–9 is not superfluous to what is said just before it in a6–7 ("it cannot be that the multiple that is commonly predicated be separate"), and it indicates no problem or lacuna in the text, contra Woods (1992: 71–72, following Allan), but not Rowe (1974: 22) or Dirlmeier (1962: 202–203). Rather, as is clear, a8–9, being the negation of a6–7, serves but to complete the formal structure of the argument: if a is b (if the double is first), then c cannot be d (the common cannot be separate, a6–7), for if c is d (if the common is separate, a8–9), then c and not a will be b (the common and not the double will be first).
7. Aristotle is presumably expecting his philosophical audience to be familiar with this fact as well as others about the categories (which is why he introduced the theory so briefly earlier and referred instead to other sources for the details).

8. As so analyzed, Aristotle's argument is both straightforward and sound. Other analyses, as Wood's (1992: 70–72, with references), make it neither straightforward nor sound.

9. The interpretation given here differs from others in this respect, apart from a brief remark in Woods (1992: 74).

10. Retaining, at 1218a16, the MS reading *homologoumenōn* (things agreed . . .) and not emending it, as other commentators do, to *anhomologoumenōn* (things not agreed . . .). The stress is on the difference Aristotle draws between *have* and *be*.

11. An argument that may not go back to Plato but only to some of his followers in the Academy, Dirlmeier (1962: 204–206), Woods (1992: 76). Dirlmeier also suggests that by "monads" here are meant points, which fits nicely because points are the first units of order.

12. Woods (1992: 74–76, following Brunschwig, in Moraux and Harlfinger) constructs a more elaborate argument stretching into the next paragraphs of Aristotle's text. But such a construction is forced on Woods in part because he accepts, at 1218a16, the emendation *anhomologoumenōn*.

13. A view not too dissimilar is found also in Plato's *Timaeus*, but then the *Timaeus* presents the Ideas rather as exemplars than as separated common terms.

14. Aristotle does not hold all desires to be appetites that presuppose life, for the desire, or innate tendency, of earth and fire for their natural places does not presuppose life. But that numbers, which are mathematical abstractions, should desire even in the way earth and fire desire their natural places is going to be hard to credit.

15. Other plausible suggestions are that it is also, or instead, a reference to one of Aristotle's lost work as *On Ideas* or *On Divisions* or the like, Dirlmeier (1962: 209–11), Von Fragstein (1974: 40–41), Woods (1992: 77), Gaiser (1967: 322, 340–41, 345) suggests the reference is to the *Protrepticus*.

16. Dirlmeier's (1962: 212) translation of the Greek for "Nor yet the common good likewise. . . ." does not follow the translation given here, but he rightly notes the significance of "likewise."

17. Contra Woods (1992: 79).

18. Dirlmeier (1962: 16, 212), Rackham (1961: 231), Rowe (1971: 23), and Woods (1992: 10). Some also want to emend the Greek from *auto agathon* ("good itself" or, as in the translation, ". . . it good") to *auto to agathon* (the good itself).

19. As Woods (1992: 80) ably shows, contra Dirlmeier (1962: 212); but cf. Rowe (ibid.).

20. Aristotle does, of course, deny, because of his doctrine of the categories, that the term good has a univocal as opposed to an analogical sense, but he does not deny that the term good is predicable of all goods.

21. If this argument is what Aristotle intends, then it is stated in highly compressed form. But compression of argument seems to be a feature of *EE*.

22. Again, contra Woods (1992: 81).

23. Dirlmeier (1962: 194, with references), Gigon (1959: 196).

24. Following Dirlmeier (1962: 212) in marking here the start of the next section in the text, against Woods (1992: 81) whose interpretation, as he admits, makes it hard to see the relevance or sense of the remarks that follow.

25. A division Aristotle uses extensively, for instance, in his discussions of friendship (*EE* 7, *NE* 8–9, *MM* 2.11), which, oddly enough, Von Fragstein misses (1974: 41) despite his being otherwise very careful about Aristotle's divisions.

26. So *Meta* 13.3.1078a31–32, contra the interpretations of Dirlmeier (1962: 16, 213) and Woods (1992: 10, 81–82), though Woods does give the reference to the *Metaphysics*, and Dirlmeier does note the two kinds of noble and that the noble that is for the sake of which and doable is the beauty of virtuous deeds.

27. Keeping to the Greek of the MSS and reading *to en tois akinētois phaneron, hoti* . . . (the one manifest in changeless things, because . . .) and not, with others, emending to *to en tois akinētois. Phaneron <oun> hoti* . . . (. . . that in changeless things. It is manifest, therefore, that . . .).

28. Sc. and not as *object* of the end. The end is doable, but the object of it might not be, for God is not doable, yet he is the ultimate object of contemplation, and contemplation is the end and doable.

29. The example is suggested by Woods (1992: 84). There is the question, though, as to how we would know that health was part of happiness, and if the answer was, as is likely, that health was one of the human goods, then the goodness of health would be being assumed as self-evident after all.

30. So Dirlmeier (1962: 216–218), who prefers changing "how many ways" to "how" but otherwise keeps the text as it is, includes the final "taking after this another beginning" (which is repeated at the start of the next book). Woods (1992: 84) adds "it is said (or called)" to "how many ways" but considers the sentence rather ponderous and likely spurious. He also omits "taking after this another beginning." Rowe (1971: 24) thinks the sentence confused but otherwise follows Dirlmeier. Von Fragstein (1974: 45) attractively suggests marking a new sentence at the beginning of 1218b26 ("we must examine"). This new sentence will then, to be sure, lack one of the particles that are normally found at the beginning of a Greek sentence, but Aristotle does occasionally omit such particles.

Book Two: Virtue in General

Chapter 1

Virtuous Doing Is the Best End
Proof

The beginning is the classification of human doable goods, for the aim is to 1218b31–36 see how many ways the best doable is the best doable, which requires that we know what the doable goods are. Since human doing is an act of soul, doable goods must be something done either outside the soul or within it. Further, of these goods, those within the soul must be better than those outside it, for which the proof is what is said in exoteric works and what has been said here, that the three things people say are the end—prudence and virtue and pleasure—are all in the soul (from which it is evident that things within the soul means things within the living animal, for bodily pleasures, which some say are the pleasures of happiness, are in the body but in the body as animated by soul).[1]

The exoteric works referred to (b34) must include the *GE* 1.3, where such a distinction is drawn and where goods within the soul are divided as here into prudence, virtue, and pleasure, while goods outside the soul are listed as things like wealth, rule, and honor. That the former are best is there asserted as obvious, which it is, for it is obvious that people seek wealth, rule, and honor for the sake of pleasure or the exercise of their abilities, as in particular the exercise of virtue (including skills) and prudence. Here in *EE*, Aristotle expressly adds that people hold one or more of the goods within the soul to be the end, perhaps because here these goods constitute the rival claims to happiness under investigation. In *GE*, by contrast (because of the nature of its audience), the correctness of the claim of virtue is being taken for granted.

Things within the soul are habits or powers, on the one hand, and activities or changes on the other. Virtue and prudence are habits or powers and pleasure would seem to be some sort of activity or change (pleasure was earlier set aside as something to come back to later, so its status is not pursued here).

This opening paragraph gives us the following theses:

(1) goods are divided between those in the soul and those outside it;
(2) those in the soul are better;
(3) things in the soul are divided into powers and acts.

Premise (1), being a division by contradictories, is a necessary truth. Premise (2) is a matter of fact from common opinion (and from the exoteric works).

Premise (3) may also be considered a necessary truth. The goods in question now are doable goods, but doable goods can only be found in things in the soul that relate to doing, which must of necessity be the soul's powers for doing and its actual doing. The conclusion follows: since we are looking for the best of doable goods, we must look for them in the soul's powers and acts.

Aristotle is peculiarly flexible in the words he uses for (3), speaking of habits (*hexeis*), powers (*dunameis*), activities (*energeiai*), changes (*kinēseis*), and (at b38) of dispositions (*diatheseis*). The terms have precise distinctions: dispositions are certain states of a power, habits are certain kinds of dispositions, and activities are not the same as changes. Aristotle ultimately wants to preserve these distinctions (as that virtue is a habit, that a habit is a stable disposition of a power [2.2], and that pleasure is an activity and not a change or a becoming [6.12]).[2] Why does he not say so here? Perhaps because his argument does not yet need the distinctions, though it does need some differentiation between powers and acts, and such differentiation cannot be made without employing one or more of the terms. Aristotle employs them all, therefore, lest perhaps a philosophic audience (who could be expected to be familiar with the precise sense of the terms) think he is ignoring the distinctions when really he is not now in need of them.[3]

1218b37 A further thesis is laid down:

(4) virtue (including also prudence) is the best disposition or habit or power of what has a use or work.

The thesis is proved through induction from examples (even if in English we would not happily apply the word virtue to them), that a cloak, a ship, a house are all things with a use or work and that the virtue (or excellence) of each is the best disposition of each with a view to that work. Hence, in the case of the soul, which has a work, its virtue will be its best disposition in the same way. The argument is straightforward:

(4) virtue is the best disposition of each thing that has a work;
(5) the soul has a work;
(6) therefore, the virtue of the soul is the best disposition of the soul.

Premise (4) was proved through the examples. Premise (5) is proved shortly. The conclusion (6) achieves a further focusing of the search: the goods in the soul we are looking for must be those powers or dispositions in it that are virtues.

1219a6/13 Further theses are now added:

(7) the better habit has a better work, or generally, the works are to each other as the respective habits are;
(8) a thing's work is its end.

From (8) follows:

(9)   the work is better than the habit, because
(10) the end is best (the end was so defined at the end of the previous book).

Premise (7) has not yet been used. It is returned to later. The conclusion (9) also further focuses the search: the goods we are looking for are the habits, but the habits as exercised or at work and not merely as had.

But work is said in two ways, either as the product of some use or act or as the use and act itself. The distinction is clear: a house is the work of the art of house-building as what results from using the art; the work of eye and science is the very using of them and not something further. Hence a specification of (9) follows:

(9a) the using is better than the habit in the case of things whose work is the using.[4]

A further distinction is now made about work, between the work as of the thing and as of the virtue of the thing. A shoe is the work of the shoemaking art but a good shoe is the work of good shoemaking. So, if there is a virtue or an excellence in shoemaking and the good shoemaker, then the work of this virtue will be a good shoe (whereas the work of a poor shoemaker, who lacks the virtue, will be a poor shoe). The same will hold in all other cases, that is, both when the work is a product, as in the case of a shoe, and when it is the use, as in the case of seeing and studying. Hence, the work of the virtue of an eye or of a student will be good or excellent seeing and studying. Thus we may state, as another general thesis: 1219a18

(11) the work of a thing is also the work of its virtue, and the work of its virtue is virtuous or good and excellent work.

Aristotle now returns to premise (5) that the soul has a work, which he proves   1219a23
less by argument than by illustration of its meaning. Soul is just a name for the principle of life in things that live, and what it does in them is make them live (in the sense of formal and not efficient causality, as health—and not medicine—is said to make things healthy). Things are made to be alive by soul even when asleep, but soul is at work rather in using life and being awake (sleep is more like a not working or a resting). Hence we may specify (5) as:

(12) the work of soul is life,

and we may conclude from (11), or from its restatement here (the work of the soul must be one and the same as the work of its virtue) that:

(13) the work of the virtue of the soul is virtuous life.

From this Aristotle concludes further and finally that:

(14) virtuous life is the final or complete good (which was happiness).

1219a28   This conclusion is the one we were in search of, but it does not follow directly from (13). We have to combine (13) with the earlier premises and conclusions. Aristotle therefore gives a quick restatement of the argument. First he recalls (from the previous book) that:

(15) happiness is the best.

Secondly he recalls, from (1), (2), and (3), that the goods or ends in the soul, its habits and activities, are best. He then argues:

(9, 9a)   the work or activity is better than the habit or disposition;
(7)   the best activity is of the best habit;
(6)   virtue is the best habit of the soul;
(16)   therefore, the activity of the virtue of the soul is best, but
(15)   [repeated] happiness was best (the stress is perhaps now on the word "best" and not "happiness");[5]
(17)   therefore, happiness is activity of a good soul.

There are problems with this restatement. Conclusion (16) does indeed follow from its premises, with (7) now put to express use (for if the best is in goods of the soul, and if in these goods the activities are better, and if the best activity is of the best habit, which is the virtue, then the activity of virtue is best). The difficulty is to see, first, how the restatement supports or entails (14), for (17) does not strictly say the same as (14); second, what role (13) is supposed to be playing (for it has not been expressly used and it does not entail (14) by itself); and, third, how (17) anyway follows.[6] For what follows from (15)—or its valid converse, for it is a sort of definition—and from (16) is this other conclusion:

(18) happiness is the activity of the virtue of the soul.

We may begin by noticing, therefore, that (18) entails (14), or part of it (excluding the reference to completeness), when combined with (13):

(18) happiness is the activity of the virtue of the soul;
(13) the work, or activity, of the virtue of the soul is virtuous life;
(14a) therefore, happiness is virtuous life.

We may also notice another inference entailed by earlier premises:

(12) [the specification of (5)] life is the work of soul;

    (11)   the work of the soul is one and the same as the work of its virtue, which work is excellent or virtuous work;

    (19)   therefore, virtuous life is the work or activity of the soul as possessed of and using the virtue.

The necessity of conclusion (19) is made clear by the example of shoemaking, for it is only a shoemaker possessed of and using the virtue of shoemaking who makes a good shoe. The same example of shoemaking enables us to argue further:

    (20)   a soul possessed of the virtue and using it in its work is by definition a good soul (as a good shoemaker is a shoemaker who uses his excellence in making good shoes);

    (21)   therefore, from (19) and (20), virtuous life is the work of a good soul;

    (14a) happiness is virtuous life;

    (17)   therefore, happiness is the work or activity of a good soul.

Aristotle's restatement of his argument thus proves (14a) and, through (14a), proves (17), which is the conclusion he states. We might say that (14) or (14a) is enough and that we do not need to go to the bother of deriving (17) as well. Perhaps (17) is in a way obvious (at least from examples, as that of shoemaking), but it does hold. Moreover it holds in such a way as to stress the idea that the virtuous life of happiness is not something that happens to the soul (in the way that fortune and external goods can), but something that the soul itself does by exercise of its own powers. Happiness is possessed from within, not from without.

What is striking about Aristotle's presentation of this argument is how complete it is in its materials but how incomplete and indirect in its expression. The necessary premises are there, explicit or implicit, but they are not brought together in neat syllogisms. Some of the syllogisms are indeed rather obvious, but others are not. Perhaps Aristotle, then, is writing with an eye to his philosophical audience and to their predilection for arguments to exercise their wits. So here, he says, is an important argument, perhaps the most important in terms of the treatise, the proof of happiness. However, the premises are not stated in linear order and some are missing while others seem irrelevant; so have philosophical fun with it and see how it is all meant to hang together.

Proposition (17) says nothing about completeness, nor does (14a), but (14) does, since it identifies virtuous life with happiness by identifying it with the final and complete good. Happiness is by definition complete, for it is by definition best and anything incomplete would, if it were made complete, be better than it is and so could not be best. But the question of completeness is only relevant or only worth drawing attention to if the thing in question admits of completeness and incompleteness. Happiness has been defined as

1219a35

virtuous life and both virtue and life, he says, may be complete or incomplete, so happiness must be specified as complete in virtue and in life.

The meaning of "complete" is unclear. That virtue and life can be complete or incomplete Aristotle asserts on the grounds that they admit of being a whole or a part (and parts are incomplete without the whole). Time, at least as to its beginning, has something to do with completeness, for a child is not happy (as Aristotle indicates shortly [b5]), but it is not clear that an ending of time is required as well. For since physical growth, in height and bulk, has an end not when life ceases but when life is at its bodily peak, perhaps the same is true of life at its moral peak of virtue. Happiness is such a peak, for it is a peak of goodness, so life and virtue will be complete and happy, not when they end, but when they are best. The termination of life at death, then, seems to be an irrelevant consideration that reflects material necessities, not moral ones.

Aristotle says little further here. What is meant by complete virtue can only become clear after the detailed treatment of virtue itself has been given. There are, however, two express places later where completeness is discussed: completeness of life in the chapters on friendship (esp. 7.12) and completeness of virtue in the chapter on the gentleman (8.3).[7] Before those passages are reached, the word "complete" must be left indefinite, and "complete virtue" and "complete life" must be left to mean whatever they must mean if happiness is to be complete. Taken thus indefinitely, Aristotle's argument does not, despite appearances, trade on ambiguity in the word complete, nor is it too quick.[8] Complete means the same when said of life and virtue as when said of happiness. That we are as yet ignorant of precisely what that meaning is does not invalidate the argument.

Confirmation of the Proof

1219a39/b16   In accordance with the method laid down in 1.6, to use the appearances as evidence and example, Aristotle proceeds to show that the definition of happiness just given coheres with the appearances, that is, the prevailing opinions. The appearances are evidence, he says, both of the genus (activity) and of the definition (complete virtuous activity).

The opinion that happiness is doing or living well confirms the genus, for living and doing are activity (as the arts show, for the acting art is the art that uses what the making arts make).

The opinion that a happy man is not so for a day or as a child confirms the definition that happiness is complete. Solon's remark not to call a living man happy but when he has reached his end is approved by Aristotle on the grounds that nothing incomplete is happy because it is not whole. Reaching the end means being whole and not, as the story about Solon has it, being dead. For Solon applied his remark to death because of completion, for death was how he judged completion. But if completion could be reached and judged before death, even Solon would agree to call it happy. By glossing end as whole, and not as death or cessation, Aristotle gives to understand that not to call a living man happy must be taken to mean that one should not call a man happy qua living but only qua whole in living. Whether death is needed for wholeness is another question. (Aristotle answers it in the negative in the last chapter of this whole treatise when he treats of the completeness of the gentleman.)

The opinions about praise and encomia and victory (that these go to deeds and not capacities) confirm that activity is better than capacity and hence confirm the genus, again, that happiness (which is better than anything else) must be activity, not capacity, and they confirm the definition that the activity must be good enough to deserve praise.

The opinions about happiness being felicitated and not praised confirm the same point, that happiness is something complete and excellent. Deeds are praised in view of happiness, as parts of it or steps to it, for encomium focuses on some particular excellent deed and praise focuses on character, as shown repeatedly in excellent deeds. But happiness, because it is an end, is a matter of felicitation or congratulation. Aristotle's remarks here should be taken as applying to the thing, not the words (for the words can have a certain looseness in ordinary speech). An example from sports may help. Encomium would be when a player makes a superb stroke in tennis, and the stroke is lauded as superb even if the player plays normally at a lower level. Praise would be of a player who plays regularly at a high level and is praised as an excellent player, even if he occasionally makes a bad shot. But while both players are thus praised for particular strokes or general performance, they are only congratulated or felicitated if they win the game or the tournament. The praise is of the deeds in view of the end; congratulation or felicitation is of the end. Because happiness is felicitated it is an end or completion of excellence (though the end in the case of happiness, since it is activity, is not something attained when activity ceases, as the victor's crown in a tennis tournament, but something attained when activity is full, as the unimpeded exercise of an achieved mastery).

The opinion about sleep (in sleep there is no difference between the virtuous and the base) confirms the genus that happiness is activity. For the virtuous and the base differ in virtue when asleep but do not differ in happiness or misery, thus happiness cannot be virtue but must be activity of virtue. Hence it must be activity of virtues that are not operative in sleep, unlike the virtues of the nutritive soul. Further, happiness cannot be the virtues of the body, as health and beauty. For those who say happiness is bodily pleasure only include health and beauty in happiness insofar as health and beauty are used in activities of bodily pleasure (health and beauty exist in sleep, yet actions of bodily pleasure are not then done or enjoyed). A full and peaceful sleep can contribute to action and to pleasure, but as providing rest from past action and strength for future action, not as being itself either action or enjoyment (except insofar as such sleep may also produce pleasant dreams).

One should perhaps note about all these points of confirmation that they only show that Aristotle's definition of happiness saves them, not that it alone saves them.[9] Perhaps some other definition could save them too, or some of them. But that the definition is correct was shown by the argument in the previous section. What Aristotle is doing now is showing that none of the appearances or opinions about happiness is incompatible with it. Therefore, as he said in 1.6, all men will be able to agree with it when they follow it through, because they will see that it conflicts with nothing they otherwise believe.

What Happiness Is in Particular
Parts of Soul

1219b26/b36 Aristotle has completed his account and definition of happiness in general, and he now turns to discussion of it in detail, in particular about soul and virtue. The discussion, however, is taking place against the background of the three goods that claim to constitute the happy life: virtue, prudence, pleasure. Virtue and prudence are the immediate focus (1.5); the question of pleasure has been temporarily deferred. Books Two to Four are about virtue, and Book Five is about prudence (and the other intellectual virtues in relation to prudence). Book Six is about continence and incontinence and includes a treatment of pleasure at the end. But continence and incontinence are also about pleasure, for both are cases of giving into or resisting pleasure, especially bodily pleasure. Further, the treatment of pleasure shows that there are pleasures in addition to the bodily ones, and that these other pleasures are pleasanter and properly belong to happiness. Book Six thus fulfills that part of Aristotle's program, which is to deal with pleasure.[10] Further, Books Three to Six taken together show that the goods of virtue and prudence and pleasure are all integral to the happy life, and hence that happiness is noblest because it is virtuous and prudent, and that it is pleasantest because it is full of the best pleasures. Thereby happiness will also be shown to be best, provided the life of virtue and prudence and pleasure is complete in goodness. Book Seven is about complete life (it is about friendship, without which human life is not complete), and Book Eight is about complete virtue. Books Seven and Eight are, then, about the completeness of the happy life and how this life, being complete, is best. The overall program of *EE* and how its parts fit into this program thus seem clear.

As regards the first question of the soul and its virtue (including prudence), virtue, says Aristotle, belongs to the soul non-accidentally (b27) because, presumably, the virtue in question now is the virtue of man as man (and not any virtue that may belong to him not as man but merely as animal or nutritive). The acts we do that are distinctively human are those done with reason or with some understanding and awareness. The soul has two parts, which share in reason, though dissimilarly, the part that commands and the part that obeys by hearing the command. But the term part should not be pressed. The question is not about the soul's divisibility but about its powers, for even if the soul is in some sense divisible or indivisible (in what sense is not relevant here),[11] it surely has the distinct powers just mentioned (of commanding and of obeying). These powers should be accepted as evident phenomena of experience, and that there can be separate powers without separate souls is clear from the examples of concave and convex and of white and straight (which are not separable on a curve or a line yet are different properties or powers).

So much shows that the soul can be one and have distinct powers (and so distinct virtues), but that the powers mentioned are the relevant ones needs to be shown also. There are disputes about the Greek at this point (b36–40). The translation is designed to follow the manuscript readings as they are without emendation or addition.[12] The argumentation is as follows: First, any part of the soul that is not involved in reason, as the "natural" part, is to be removed from consideration. The term "natural" here is being used in contradistinction to "rational" and to be referring back in particular to the nutritive part of the soul mentioned earlier. The rational parts of the human soul, by contrast, are proper to man. Thus, the virtues of the nutritive and appetitive parts are not proper. For these parts belong to the natural as opposed to the rational part in man (appetite exists in the other animals that are incapable of properly human virtue),[13] and we can only speak of human virtues when reason is involved. Hence we must dismiss any virtues even of the appetitive soul that, as in the case of animals, are there when reason is not. The virtues proper to man can only include those virtues in the appetitive soul that are obedient to reason and not any that are independent of it.

Second, Aristotle gives a proof. A man must, if he is a man, have in him reasoning and rule and action (man, by definition, is an animal possessed of reason, and since as an animal he is a self-mover and as rational he directs his own moving, he must possess rule and action as well as reason). A man in his moving, therefore, must have a part that rules by moving and a part that is ruled by being moved. The reasoning part is clearly the part that rules, but not, in the case of motion, over reasoning;[14] rather, as is plain, over appetite and passion (these are the immediate drivers of motion in any animal, rational or irrational). Appetite and passions must, therefore, be proper to man, but proper as subject to the rule of reason and not simply (the way they are in the other animals). Hence, if these parts of the soul as subject to reason, along with the part of the soul that is reason, are proper to man, then these parts must be the relevant ones for understanding human virtues—which was the hypothesis laid down.[15]

This result, that virtue is twofold as the parts in which it exists are twofold, is confirmed with an analogy from good physical condition, that as such condition is a matter of combining virtues in the several parts of the body, so also is virtue of the soul a matter of combining virtues in the soul's several parts. There are two kinds of virtue, then: the moral virtues in the appetitive part that obeys reason and the intellectual virtues in the rational part that commands.

1220a4/8   That the intellectual virtues must indeed be virtues is shown from the fact that we praise people who act on these habits as well as those who act on moral ones, and virtues and their works were earlier set down as things that are praised in this way (1291b8). The Greek of the next phrase about "these" not acting but having activities (a6–7) is ambiguous. The "these" could be a reference to both moral and intellectual virtues, in which case the meaning will be that virtues are not activities but dispositions or habits that issue in activity when exercised. Or it could be a reference to the intellectual virtues alone, in which case the meaning will be that although these virtues are not active as the moral virtues are (for they refer to our thinking and not our doing), yet they do have a work. Their work is their internal activity, the act of thinking or reasoning and ruling, and not some external action as in the case of the moral virtues.[16] Hence since, as said before, a virtue is the best condition of what has a work, the best condition of the intellect with respect to its work must be virtue. The former interpretation is perhaps more likely but the latter is not impossible. Not much seems to hang on the difference.[17]

The claim that virtue divides into moral and intellectual only may seem to beg the question against those, like Sardanapalus, who say the happy life is the life of bodily pleasure. For why could there not be virtues that are about enjoying these pleasures to excess and why could not the activity of these virtues be the complete end that is happiness? Such activity, to be sure, might not be noble, but it could be pleasantest and, as pleasantest, best. Strictly speaking, Aristotle has not excluded this option, and he does not exclude it until he examines pleasure in Book Six. For while it does turn out in what follows that there is no virtue for an excess of bodily pleasures but only a virtue (temperance) for moderating them according to the measure of reason, yet from this fact alone one cannot argue, and Aristotle does not argue, that moderating these pleasures is pleasanter than having them to excess. Most men conclude the opposite, of course; for while in their praise they speak of temperance as noblest, in their deeds they pursue license as pleasantest. That they hereby err, because temperance is far pleasanter, is something that Aristotle has to argue separately. But in order to do so he first has to say what moral virtue is and specifically what temperance is, since it is from what these are that the arguments about their pleasantness will be drawn. Therefore the discussion of virtue must precede the discussion of pleasure.

Virtue of Character
In General
What It Is
That It Is Caused by and Does the Best Things

1220a13   Having distinguished the two parts of soul and the two kinds of virtue, Aristotle proceeds to deal with each in turn, and first with moral virtue (intellectual virtue is dealt with in Book Five). He begins, as is his wont and as the method of science requires,[18] by looking for the definition. From the definition once found he proceeds to divide moral virtue into its kinds[19] and to consider its properties, that it is voluntary and by choice. These matters he discusses first in general in this book and then with respect to the individual virtues in the two following books.

Aristotle begins by recalling his methodological remarks (from 1.6), that we must start with truths we have already got hold of, but not clearly, so as to reach what is both true and clear. In other words, he is going to start, as before in the case of defining happiness, from the prevailing opinions that, in ethics, are the relevant phenomena. An example about Coriscus makes the point. But its interpretation is disputed.

A first interpretation is to say that if we only know about health that it is the best disposition of the body, or that Coriscus is he in the marketplace with the darkest skin, then we do not know what health is, for we do not know which disposition is best or what role spending time in the marketplace and having dark skin play in having, or not having, the best disposition.[20] Still, it is worthwhile and not useless to know that health is the best disposition of the body and that Coriscus has the darkest skin among those in the marketplace. For on the basis of these facts we can proceed to investigate what part of health they are, as, say, that good quality of body is the substance or essence of health and darkness of skin an effect or property or sign of health in the marketplace (because, say, those with dark skin are best able to endure and work in the sun). From these results we can then, perhaps, proceed further to examine best dispositions of bodies and darkness of skin among those in the marketplace and come to a clearer grasp of what health is. Accordingly Aristotle talks first about what is involved in saying of something, whether health or virtue, that it is the best disposition, and then adds a sign or effect from pain and pleasure about the best disposition in the case of virtue. He then proceeds, in the next chapters, to develop both points in detail.

A second interpretation is to say that we are placed with respect to virtue the way we would be if we knew that health was the best disposition of the body and that Coriscus was the darkest man of those in the marketplace. Our knowing these facts does not tell us what health is or who Coriscus is, but does help us to recognize them and so to learn what or who each is. We can do the same, then, with virtue and from general facts proceed to more detailed knowledge. This interpretation gives a reasonable sense but not, perhaps, the sense that best fits what Aristotle does next. Moreover it requires some emendation of the Greek.[21] The other interpretation therefore seems preferable.

Aristotle begins with the known fact that virtue is the best disposition, and from it he lays down certain other facts plain from induction. The facts are (1) the best disposition is brought about by the best things; (2) the best

1220a22/34

things are done in each case by the virtue of each thing. The induction is from the example of physical exertion and diet: those who have the best diet and exert themselves in the best way have the best physical condition, and those who have the best physical condition have the best diet and exert themselves in the best way. A further fact is (3) every disposition is brought about by the same things that also destroy it as these things are differently applied. The induction is the example of health, which is brought about and destroyed by diet and physical exertion and seasons (of the year or perhaps one's time of life), for if one eats this food and does these exertions in this way at this time one becomes healthy, and if one eats or does them at some other time in some other way, one becomes unhealthy.

Applying these facts to virtue, which is the best disposition of the soul, we get (1) it is brought about by the best movements in the soul; (2) the best works and passions are done by it; and (3) it is brought about and destroyed by the same things (virtue is increased and destroyed by the same things that its use is for).

The final sentence (a34) is ambiguous, for it is unclear what is being said to be a sign of what and, accordingly, what the practice of punishment is supposed to be confirming. The meaning could be that what has just been said is a sign that virtue and vice are about pleasures and pains. Or it could be that virtue and vice being about pleasures and pains is a sign of what has just been said (where, in each case, the practice of punishment, or the use of pleasures and pains to end vice and generate virtue, confirms the alleged fact). Or it could be that punishment is a sign that virtue and vice are about pleasures and pains.[22] All three interpretations make the sentence say something true but not, it seems, something particularly relevant. For it is odd that pleasure and pain are mentioned here at all. The point seems out of place because it introduces something new to the discussion and something that seems properly to belong to the later discussion in chapter 4.

Relevance and sense can be given to the sentence and to its position if, by a fourth interpretation, we return to the example of Coriscus. For as the color of Coriscus among those in the marketplace is helpful for understanding health (though how, or what part of health it is, we may not know), so pleasure and pain are helpful for understanding virtue. We know that Coriscus' color is in some way relevant to health because of what we know of Coriscus, that he is, say, healthiest among those who spend time in the marketplace. In like manner we know that pleasure and pain are in some way relevant to virtue because of what we know of punishment. For punishment, which is painful, is a cure of vice and, like cures generally, works through opposites. Hence pain and pleasure are in some way cause of virtue (for they are in some way cure of vice—pain being given for bad deeds and pleasure for good). Therefore pain and pleasure are in some way what virtue is about, for, as just noted, the use of virtue is for things that bring it about and destroy it, and that virtue is the best disposition for. Thus pleasure and pain, while something new in the discussion as regards content, are not new as regards logical role. They are introduced, like Coriscus' skin color, as an additional known factor for determining the best disposition. They are a sign of virtue (in the way that Coriscus' color is a sign of health) and will be used in due course in chapter 4 to advance understanding of what the best disposition of virtue is.

Notes

1. Contra Woods (1992: 88) and perhaps Von Fragstein (1974: 53). Goods of the body, like health and beauty, are perhaps outside the soul as states of the body but within the soul as used by the soul in acts and pleasures.
2. These distinctions are also drawn elsewhere, as that between disposition and habit in *Cat.* 8, and that between activity and change in *Meta.* 9.6 and *NE* 10.4.
3. Thus may we explain the puzzles about Aristotle's use of terms here noted by Dirlmeier (1962: 221–22) and Woods (1992: 87–88); also Von Fragstein (1974: 54).
4. One might also say that the using is better than the habit in the case of things whose work is a product because it is only through the using that the product is produced, so that the habit must be for the using as the using is for the product. But this point, while true, is irrelevant to the present argument.
5. So Von Fragstein (1974: 57).
6. The puzzles are noted by Woods (1992: 87–88). About the first he says that (14)—which, because he gives separate numbers to Aristotle's repetitions, he lists as (19)—and its immediate premises are not part of the main argument but independent of it; about the second he simply notes its presence with a question mark; about the third he says that Aristotle assumes what is necessary to get (17) from (16)—or in his numbering (24) from (23).
7. Dirlmeier (1962: 227).
8. Woods (1992: 90), also perhaps Dirlmeier (1962: 226).
9. Contra Woods (1992: 92).
10. Dirlmeier (1962: 177–78, 361–65) doubts that *EE* follows the division of the three lives, because he does not think the three books it has in common with *NE* really belong to it.
11. It is dealt with in *De Anima* 2.
12. At 1219b40 the Greek reads *ēi* (is) or *hēi* (qua). The MSS do not clearly disambiguate the two readings. Adopting the former is grammatically easier and does not require supplying anything extra to the clause. A scholarly emendation would also alter *orektikou* (appetitive) at 1219b39 into *auxētikou* (growing) so as to have the text mention two of the parts that belong to the *phytikon* (vegetative) part of the soul. This emendation requires a prior emendation at 1219b37 of *physikon* (natural) to *phytikon*. See Dirlmeier (1962: 233–34), and Woods (1992: 95).
13. *GE* in a parallel passage may be adopting this position, 1185b11; Dirlmeier (1962: 234).
14. Reasoning can no doubt rule reasoning when it comes to thinking, for reason can direct its thinking according to the rules of logic, which are rules reason imposes on itself so as to think correctly.

15. Woods (1992: 94–95) offers a not too dissimilar analysis of the argument though his translation, because he accepts the emendations, differs considerably from mine.
16. Cf. the argument in *Politics* 4(7).3.1325b16–30.
17. Discussion in Dirlmeier (1962: 235), also Woods (1992: 96), both of whom accept the first interpretation. The second interpretation comes from Maurus (1668/1886: 396 *ad loc.*).
18. See Natali (2007, 2010).
19. Thus may one interpret the word "parts" (a14) in the Greek (because of what follows in chapter 3). But the reference could be, not to the kinds of virtue, but to the elements in its definition, so Dirlmeier (1962: 236) and Woods (1992: 96).
20. Perhaps Woods (1992: 97) has something of this sort in mind in one of his proposed interpretations of the example.
21. As in particular that "of it" (*autēs*) at 1220a21 be changed to "of them" (*autōn*) or "of the two of them"(*autoin*). See the details in Dirlmeier (1962: 236–37), who, while accepting the emendation, points out other difficulties with the text as so read. Von Fragstein (1974: 62) keeps *autēs* but has it refer back to virtue, not health, taking the clause to mean, along with what follows, that thus positioned (that is, knowing virtue to be the best disposition) we can come to know each of the two forms of it (intellectual and moral). This interpretation is better than that of Dirlmeier and others in not requiring any emendation of the Greek, but it has the disadvantage of making the discussion still to be about both kinds of virtue when Aristotle has just said at 1220a13 that he is now going to discuss moral virtue only.
22. The question is nicely discussed by Woods (1992: 98), who opts for the first interpretation. Dirlmeier (1962: 238–39), Rowe (1971: 40), and Von Fragstein (1974: 63) opt for the second. Solomon (1984: 2.1932) and Allan (1961: 312n3) opt for the third (though Allan thinks the sentence thereby out of place).

Chapter 2

That It Is an Acquired Habit

1220a38   We have a hold on two facts about virtue: it is the best disposition, and it concerns things pleasant and painful. The best disposition at issue here is that of moral virtue, which, as has just been said, is brought about by the best movements in the soul and does the best things. The first point to note, then, is how these best movements bring it about, which, as the name "moral" or "ethics" itself indicates, is by custom.[1] What gets to have a custom is something, which when moved repeatedly a certain way under a guidance not innate to it comes to be an activating principle with respect to that movement. The point is clear from the contrast with lifeless things that cannot be made to act differently by custom (as stones that cannot be accustomed to go upward rather than downward). Living things, by contrast do develop customs (plants can be trained to grow in one direction rather than another and animals to behave in one way rather than another), and we ourselves develop customs under the external guidance of parents and teachers, thus becoming activating principles of different behaviors. A moral character, then, being a custom, is an activating principle so generated in the soul, and also, because best disposition is at issue here, one that is in accord with command-giving reason. It will be produced by the best movements and do the best works and passions, namely those commanded by reason.

The definition of moral character can now be collected from what has been said. It is a quality of soul (it is a property acquired through custom and custom does not arise save in things with soul) that is in accord with a reason that gives commands (the custom comes about through extrinsic guidance), and what receives the commands is a something able to follow reason (else it could not respond to the guidance and become itself active in following reason but would, like the stone, keep behaving the same way).

There is an implication here, left unexpressed, that this process of habituation not only implants a quality in the part of the soul that follows reason but also implants correct commanding in the part of soul that reasons, so that he who learns right behavior also learns right judgment at the same time. The point becomes explicit later; it would complicate the exposition to make it explicit now.

The next question naturally to ask is what qualities these are and in accord   1220b6/b10
with what in the soul (what materials in the soul the customs are customs of). From what was said earlier about moral virtue (it belongs in the appetitive or passionate part of the soul) and from what has just been said (it is generated by custom), these qualities must be in accord with the soul's powers for feeling passions and in accord with its habits, or with the ways people get accustomed to feeling or not feeling the passions.

But these remarks are still very general. Aristotle's method, as he has just recalled, is to begin with truths already known but unclearly so as to reach truths that are clear. The thing to do next, then, is to turn to what we already know about passions and habits and use it to advance to something clearer. Accordingly Aristotle next appeals to some such collection of data and a division of passions and powers and habits, and uses it to answer the two questions, what sort of qualities moral characters are and according to what in the soul. In this chapter he uses it to answer the second question, listing the sorts of things we mean by passions and powers and habits that the custom of moral character accords with. In the next chapter he uses it, along with further examples, to answer the first question, explaining how the habits divide according to the more and less of the passions that the powers have become accustomed to display, and how some of these accustomed ways are what we mean by moral virtues and others what we mean by moral vices. That this collection of data is, or includes, *VV* was argued in the Introduction and will simply be assumed here.

The summary Aristotle now gives generally follows *VV* and roughly anticipates the list he gives in the next chapter. So, for instance, he mentions passions, such as spirit, fear, shame, desire, or things that perceptible pleasure and pain[2] essentially follow on. By the "things" that he puts last here, he would seem to mean various external goods, as money and glory,[3] for which people have passions because they have about them palpable feelings of pleasure and pain.[4] So in the next chapter, when he lists the means and extremes of passions, he follows the order given here, beginning first with spirit, fear, shame, and desire, and then proceeding to passions to do with money, fame, power, and the like. Powers and habits are described relative to passions, as they are effectively in *VV*, so that powers are what people are active by in respect of feeling the passions, and habits are what set their being thus active[5] in accord with or against reason.

Notes

1. "Moral" and "ethics" come from Latin (*mos*) and Greek (*ethos*) words meaning custom. Because of the mention of best movements in the previous chapter, this chapter does not seem, contra Rowe (1971: 40), to be a digression but the next step in the process of thought. The Greek text at a39–b6 is disputed and subject to much emendation; details in Dirlmeier (1962: 239–41) and Woods (1992: 99, 188–89). The translation is meant to be accurate to the Greek, as it is without emendation, and to give the whole a defensible philosophical sense.

2. Cf. Leighton (1984: 135–38), also Woods ad loc.

3. So, unlike Woods (1992: 100–101), not taking "things" to be a reference back to spirit, fear, shame, and desire but rather to be an item additional to them in the list.

4. The tight connection between passion on the one hand and pain and pleasure on the other is evident in the definitions of the passions given in *Rhetoric* 2.2–11.

5. The Greek at 1220b18 is ambiguous and simply says "these" (*tauta*), which could be a reference back to the powers or the feelings or both. Little seems to hang on the ambiguity for a habit will in any event be a quality in accord with or against reason, whereby the power of a passion is exercised this way or that in actual feeling of the passion.

Chapter 3

That It Is a Mean

1220b21 The argument that virtue is a mean and the vices extremes proceeds in two stages, first that all continuous things admit of a mean and extremes, and second that the mean is best for us. The argument for the first stage is by way of example from the sciences and arts and human actions generally (including those not done with art). The examples, which are of habits and of actions, pick up from what was just mentioned in the previous chapter and illustrate how there is in them an excess and deficiency and a mean because they are continuous quantities. That passions and powers and habits are such quantities is obvious enough (it would be obvious from summaries of the sort to be found in *VV*), for each of these is a continuous quantity (we have the power to feel the passions a lot or a little).[1] But the point is reinforced, as well as extended, by the examples of the sciences and arts, which are also habits, and by the examples of actions that, whether done with art and science or without, can be done more or less or in between, and either relative to themselves or to us (exercising for two hours is a mean between exercising for one hour and for three, and exercising for two hours may be a mean for one person but not another).

That Aristotle expressly mentions actions and expressly adds an argument to show that they are continuous quantities (they are cases of change, and change is a continuous quantity) is perhaps because the conclusion he is intending to draw, at 1220b34–35, is that virtues are not only mean states but are also about certain means, and the means they are about would seem to be actions (courage is the mean state in feeling fear and daring, and courageous actions are the mean in facing dangers).[2] These actions will be means not only as individual continuous acts (because they go thus far and no further) but also as sets of discrete actions (because they are repeated thus often and not more). Aristotle presumably intends to include both kinds of quantity (continuous and discrete), for both appear later in the chapter, and he opened it by speaking of everything "continuous *and* divisible" (b22) and discrete quantities are divisible, at least in number.

The second stage of the argument, that virtue belongs with the mean, can be schematized thus:

(1) in all of them (actions, passions, habits) the mean relative to us is best;
(2) for this is the way science and reason command;
(3) this makes the best habit;
(4) this is plain from induction and argument;
(5) for opposite things destroy each other;
(6) and the extremes are opposite both to each other and to the mean;
(7) for the mean is either to either, as the equal is greater than the less but less than the greater;
(8) therefore, moral virtue must be about certain means and be itself a mean state.

A puzzle here is what the three instances of "this" in propositions (2) to (4) refer to:[3] whether to the mean or the best in (2), whether to the mean or to reason's command in (3), and whether to proposition (2) or (3) or both in (4). In the case of (2), it perhaps makes little difference which way we take the "this," or indeed whether we take it both ways, for it must be taken both ways to constitute an argument for (1). The argument is supposed to prove that the mean is best, and the middle term for this purpose is science and reason. We need a premise, then, that says science and reason command the best things and another that says the mean is the things that science and reason command. But if "this" refers to the best, we are only given the first premise, and if it refers to the mean, we are only given the second; hence in either case we must supply the other. Better, perhaps, to suppose Aristotle intends to give us both premises at once by making the "this" do service for both at once. Both have to be assumed anyway from experience and obvious examples (as that, in culinary science, reason bids the ingredients to be mixed and cooked best, which is that they be mixed and cooked neither too much nor too little).

As for how to take the "this" in (3), whether as referring also to the mean as best or more broadly to the command of science and reason, the difference is slight, for the mean or the best is what, from (2), we must understand science and reason to command. We may again suppose that Aristotle intends the reference to go either or both ways indifferently.

The importance of (3) is its introduction of the idea of habit, or the claim that "this" (the mean as best and commanded by science and reason[4]) makes the best habit, which, Aristotle says in (4), is plain from induction and argument. As for the induction Aristotle presumably intends us to refer back to the cases of science and action he mentioned just before (1220b23–26), where the fact is obvious (doing what science and reason say is the way to acquire the best habit in each case, as that one becomes a good chef by following what the science of cooking says). So we should regard the "this" in (4) to be referring to both (3) and (2), or to (3) in the light of (2) and also (1). As for the argument, it consists of the following:

(5) for opposite things destroy each other;
(6) and the extremes are opposite both to each other and to the mean;
(7) for the mean is either to either, as the equal is greater than the less but less than the greater.

Proposition (7) proves the part of (6) about the mean (the part about the extremes is obvious and, anyway, not important for the argument), for if the mean is both less and greater, each extreme is opposite to it. The point of (7), however, is double. For if the extremes are opposite to and destructive of the other extreme and the mean, the mean is opposite to and destructive of the extremes[5] (cooking the right amount, for instance, opposes and destroys cooking too much and cooking too little). But the mean is best and is what science and reason are about, from (1) and its proof in (2). Hence, since the habit, as just said in the previous chapter, is a custom generated by repeated doing of the acts of the habit, the mean makes the best habit, which is (3).

By the same token, then, this best habit is itself a mean state, for the habits in question are in the appetitive part of the soul, and to have appetites or passions for things according to the mean of the things is to have passions for these things neither too much nor too little, which is the mean state. But the best habit is the virtue. Thus virtue is a mean state and is about certain means, which is (8), the conclusion Aristotle intended.

The conclusion is stated in general terms (despite the sort of details to be found in *VV* that must lie behind it). The next step is to specify the sort of mean state and the sort of means that virtue is and concerns, which Aristotle proposes to do from the outline or list that follows. The list is peculiar in several respects, for it lists things, like prudence, that do not appear to be *moral* virtues; it lists some things, as luxury (*trupherotēs*) that are not further dealt with; it lists things, such as shame, righteous indignation, truth, friendliness, and dignity, that though allowed to be means are later called means of passion and not of virtue; it lists others, like endurance, that are parts of continence only and not properly virtues. Also the list looks not to have a clear order, or no order is given.[6] 1220b35/21a28

We should begin, perhaps, at the end of the list, where the items in it are called, not vices and virtues, but passions (1221a13). We should also note that the list does follow a sort of order, the order in which the passions were listed at the end of chapter 2 (1220b12–13). For the first four listed there (spirit, fear, shame, and desire) correspond to the first four listed here: angriness (which belongs to spirit), boldness (which is about fears), shamelessness (which is lack of shame), and license (which is excess of desire). Further, the general category of passions listed fifth there, described as "things generally that are for the most part essentially followed by a perceptible pleasure or pain" (1220b13–14), corresponds, in a way, to all those listed next here, which are all things, or all about things, on which pain and pleasure follow. So envy, gain, and prodigality concern prosperity and the pleasure or pain its possession and use excite; boasting, flattery, and fawning are about personal merit and the pleasure or pain of it felt by oneself or excited in others; softness is about the pain of toil and the pleasure of escaping or enduring it; vanity is about fame or reputation, as is also extravagance in a way (for expensive gestures bring reputation) and the pleasure and pain of having it or not having it; unscrupulousness is about ways of getting prosperity and fame and other external goods and the pleasure and pain felt in doing so. Most of these items also appear in the discussion that immediately follows the list, but, at least after item four, not in precisely the same order. These items are only collected under a general head and not given a particular order among themselves.[7]

The focus of the list, then, is on passions and the objects of passion, and it has a rough order that it roughly follows. This focus, further and importantly, is on how these passions fall into extremes. For if they do, then it is obvious that they must also admit of a mean. Hence in the discussion that immediately follows Aristotle talks only of the extremes and not also of the mean. He leaves the mean rather to be read off from the list. For, by showing, in each case, how the passions can go too far or not far enough, he automatically gives to understand that there is a mean and that this mean is better than either extreme. There is thus no need for the list to correspond to the number or order of virtues and vices given later. It is sufficient if it shows, and in manifold ways, the division of passions into extremes and therefore means. For the point of the list is less that it be complete or precise or organized than that it be informative and suggestive, both about the particular passions mentioned and perhaps about others too that might, in some circumstance or other, be considered relevant to living well.

Note too that logic does not require that, if all moral virtues and vices are means and extremes of passion, therefore all means and extremes of passion are moral virtues and vices. And indeed, as shown later, not all are. So as regards prudence, for instance, which is properly an intellectual and not a moral virtue and so not a mean of passions as moral virtues are, the mention of it here at 1221a12, 37–38 seems to concern its role in counseling the mean of acquiring external goods and so its role in counseling what are later identified as acts of liberality (3.4). Prudence is thus a mean in what it counsels because it counsels neither the too much of the unscrupulous man nor the too little of the simple man. But prudence precisely understood counsels the mean in all the virtues and not in liberality alone (prudence is the right reason of all the virtues). This precision is given later when prudence is discussed (Book Five), but here it is omitted as not being needed for making the present point about extremes and means. Something analogous may be said about the mention of endurance (1221a9, 28–29).[8]

1221b4–26   The chapter ends with some methodological remarks. The first concerns the fact that things are not accidentally thus in each case, which, however, says Aristotle (adding dismissive remarks about sycophants), it is superfluous to define in the case of science. The point is obvious enough but its relevance is less so.[9] Perhaps, then, the relevance is that some verbal quibbler might say that the science of ethics cannot be about the quantities of the passions, and so cannot be about the mean and extremes, because quantities are accidents of passion (the passion of fear is still the passion of fear no matter how great it is in a given case). That there is only a quibble here is plain because ethics is about passions not qua passions but qua ingredients of happiness and living well. But they are such ingredients because of possessing quantity. Virtues, which have already been proved to be part of happiness, differ from vices according to quantity of passion. The fact is evident from the list just given and also from the sort of abstracts (as especially the *VV*) referred to at the end of chapter 2. Hence quantity of passion, while it may be accidental to passion, is essential to virtue and vice, and it is as essential to virtue and vice that it is considered in the science of ethics. The only reason to make the point explicitly is to dismiss sycophantic quibblers who are trying to impress an audience with verbal tricks. The science itself has no need to do so, for the thing is obvious from the definitions it gives of the habits. These definitions will have to be made precise later, but here the simple fact that they are extremes and means is enough.

To drive the point home, as it were, and also to anticipate something of the precise definitions, Aristotle adds further methodological remarks, this time about how the quantities of the extremes and mean are to be understood. The quantities do not simply concern amounts of passion (as feeling too much anger), but also time (as feeling it too quickly or keeping it too long), and intensity and occasion (as reacting to provocation too forcefully). The case of adultery reinforces the point, because here the extreme lies in the object (another's spouse) and not in how much or how often one feels the passion (adultery will be one of the things that produce a passion [1221b11–12]).[10] Evidence is provided by the fact that people accused of adultery (or wanton violence) defend themselves by saying, not that they did it only a little, but that they did it through ignorance or force (the vehemence of the temptation, perhaps), and not voluntarily. In other words, they admit the error is in the deed and the passion for it, not in the amount.

Notes

1. Aristotle speaks of *all* continuous and divisible quantities (1220b21), but he presumably intends us to be thinking primarily of the things he has just talked of, where a mean relative to the things is as obvious as a mean relative to us (e.g., a certain degree of anger may be too much simply or too much for this or that person). He does not (contra Woods [1992: 102]) intend that all quantities whatever must admit of *both* kinds of mean (for the several revolutions of the planets are large or small or in the middle, though hardly relative to us), but only that they must admit of at least *one*. That passions and actions admit of both is obvious by itself, as well as from the examples given.
2. *EE* will thus agree with *NE* (1106b16, 1109b30) in making the mean of virtue to concern both passions and actions. It will differ only by being more precise in saying virtue is a mean state *in* passions *about* a mean in actions, as Woods suggests (1992: 103–104, 114), despite doubts; see also Dirlmeier (1962: 262–63). Von Fragstein (1974: 74–75) says that the reference of the "about" is not to actions but to the table of virtues and vices that immediately follows, so that the means virtue is about are the several virtuous means that lie between opposed vices. But this interpretation takes the reference of the "about" to be to the species of a genus, and also makes the conclusion depend on what follows in the text and not on what precedes. In both respects it seems forced.
3. Woods (1992: 104).
4. Woods (1992: 105) understands (3) to say that the mean state is the best habit. This interpretation is possible but perhaps fits the context less well, which, as the conclusion (8) shows, is about how the mean state is best as being about things in the mean that are best.

5. Rowe (1971: 40).
6. Dirlmeier (1962: 246–48).
7. Most of the passions in the list, or elements relating to them, appear in *VV* but not precisely in the same order. *VV* is, by express intent, an ordering and description of virtues and vices and only of passions and powers by relation to them.
8. Dirlmeier (1962: 246–47, 251–53) is therefore right to retain the passages about prudence and endurance, contra Spengel and Fritzsche (Susemihl, 1884: 24) and Woods (1992: 106), who would delete them as spurious.
9. Woods (1992: 108); contrast Dirlmeier (1962: 254–55).
10. Contra Woods (1992: 110).

Chapter 4

That It Concerns Pleasures and Pains

1221b27/b37 That virtue and vice concern pleasures and pains was said before (1.1220a34–37). The point is repeated here not as to the fact but as to the reason, namely the doctrine of the mean and extremes (that pursuing and avoiding pleasure and pain as one should or should not produce and characterize the virtues and vices). The reason is given in two stages, first as to its source in the division of the soul and second as to its reality in facts and common opinion.

The division of the soul is as given before (1.1219b28–31), into the rational part of the intellectual virtues and the nonrational and appetitive part of the moral virtues. Pleasure and pain are typically understood by reference to appetite (pleasure is what attracts appetite and pain what repels it), so that wherever appetite is found pleasure and pain must also be found (which need not mean that each individual case of appetite is actually pleasant or painful, for some might perhaps be neither, but only that each is potentially or generically so).[1] Hence virtues and vices, being in the appetitive part of the soul, must be characterized in general by pursuit and avoidance of pleasure and pain. This reason is confirmed by the same divisions as before of habits and passions and powers (b34–35 referring back to 2.1220b10–12). The reference to the divisions again fits *VV*, for, in addition to that work's several mentions of pleasure, the way the virtues and vices are described is in terms of things that give pleasure or pain, whether to those who have them or to those who experience them from others.

The fact is confirmed by other things said earlier (b37–38, likely a reference to 1.1220a22–37),[2] that souls find their pleasure in what they naturally tend to be made better or worse by (as the glutton becomes a glutton by indulging his pleasure for food).[3] The same fact is also confirmed by the way people are said to be base because of wrongly pursuing and avoiding pleasures and pains (as with the glutton again), and by the ready definition everyone has[4] that

254

virtues are states of rest and vices the opposite (as the glutton is set aflutter by abundance of food while the moderate man remains unmoved).[5] Each of these observations[6] confirms the point at issue: virtue and vice revolve about pleasure and pain and the avoidance or pursuit of them.

Notes

1. Woods (1992: 112) thinks Aristotle must mean that the passions are always individually pleasant or painful, but the argument hardly requires something so strong.
2. So Dirlmeier (1962: 259–60), followed by Woods (1992: 113).
3. Following, against most commentators, Von Fragstein's (1974: 109) defense and interpretation of the MS readings at 1221b39–20a1.
4. Or that everyone gives offhandedly. The definition is strictly inaccurate but points to something correct: the virtuous are controlled in their passions and the vicious not.
5. *VV* speaks along these lines, 8.1251b26–28, 37.
6. Woods (1992: 112–13), because he rejects the MS readings at 1221b39–22a1, thinks these observations constitute rather one argument than several.

Chapter 5

That the Mean Is Not a Middle

Aristotle next shows that the mean must be understood relative to us and not to the things, or that it is not a matter of calculating a mathematical middle. The argument is in several stages. 1222a6/a38

First (a6–17), from what has just been said about pleasure and what was said before about virtue being the mean state whereby people live best, the conclusion is drawn that virtue will be (subjectively) a mean state in feelings of pleasure and pain or (objectively) about means in pleasant and painful things.[1] This mean state may be in pleasures or pains or both, as is shown from those who go to extremes of pleasure (as the licentious) or to extremes of pain (as the irascible do, perhaps, for anger is painful).

Second (a17–22), these several states of mean and extreme pleasures and pains are opposites. The case Aristotle introduces to prove the point is obscure. It is either of some single habit where the possessor takes partly the excess and partly the deficiency of the same thing, or of two habits where in one the possessor takes the excess and in the other the deficiency. We might understand both options of courage (which concerns the pain of fears and dangers): either the coward takes an excess of fear and the rash man a deficiency,[2] or the brave man takes both an excess and a deficiency according to occasion (being fearful and retreating when he should, and being fearless and standing firm when he should). If the latter, courage is the single state of having a lot of fear on some occasions and a little on others; if the former, cowardice and rashness are the two states, respectively, of having a lot of fear and of having a little. The point is the same in either event: excessive and deficient fears are opposite to each other and to the mean, whether in persons or in occasions (being fearful and retreating is opposite to being fearless and standing firm, and either, if always done, would be opposite to the other and to the mean of variously doing both). Hence the habits relative to them are opposite to each other and to the mean of virtue.

Third (a22–b4), the opposition between these things and states is not straightforward, but sometimes one opposition may be more obvious than another because the transition from extreme to mean is quicker in one direction than in another (thus the other extreme will seem alone to be the opposite). So, in the case of the body, since we can pass more quickly from the extreme of too little food to the mean of the healthy amount, the extreme of too little is close to the mean and the extreme of too much is the one opposed to it; the converse holds with physical toil. The reason that the mean is closer to one extreme, adds Aristotle, is that our nature favors the opposite extreme. Getting to the mean is more a matter of avoiding that extreme than of avoiding the other. The same holds of the soul where again, as with anger, those extremes alone are held to be opposite that we and the many favor, and those in the other direction, because rare, get overlooked.

This third stage of the argument is the decisive one for showing that the mean is the mean relative to us. The first two stages show that the mean and extremes are states of pleasures and pains, and that these states must be opposed as the degree or mix of pleasures and pains are opposed. The third stage shows that since we naturally favor pleasures and shun pains, we will find ourselves drawn to the extremes of more pleasure and less pain, while the respective means, even if in quantity they chance to be at a midpoint of pleasure and pain, will, for us, be further from the favored pleasure and closer to the shunned pain. Hence the mean must be the mean relative to us. For even if it is also in some cases a mean relative to the things, we will have to note and judge and pursue it as it relates to us.[3] The example of spirit not being a flatterer (b4) confirms the point. Flattery is further on the other side beyond mildness than the extreme of insensibility, for where the insensible man should get angry but does not, there the flatterer showers praise. Therefore if the mean for us in spirit is closer to not having than to having anger, the spirited, who will thus find it hard even to be mild, will find it well-nigh impossible to be flatterers.[4]

Summary

1222b4   The summary stresses again that the collection or list was of passions as divided into means and extremes of deficiency and excess (the list was not *as such* of vices and virtues). As Aristotle's remarks indicate, the point of it, and

256

of the intervening discussion of the extremes and the opposed means of right reason, was to show that the moral virtues and vices are about extremes of pleasures and pains (the virtues avoiding them, the vices falling into them), and that since the best habit in each case is the mean, the virtues will be in these mean states (though perhaps not all the mean states need be virtues). The reservation at the end (b13) about some virtues not belonging to mean states,[5] probably relates to the moral virtue of justice. For justice, while it is about a certain mean (the mean between gain and loss), is not itself a mean state between two vices. He who gains is unjust, but he who loses is not unjust in the opposite direction; rather he *suffers* something unjust.

Notes

1. The terms "subjective" and "objective" are borrowed from Dirlmeier (1962: 262); also Von Fragstein (1974: 110).
2. Dirlmeier's interpretation (1962: 263).
3. A point that Woods in his criticism (1992: 115) seems to overlook.
4. Read thus, Aristotle's point seems clear; see Von Fragstein (1974: 113), who is right to keep the MSS reading against the doubts of Dirlmeier (1962: 265).
5. If, unlike Woods (1992: 115, 191), we keep to the MSS reading. Woods would have it say that not all means need be virtues, which is correct, but so is the point about justice not being a mean state.

Chapter 6

Through What It Comes to Be
That Man Is Voluntary Cause of Actions and Habits

The discussion so far constitutes an account of what virtue is (a mean state in 1222b15/b37 pleasures and pains). This account is not complete. The fuller account given later (10.1227b5) adds the factor of choice, which is derived from the consideration (given now) of how virtue comes to be. Since, therefore, Aristotle speaks here of making another beginning, we would seem best advised to mark a change of focus in the analysis from the what of virtue to the how of its coming to be. The argument that follows turns on how man is a cause of actions (and so therefore of virtue and vice as habits generated by actions). The argument rests on several premises.

First (b15–20) there is the evident fact that substances are principles that produce things, as man and animals and plants produce their own kind, and as man, but not animals, produces actions.

Second (b20–29) some principles are sources whence changes first emerge and these are *controlling* principles. Especially so are those from which there is no possibility of being otherwise, as God perhaps (b22–23). The point of this remark, which is disputed,[1] would seem to be that those principles of change are most of all principles where what results, although it is a change, is eternal and regular. So the God that is the unmoved mover of the heavens (the God of *Physics* 8 and *Metaphysics* 12) causes changes but ones that are eternal and regular, like the motions of the heavens (and not the irregular and temporal changes of the sublunary world where men and animals and plants live). To explain what is meant by a controlling cause, Aristotle uses an example from mathematics, where the principles, despite not being controlling causes, have a likeness to controlling causes, and this likeness, as it turns out, enables us to see what controlling causes are. The principles of mathematics are not controlling causes because they are unchanging. The remark is problematic because God too is unchanging, yet he is a controlling cause. Probably Aristotle is just being loose and means, not unchanging principles, but principles of unchanging things (as mathematical principles are),[2] and not principles of changing things (as God is, for God, though himself unchanging, causes the change that is the motion of the heavens). The point, in any event, concerns less what causes and what is caused than the dependence of the caused on the cause: if there is a change in the cause, there will be a change too in everything caused.

The obscure parenthetical remark (b26–28)—"but they [sc. the conclusions] do not cause themselves to alter if one of them is assumed under the other, except by assuming the hypothesis and proving through that"—confirms that the stress is on causal dependence. It can be glossed as follows: conclusions from causes, even if one of them is assumed under another, do not cause each other to change, or not unless they are also assumed under the cause ("the hypothesis") and the cause is used to prove them. The example of triangles and quadrilaterals can explain the remark. Take as cause that a triangle has angles equal to two right angles. Take as one conclusion that a quadrilateral has angles equal to four right angles, and take as a second conclusion that the angle in a semi-circle is a right angle. If we put these conclusions under each other, one of them will not change because the other does, for the conclusions qua conclusions are independent of each other. A change in one will only cause a change in the other if we assume both under their common cause (that triangles have angles equal to two right angles), and we use that cause to prove them. For then, to change one of them would be to change the cause, and hence, by that fact, to change the other.[3]

At all events, man is a principle of change, for he is cause of action, which is a change (b28–29). So man, like God, is a controlling cause because he is a cause of change.

Third (b29–37), causes (whether controlling or not) are related to effects as premises to conclusions in proofs. Thus, the proof that a quadrilateral has angles equal to four right angles depends on its cause, which is that a triangle (two of which combined make a quadrilateral) has angles equal to two right angles. Thus, if the triangle changes in its number of angles so must the quadrilateral, and if the quadrilateral does not change in its number of angles, neither can the triangle. The truth is confirmed from the *Analytics* (*Post. An.* 1.1), but Aristotle declines to go into the details. The reservation is presumably that while the example is enough for present purposes it is not strictly of the first cause. For the triangle itself has causes of its having angles equal to two right angles, so that it is not the first cause of the angles of quadrilaterals. Nevertheless, if we suppose it is for the sake of argument,[4] it illustrates what needs to be illustrated, namely how things that follow principles depend for what they are on those principles, and how, if what follows does not change, neither can the principles change.

Fourth (22b40–23a9), these points are applied to man and mans' actions:

(1)   if some of the things that are can be in the opposite state, their principles also must be of the same sort (the outcome of the necessary is necessary, but opposite outcomes are possible from these principles, so these principles cannot be necessary);

(2)   there are many such opposites in man's case as regard what is up to him, and he is controlling principle of them;

(3)   therefore, man can come to be (active) or not as regards all actions he is controlling principle of; and

(4)   it is up to him whether the actions whose being he is controlling principle of come to be.[5]

The inferences are clear: (1) has just been proved (with the mathematical example); (2) was stated at the beginning of the chapter (man is able to produce and not produce offspring and actions). These two together entail (3) and (4), at least as regards those actions man is controlling principle of (and man is manifestly controlling principle of some actions, for men are forever acting first in one way and then in another).

The conclusion is very strong: (4) says man's actions are up to himself and (3) that his acting is up to himself. Hence, in all respects, what man does is up to him and not necessitated. Aristotle seems to stress this fact by what he next adds:

(5)   all things where it is up to man to produce or not, these things he is cause of;

(6)   all things that man is cause of are up to him.

These two propositions are the union of (3) and (4) but stated, as it were, in both directions: man is cause where it is up to him to act or not, and conversely, where man is cause, there it is up to him to act or not. The conclusion follows necessarily from (1) and (2), and (2) is undeniable (even those who deny that man acts freely do not deny that man acts), and (1) was proved from the mathematical example. So it must be up to man, and not to anything else, both whether to act at all and, if so, what act to perform.

One might, perhaps, respond that even if man causes his acting and not just his acts, yet there must be some further cause to explain that causing. In addition, one might say that the phrase "can be in opposite states" in Aristotle's argument above may be taken in two ways: either that a certain thing can be in opposite states, or that that thing makes itself to be in one or other state. If the first, then a strong sense for (3) and (4) does not follow. For although the thing can be in either state, which state it is actually in is determined by something else. But, in response, note that, as (1) says, the something else or further cause will either be necessary and produce unvarying results, or it will not. But, as (2) says, man's actions vary, sometimes being this way and sometimes the opposite. Therefore any cause behind his causing must also be variable. But if we must thus stop at a variable cause (and not proceed to anything necessary), there is no reason not to stop at once with man as that cause, and thus no reason to say he must act necessarily or is not controlling cause.

1223a9　　This result does not yet, however, go far enough; for the behavior of animals is also variable, so hence it too, for the same reason, cannot be necessary. But Aristotle's concern, since it is ethics, is with action, not behavior, that is, it is with things that the agent can be praised and blamed for. So he applies his argument now to virtue and vice and their deeds:

(7)　virtue, vice, and their deeds are praiseworthy and blameworthy, as is shown by the fact (7a) that people praise and blame them;

(8)　they are so because of what we and not necessity or chance or nature are cause of, as is shown by the fact (8b) that where someone else is cause he gets the praise and blame;

(9)　therefore, virtue and vice are about things where we are cause and principle of actions.

The argument is clear but its structure and conclusion need to be noted. It does not argue that because vice and virtue deserve praise and blame, and because praise and blame are of things we cause, therefore vice and virtue have us as cause. Rather it argues that because "virtue and vice and the deeds they are the source of" (a9–10) deserve praise and blame and do so "because of[6] what we ourselves are causes of" (a12), therefore virtue and vice "are about things where one is oneself cause and principle of actions" (a14–15). The former way of arguing is perhaps acceptable as far as it goes, but it suffers from several defects. First, virtue and vice are habits, and we are not directly cause of habits but only of the actions that, by constant repetition, cause them. Second, for the same reason, the actions that cause virtue and vice are not the same as the deeds that have virtue and vice as source, for the latter flow from habits already acquired and the former precede, by causing, the acquiring of those habits, and if the former are clearly deserving of praise and blame, the latter are less clearly so. Third, virtue and vice are not about things where man is simply cause but where he is cause of *actions*, for animals too are causes (they are variable causes of variable behavior), but, as was remarked at the beginning of the chapter, they are not cause of actions. The latter way of arguing, the way Aristotle actually follows, avoids these defects and does so because of the complicated precision of its wording. It avoids the third defect because it says virtue and vice are about things where man is cause of *actions* (and not where he is cause simply); it avoids the second because it says that virtue and vice, and the deeds they are the *source* of, deserve praise and blame (and not because it says the actions that *cause* virtue and vice do); it avoids the first because it says that virtue and vice deserve praise and blame *because of* things of which we are cause (and not because we are direct cause of virtue and vice). We should not, therefore, seek to emend the text. The manuscripts that preserve for us its complicated wording are, here as often elsewhere, remarkably accurate. They confirm one of *EE's* more striking features (especially in comparison with *EN*), namely its compressed and precise argumentation. They also confirm, incidentally, that the present topic must be glossed as the *sources* of virtue. For this chapter and those that follow are less about how virtue and vice are up to us than about how our actions, which are the sources of virtue and vice, are up to us.[7]

The next question, at any rate, turns on what these sources are or what sort of things we are dealing with when we are active as cause and principle. Merely that these things must be actions is not enough; they must be actions such that we are cause of them, and these actions, as all agree, are the voluntary and chosen ones. Things involuntary we are not cause of, nor do we choose them (what is done by choice is voluntary). Hence the actions that vice and virtue are about must be voluntary ones. The matters to discuss, then, must be the voluntary and that part of the voluntary that is choice. The rest of the book divides accordingly, chapters 7 to 9 being about the voluntary and chapters 10 and 11 about choice.

1223a15

Notes

1. Woods (1992: 21), Dirlmeier, Von Fragstein, Rowe, ad loc.
2. Woods (1992: 117), rightly. The looseness is the figure of speech known as hypallage.
3. Woods (1992: 117) interprets the example differently but, as he has to admit, not satisfactorily to the context.
4. Which is all Aristotle here needs to do, contra the doubts of Woods (1992: 118).
5. This interpretation depends on construing the Greek as in the translation. Standard construals produce inferences whose relevance and validity are rather obscure, Woods (1992: 118–19). Kenny (1979: 9–10) gets the sense of the passage right but not the particular construal.

6.   Provided we keep the *dia* of the MSS at 1223a11 and do not delete it as some scholars wish.
7.   Contra Rowe (1971: 41).

Chapter 7

The Voluntary and the Involuntary
That They Are Not According to Appetite

_{1223a21/a28} As regards what the voluntary and involuntary are, Aristotle begins, as is his wont when looking for definitions, with a division of what they could fall under and then examines which one or ones they do in fact fall under. So, they must belong with appetite (or inclination in general) or choice or thought (these being the factors operative in human action), and if with appetite, then with will or spirit or desire. Aristotle examines each in turn and, again as is his wont, argues dialectically on either side. These dialectical arguments need not be arguments he himself accepts. It is sufficient if they are probable and draw attention to important features of the question in each case.[1]

He begins by considering if the voluntary belongs with desire (one of the divisions of the division of appetite) and gives two arguments that what accords with desire is voluntary. The first runs:

(1)   the involuntary is all forced;
(2)   the forced is painful (and so also is all that men are forced to do or suffer);
(3)   so that if something is painful it is forced, and if forced painful;
(4)   what is against desire is all painful;
(5)   for desire is of the pleasant;
(6)   so that what is against desire is forced
(7)   and involuntary;
(8)   therefore, what is in accord with desire is voluntary,
(9)   for these are opposites.

There are puzzles with this argument. First the obvious inference from (1) and (2), that (10) the involuntary is painful, is not stated. Second, the first part of (3), if something is painful it is forced, does not follow from (2), and the second part of (3) just repeats (2). Third, (7) only follows if we assume (6), which rests on (4) and (5) and the first part of (3), and if we also assume, not (1), but the converse of (1), that the forced is involuntary. Fourth, the conclusion (8) follows more simply and directly from (10) and (5): the involuntary is painful; desire is of the pleasant; therefore desire is not involuntary; therefore (because (9) the voluntary and involuntary are opposites) desire is voluntary.[2] Fifth, some of these propositions are rejected by Aristotle elsewhere, as (1), for the involuntary also includes things done in error (9.1225b6–7), and (3), for not all painful things are forced or involuntary (1224b15–29). Sixth and finally, (8) does not seem to follow from (9) and (7), for a proposition that has both terms opposite to those of another proposition is not entailed by that other proposition (all A is B does not entail all not-A is not-B, for all A being B is compatible with some not-A also being B).[3]

The fifth puzzle is fairly easy to deal with because in dialectical arguments it is not necessary that the premises be true but only that they be in some way plausible.[4] An answer to the second and third puzzles would be that (3) is not meant to be taken as an inference but as a stipulation about (1), or at least (2), so that these are to be taken as equivalences and to be read in both directions: the involuntary is forced and the forced involuntary; the forced painful and the painful forced. The equivalences are both plausible (which is all dialectical argumentation needs), for it seems no less plausible that the forced is involuntary and the painful forced than that the involuntary is forced and the forced painful. Further, the word "all" in (1) is ambiguously placed (does it go with the subject or the predicate or both?), and the quotation from Evenus too, having the ambiguity of poetry, allows for multiple interpretations.

The first and fourth puzzles are more problematic. For the simple and direct argument, since it dispenses with (2), (3), (6), and (7), would, if presented, get rid of all five puzzles at once. The conclusion must be that Aristotle wants the more complex argument with its equivalences, and a reason may be suggested. He uses the equivalences again later in arguments on the other side, which conclude to the opposite of (8), that what accords with desire is not voluntary. For (7) relies on the converse of (1), as well as on the converse of (2), which is the first part of (3). It is stated at 1223b16–17 in the course of an argument that if (7) is true then the continent man will act voluntarily and involuntarily at the same time, which is impossible. Hence (7) cannot be true, and thus not (8) either, which depends on (7).[5] Further the converse of (1) is stated at 1223b20–21 in an argument about spirit that is also, by extension, applicable to desire, and the first part of (3), the converse of (2), also has to be assumed in the same argument.[6] Dialectical arguments are more valuable philosophically if opposite conclusions can be drawn from the same premises, for thus one is forced to look more carefully at what is going wrong to find out where the truth must really lie.

One answer to the sixth puzzle would be similar to the answer to the fifth, that the appeal to opposites is not meant to be decisive but only probable, that while opposites might share the same feature (as when both A and not-A are B), yet it is not unlikely that they have opposite features.[7] A second and better answer is that the thesis that opposites have opposite features will be true when the feature in question is meant to be the difference, which when added to the genus completes the definition; for opposites in the same genus are defined by opposite differences (as humans and brutes, which are in the genus of animal, are defined by the opposites of rational and irrational). Since Aristotle is investigating the definition of the voluntary here, he is entitled to take this principle about definitions for granted in his presentation of arguments, dialectical or otherwise. Indeed he seems to reference the principle at 1223a25–26 with the remark: "the voluntary being in accord with one of these [appetite, choice, thought] and the involuntary contrary to one of them," for contraries are only going to accord thus with contraries when what is in question is their definition.

That defining properties are what Aristotle has in mind in this argument is perhaps indicated by the wording of (4), which is again ambiguous as to whether the "all" goes with the subject or predicate or both. For if it goes with both then the painful is being made the defining difference of what opposes desire, and the pleasant the defining difference of what accords with desire. Nevertheless, whether Aristotle is thinking of defining differences or not, he does not consider either (7) or (8) to be ultimately true, for, in the case of the continent, what is against desire (or some desire) can be voluntary, and, in the case of the ignorant, what is in accord with desire can be involuntary (as with the woman who, out of love, gave her lover a potion that she did not know was lethal and killed him).

1223a36   The second argument to the effect that what accords with desire is voluntary runs as follows:

(1)   all wickedness makes one more unjust;
(2)   incontinence seems to be wickedness;
(3)   the incontinent man acts according to desire against calculation, and he is incontinent when acting according to desire;
(4)   acting unjustly is voluntary;
(5)   so that the incontinent man acting according to desire acts unjustly;
(6)   so the incontinent man acts voluntarily;
(7)   and what accords with desire will be voluntary;
(8)   for it is odd if they who become incontinent will be more just.

Here (1) and (2) yield (9), that incontinence makes one unjust. Also (3), because of the peculiarity of its phrasing, amounts to the claim that the incontinent man is an acting-according-to-desire-incontinent man, which in turn, because it is equivalent to a definition, yields its converse (3a), that the acting-according-to-desire-incontinent man is incontinent.[8] From (9) and (3a) there follows (5), for (5) is equivalent to the claim that the acting-according-to-desire-incontinent man acts unjustly. From (5) and (4) there follows (6), for (6) is equivalent to the claim that the acting-according-to-desire-incontinent man is an acting-voluntarily-incontinent man, which is to equate acting according to desire with acting voluntarily, which is (7). The remaining proposition (8) removes an objection to (6), that the incontinent is not acting voluntarily although acting according to desire. For to deny (6) is to deny (9) and therewith also one or both of the premises it follows from, (1) and (2),[9] for one can hardly be accused of being wicked or unjust if one's act, though wicked and unjust, is involuntary. But to deny (9) and either (2) or (1) is to say that a man who does an unjust act is excused of injustice if he is incontinent; so it is to say that incontinence stops a man being unjust, which is, as far as it goes, to make him more just, for it makes him more just than he would have been had he acted without incontinence.

This argument is dialectical because (9), (2), and (1), while plausible, are not propositions that Aristotle finally considers true. Incontinence is not fully a wickedness or a vice, but a state between virtue and vice that tends toward vice (Book Six). He also later clarifies the idea of justice so that while there is a sense in which, as here, injustice includes all vices and justice all virtues so that any vice or wickedness makes one unjust, there is also a sense in which it is a particular vice and justice a particular virtue (Book Four) so that not all kinds of vice or wickedness make one unjust in this sense.

Aristotle turns now to argue the opposite, that what accords with desire 1223b4 is not voluntary, and again gives two arguments. The first runs:

(1) everything that someone does voluntarily he does wanting to do it, and what he wants to do he does voluntarily;
(2) no one wants to do what he thinks is bad;
(3) the incontinent man does not do what he wants;
(4) for to be incontinent is to do because of desire the opposite of what one thinks best;
(5) therefore, the same man will be acting voluntarily and involuntarily at the same time, which is impossible.

Here (3) follows from (2) and (4), and from (3) and (1) follows (6), that the incontinent does not act voluntarily. But the arguments just given were that the incontinent man acts voluntarily by acting according to desire; hence, by combination of both conclusions, (5) follows. But (5) is clearly impossible. So to keep (6), the conclusion implied here, one has to reject the earlier conclusion and deny that what accords with desire is voluntary.

The second argument draws the same conclusion from the opposite case 1223b10 of the continent man:

(1) the continent man does what is just;
(2) for continence is a virtue,
(3) and virtue makes people more just;
(4) one is continent when one acts contrary to desire in accord with calculation;
(5) doing what is just is voluntary (for doing what is wrong is voluntary and if one of these is voluntary so must the other be);
(6) acting against desire is involuntary;
(7) therefore, the same man will do the same thing at the same time voluntarily and involuntarily.

Here (1) follows from (2) and (3), and from (1) and (5) follows (8), that the continent man acts voluntarily, and from (8) and (4) follows (9), that the continent man acts voluntarily in acting against desire. But (6) was concluded by the first arguments, and (7) follows from (9) and (6). So again, since (7) is impossible, we have to deny (6) in order to keep (9). This argument is clearly dialectical for Aristotle does not finally accept (2) as true, and only accepts (1) as true in the sense that the continent man does the just thing, but not in the sense that he does it as a virtuous man would, for the continent man, while good as far as he goes, is not yet virtuous.

1223b18   Aristotle now argues for and against the identification of the voluntary with spirit, using incontinence and continence as middle terms:

(1)   what is contrary to spirit is painful;
(2)   being held in check is forced;
(3)   so if the forced is involuntary, then
(4)   that which accords with spirit would all be voluntary;
(5)   but, if it is impossible for the same thing to do at the same time things voluntary and involuntary in regard to what accords with the same part of the thing, then
(6)   what is in accord with will more than what accords with desire and spirit will be voluntary.

The argument is elliptical but what needs to be supplied to complete it is clear from what has been already argued. So, first, (1) and (2) do not, as such, connect what is contrary to spirit with (3). The further premise (7), that what is contrary to spirit is forced, is needed for that purpose. But (1) and (2) can each be used, and in separate ways, to prove (7). For if we supply from the first argument about desire that (8) what is painful is forced (which was numbered [3] in that argument [1223a33]), then (7) follows from (1) and (8). Further, if we supply the obvious premise (9) that what is contrary to spirit checks spirit, then (7) follows from (9) and (2). In fact, (9) perhaps does not need to be supplied for it can be proved from the Heracleitus quotation. For that quotation gives (10), that what opposes spirit is painful, and (10) and (8) prove that what opposes spirit forces spirit, which is equivalent to (9). At any rate, (7) and (3) will give (11), that what is contrary to spirit is involuntary. So if we also assume (from the same earlier argument from which [8] comes) the further premise about opposites, (12) that opposites have opposite features (numbered [9] in that earlier argument), then (4) follows, that what accords with spirit is voluntary.

The way Aristotle is implicitly appealing back to premises in an earlier argument suggests the same answer as before about why he gives two ways to prove (7). Dialectical arguments that come to conflicting conclusions form the same premises are more philosophically rewarding because they stimulate more to the search for truth. In this case (8) and (12) are such same premises.

Not only have they just appeared in the argument that what accords with desire is voluntary, but they must also be assumed for the next argument that what accords with spirit is involuntary. This argument is what is given in (5) and (6), and since it is just an application of the phenomenon of incontinence and incontinence to spirit, it has to make the same assumptions as were made when the same phenomenon was applied to desire. The argument about desire was that if acting according to will, which the continent man does and the incontinent man does not, is voluntary, then acting according to desire cannot be voluntary. So since there is continence and incontinence in spirit, it follows, by the same reasoning, that if acting according to will is voluntary, then acting according to spirit cannot be voluntary. For, as (5) repeats, people cannot act voluntarily and involuntarily at the same time; and, as (6) repeats, of the two of acting according to desire or spirit and acting according to will, the latter, if we go by the phenomenon of continence and incontinence, is voluntary rather than the former.[10]

The peculiar phrase in (5) about the same thing not doing at the same time things voluntary and involuntary "in regard to what accords with the same part of the thing" (1223b25–26)[11] seems just to state, in a wholly general or impersonal way, the impossibility of the same thing acting voluntarily and involuntarily at the same time in the same respect of itself. To state it personally, then: it is impossible for the same man to act at the same time voluntarily and involuntarily as to what accords with the same part (desire or spirit) of his soul. The reason for the remark is perhaps to answer the objection that the continent and incontinent could act voluntarily and involuntarily at the same time if they did so in different respects. But this objection fails if the voluntary is located, as the arguments just given have tried to locate it, in desire or spirit. For then acting voluntarily and involuntarily at the same time will mean acting voluntarily and involuntarily "as to what accords with the same part" (desire or spirit), that is, precisely in the same respect at the same time. Hence the contradiction remains.

At all events the upshot is the same in the case of spirit as in the case of desire: there are arguments on one side that acting according to spirit is voluntary, and arguments on the other side, based on some of the same premises, that acting according to spirit is not voluntary.

So far the discussion has resulted in an impasse: the voluntary is and is not desire and spirit. Aristotle turns next to consider the third option: will. 1223b27 The first point he makes (about the sign), though brief, both follows on from what he has just said and prefaces what follows; for it looks to be meant to resolve the preceding dialectical impasse by saying that the voluntary cannot really be identified with either desire or spirit.[12] It appeals to the fact that we do many things voluntarily without anger or desire, which makes it clear that the voluntary cannot be simply identified with either. Thus, we need to consider if the willed is the voluntary. The argument, which in its first two premises is the same as the first one against desire, runs:

(1) wickedness makes people more unjust;
(2) incontinence appears to be a sort of wickedness,
(3) but the opposite will result,
(4) for no one wants the things he thinks are bad;
(5) but a man does do these bad things when he becomes incontinent,
(6) so if doing wrong is voluntary, and
(7) if the voluntary is what accords with will, then
(8) when he becomes incontinent he will no longer be doing wrong, but
(9) will be more just than before he became incontinent, but
(10) this is impossible.

First, (3) must mean that the result will be the opposite of what follows from (1) and (2), which is (11), that incontinence makes people more unjust. For (4) and (5) entail (12), that the incontinent man does when incontinent the things he does not want or will; (6) and (7) entail (13), that doing wrong accords with will; (12) and (13) entail (8) that the incontinent is not doing wrong when incontinent, and hence (9) that he is more just than he would otherwise have been. But (9) is contrary to (11), and so is impossible, which is (10). Thus, the premises that entail (9), namely (8) and (7), must be rejected, and the voluntary must not be what accords with will.

There are not the same problems with this argument as there were with the previous ones. The impossibility follows from premises Aristotle would accept. For, first, the premise about incontinence being wickedness is stated with a qualifying "sort of," which accords with his later view that incontinence is something bad but not a vice.[13] Second, the point of (9), which may look odd,[14] seems to be merely that incontinence, if it excuses from injustice, will be, say, like ignorance. For ignorance excuses an unjust deed by making it not to be unjustly done. So it makes the doer more just by making him not the unjust doer he would have been had he not been ignorant. Incontinence will do the same, then, which is incompatible with its being a sort of wickedness or something that should make its possessor worse.

1223b36 The upshot of the chapter is that the voluntary cannot be acting in accord with appetite (desire, spirit, will), nor the involuntary the opposite. Or at least it is manifest that no simple such identification can be made.[15] For the answer Aristotle eventually comes to does allow that appetite plays a role in determining the voluntary, but only with certain qualifications. Here he has only considered, and his concluding arguments have only rejected, the unqualified identification of the voluntary with appetite.

Notes

1. So Kenny (1979: 22–23).
2. This argument is actually given in *GE* 1.12.1188a1–5.

3. The second, third, fifth, and sixth puzzles are discussed by Woods (1992: 122–23) and Kenny (1979: 15, 21).
4. Kenny, ibid.
5. The same argument on the other side does not appear in *GE* in this way, though something equivalent does, 1.12.1188a5–10.
6. See the discussion on this passage later at the paragraph which begins with the reference 1223b18, and Woods (1992: 126).
7. In the corresponding passage in *GE*.1.12.1188a19–20, (7) is inferred from (8), but the passage is dialectical again and the inference is stated only as a hypothetical.
8. Contra Woods (1992: 123).
9. As Dirlmeier shows (1962: 272) there is no real problem either with (6) itself or its placement here, *pace* Woods (1992: 123–24).
10. Kenny (1979: 22) takes (6) as going with the argument that follows and not with the one here. Grammatically it must go with the one here, but in sense it can also go with the next. Perhaps then it should be taken as going with both.
11. The Greek has been doubted by scholars and several emendations proposed; discussion in Dirlmeier (1962: 274). But no change seems necessary. The wording may be peculiar, but the logic is fine.
12. So Kenny (1979: 22–23).
13. See Kenny (1979: 24n1).
14. As it does to Kenny, ibid.
15. Kenny rightly (1979: 24–25), against Woods (1992: 121–22).

Chapter 8

That They Are Not According to Choice

The second of the three general accounts of the voluntary was choice, but a   1223b38
simple identification of choice with the voluntary is also impossible. Aristotle begins by stating results from the previous discussion: first, that what accords with will is not involuntary but voluntary (1223b39–4a1); second that we can act voluntarily even when not willing (1224a2–3). The first point comes from his statement that what accords with will is voluntary rather than what accords with desire or spirit (1223b26–27), and the second from his conclusion that the incontinent man must still be acting voluntarily even though he is going against his will (for otherwise his incontinence would excuse him and make his action better, not worse [1223b2–3, 33–36]). For these two points show that what is willed is not involuntary but voluntary (for the continent does voluntarily what he wills), and also that not everything voluntary is willed (for the incontinent does voluntarily what he does not will).[1] Aristotle adds that this fact has alone been shown, for it has only been shown that *some* voluntary things are not willed, which is compatible with all willed things

269

being voluntary.[2] So, if all willed things are voluntary and some willed things are not chosen (as when we will suddenly, for we do not choose suddenly), then, necessarily, some voluntary things are not chosen. Hence the voluntary cannot be the same as what accords with choice.

That They Are According to Thought
Force
Impulse and Reason and Appetite

1224a4 Of the three options, appetite and choice, only one is left, that of thought. So the voluntary must in some way be identified with thought. The question is in what way? That Aristotle turns first to consider force may seem odd, for force has not so far appeared as an express theme but only as premises in earlier arguments. But Aristotle himself explains its introduction now, namely that the forced is involuntary and the involuntary forced (which have both just appeared as premises, though the latter is not something Aristotle will finally accept as true, since ignorance can also make things to be involuntary). For if so, an account of the voluntary must include an account of force. Further, force has implicitly been involved in the arguments about continence and incontinence, for the claim that incontinence is involuntary, although Aristotle has rejected it, gets its plausibility from the idea that the incontinent man is forced by desire to do what he does.

1224a13 The first thing is to say what being forced means, and, as regards the present topic (people and their actions), the forced and the necessary seem to be opposed to what is voluntary and by persuasion. But the way the term "force" is applied beyond this topic is also relevant. For the forced in the case of lifeless things means what they are made to do against their natural inclination (as stones going upward or fire downward), and the same in the case of animals, when something from outside moves them opposite to their impulse.

1224a20 There is a difference between force in these cases and in man. The former things are simple in having only a unitary impulse (natural tendency or animal appetite), which they can be forced by something external to go against. In man's case the impulse is not unitary but, after a certain age anyway, reason and appetite both exist and can each be in opposition to the other.

1224a30 Nevertheless, even here the forced has the general characterization of being painful (animals and children too are pained when forced). The difficulty concerns the phenomenon of continence and incontinence, where reason and appetite are opposed and where following one means forcing the other. Hence dispute arises, for while thus they seem to be forced, they also seem, on the other hand, not to be forced. The incontinent seems not to be because he does not suffer pain (rather he gets the pleasant thing he desires), and the continent seems not to be because he follows persuasion, which is contrary to force, and because desire too works against persuasion (so that, to this extent, he is acting against force, the force of desire).

Still the continent and incontinent are the only cases where acting seems to be forced, namely because of the likeness to force in lifeless things.[3] The dispute is solved, however, if one adds the qualification (necessary even in the case of lifeless things) that the force must not just be what opposes impulse but also what operates from without. In the case of the continent and incontinent, however, the force is from within, since one inner impulse, appetite, opposes another, reason. Thus, the analogy with lifeless things requires one to say that the continent and incontinent act voluntarily and not by force, and that they only act by force when the impulse is from without (as when someone else seizes one's hand against one's will and desire and strikes another with it).

1224b2

The plausibility in saying that each nevertheless acts by force comes from the fact that each suffers pain (the incontinent future pain and the continent present pain), and because each does suffer force in one part of himself. The error is to apply the force in a part of the soul to the whole soul, whereas one should really do the opposite. For the action that is eventually done is done by the whole soul, despite the conflict in the parts, and the whole soul (following, as it is, an internal impulse) is acting voluntarily.

1224b15

That appetite and reason are both internal is evident from the fact that they are in the soul by nature (and the natural is obviously internal to a thing),[4] either from birth in the case of appetite or by later development in the case of reason (for age and gray hair too are natural, and they can only be natural by later development). Hence the continent and incontinent do, in a way, act against nature, but against a different nature, or part of nature, and not the same one. Simply, though, they do not act against nature, for their whole soul ends up going with one of the parts of the soul, and this part is natural.

1224b29

Therefore, the puzzles from the previous chapter are solved: the incontinent and continent appear, because of their divided parts, either not to act voluntarily but by force, or to act voluntarily and involuntarily at the same time. In fact, however, the acts of both are voluntary simply.

1224b36

Threats and Passion and Argument

Continence and incontinence are one way in which people are said, falsely, to act involuntarily. Another way is when people do something because of threats if they do not do it, for here too they are said to be forced. In fact, though, they are not forced for they have a choice, however limited or painful, between either doing the thing or accepting the threatened suffering.

1225a2

At least so it is in those cases where it must have been up to oneself whether this sort of choice obtained or not. Instances might be where one chooses to set sail hoping to outrun a threatened storm, or where one assists a friend to seize power hoping to enjoy the benefits. In fact, however, one fails to outrun the storm or the friend turns tyrant, and one finds oneself having to choose between shipwreck and throwing the cargo overboard, or between doing as

1225a8

the tyrant bids and suffering death. Here one is oneself responsible for being in the relevant situation (for one need not have set sail or assisted one's friend), so that one is also responsible for being forced to choose between the painful alternatives. Hence, whatever one chooses, one's act is voluntary and not forced.

If, on the other hand, one is not responsible for the situation (the storm arose beyond all expectation, or the tyrant seized power on his own), then one's action is in a way forced and in a way not. It is forced because one does not choose the loss of cargo or the tyrant's bidding; it is not forced because one does choose the end[5] that loss of cargo or the tyrant's bidding brings about, namely one's own safety.[6]

1225a14   At least such is what one must say when the situation is serious and not the ridiculous one, mentioned now, of killing someone to prevent being caught in a game of blind man's bluff. A choice that can truly be said to be forced must be one that avoids a greater and more painful evil, and being caught in a game of blind man's bluff is not a greater or more painful evil. When, however, one does face such an evil, then, "being thus under necessity and not under necessity, one will act by force, or not by nature" (a17–18).[7] The sense is that one is and is not under necessity because one does have a choice, but a choice limited by necessity to unpleasant alternatives, and so one acts by force, or not by nature, because the necessity is forcing one to choose what one would not naturally choose (as jettisoning the cargo, which one would not choose naturally but only under necessity). Thus, to this extent, one also acts involuntarily, for the assumption now is that the circumstances of the necessity were not up to oneself.

1225a19   The point is continued with other cases where the force comes from something outside one's control and action is judged to be involuntary and forgivable, as with passions of love and anger that are so strong they naturally overwhelm nature. For the same reason, avoiding strong pain rather than weak seems more involuntary, and avoiding pain, like the incontinent, than avoiding pleasure, like the continent (so the former seem more forced by their desires than the latter by their calculation). The question of force here turns on what nature can bear. For although in these cases the force comes from within (and not without, as was said about force earlier [1224b11–15]), yet it is as if it came from without because it comes from without or beyond one's nature.

1225a27   Not only appetite but reason too can be beyond nature in this sense, as with the inspired or possessed who speak and do what is not in their control, yet they are acting by thought and not desire. Hence some thoughts too, and not just desires, must be posited as too strong for nature and as operating by force and not voluntarily.

Such then completes the discussion of force in the context of the voluntary and involuntary. The discussion was only necessary because of the cases examined here (of acting under duress or by internal impulse too strong for nature), where action seems to be both forced and voluntary.[8] The voluntary cannot be sorted out if these are not sorted out.

Notes

1. Doubts about the Greek and the logic of this passage are unnecessary, see Dirlmeier (1962: 275–76), contra Woods (1992: 128, 191–92).
2. Aristotle is also, in fact, going to conclude (later in this chapter) that all things done with desire and spirit are voluntary (save for certain extreme cases, 6.5–6).
3. They are the only cases where *acting* seems forced; when one is forced from without, one does not act but is acted upon. The Greek does not need emendation, contra Woods (1992: 192).
4. Contra Woods (1992: 132), who doubts the relevance of the appeal to nature.
5. There is no oddity in Aristotle saying here that one chooses the end although he says elsewhere that choice is of the means and not of the end. For here one is choosing, not between means to a given end, but between means that have different ends (obeying the tyrant so as not to die; not obeying the tyrant so as not to be unjust). Hence one is choosing between ends (life or justice), but in view of some further end to which these ends are means (happiness).
6. Kenny (1979: 41–42) again seems right as to the sense if not as to the particular construal of the Greek. A difference between *EE* and *EN* is that *EN*, while it recognizes the class of actions done to avoid a greater evil (1110a9), does not distinguish this class further in the way *EE* does. This further distinction is, to be sure, of philosophical interest, which is why it is here in *EE*; but as making it and judging according to it would belong to equity rather than to law, it has little legislative interest and so is not in *EN*, which is directed to legislators.
7. If the Greek is not translated thus, one is forced into emending it, so Woods (1992: 193–92), Dirlmeier (1962: 284).
8. If such is what the Greek at 1225a35–36 means; discussion in Dirlmeier (1962: 285–86), Von Fragstein (1967: 127), Woods (1992: 194).

Chapter 9

Thought

The treatment of force, while necessary, has intervened in the process of discussion, which at the beginning of the previous chapter had reached the point that the voluntary could not be appetite or choice and so had to be thought (1224a4–7). This conclusion does not exclude appetite from the voluntary altogether, for things done by appetite are voluntary (provided the appetite is not too great for human nature). It only excludes appetite from being sufficient to define the voluntary, but something sufficient is what Aristotle is looking for. So he returns to the point about thought and argues thus:

(1) the voluntary is opposite to the involuntary;
(2) what is done in ignorance of the whom, the what, and for the sake of what is opposite to what is done without ignorance of these things;

1225a36

(3)   what is done in ignorance of these things is involuntary;
(4)   therefore, the opposite (what is done without ignorance of them) is voluntary;
(5)   therefore, everything done by oneself without ignorance when it is up to oneself not to do it is voluntary, and the opposite is involuntary.

The argument as thus stated is not valid. Conclusion (4) does not follow from the preceding premises. Merely because actions done voluntarily and actions done involuntarily are one pair of opposites, and actions done in ignorance and actions done with knowledge are another pair, does not entail that the two pairs coincide. If it did it would also entail, since actions done virtuously are opposite to actions done viciously, that these would have to coincide with the voluntary and involuntary, but they manifestly do not for both are voluntary. We need to add further premises.[1] In particular we need to add the one with which the chapter begins, that (6) the voluntary and involuntary are both defined by thought (and not by appetite or choice). Another premise, therefore, can at once be supplied from the logic of definitions (as mentioned earlier), that (7) opposites must be defined by opposite differences. With these two premises added the following argument can be constructed: from (1) and (7) follows (8), that the voluntary and the involuntary are defined by opposites; from (8) and (6) follows (9), that they are defined by opposites in thought; from (2) and (3) follows (10), that the involuntary is defined by one opposite in thought, namely ignorance; from (10) and (9) follows that the voluntary is defined by the other opposite in thought, namely knowledge, which is (4). But (4) is not yet enough for it does not take account of the results of the previous chapter about force, that (12) the voluntary is up to us (in the sense there clarified). From (4) and (12) follows (5), that the voluntary is things up to us done with knowledge.[2]

1225b11   Two final qualifications are in order: that the ignorance can be either not using the knowledge one has or not having the knowledge, and that ignorance does not make an act involuntary if one is oneself responsible for it through carelessness or pleasure or pain—at least of the kind that does not exceed human nature (which may be what Aristotle means by adding that the act must be done "of oneself" (b9), that is, not by overmastering passion).

The qualifications may be taken to explain preceding remarks, as that the involuntary is when the act is done in ignorance *and* because of ignorance (b10). For if it is done in ignorance but because of carelessness or the like, so that the ignorance is not the cause, or not the first cause, then it does not make the act involuntary. Likewise, the remark that the ignorance must be non-accidental (b6) perhaps refers to the same point, that the ignorance must be the cause of the action and not merely something that accompanies it or is caused by something else.[3]

Notes

1. Woods (1992: 135–36) notes the invalidity but not how to remove it.
2. Conclusion (5) also says the same, in different words, as *EN* 3.1.1111a2–24, where the voluntary is defined as that which is done neither in ignorance nor forced. That *EE*, unlike *EN*, does not list all the items ignorance of which makes something involuntary may be again because *EN*, being directed to legislators, needs to take more cognizance of what is relevant to legislation. *EE* can content itself with providing the principal points alone.
3. Discussion in Woods (1992: 136–37).

Chapter 10

Choice
What Choice Is Not

The question of choice next naturally arises, for although it has been shown   1225b18
not to be the same as the voluntary, it was said earlier to belong to virtue
and vice. Hence an account of it is necessary. Aristotle proceeds first from
common opinion and experience and shows, in the light of them, what choice
cannot be, and then, using that result, what it must be instead.

Common opinion and experience suggest that choice is appetite or opinion.   1225b21/6a1
That it is not appetite Aristotle shows by showing, as before, that it cannot
be any of appetite's three kinds: desire, spirit, will. The five reasons he gives
(four about desire and spirit, one about will) are clear and need little comment, save that, as earlier with the arguments about the voluntary, they are
not meant to show that appetite has nothing to do with choice but only that
appetite cannot be the defining difference in choice. The same holds for the
two arguments he gives about opinion.

The next reason is about opinion and will together,[1] that they are of the   1226a6
end but choice only of what is for the end, as that one wants health and thinks
one should be healthy, but that one chooses only what is for health. The problem here is that it seems one can choose to be healthy, for one can choose
not to be healthy (say if one chooses to starve oneself as a way to commit
suicide).[2] Aristotle's point, however, seems to be a purely formal one, that in
any choice there is an end presupposed, which, within *that* choice, one does
not choose but for which one chooses other things. For nothing prevents a
thing that is an end in one choice becoming for an end in another choice,
as that bridles are the end for which the bridle maker chooses his materials
and tools, but bridles are chosen by the horse rider for the end of horse rid-
ing (the example comes from *EN* 1.1.1094a9–14). Nevertheless the formal
structure of choice remains the same in every case: choice is *of* something

for an end. Hence whatever and whenever one chooses, what one chooses is not the end; rather the end, being that for which one chooses, grounds and guides what one chooses.

What Choice Is

1226a18 In looking for the definition of choice, Aristotle follows his wonted method and goes through a series of divisions. He begins with things that are capable of being and not being, for choice concerns contingent things and not necessary ones. Choice also concerns things we deliberate about, and not everything contingent is of this sort, but only things that are up to us to bring about (or that we think, if falsely, are so). So contingent things caused by nature (as the weather, say) or chance or other people (as things in faraway countries) we do not deliberate about because they are not up to us (though we can deliberate about things that in some way relate to them, as what to do if it rains rather than shines). And necessary things (as theorems of geometry) we do not deliberate about because they are not even doable to begin with.

1226a31 But, further, deliberation is not about all the doable things up to us. The reason (which Aristotle insinuates by saying that hereby choice is shown not to be opinion) is that some doable things up to us we just think about and do not also act on. Or, as he says (a32–33), choosables are in fact doables, that is, things we are actually treating as doables because we are doing or planning to do something about them.[3] The puzzle about the different behavior of doctors and grammarians, and the answer to it, illustrate the point. Doctors deliberate when acting on their science because their science requires them to deliberate what to do and also to do it, as working out the right kind and amount of medicine and actually administering it, and they may make mistakes in both ways. Grammarians, by contrast, only have to act on their science, for everything has already been decided by its rules. So if we make a mistake in spelling or syntax, it is not because we failed to deliberate how to spell or pronounce a word or combine nouns and adjectives (these things are fixed), but because we made a mistake in the actual writing down or speaking. Further, we do not examine the mistakes that are possible in this way, for they are endless. We make corrections as we goes along, following what we perceive ourselves doing or saying. The reason for the difference, then, is that in grammar what to do is not a doable and does not admit of mistake or need deliberation. In medicine it is and does.[4]

1226b2 Choice, then, concerns contingent things that are up to us and doable, and treated as doable. But it is not opinion or will, as was proved earlier and has just been proved again about opinion. There is a way, though, that it is each of them—not by being them, but by being *from* them. It cannot be both, for choice is not sudden but opinion and will can be sudden; yet it must contain both, for both are present in someone when choosing (a chooser is someone who wants something and is at the same time thinking how to get it). So if it is not both but contains both, it must somehow come from both. The question is how, and an answer is suggested already by the name "choice," which means taking or preferring one thing over another and such preferring is not possible without some examination of the alternatives along with the will to take one of them. Hence choice must follow or come from such examining, that is, from deliberating opinion.

Deliberation is not of an end but for an end already assumed, as said before, 1226b9 and is about what thing will lead to it and about how that thing can be realized. Deliberation proceeds until we reach something whose coming to be lies now in our power and that therefore we can start doing. Consequently if no one can choose without preparation and deliberation (for even those who do both badly are still doing them),[5] that is, without setting himself going for something and deliberating how to get there from something up to himself, so that these are essential to choice, then choice must be a willing that deliberates, or a deliberative appetite, of what is up to us.

Aristotle confirms the conclusion by his next remarks. Choice must be something deliberative, for we all deliberate about what we choose. But it must be more than deliberation, because we do not choose all we deliberate about (some of the things we deliberate about we reject in favor of other things).[6] So appetite must be added, namely the actual wanting of this thing rather than that thing. But such wanting cannot be choice unless and insofar as it comes from the deliberation. Hence, adds Aristotle, appetite is deliberative when it has deliberation as its principle and arises from the deliberation (that is, as to its specification to this thing wanted now).

It follows from what has just been concluded that choice cannot exist 1226b21 in animals or children or even some men, for these lack deliberation and a concept of the "why." They can have opinions about what to do, but not by reasoning out what to do. That they can have opinions must here simply mean that they can perceive something as doable or as an object of action (which even animals do, as when they perceive prey and hunt or pursue as a result). But that they cannot have these opinions by reasoning out what to do, Aristotle argues thus:

(1) the deliberative part of the soul studies a certain cause, namely the cause "for the sake of which";
(2) a cause is a "why";
(3) what something is or comes to be for the sake of is a cause;
(4) walking to fetch merchandise is an example of such a cause;
(5) therefore those who have no posited aim are not deliberative.

The argument is elliptical but can be expanded as follows: from (1) and (2) follows (6), that the deliberative part of the soul studies the "why" of the "that for the sake of which"; from (3) and (4) as generalized (for (4) states a feature that holds as such of doing something for the sake of something) follows (7), that doing something for something is doing it for the "that for the sake of which"; from (6) and (7) follows (8), that deliberation studies the "why" of doing something for something; from (8) and the obvious (9), that the "for something" of doing something for something is an aim, the conclusion (5) follows, that those who have no aim posited do not deliberate. But it has just been said (at b10–13) that (10) deliberating is a matter of reasoning things out, and from (5) and (10) follows (11), that those who have no aim posited do not reason things out; but further, it was also just said (at b22–23) that (12) animals, children, and some men do not have a concept of the "why," and the second part of (6) has said that the aim is a "why," and from (12) and (6) follows (13), that animals, children, and some men have no posited aim; and from (11) and (13) follows (14), that they do not reason out what to do, which is the conclusion Aristotle was intending to prove.

The conclusion and its premises must be taken strictly. The point is not that animals and children and the like do not have aims or ends and do not pursue them (for manifestly they do, as when animals hunt prey), but rather that they do not grasp or conceive these ends as posits and so do not proceed to the deliberative process of investigating how to attain them.[7] They just act straightaway (and sometimes foolishly too). Hence nothing prevents them having opinion and acting on that opinion (b23–24). As Aristotle has already twice remarked (1226b3–4, 1224a4), opinion can happen suddenly but not choice. Choice requires reasoning out and so time, but opinion, and acting on opinion, do not.

1226b30 Aristotle now draws a further conclusion that answers a question posed earlier about the relation between choice and the voluntary (1225b20–21, 1226a19–20). Choice is of things up to us, and these are voluntary (provided the two earlier conditions are met, that the action be our own, not forced from without, and that it be done with knowledge and not through ignorance); but some of what is voluntary we do without deliberation and the thinking ahead that deliberation necessarily involves (the thinking ahead of how next to get the end we have conceived); thus what is chosen must be voluntary but not everything necessary need be chosen.

1226b36 The distinction, therefore, between the chosen and the voluntary, and between the voluntary and the involuntary, shows that those legislators are on the right lines who draw the same distinction in the passions.[8] That they are not entirely correct is perhaps a reference to the fact, discussed in the chapters on justice (esp. 4.8), that the distinction between the voluntary and involuntary is complex (it involves questions of force and ignorance and of kinds and degrees of force and ignorance) and maps on to the just and unjust in a complex way, so that precision would require further distinctions.

As for choice itself, the discussion ends with a summary: it is opinion and appetite as brought together in a conclusion through deliberation, that is, a conclusion now to act for what we want by doing the thing that deliberation has settled on.

Virtue and Choice
In the Definition of Virtue

The discussion about choice and the voluntary began from the question of 1227a5 virtue and how it comes about. Aristotle returns to that question and shows how the results now reached provide an answer to it. He first recalls and repeats the point about the end, that it is not what one deliberates about but what one deliberates for, so as to find something one can do now to attain it (as one deliberates about starting a given war so as to get wealth, or even pleasure—the pleasure, perhaps, of fighting, or at least of dominating the conquered).

This fact about deliberation and the end bears repeating because, as 1227a18 emerges, the way choice relates to virtue turns on the way it relates to the end. The next point, then, to make about the end in this regard is that it is by nature a good, as the examples of doctor and general show, who are each looking to do the naturally best thing in each case. But by distortion and against nature it can be the apparent good, and so a bad. This possibility does not hold of everything (as not of sight, for there is sight only of things that can be seen), but it does hold of science, which is of opposites, though not equally so. Medicine is naturally of health, but to know health is also to know disease, so that medicine can also be used, unnaturally, to produce disease.

The same holds of the will, which is naturally of and wants the good but 1227a28 against nature also the bad. Aristotle seems to mean this point to be taken with the previous ones: that the bad that is willed against nature is the opposite that is against nature in the case of a science, and that this opposite, while not good, can appear to be good. Hence he would seem to intend the additional implication that will can only focus on a bad because it follows knowledge. For, unless it did so, the fact that science is of an unnatural opposite would not be relevant to will's being of an unnatural bad. Further, there can be no wishing of bad against nature if there is no prior knowing of good according to nature (as presumably in the case of animals and the like, which, as just argued in 1226b21–30, have no conception of the good as a "why" of action).[9]

Aristotle himself draws an inference that seems to presuppose the connections between bad and nature and knowledge. Distortion and destruction, he says, are not to just anything but to opposites and things in between, and he gives as reason that deception too, which is error in knowledge, is to opposites in the science. The doctrine that destruction is to opposites may be a general one (*Physics* 188a30–b26, *De Caelo* 310a24–27), but the reason proffered is only a reason for perversion in the will if the bad that one unnaturally wills is the unnatural opposite in knowledge.

From these general points the discussion is brought back to virtue. The 1227a36 remark that "deception too and the choice" must be from the mean to the opposites is presumably about the deception that occurs in choice when a bad is chosen under the appearance of good, and the opposites in this case are from the mean of virtue to the extremes of the more and less. The extremes are naturally bad and the mean naturally good. But what makes the natural bad to appear good is pleasure and pain. The pleasant appears good, the pleasanter better, the painful bad, and the more painful worse. Aristotle's point cannot be that the pleasant is not really good and the painful not really bad, for his view (stated at the beginning of the treatise and argued for in his discussion of pleasure, 6.12–13) is that the best is also the pleasantest. Rather his point must be that real pleasure is found in the mean and only apparent pleasure but real pain at the extremes. Hence he repeats what was said before (2.4), that virtue and vice concern pleasure and pain, but here he gives as reason that they concern what is choosable and that choice is about good and bad and their appearances, which pleasure and pain by nature are. His meaning must be that pleasure and pain by nature both are and appear to be good and bad. That pleasure and pain appear good and bad is manifest, but that not all of them need really be good and bad is also manifest, at least as regards pleasures and pains in the passions, which, as remarked before, are things on which perceptible pleasure and pain generally follow (2.2.1220b13–14). For vice, which is the bad in the passions, is sensed as pleasant by the vicious, or by those not yet virtuous (as the continent and incontinent), while virtue, which is the good in the passions, is sensed as painful. To the virtuous it is the reverse, and the good in the passions is sensed by them as pleasant and the bad as painful. Pleasure and pain thus are and appear to be good and bad to the virtuous, but appear to be and are not good and bad to the vicious.

From this result it follows, incidentally, that the pleasures of the virtuous, however intense they are and are felt to be, can never be bad, while the pleasures of the vicious, however mildly felt they are, can never be good. For the pleasures of the mean will never be in excess, for there can be no excess of the mean; but the pleasures of the extremes are always in excess, for the extremes are by definition the too much and the too little. If there is a life, then, that is both pleasantest and best, it cannot possibly be the vicious life.

1227b5   Fittingly, therefore, does Aristotle end the chapter by drawing together, in a final definition, all the things he has said about virtue and vice in the previous chapters, including now the element of choice: virtue is a habit of choosing the mean in those pleasant and painful things that, by the way one enjoys or is pained by them, are determinant of character. Aristotle notes especially about the addition of character in the account of virtue (and vice) that it excludes mere habits of taste. There is nothing intrinsically bad, or good, about preferring the taste of sweet things over bitter or bitter over sweet (or of spicy over mild), for there is nothing in this preference that intrinsically agrees with or opposes the mean of virtue. A temperate man could, without going against the mean of temperance, prefer sweet foods and drinks to bitter ones, or vice versa. Only if his taste for sweet things made him take (or avoid) food and drink to excess would he fall into vice.

Notes

1. So Von Fragstein (1969: 134) and Woods (1992: 140), against Dirlmeier (1962: 38, 289), who regards this argument as a continuation of what has preceded and not as a new argument.
2. Discussion in Woods (1962: 140–41), Dirlmeier (1962: 289).
3. The Greek makes sense here without need for any transposition of sentences; Dirlmeier rightly (1962: 291–92), contra Woods (1992: 194).
4. This reason, which is implied in what Aristotle says and by the context, is not noted by Woods (1992: 142). It parallels what is said in *GE* 1.16.1189b19–25, contra Von Fragstein (1969: 137–38).
5. There is no reason to change the *ē* (either) of the MSS at 1226b15 to *ei* (if) to give the sense, "... deliberated if it is worse or better ...", for *ei* adds nothing important (deliberation is of course about what it is better to do), but keeping *ē* provides confirmation for the universal judgment: if even those who are bad at deliberating still deliberate when choosing, then there is no one who does not so deliberate.
6. The replacement of "deliberation" here by "wish" found in some MSS and favored by some scholars, as Dirlmeier (1962: 295–96), Rowe (1971: 44), ends up making the same point but in the opposite direction: it specifies appetite by deliberation rather than deliberation by appetite.
7. Contra Woods (1992: 145).
8. Some scholars wish to change "passions" at 1226b37–38 to "actions." But perhaps the word for passions could be translated as experiences, or perhaps Aristotle's imprecision arises because the legislators in question speak of passions when they should speak of actions. Dirlmeier (1962: 297) defends the MSS reading.
9. Contra Woods (1992: 149–50), who thinks these inferences are not implied.

Chapter 11

In Rightness

So much is enough to show how choice falls into the account of virtue, both 1227b12
as to what virtue is and as to how it comes to be (in both respects virtue is up to us as choosing agents). The question remains of how virtue falls into the account of choice, or rather of virtuous choice (for choice does not have to be virtuous to be choice). Virtue is a habit whose exercise is keeping to the mean in doing and feeling, and this mean is what, in each case, is right. So does virtue make choice to be without error and its end right, so that we choose for ourselves what we should, or does it just make reason to be so?

The way the question is phrased is puzzling.[1] Choice was defined as the bringing together of appetite and opinion in a deliberated conclusion

(1227a3–5). Hence choice involves both appetite and reason. But virtue is a habit in the passions or the appetite, so that the question one would expect about virtue and choice is not whether virtue makes reason right and not appetite (for it seems to make appetite right by definition), but whether it makes appetite right alone but not reason as well (and reason is made right by something else). This puzzle, however, leads to another one, for the question as asked is deceptively simple. It looks like two questions: first whether virtue makes both choice and the end right, and second whether it makes reason alone right. In fact, however, it is more, for the first, as emerges at b19–23, is ambiguous. Choice is both for the sake of the end and also of what is for the end, and the question whether virtue makes choice right must accordingly divide into whether it makes what choice is *for* right (the end) or what choice is *of* right (the actual thing chosen), or both. The question about reason is now itself ambiguous in the same way. For when reason is right, is it right about what choice is *for* or what choice is *of*, or both?

Clarification comes from the answer Aristotle gives to the question about reason. The continent man, he says, has reason right yet is not virtuous. The continent man is praiseworthy for, unlike the incontinent man, he does the right thing (which is why some people think him virtuous). But he is not praiseworthy as the virtuous man is, for the continent man has appetites against virtue, while the virtuous man does not. (The point is discussed at large in Book Six.) So virtue cannot make reason alone right; it must make appetite right too. This answer, however, does not say what reason is right about when it is right. For the continent man, since he does what is right, is right both about the *for* and the *of* (he chooses the right thing for the right end). So if virtue does more than make reason right (because it does more than make people continent), it must do more than make choice right about the *for* and the *of*. The only thing more it can do is make appetite right. Accordingly, when Aristotle asks in his opening question whether virtue makes reason right, he asks it first as others ask it (those who think continence is virtue), namely whether virtue make reason right and not appetite, but ends by asking it as he would ask it, namely whether virtue makes reason right as well as appetite.

Consequently the way that question is phrased is not in the end puzzling, for when it is properly understood (does virtue make reason as well as appetite right?) it is not puzzling. Of course virtue makes appetite right. What needs asking is whether or how it makes reason right. The initial puzzle and the diversion through continence were a way, a highly compressed way, to focus the question properly. Moreover, once the question is properly focused, the ambiguities are clarified too. For the question about reason collapses back into the question about choice: since choice is a combination of reason and appetite, and since virtue makes appetite right, then, if it also makes reason right (and so the whole of choice right), does it make reason right about what choice is for (the end), or about what choice is of (what is for the end), or both?

Or, if this analysis is thought to import too much compression into the text, an alternative might be to take the question about virtue and choice to be about the end only, and the question about reason to be about both the end and what is for the end. The remarks about continence will then be directed against those who say that virtue's job is to make reason right both about the end and what is for the end and that whether one has good appetites is not part of virtue. Aristotle's response will then be both that having good appetites is part of virtue, and that one's answer to the question about appetites does not settle the question about ends and what is for the end, for whether appetites are part of virtue or not, there is still the question whether virtue makes the end and what is for the end right or only one and not the other.

This question Aristotle next raises. He first answers that virtue must at least make the end or aim right, for there is no argument or calculation to get one to what the aim is. Instead, as the examples show, the aim has to be laid down or assumed as a first principle. The point of this remark cannot be that the assumption is arbitrary, for an arbitrary end need not be right, but the end must be right. Rather the point must be that thinking[2] does not argue *to* the end but *from* it. The end, says Aristotle, is the beginning of thought, but the ending of thought is the beginning of action (thought about what to do proceeds from the thing aimed at to a conclusion that this thing here is to be done now in order to get it). The end, then, must be made right by virtue and be laid down for practical thinking as hypotheses are laid down for theoretical thinking. (How to determine the rightness of the end was explained, and carried out, before in the discussion of what the best for man really is; but that the best for man is the end for man, from which that discussion began, is a self-evident principle and superior to all proof.)

Virtue, then, and not reason makes the end right, and hence reason cannot be the cause of complete rightness. But neither, as Aristotle now argues, is virtue cause of complete rightness, for while it (and not reason) is cause of the end being right, it is not cause of what is for the end being right. Or, as Aristotle puts it here, virtue makes choice to be right about what it is for the sake of but not about what it is of. The Greek of what he says, however, is rather complex and obscure. The following may be suggested:

(1) an end is that for the sake of which;
(2) choice is of something and for the sake of something;
(3) what choice is for the sake of is the mean (sc. of virtue);
(4) what virtue is cause of is choosing for the sake of which;[3]
(5) choice is not of the mean (of virtue) but of what is for the sake of it;
(6) hitting on these things belongs to another power;
(7a) hitting on the end being right—(7b) of which the cause is virtue—belongs to choice.[4]

1227b19

1227b34

In this series of propositions (1) and (4) are of the nature of parenthetical reminders repeating what has already been said, that virtue makes the end right that choice is for the sake of and not, or not yet, that it makes what choice is of, or what is for the end, right. Proposition (5) follows from (2) and (3); and (7a) follows from (4) and (7b). For if (4) virtue is cause of what the end is that choice is for the sake of, and if (7b) it is also cause of the end being right, then it follows (7a) that hitting the right end in actions belongs to choice—not in the sense that choice makes this end right but that it possesses this right end as that part of itself that is its "for the sake of." Or, to put it in other words, virtue gives choice its essential form (because it gives it is end), and choice gives virtue its concrete expression (because it realizes it in concrete actions).

This result will neatly explain what Aristotle argues in the next lines (a2–4), but first there is proposition (6) to consider and also what role in the whole argument is being played by (5). Proposition (6) is perhaps not strictly entailed by any of the other propositions but its possibility is. For (2) asserts that there are two parts to choice: what it is of and what it is for the sake of; (4) asserts that virtue determines what choice is for the sake of; and (5) asserts that choice is not of virtue but of what is for the sake of it. Hence, if we can press (4) and (5) to mean, or at least to suggest, that virtue does not determine what choice is of, then (6) follows, that some other power must determine it. No reason is given for leaving the inference to (6) somewhat vague. But a reason for no reason being given is given. For if what is for the end belongs to another power, and if what is in question now is how virtue enters into the rightness of choice, and if virtue enters into such rightness only as the end it is for the sake of (the virtuous mean) and not also as what it is of, then this other power is not properly in question here.[5] This other power, an intellectual and not a moral virtue (prudence), belongs to the later discussion in Book Five.

1228a2 As for what is in question here, virtue and choice, Aristotle shows how his conclusion (glossed earlier as virtue being the form of choice and choice being the expression of virtue) explains the way we judge people's character, namely from their choice, or what they do things for, and not merely from what they do. The same, therefore, holds of vice too, that it, like virtue, forms what choice is for, and thus that we judge vice from the "what for" of the choice and not from the "what" that is done. But we can nevertheless judge the "what for" from the "what," provided the "what" that someone does is in his power. For if it is in a man's power to do the noble thing and he does the base thing, then we know that the "what for" of his choice was not the noble; for if it were, he would have done the noble thing. Hence we know he does not choose for the sake of the noble, and thus we know he is not virtuous (for virtue is in the "what for" of choice). The deeds in this case (though not necessarily in others) are a clear manifestation of character. Further character,

or vice and virtue generally, must be voluntary, for they are only manifest in voluntary deeds. Were the deeds necessitated, they would reveal nothing about the "what for" of choice and thus would reveal nothing about virtue and vice (since, as just shown, virtue and vice are precisely this "what for").

This voluntariness of virtue and vice are shown by several different considerations. First, good and bad things that are not voluntary cease by that fact to be deserving of praise and blame and so cease to be good and bad, at least qua attributable to goodness or badness in the doer (though as external deeds they may be good or bad). Second, there is the opposite circumstance, that we praise and blame people more for what they choose to do than for what they actually succeed in doing, even though the point of virtue is deeds and not the habit by itself. Third, when people do base things under compulsion (as from threats and the like as mentioned before), they are not choosing to—on the contrary, if offered a way out, they would take it (hence we do not blame them, or not very much). Nevertheless fourth, and despite such cases, we judge character by deeds because deeds are easier to judge than choice (we cannot see choice independently of deeds, however inchoate the deeds may be). That is why, fifth, we prefer the good act (for the act is what makes the difference and brings about good) but we give more praise to the choice (for the choice reveals the goodness of the person).[6]

All these results both follow from the analysis of virtue just given and, as is manifest, are in agreement with what we do and say. They confirm, therefore, the truth of the analysis. The analysis also gives the solution to the fact that some states of passion, while good, are not properly virtues, because they are not also states of choice (3.7.1334a23–25).

Notes

1. Woods (1992: 152–55) has an extended discussion. His basic analysis is followed here but not all the details.
2. Practical thinking, that is. Theoretical thinking, as thinking what the end of man is, can argue to the end, or to an account of what it really is.
3. That the Greek at 1227b38 should be translated thus is controversial, but at least it does not require any emendation of the Greek; discussion in Dirlmeier (1962: 306), Von Fragstein (1974: 120), Kenny (1979: 86–87).
4. The Greek naturally lends itself to such construal if it is taken in context; Von Fragstein (1974: 120–21) already came to the same conclusion. Kenny (1979: 87n1) criticized the construal but unfairly.
5. The same point is made by Kenny (1979: 87–88).
6. One may regard this observation as Aristotle's answer to Kant's well-known claim that there is nothing better than the good will. Aristotle would say rather that there is nothing more praiseworthy than good choice, but that nevertheless good deeds are better.

Book Three: Particular Virtues

Chapter 1

In Particular
Bravery
What It Is a Mean State About

Aristotle's detailed discussion of the virtues is a sort of phenomenology of 1228a23 happiness. It describes in concrete detail what it is like to live the happy life of virtue. In particular it shows how such a life is a balance or a mean between extremes of vice, and so, in anticipation of later books, how it is a life of wise judgment or prudence. Any phenomenology begins with manifest and acknowledged facts. Of all virtues courage or bravery is perhaps the most manifest (for the deeds of brave men in war are, from our earliest years, the most celebrated in song and story). The phenomenology of virtue suitably begins here.

Aristotle's discussion of bravery divides, as he summarizes at the end of the chapter (1230a33–36), into the treatment of three questions: what bravery is a mean state about; what it is of and why; what power fearful things have. His answer to the first question is fear and daring; to the second, things simply fearful and for the sake of the noble; to the third, cause of destructive pain. Accordingly the translation and commentary are divided at the points where these questions are successively raised.

The discussion begins with the manifest facts that bravery has to do with 1228a26/a36 fear and boldness; that fear and boldness are opposites (as noted before in the table of passions in 2.3); that they thus give rise to opposite habits, as the coward who fears too much and dares too little and the rash man who does the reverse. Since, then, bravery is the best habit in these passions, and since one should not be as the cowards and rash are but keep to the mean between them, the mean disposition, and not either of the extremes, is bravery, "for this is best" (b4–5).

The reference of "this" is ambiguous and could be either to bravery or to the mean. If to the former, the argument is: bravery is best, the best is the mean, and therefore bravery is the mean. If to the latter, the argument is: the mean is best, the best is bravery, and therefore the mean is bravery. Perhaps it matters little which way the argument is taken, for the premises, since they assert identities, must in any event be convertible. Virtues by definition and common usage are names for the best habits, so that the best habit is the virtue and the virtue the best habit. Likewise with the mean, for though it is neither a matter of definition nor of common usage that the mean is best, nevertheless we will typically come to recognize the mean and the best at the same time as each other. The case here of fear and daring nicely illustrates the fact, for to see that there is a mean in these passions between too much and too little is to see at once that this mean is best and that the best is this mean. Hence it is to see at once (because of the identity of the best and virtue) that this mean is the virtue and the virtue this mean. Aristotle seems not to care too much, in what follows, which way he draws the inference, from the mean being the best or from the best being the mean.

In either case, however, he draws the inference, that virtue is a mean or the mean a virtue, through the middle term of the best. That some habits and characters are good and others bad is obvious, for we all naturally praise virtues and blame vices. That these habits and characters concern the different passions is also obvious, for what we praise in virtues and blame in vices is the good and bad way people act on and feel their passions. Once, then, we notice that this good and bad way is a matter of the just right of passion and behavior, on the one hand, and of the too much and the too little on the other, the step to identifying the virtue, the best habit, with the mean is easy. The step then to seeing that each virtue must be opposed by two vices, one at either extreme (even if both extremes are not equally obvious), is then also easy.

What It Is of and Why

1228b4/b18 The phenomenology of fear shows the brave man resisting fears and the coward yielding to them as regard both the kind and the manner of fear. The first problem then concerns what fears the brave man confronts, whether things that others find fearful or that he does. If the former then there seems nothing special about him (the brave man only faces fears that other people face). If the latter then the fearful things the brave man faces must be great ones (greater certainly than those of others), and fearful things cause fear in those they are fearful to,[1] so that the brave man must go about finding things to face that will cause him a lot of fear. But, on the contrary, the brave man is supposed not to fear, or not much.

The problem arises from a failure to distinguish between the *simply* fearful and the fearful *for*. Things that are simply fearful are things that most people fear and that are fearful for human nature (death or maiming, for instance, as opposed to pin pricks), and these are what the brave man is fearless about. Thus, contrary to the dilemma just posed, he can both be fearless and face fearful things. For the things he faces are fearful for man (they are fearful simply), but they do not cause fear, or not much, in him. The dilemma was supposing, falsely, that things are only to be called fearful if they are causes of fear for him who faces them. But while the fearful *for* is always fearful thus, the fearful *simply* is not, and bravery makes the simply fearful not fearful for the brave (cowardice will do the opposite, making the simply not fearful fearful for the cowardly).

The comparison of the brave with the physically strong and healthy is natural enough but ambiguously expressed. The fact that the strong and healthy are able to do and bear what most people cannot and that, conversely, the sickly and weak are more affected by more sufferings than most people excite no surprise; but it does excite surprise that the sickly and weak are not affected, or not much, by what affects most people. One suggestion, therefore, is to fault the text and mark a lacuna.[2] Another is to accept the text and refer it to the phenomenon that those already sick with one disease are not liable to fall sick with another that might have afflicted them were they otherwise healthy.[3] This phenomenon seems genuine, but its relevance to the context is not clear. A third suggestion is to adapt the idea of the second by referring it instead to the phenomenon that the sickly and weak are not affected by *good* things that the strong and healthy are affected by, as the finer perceptions of taste and sound and sight and the like (for the senses of the sickly and weak may be too dulled or corrupted to notice them).[4]

In fact this other phenomenon is what Aristotle next talks about in the puzzle of whether the brave will feel any fear. They will, he says, in the way stated, because they will follow reason and so fear and not fear as reason bids, that is, for the sake of the noble. The reference of "in the way stated" (1229a1) may be to remarks in previous chapters (2.1.1219b30, 2.1220b5, 3.1220b28) about the role of right reason in virtue.[5] But it is perhaps rather, or also, to what has just been said about the weak and sickly, for the cowardly and rash are like the weak and sickly and unlike the brave in failing to be affected by reason and the noble. Hence some things will be fearful for the brave and the brave will fear them, but these will be things that reason bids one fear and not those reason bids one not fear. The brave are thus again shown to be a mean between the cowardly, who fear what they should not, and the rash, who do not fear what they should, but now with the important addition that the "should" in each case is determined by reason, which the brave follow and the extremes do not, though in opposite directions.

Reason and the noble also mark off likenesses of bravery from real bravery. They are called *likenesses* of bravery, and not, say, the vices of cowardice or rashness, because they do *what* bravery does (as cowardice and rashness do not), but not *why* bravery does it. Brave deeds are done in these cases for reasons other than the noble. They can be useful, then, and serve as encouragements in danger, but they do not count as true acts of virtue. The truly virtuous man is he who does the virtuous thing because it is fine and noble. The other braveries would become true bravery if the right motive were added to the right deed. We may conjecture that most truly brave people do become brave thus (especially if most people do virtuous things because of the law [1229a29–30]). Habits of virtue are caused by repetition of the deeds

1228b30/b35

1229a11/a20

289

of virtue, and hence the deeds must in some way precede the habit and so also the perfection of motive that is the habit.

What Power Fearful Things Have

The fearful things of bravery are, then, the simply fearful things, but the phenomenon of fear is not thus sufficiently identified. The object of fear must be further specified as pain and as the sort of pain that is destructive of life. These pains are the dangerous ones that the brave man faces fearlessly.[6] To face other pains fearlessly is not a mark of bravery, as Aristotle shows by doing the phenomenological exercise of considering cases and varying the pains. Moreover the same phenomenological exercise shows that some of the fearful things (those that exceed human measure) must be fearful for everyone, including the brave, who see things as they really are and do not, like cowards, fear what is not fearful nor, like the rash, fail to fear what is fearful.

The phenomena, viewed in their varying forms, thus show that it is not brave to face dangers out of spirit, as barbarians do, or pleasure, as the incontinent would if death were pleasant, as some of its causes are (overeating and excess drinking), or flight from pain, as some like Chiron do, or experience, as professional soldiers do (who face dangers because they know how they can be made not dangerous), or abundance of resources, as the strong and wealthy do. Nor is it bravery to face danger out of shame before one's fellows, as citizens do and as Hector did when he faced Achilles.

All such varying of cases shows that true bravery, since it is a virtue, must lie elsewhere. Virtue lies in choosing for the sake of the noble, so that bravery must be found in choosing to face danger, real danger, because it is noble and for no other reason. This point about the noble is one of the conclusions Aristotle had expressly come to at the end of the previous book, and it is clearly determinative for deciding all cases of supposed and real bravery. Thus, for Aristotle, not only Hector but Achilles, too, cannot count as truly brave, for Achilles fought out of passion to avenge his beloved Patroclus and not from choice of the noble.

Of the people mentioned by name in this chapter, only Socrates, who notoriously faced death without fear in the courtroom, could count as having done so for the sake of nobility, the nobility of philosophy and the truth. Socrates may have been wrong in his thinking about bravery (at any rate as regards its likeness in soldiers), but not, it seems, in doing it.

Notes

1.   Some scholars, as Dirlmeier (1962: 311), want to emend the Greek at 1228b11–13, but unnecessarily, as Von Fragstein notes (1974: 124).
2.   See the *apparatus criticus* in Susemihl, also the translations of Solomon (1984: 2.1946) and Rackham (1961: 312–13).

3. Dirlmeier (1962: 312), with reference to Thucydides who noted the phenomenon about the plague at Athens.
4. A possibility that Dirlmeier, ibid., seems perhaps to hint at.
5. The view of Dirlmeier, ibid.
6. Interestingly, *EE* does not speak of bravery as at its best in facing death in battle, unlike *NE*, which does so speak (3.6.1115a24–35). The difference is explicable on the ground that *NE* is directed primarily to legislators whose concern is the city, for battle is a matter of great moment for the city.

Chapter 2

Temperance

Aristotle's discussion of temperance is similar to that of courage in first iden- 1230a37/b13
tifying the habits and the objects and then in speaking about both in more detail. It differs by being more elliptical in the way it does so, requiring the reader to fill things in from the model of the treatment of bravery.

The phenomenology begins with the obvious habits, temperance and license, and first with license and the ways of being licentious, either by lacking the necessary correction (as undisciplined children) or by being incapable of it, and that either altogether or with difficulty. The habit of temperance is obvious by contrast, that it must be the opposite of these. The phenomenology continues with the objects, that these are pleasures and pains and that the types of license differ by the dispositions toward them just given. Hence becomes manifest the unobvious habit of insensibility on the other side, that it is the failure to be moved by these pleasures instead of the failure to be held back by correction in the pursuit of them. Comedies of manners (like those of Menander, a student of Aristotle's successor Theophrastus) show the possibility of the type even if living examples are lacking.

The pleasures and pains of temperance are next more precisely specified (as 1230b21/31a18
were the fears of bravery in the previous chapter). That they are the pleasures and pains of touch and taste, and really of touch (the pleasures of taste being, as shown shortly in the case of Philoxenos, more a matter of touch than of taste), is shown by a series of illustrations taken from both men and beasts. The illustrations reflect the phenomenology of sensation and the observation of facts and speech; their truth will be assessed in the same way.

It remains to note how the virtue of temperance, like that of bravery, is a 1231a26/a34
mean. The argument is, as before, through the middle term of the best. There are extreme states and a mean here, and this habit (the mean) is best, therefore temperance is best. However the conclusion is expressed in a complex way (a36–38)[1] and includes in it two parts, both that temperance is a mean

between opposing extremes and that it is a mean in the pleasures of touch. It may be put in formal manner thus:

(1) there is a temperance that is the best habit about things the licentious man is about;

(2) there is a temperance that is the mean state about the pleasures of sense mentioned (those of touch);

(3) the temperance stated in the first premise is the temperance stated in the second.

The conclusion is perhaps stated in this complex way because Aristotle has seemingly just allowed that there can be a temperance (because there can be an excess) in sights and sounds and smells (1231a22–26), but temperance in these things is not the temperance that concerns the pleasures of touch because it is not the temperance that opposes the excess of the licentious man.

However, what is also of interest is how Aristotle intends to reach the identification of the two temperances mentioned in (3). For when we add the further points needed from the context, that (4) the things the licentious man is about are the pleasures of touch and that (5) this habit, the mean, is best, there are two arguments that can be constructed. From (1) and (4) follows (6), that the temperance that is the best habit about what the licentious man is about is the best habit about the pleasures of touch. From (2) and (4) follows (7), that the temperance that is the mean state about the pleasures of touch is the mean state about what the licentious man is about. Now both (6) and (7) will give (3) or its converse, depending on whether (5) or its converse is taken. For if (5) is taken as is, then (5) and (7) give (8), that the temperance that is the mean state about the pleasures of touch is the best habit about what the licentious man is about, which is to say that the temperance of (2) is the temperance of (1), which is the converse of (3). If (5) is taken in its converse (5a), namely that the best is the mean, then (5a) and (6) give (9), that the temperance that is the best habit about what the licentious man is about is the mean state about the pleasures of touch, which is to say that the temperance of (1) is the temperance of (2), which is (3).

Both ways of taking the argument require one to take something Aristotle says but in its converse form, either conclusion (3) in the first way or premise (5) in the second. The conversions are valid so no logical problems arise. But Aristotle states the argument with neither conversion, though one or the other is strictly required. Since he implicitly uses the converse (5a) shortly (at 1231b24–25), perhaps his point is that because nothing with respect to validity hangs on which way we argue from an identity, we should, in each case, argue from it as best suits the topic and our knowledge of it, which will be sometimes one way and sometimes the other.

Note

1.   There is no need, contra Dirlmeier following Spengel (1962: 327), to alter
      the text to get the sense required. The Greek is compressed (as is typical
      of *EE*) but nevertheless intelligible. Perhaps, indeed, one could capture the
      Greek best by liberal use of hyphens: "temperance the-best-habit-about-
      what-the-licentious-man-is-about would be the mean-state-about-the-
      pleasures-of-sense-mentioned temperance."

Chapter 3

Mildness

The treatment of mildness follows the pattern of treatment for temperance   1231b5/b15
and is accordingly brief. The relevant object (the pain associated with spirit
or anger) and the extreme and mean ways of reacting or not reacting to it are
again illustrated by a phenomenology (of facts and patterns of speech). The
argument that the relevant virtue is a mean is again through observation of
the best: the best is the mean (implicit at b24–25); mildness is best; therefore
mildness is the mean.

Chapter 4

Liberality

Aristotle begins by mentioning all three of the next virtues to be discussed,   1231b27
giving something of the impression that they together constitute a new section in his treatment. If so, he states no reason.[1] One may note nevertheless a
certain shift of focus in the presentation. For these next three virtues require
more attention to the external objects of the virtue and are not dealt with, as
the first three were, by focusing on feelings of pleasure and pain. They seem to
be virtues with a more extrinsic orientation (though they do involve feelings).
Aristotle, however, while hinting at this difference, does nothing expressly with
it. Whatever the natural orientation of the virtue, whether on feelings or acts,
his orientation remains on the dispositions of the virtuous man. A possible
explanation is that *EE*, being directed to philosophers (who as such transcend
the city), is about how virtue perfects the soul of the man and not how virtue
perfects, through its deeds, the life of the city.[2] The shift of focus allows this
fact about deeds and the city to emerge, but by not being discussed, it perhaps
also allows to emerge its subordination to the other fact about the man.

The discussion of liberality opens with where the discussion of the two immediately preceding virtues ended, with a proof, from phenomenology and the best, that it is a mean between extremes (where the premise used about the mean is that it is best (b35), and not, as just with mildness, that the best is the mean). A point of difference is that an extra premise is added, that the best is single as regards each kind of thing (b35–36). The Greek is ambiguous and the premise could read instead: the best is one in kind as regards each thing (or even, by implied reduplication: the best is one in kind as regards each kind of thing). The meaning, however, seems not to differ, for the point seems to be that while there can, in a given case, be more than one individual best, there cannot be more than one *kind* of best. Two individual runners could be equally best in a contest because they are equally quick, but they could not be equally best because, say, one was quicker and the other more beautiful. Beauty and speed could only count as best in different kinds of contest (where a different task or work was in question).[3] Failures to be best, however, can be several (a runner could be too slow or start too late or run in the wrong direction or wear too heavy shoes). The same point will hold, then, where the several passions are concerned, that there will be one best in each kind or work.

That the extra premise is stated now and not earlier is perhaps because here several kinds of vice are found at either extreme to the mean so that if the extremes are several, perhaps the bests are too, and the best that the virtue is might not be the best that the mean is. The premise blocks that possibility. Similar possibilities in the case of bravery and temperance were blocked in different ways. That there could be several bests or means in bravery arose because of the several likenesses of bravery (of soldiers, of citizens, of the impassioned and the like), but these were ruled out by the premise that they were not for the sake of the noble and so were merely likenesses and not the virtue proper. That there could be several bests or means in temperance arose because of pleasures in smells and sights and sounds, but these were ruled out by the premise that the temperance in question was about the pleasures only of touch. In the case of mildness no such possibility was mentioned, but to the extent it could have been (because the extremes are several, as feeling anger too much or too quickly or for too long a time, or the opposite), it would be ruled out by the premise stated here (the chapter immediately following upon the chapter on mildness).

1231b38/32a10   The point about the per se and per accidens use of property (a shoe is used per se as a shoe for wearing, per accidens as a shoe for exchange, and not at all as a shoe for measuring something) is introduced to explain the phenomena of illiberality.[4] Hoarding coinage or money is a case of illiberality because money, as a medium of exchange, gets its raison d'être from the practice of getting and spending even though the hoarder hoards it as if it were the object and not the instrument of getting and spending. Hoarding property for oneself is also illiberality, even if one is extreme in spending money to get it. Not keeping enough property for one's needs (or money to exchange for one's needs) is to fail of liberality on the other side. The liberal man avoids both extremes by keeping enough of what he gets for his needs and using what he has left over for giving away.

Notes

1. The peculiarity is noted by Von Fragstein (1978: 132), who suggests as the reason that these three virtues concern man as great or "noble" while the first three concern man as patient of certain passions.
2. *EE* speaks (in the list in 2.3) as if the means were always of passions, whereas *EN* is explicit that virtues are means in passions and actions (2.3.1104b13–14, 2.6.1106b16–28), Woods (1992: 103). *EN*, being directed to legislators and so to how virtue perfects the city, has to be explicit about how virtue, by its deeds, makes the life of the city good. Hence, as noted earlier, it expressly speaks, as *EE* does not, of bravery as at its best in facing death in battle (3.6.1115a24–35), for the life of the city often depends on its citizens facing death fearlessly in battle.
3. Cf. *Politics* 3.12.1282b14–83a22; Simpson (1998: 171–74).
4. The distinction is explained more at large in *Politics* 1.9.1256b40–57a14; Simpson (1998: 50–57); discussion relative to the present context in Dirlmeier (1962: 333–35).

Chapter 5

Magnanimity

The chapter begins with interesting methodological remarks about how to determine magnanimity, or its cause: that we must do so from the features of the magnanimous man. A first point to note is that the scholarly emendation, at a20, of "cause" (*aition*) to "property" (*idion*),[1] although not impossible, is neither necessary nor justified. As the chapter later makes clear, determining magnanimity is indeed a matter of determining its cause, namely what it is about (things of worth and honor), since it is because there are such things that there is also a distinct virtue about them. A second point to note is that the remarks about methodology are going to enable us to determine this cause, or to see that it is a distinct object with a distinct virtue. The point is apt to be missed because the likeness up to point between things can obscure the real difference between them even when they move further apart. Aristotle gives examples from the virtues and the vices where one of the vices claims to be the virtue because the partial likeness of one to the other obscures the real difference (as the likeness between the rash man and brave man in facing dangers obscures the fact that the brave man does so according to right reason and the rash man not). The same is true of magnanimity, but as emerges, Aristotle's meaning is not that magnanimity is partially like one of its vices, but

1232a19

that magnanimity is partially like all the virtues and that this likeness obscures the fact that it is really a distinct virtue. The way to remove the obscurity is to approach magnanimity, not directly, but through the features of the magnanimous man. We should expect the arguments that follow, therefore, to be from the magnanimous man to magnanimity, and, properly interpreted, so they are.

1232a28   The first argument proceeds from the etymology of "magnanimous," that it connotes someone great in soul and power (a point as true of the Latin root behind the English word—*magn-animus*—as of Aristotle's original Greek—*megalopsuchos*). The first part of the argument may be summarized thus (a28–31):

(1)   the magnanimous man is spoken of as great in soul and power;
(2)   the man of dignity (or perhaps the "reverend" man [the Greek is *semnos*]) is great in soul and the magnificent man in power;
(3)   therefore the magnanimous man is deemed to be like both.

This conclusion is plausible enough as far as it goes (it does draw attention to a likeness that would incline many people to associate the characters mentioned), but it does not go far enough. For in fact (a31–33):

(4)   the magnanimous man[2] follows or appears to follow *all* the virtues and not just the two of dignity and magnificence.

Aristotle turns next to show why, and states the following propositions (a32–35):

(5)   it is praiseworthy to judge rightly the great and small things among goods;
(6)   those goods are deemed great that he pursues who has the best habit with respect to such things (even if they are pleasant);
(7)   magnanimity is best.

The argument is compressed and in addition there is dispute about the Greek. The parenthetical remark in (6), at a34, requires a change in the manuscript reading from "to be pleasant" (*einai hēdea*), which makes no sense in the context, to "even if pleasant" (*ei kai hēdea*). Should the emendation be accepted, it should be read as clarifying the point of (6). What makes the pursuit of these goods by this man a mark of their being great is that he has the *best* habit about them and not that they are *pleasant* (as they would likely also be). For people without the habit could as easily pursue them for their pleasure, and if he pursued them for their pleasure, and not because of his habit, they would not thereby be shown to be great. Should the emendation not be accepted, the words are probably best deleted,[3] and in that case the meaning of (6) will remain pretty much the same. If "to be" (*einai*) is deleted but "pleasant" (*hēdea*) kept,[4] the phrase "with respect to such things" will become "with respect to such pleasant things." The trouble here is that (6) requires no reference to the pleasantness of the things in question, since its meaning turns on greatness and not on pleasure. It is better, therefore, to delete the word or emend as suggested.

As for the argument itself, since it is summarizing what people think, it need only be construed as probable and not as determinative. The following analysis, then, may be suggested. First of all, there is ambiguity about what would follow from (5) and (6). If (6) is meant to be praising the man with the best habit, then the conclusion would be drawn that (8a) he judges rightly as great the goods he pursues. If (6) is meant to be saying that the goods this man pursues are rightly judged great, the conclusion would be drawn that (8b) he is praiseworthy. Perhaps both conclusions should be drawn, or rather, since it is likely that each will be drawn by different groups of people according to which other belief they put first, Aristotle wants to allow for both. At any rate from (7) and (8a, 8b) it follows that (9) he who has magnanimity with respect to the great and small among goods has right judgment about them and is praiseworthy. But the goods in question are all the goods, or all the goods about which people suppose there is right judgment of the great and small; so that he who has magnanimity has right judgment and is praiseworthy about all the goods, which must include therefore the goods of all the virtues. So the man with magnanimity has right judgment and is praised about the great and small among the goods of all the virtues. Hence he does indeed, as (4) says, appear to follow all the virtues, because wherever there is a virtue he is praised and has right judgment about what is great in respect of it.

But now the application of the method Aristotle opened the chapter with is clear, for an inference from the magnanimous man to magnanimity readily follows (a35–38):

(10)   the virtue in each case judges rightly the greater thing and the lesser (which is just what the prudent man would command as well as the virtue);

(11)   hence all the virtues follow on magnanimity or it on all the virtues.

What (10) basically says (as highlighted by the parenthetical remark) is that what people make right judgment by when they judge the greater and lesser in each case is the relevant virtue; hence from (10) and (9) it follows that (12) the virtues are that by which he who has magnanimity judges rightly the great and small in each case; hence, equivalently, to have magnanimity is to have all the virtues or to have all the virtues is to have magnanimity, which is (11).

Aristotle now comes to a second argument in proof of (11). The structure of it is simple, but illustration of the premises requires elaboration. It may be summarized thus:

(12)   the magnanimous man looks down on things (a38–39);

(13)   virtue makes people look down on things great that are against reason (a39–b4);

(14)   the magnanimous man looks down on things because he is serious about few and great and honorable things (b4–14);

(15)   the magnanimous man's disdain of the many is because the honor he is serious about is honor awarded him by the few worthy for goods truly great or truly honorable (b14–23);

(16)   no virtue is without greatness (b23).

Proposition (15) is an elaboration of (14), which is an elaboration of (12). Proposition (16) follows as a conclusion from (15) and (13); for virtues are among the goods and, if they make one look down on things great that are against reason, they make one look down on things that appear great but are not, which is what the magnanimous man does. So the virtues must themselves possess greatness (the greatness of not making one honor and think great what is not great and not honorable). But (16) is equivalent to (11), that magnanimity follows on all the virtues or all the virtues follow on it (as Aristotle himself indicates by effectively referring back to it [b23–25]). Note too that this argument proceeds, as the chapter's opening remarks required, from what is true of the magnanimous man (he thinks great only what is really great) to what is true of magnanimity (it goes with all the virtues, or all the virtues with it, for all the virtues are cases of thinking to be great what is really great in respect of the virtue).

1232b25   So far only that part of the chapter's project has been handled that involved determining magnanimity from the magnanimous man. The other part was to use the determinations thus reached to show how magnanimity is not some other thing that it is like, and that, because of this likeness, it still appears to be even as it progresses further away. What has been shown so far, then, is that magnanimity appears, because of its being about great things, to be the same as all the virtues taken together in respect of what in them is great. Hence it appears not to be itself a virtue but just a name for all virtues.[5] In fact the appearance is deceptive because there is a class of goods, and a passion about them, which magnanimity relates to, namely honorable goods or rather the great ones among them. The virtues will no doubt fall into this class but to be about the virtues because they are honorable is not to be about what the virtues are themselves about; hence magnanimity cannot be the same as them because it has a different object (or a different "cause" as stated at the beginning of the chapter).

1232b31   Aristotle has just remarked, recalling what he said just before (b17),[6] that honorable things can be small as well as great. He says then that there must be four options: being worthy and thinking oneself worthy of great things; being worthy and thinking oneself worthy of small things; being worthy of small things and thinking oneself worthy of great things; being worthy of great things and thinking oneself worthy of small things. The phenomenology of honor and worth and the fact that here too the mean state, the first option listed, shows itself as best enables Aristotle easily to conclude that the virtue of magnanimity, being best and being about honorable things, must be this mean (a4–9), with the third and fourth options being the vices on either side (a9–16).

The second option only is left for analysis. But worth noting first is that there could in theory be at least two other options: being worthy of great things and thinking oneself worthy of *greater* things, and being worthy of small things and thinking oneself worthy of *smaller* things. One could indeed assimilate these options to two of the four: the first to the option of being worthy of small things and thinking oneself worthy of great things, and the second to being worthy of great things and thinking oneself worthy of small things. But in that case we should also be able to assimilate being worthy and thinking oneself worthy of small things to the option of being worthy and thinking oneself worthy of great things. In fact Aristotle does in a way make these assimilations. He says next (a16–25) that the man who is and thinks himself worthy of small things is the same by nature as the magnanimous man, the man who is and thinks himself worthy of great things (33a22–23). He also mentions the option of being worthy of small things and thinking oneself worthy of smaller ones and uses it to sharpen his condemnation of the man worthy of great things who thinks himself worthy of small ones (a26–28). In *NE* these two options seem to appear as the mean and deficiency of a distinct virtue, the virtue of ambition or proper pride (4.4.1125b1–25).[7] The man who is worthy of great things but thinks himself worthy of greater is perhaps a mere notional possibility. For if he thought himself worthy of more than he was worthy of, he would not, after all, be worthy of great things, since he would lack magnanimity and to lack magnanimity is not to be great. Hence he would really be a man worthy of small things thinking himself worthy of great ones, that is, he would be the same as the third option originally listed.

The notable thing, however, about the discussion of magnanimity in *EE* is that, unlike *NE*, it refuses to say the second option is a virtue even though the state is not altogether blamed and in fact is in accord with reason (a17, 22). Speculation among scholars as to why has centered on the idea that the *EE* is the earlier writing and that Aristotle changed his mind later.[8] An alternative suggestion is to consider difference of audience. The *EE*, if directed to philosophers, would be directed necessarily to people who are great (for philosophy is great, if not indeed the greatest thing), so that someone who was and thought himself worthy only of small things would not be a philosopher. Hence he would not be a concern of the present treatise, or only a concern insofar as, having at least a disposition in accord with reason, he would be suitable material for being made into a philosopher. The *NE*, by contrast, being directed to legislators whose job is to educate citizens in virtue, must be concerned with and so teach all the virtues proper to citizens, which must therefore include the virtues of those who do not have, or not yet, any greatness, including the greatness of philosophy.

1233a28   This suggestion is perhaps not as speculative as it may appear, for in a way it lies behind the chapter's concluding remarks, about the resident alien not being small-souled if he does not claim the honors of political office but rather he being so who is well-born and thinks rule a great thing. The remarks, while general, apply particularly and especially to Aristotle himself, a resident alien at Athens, and to Plato and Socrates, well-born citizens there. They would also apply to Eudemus who was, like Aristotle, a resident alien at Athens. All four, being philosophers and knowing the worth of philosophy, would have that about them that made them great and great-souled. Why then did they not seek the honors of political office? Resident alien status explains the fact readily in the one case, and that rule is not, after all, a great thing and known by philosophers not to be a great thing readily explains it in the other. Philosophy, by contrast, is a great thing and all four did openly seek its honors: Socrates by revolutionizing life at Athens and turning so many young men, including especially Plato, to philosophy, and Plato and Aristotle and Eudemus by setting up schools of philosophy, the first two at Athens and the last in his home of Rhodes.[9]

Notes

1. Dirlmeier (1962: 338); the emendation comes from Bonitz.
2. The prevailing scholarly view, Dirlmeier (1962: 339–40). That the subject of *phainetai* at a31–32 must be magnanimity and not the magnanimous man is unwarranted, so Von Fragstein (1974: 137n). Apart from forcing emendations on the text, it is in conflict with the method Aristotle has expressly said he is going to follow, to determine what is true of the virtue from what is true of the man.
3. As by the *OCT*.
4. As by Dirlmeier (1962: 340), Rackham (1961: 338), and Solomon (1984: 2; 1952, with a slight additional emendation).
5. The same point is made in *NE* 4.3.1124a1–4.
6. Dirlmeier (1962: 343) thinks the reference is rather to *GE* 1.2. The *GE* is no doubt in the background of the thought, but the reference itself seems to be to the previous lines.
7. This virtuous mean seems to be referred to as a sort of temperance at 4.3.1123b5 (in fact the reference is repeated in the chapter on proper pride at 1125b12–14); Dirlmeier (1962: 345), Von Fragstein (1978: 141).
8. Rowe (1971: 50–51), Von Fragstein (1978: 140–41, 150–51).
9. Dirlmeier (1962: 345) says these concluding remarks refer to the second option in Aristotle's list, the person of little worth who thinks himself to be so. The suggestion is unconvincing. It might apply to a resident alien who was not a philosopher, but hardly to a well-born citizen or an alien who was a philosopher.

Chapter 6

Magnificence
Magnificence evidently poses fewer problems of analysis than magnanimity 1233a31/b13
and Aristotle returns to his earlier pattern: a brief description of the virtue,
its objects, its opposed vices, examples to illustrate the point. He omits,
however, the argument that the virtue is a mean because it is best, but the
inference is sufficiently implied.

The main problems concern the grammar of certain lines of the Greek
(33b8–15) and their exact meaning. The Greek may be corrupt, as scholars
think,[1] but a certain sense can be squeezed out of it (as in the translation).

The sense given to the final two sentences (b13–15), if correct, recalls the
end of the previous chapter. For the example of someone who would be like
the liberal man if or when circumstances permit shows that some virtues
require not only a certain habit of choice but also extrinsic factors outside
one's control. If the factors are not present, if one is "as chance has it," then
one is, with respect to this virtue, a "nobody" and lacks both the virtue and
its vices. One is like the resident alien mentioned at the end of the previous
chapter, who is not small-souled even though he does not seek political office,
for his circumstances, not his habits of choice, prevent him. This limitation of
moral virtues, that they require equipment or opportunity as well as choice,
points ahead to the final book (8.2), where the role of chance is addressed and
where happiness is located in a choice that escapes the limitations of chance:
the worship of god (8.3).

Note

1.   Discussion in Dirlmeier (1962: 347–49).

Chapter 7

Means of Passion
The six means of passion listed in this chapter are handled with great brevity. 1233b16
The method of phenomenology deployed in the previous chapters, and the
standard argument about virtue and the mean being best (referred to here
expressly as "the same proof" [34a12–14]), are sufficiently familiar now as
to need no extensive application. Worth noting is that wit receives more attention than any of the others. That humor belongs to the good and happy
life and is not trivial but part of serious living is perhaps denied enough by
killjoys as to deserve some emphasis. Worth noting too is that wit consists in

taking as well as giving jokes (34a14–18), and that the measure of wit, here as elsewhere, must be the man in the mean state (34a21–23). If the butt of a joke is upset by it, the blame, if it is a good joke, lies with him and not with the person who cracked it. The solution is for him to develop a proper sense of humor and not try to suppress a part of his and others' happiness.

Some General Comments

1234a23 Aristotle ends with three general comments (all naturally related to the theme of the mean of virtue),[1] each of which however raises certain puzzles. The first comment is that the six means just described are not virtues, nor their opposites, vices, because they are without choice. The remark about choice is surprising. It seems absurd to suppose that, for instance, someone cracking jokes in a fitting way is not exercising choice; and the same with the other five. A possible answer is that the choice, while not wrong, is not made for the noble (as it should be if it is a virtue) but for pleasure, say. If so, these means will all be praiseworthy, for they are means and do not go to either extreme, but they are not, or not yet, virtues. For, as Aristotle now remarks, there are natural virtues and these means of passion contribute to them (in the ways he shortly lists [a30–34]). Natural virtues (as later remarked at 5.13.1144b4–5, 8–9, 34–45a1) are characters that people, and even animals, can have by nature and that dispose them as the virtue does, save without the intelligence or prudence that true virtues necessarily have. The following sentence (a29–30) seems meant to clarify the point (if the Greek of the manuscripts is read and not the scholarly emendation). The six means just discussed are in a way virtues, namely when, like the natural virtues, they are combined with prudence. For prudence, as said before (2.11.1227b34–28a7, 3.1.1229a1–11), is not choice merely but choice for the noble. These means, then, will become virtues when the choice is for the noble and not, say, for pleasure. The natural virtues are similar, save that, as natural, they need not yet be with any choice at all but merely instinctive (as they must be in animals); hence they become virtues "in another way," for the prudence need not, in their case, be added to any existing choice.

If this way of reading the Greek is taken, the difference between the *EE* and *NE* and *GE* on these six means can be thematically explained.[2] *NE* is unclear about the status of them but seems to allow that they are virtues, or at least does not say they are not (2.7.9–16, 4.6–9, esp. 1128b3–16). The exceptions are righteous indignation and shame, which *NE* says are passions (2.7.1108a30–b6, 4.9.1128b10–16); righteous indignation is also only discussed in its original summary of the virtues (in Book Two) but not in the fuller treatments later (in Books Three and Four). Dignity, by contrast, is not mentioned separately but seems instead to be included under magnanimity (4.3.1124b18–23), where it must of course count as a virtue or part of virtue. *GE* mentions them all but dismisses to another discussion whether they are virtues or not (1.32.1193a36–38).

NE, as directed to legislators, is about things relevant to educating citizens in virtue, and these praiseworthy means, as *NE* says but the other two works do not, concern community (*koinōnia* [1108a11, 1128b6]) in certain words and deeds, and right community is the concern of legislation. The legislator has need, then, to present these means to citizens as desirable, if not also as virtues, for them to pursue in their life in the city. That shame is said to be proper to the young will be because *NE* is about education in virtue, and learning virtue through shame is especially important for the young; so shame's role there (and not its possible continuing role in later life) deserves emphasis. Dignity gets no separate mention because, perhaps, so much is said in *NE* about magnanimity, and in such detail, that nothing specific needs to be added about it. Magnanimity in turn gets extensive treatment because, perhaps, as great and about great things, it is the moral virtue closest to philosophy, and philosophy is greatest and also the most important of all virtues for the city (10.7, 8.1179a22–32; *Politics* 4(7).15.1334a11–36). But citizens seem to have a certain resistance to thinking philosophy great, so anything that prepares the way for philosophy needs special attention from legislators.

EE, as directed to philosophers, who to a certain extent transcend the life of the city, does not have to mention these means for that purpose, which is primarily the needs of play and relaxation (*NE* 4.8.1128b3–4); so it can be open in not regarding them as virtues, or in only counting them so when pursued (as they would be in the philosophic life) expressly for the sake of the noble. *GE*, as directed to citizens, needs to present these means as praiseworthy, which it does, but it can add the remark about "another discussion" because, while this remark will pass most of the audience by, it will pique the curious who, precisely as curious, will show themselves candidates for entering the school and becoming philosophers (where they will eventually learn *EE*).

The second and third comments concern the relations between the extremes and the mean but they seem opposed to each other. The first says that the mean is more opposed to the extremes than they are to each other, and the second that the extremes are more opposed to each other than to the mean.[3] The contradiction can be readily explained. The mean is more opposed to the extremes because it is with reason but neither extreme is, and someone who is irrational in one direction and then swings to irrationality in the other remains irrational both times. His unevenness (going to this extreme and then to that) is bad because it is always irrational. The man in the mean is also uneven too, sometimes facing the enemy, or sometimes giving away money, and sometimes the reverse, but his unevenness is good because on each occasion he does as reason says (and reason does not say always face the enemy or always give money away but do so according to circumstances and the noble). The two kinds of unevenness are thus different: the first is in habits (now one extreme and now the other) and the second in actions (now this action and now that). This difference also explains how the mean can

1234a34

be closer to one extreme than the other because, though more opposed to it as a habit (reason to unreason), it can be closer to it in actions done, for the brave man more often does the same act as the rash man (facing the enemy) and less often the same act as the coward (retreating). The oppositions are different so the relations of closeness are too.

Notes

1. Dirlmeier (1962: 359–61).
2. If the Greek is read with the emendation several other differences arise, which can furnish ground for unwarranted speculations about the order of writing of the three ethical works; Dirlmeier (1962: 357–58), Von Fragstein (1978: 159).
3. The puzzle is raised but not resolved by Dirlmeier (1962: 358–59).

The Common Books in General

The question about the common books was discussed in general terms in the Introduction. The conclusion there reached was that, as far as we can see from the text, the common books are genuinely common and were meant by Aristotle to be part equally of both *EE* and *NE*. None of the arguments against this conclusion, whether based on style or structure or content, is sufficient to overthrow the witness of the ancient tradition. For whether the style and structure of the common books are more like *EE* than *NE*, or like *NE* than *EE*, and whether there are tensions or inconcinnities or even contradictions between the common books and the other books of either treatise, no such facts prove that Aristotle either did not write them or did not intend them to be where they now are. Certainly contradictions prove nothing, for it is an established opinion among commentators that Aristotle contradicts himself or repeats himself or says things in tension with what he says elsewhere, even in books and passages that the same commentators hold to be really his and really in the form in which he left them.[1] However, it can be shown that none of the alleged contradictions or tensions is really genuine (some evidence for the fact will be given below, and has already been given above about the other books of *EE*). Explanations and interpretations have long existed (going back to medieval and ancient times) that dissolve them. No doubt some of these explanations and interpretations are more persuasive than others, and no doubt the explanations and interpretations preferred by modern scholars, who analyze the inconsistencies in terms of Aristotle's philosophical development or the incompleteness of his revisions or simple failure to notice, save the phenomena just as well. The point nevertheless is that, of the many hypotheses hitherto proposed by scholars, or yet to be proposed in the future, none of them, provided each does indeed save the phenomena, can claim superiority over the others. Since, *ex hypothesi*, all save the phenomena, all are compatible with the phenomena. The only one piece of evidence that does distinguish these hypotheses, and that does make some superior to others, is the evidence of the ancient tradition. For this tradition favors all and only those hypotheses that hold the common books to be both common and authentic. These hypotheses, therefore, by the right of reason and of sound methodology, should be adjudged superior to those that hold the opposite.

In the analysis and comments that follow, this judgment will be assumed to be correct, and the hypothesis will be adopted that the common books are where they are in both works because Aristotle intended that there they should be. But since all three books have long received extensive and detailed study at the hands of innumerable scholars, no detailed commentary will here be given;[2] sufficient if certain general matters, or matters specifically relating to the role of the common books within the context of *EE*, are adverted to and discussed. For the overall coherence, organization, and philosophical integrity of *EE* as to all eight of its books, both jointly and singly, are the object of study here. The role of the common books within the context of *NE* will be generally ignored, apart from remarks of a comparative or contrastive nature.

Notes

1. The opinion of Rowe (1971) about *NE* in general.
2. Aquinas (ed. Spiazzi [1964]), Broadie (1991), Broadie and Rowe (2002), Dirlmeier (1959), Gauthier and Jolif (1958/59), Hardie (1980). See also the extensive bibliography collected by Lockwood (2005).

Book Four: Particular Virtues: Justice

That both *NE* and *EE* need a book devoted to justice is evident, and both assert (*EE* 3.7.1234b13–14, *NE* 4.9.1128b35) that such a book follows immediately on the treatment of the other moral virtues, that is, as Book Four of *EE* and Book Five of *NE*. The book on justice that we actually have and that is numbered in the manuscripts in this double way answers well to the needs of both treatises. It plays the same role in each (to complete the account of moral virtues) and no differences of context require difference in interpretation of content relative to them. The questions and problems that have engaged scholars concern the organization of the book and the relevance and consistency of certain of its parts. In what follows, questions of organization and substance will be considered together.

The opening chapters of Book Four follow the standard Aristotelian pattern of establishing first that there is such a thing as justice (from common opinion and practice) and then what it is.[1] Since in this case, however, there turns out to be more than one kind of justice, there is accordingly more than one answer to the question of what justice is. Universal or legal justice is the crown of all the virtues as being the exercise of all the virtues in relation to another, especially in the context of the city. Particular justice is that particular virtue that concerns the goods of fortune and the establishment and maintenance of equality in people's possession of them. Particular justice itself turns out to be more than one kind (namely distributive and commutative), so that it too has more than one definition or whatness. The first chapters of this book are about the existence and nature of the three kinds of justice: chapter 1 is about universal justice, chapter 2 about particular justice and its distinction from universal, chapter 3 about particular distributive justice, and chapter 4 about particular commutative justice (justice in exchange). The content of these chapters is reasonably plain and nothing more needs to be said here about them.

Note

1.   Natali (2007, 2010).

Chapter 5

How Commutative Justice Is and Is Not Reciprocity
Problems arise, however, with chapter 5 about reciprocity, for it is not immediately clear how reciprocity fits in, and thereafter with chapters 6 to the end, which seem to be little more than an amalgam of disparate themes.

These themes are all relevant to the question of justice, but they appear to be lumped together and to lack systematic organization.[1]

To begin with chapter 5, about reciprocity, it seems to serve two functions: first to criticize the Pythagorean account of justice, and second to show how equality can be measured in voluntary exchanges of buying and selling. The first function is clear. Since the Pythagorean account of justice was well-known, at least to philosophers, and presumably well regarded too, but since, further, it is misleading in the simple way it is stated, something needs to be said to show how it is misleading and how it must really be understood if it is to be correct. The problem with the simple statement, says Aristotle, is that the equal is calculated wrongly. The impression is given that equality is secured if the deeds are equalized, as that if a blow has been struck, there will be equality if a blow is struck back (5.1132b28–30). Such equality, it is clear, will not fit distributive justice, because equality in distribution is determined by merit, and is not a matter of equalizing the deeds in abstraction from the persons but of equalizing the distribution in proportion to the persons. Such equality will not fit rectifying or commutative justice either, even though it may seem to, because sometimes the worth of the person enters into the "what" of the deed. In the case of striking an office holder, for instance, the striking is more than a striking of another person but is, as it were, a striking of the whole community (the office holder represents the community). Hence equalizing requires more than a simple striking back but some further punishment besides. Likewise, if an office holder strikes someone (as in administering discipline), his deed requires no equalizing by a striking back but is itself already an equalizing (it is the infliction of a due rebuke).

The second function of the chapter, the measuring of equality in exchanges, is in a way a continuation of the first function. The error of the simple Pythagorean formula would be repeated if the exchange of goods were measured by the goods alone without regard to the persons involved in the exchange. For here too the persons enter into the "what" of the things exchanged, and if they are omitted the equality of the things will be wrongly calculated. To know what is equal in an exchange of shoes and houses, it is not enough to count the things (as five shoes against five houses); one must also proportion the things to the exchangers. A house is worth more than a pair of shoes, so in order to calculate equality of exchange between houses and shoes, one must first calculate the respective worth of house and shoe. The theoretical principle Aristotle gives of diagonal conjunction is clear. Shoes are to houses what a cobbler is to a builder, so that if, say, five pairs of shoes are to a cobbler what one house is to a builder (the example is schematic), then equality of exchange will be secured if the cobbler gives the builder five pairs of shoes for one house. The exchange will now satisfy Pythagorean reciprocity, for the cobbler will do to the builder what the builder does to the cobbler, namely give him his work back. Such reciprocity is, therefore, a case of commutative justice. It is not another or third kind of justice. Diagonal conjunction is also not another way of determining just exchange but a way of determining the measure by which to calculate equalities so that just exchange can be effected.

The theoretical principle is clear, but its application to practice is not. For how does one measure a builder against a cobbler so as to calculate the relative worth of houses and shoes? Aristotle gives two answers, one immediate to practice and one more removed from it. The first answer is that money determines the worth (5.1133a19–24): a shoe is worth a certain amount in drachmas or dollars and a house is worth some other amount. So convert the shoes and the houses to their worth in the relevant currency and give for a house that amount of shoes whose denomination in currency is the same as the denomination for the house. Cobbler and builder will thus (as reciprocity requires) get their work back if they exchange with each other at the money rate (or, as is more likely, if they directly exchange money—money they have first acquired through selling their respective products).

Such monetary transactions are the way most people most of the time carry out exchanges with each other and exchanges that are, for the most part, to each party's satisfaction. But the recourse to money does not answer the question how to measure a builder against a cobbler, for it assumes this measuring has already been done and takes the existence and the function of money for granted. How then is the measuring done? Aristotle gives here his second and more removed answer that the determination is done by need or demand (5.1133a25–29, b6–13, 20). Houses and shoes are worth the need they satisfy, for the need determines how much people are willing to give to get what they need. If the need is great and the availability of the things small, the price will be high; if the need is small and the availability great, the price will be low. We know this phenomenon as the law of supply and demand, and though Aristotle does not use these terms or state the law, it is clear he has it in mind (it is obvious enough to reflection). Hence supply and demand determine money values; money values determine equality in exchange; equality in exchange is commutative justice.

Such a diversion into elementary economics may seem irrelevant to the question of justice and its kinds,[2] but it is not. For economic exchange is an example, and a very important example, of commutative justice. It is the form of justice that is, as it were, the foundation of political community, for political community exists in the first instance for sufficiency in the mutual satisfaction of needs (*Politics* 1.2). Showing how it fits the analysis of justice in chapter 4 is no less important. Recall, however, that the diagonal conjunction that Aristotle has used in chapter 5 to explain reciprocity in exchange is not a form of commutative justice. It is that which makes possible the numerical equality, which is commutative justice. Until the things exchanged are reduced to some common measure, no determination can be made of how much A should give to B or B to A to ensure that each has after the exchange equal to what they had before.

One might, of course, raise questions about the justice of diagonal conjunction, or rather of the justice of the criterion of supply and demand used to apply it in practice. If someone powerful were to manipulate supply and demand, so as to maximize his own profits and impoverish others, would he not be acting unjustly? With what sort of injustice, then, would he be acting (for he would not be acting against justice in exchange if justice in exchange follows supply and demand)? How, then, and by whom should his injustice be corrected? Aristotle would no doubt answer that such a manipulator would be acting against political justice because he would be acting against the common good, which determines the political just, and so he would be making the political community into an oligarchy or a tyranny or the like. Correction would consist in changing the regime from its deviant form to a correct one, and the work of changing regimes belongs to the legislator (the question is treated at large in the *Politics*). Commutative justice, we might therefore say, is derivative from political justice—not in the sense that political justice requires the rulers to determine the level of prices (which would almost certainly lead to worse problems than it was meant to solve), but in the sense that political justice requires the rulers to rule for the common good. The common good is virtue, and virtuous citizens, because they will have virtuous desires, will give a virtuous form to the operations of supply and demand on which commutative justice is based.

Commutative justice will thus always be justice, for it will always ensure equality in exchange. But the equal exchange it ensures will not always be virtuous, or will only be as virtuous as the people involved in the exchanging. There can, after all, be demands in a community for prostitution and for contract killings, and diagonal conjunction could no doubt be used to determine equality between providers of prostitutes and of killers as easily as between providers of shoes and of houses. The principles of commutative justice would no doubt apply as much in the one case as in the other. But one could hardly say that such exchanges were virtuous. They would not, therefore, be just with universal justice, but they could be just with particular justice.

Notes

1.   A full discussion in Rowe, with references (1971: 100–107).
2.   Rowe, ibid.

Chapter 6

Relation of Justice to the Just Thing

The last point mentioned shows that the three kinds of justice, which Aristotle has discussed, relate to each other in a certain order. Universal or legal justice is the exercise of all the virtues as realized in and for the community. It is the political justice of the common good. Distributive justice, since it determines how rule is distributed in the city, is derivative from political justice because rule should be distributed to those who rule for the common good and denied to those who rule for their own advantage. Aristotle did not discuss in chapter 3 what the principle of merit should be to ensure that distribution is made to those who rule for the common good. He merely stated the different principles that different regimes use (3.1131a25–29), and thereafter contented himself with showing, regardless of the principle of merit chosen, what the structure of equality in distributive justice must be. He abstracts, therefore, as he said (2.1130b18–29), from universal justice when discussing distributive justice, and leaves the question of the principle of merit to the *Politics* (Book Three). He does the same with commutative justice, since he contented himself there too, in chapters 4 and 5, with the structure of equality in exchange (voluntary and involuntary), regardless of how the things exchanged came to be acquired in the first place. There is, nevertheless, a question about the justice of acquisition, but it belongs to universal justice, because it belongs to the virtue of liberality (3.4), which, like any virtue, is part of universal justice when taken in its relation to the political community (1.1129b19–31).

These facts are relevant to what Aristotle does from chapter 6 onward. For the focus of his attention now shifts, as is indicated first by his conclusion to chapter 5 (that the nature of justice and injustice, of the just and unjust, has been stated in general [1134a14–16]), and second by his opening statement in chapter 6 (that one can do something wrong without yet being unjust [a17–19]). His attention is thus turning to the relation of the virtue to the thing done and away from the nature as such of the virtue. He makes this point first only about the vice, perhaps because the problem is more immediately manifest in the case of the vice. The problem nevertheless is a general one, for a man can do a just thing as well as an unjust thing without yet being just or unjust. That this problem is not simple Aristotle shows by at once ruling out as a possible answer that someone is unjust if he does certain unjust things. The correct answer has to do rather with how the doer relates to the thing done, whether he does it by choice or passion or something else (a20–21).

Taken in this way the problem is general to all the virtues. For the courageous or liberal man is not he who does the courageous or liberal thing, but he who does it courageously or liberally, that is, from choice and the virtue.

Why cannot the same question be raised, then, about all the virtues and so why does Aristotle raise it only or specifically about justice? The answer has in a way been provided by the preceding analysis of distributive and commutative justice. The mean in the case of justice is a mean in the things, but the mean in the case of the other virtues is a mean in relation to the agent. The point is clear from the fact that the subject matter of the other virtues, or what each is about, is something that, taken by itself, is neutral. Fear and daring, or anger, or getting and spending, or the pleasures of touch, are in themselves neither good nor bad. They are only good or bad in how the agent feels or does them, whether too much or too little or to the right amount. Moreover, the agent himself enters into the determination of where this mean lies, for the mean of courage or liberality or temperance may be here for this man but there for that man. Nevertheless the mean is an objective thing, for it is relative, not to the opinions of the agent (as if an act became courageous or liberal because the agent thought it so), but to the circumstances and person of the agent (what situation the agent is in and what his age, his status, his health, and the like). Hence one can rightly judge another, say a private soldier, to be a coward even though courage for a man in his station would not be courage for a man in a higher station, as for a leading officer or general.

In the case of justice, on the other hand, the mean is in the things and is determined to be a mean by reference only to the equality of the things and not also by the how much or how little of the agent in doing or feeling it. So adultery is an inequality in the things, since it is a sort of grasping for more. Sex between spouses is an exchange of what is due as between husband and wife, but if others than spouse A engage in sex with spouse B, they are taking more, for they are taking what is not due to them. The matter of justice, in contrast with the other virtues, is not something neutrally described but something that is already a mean or an extreme (an equal or a more or a less); the matter is already some just or unjust thing. This just or unjust thing is determinable independently of the agent and the doing of it. So when someone commits adultery, he is always doing an unjust thing (an act of sex, by contrast, is itself neither good nor bad but only according to who, when, how, why, and the like); but he may not always be doing it as unjust. He may instead be doing it from passion or desire for pleasure, as the incontinent and licentious do. In this case the act is not one of injustice, though the thing is unjust, because it is not done for its injustice (for its being an unequal exchange); it is done rather for its pleasure, and the fact the person is the spouse of another is tangential to the act and not the object of the passion. Were it to be done as an act of injustice, there would have to be a choosing of the inequality of the exchange and not merely a passion for the pleasure.

The mention of choice here is significant (1134a20). Aristotle's point is not about the settled state of choice that makes the virtue or the vice and that is brought about through repeated doing of the same acts (as one becomes licentious by doing licentious things and brave by doing brave things). He is talking rather about the choice that makes an act to be an act of justice in the first place. In the case of adultery, doing it for sexual pleasure would make it an act of license; doing it for its inequality would make it an act of injustice. One could, out of passion, do it for pleasure (though one could also do it thus from choice), but one could only by choice do it for inequality, because the inequality is a matter of calculation and not of passion. One must, as it were, say to oneself, as one acts, something like: "it is because this woman is another's spouse that I want sex with her and not because she is seductive, even if she is." Only after the act of adultery has been established as of this or that sort, as licentious or as unjust, will repeated doing of it produce the habit, and produce a different habit depending on which sort the act is.

Someone, then, who commits an act of adultery from passion has done an unjust thing, but he is not unjust with the injustice of adultery, either in that act (for he did not do it as unjust but as pleasant) or in his habit (for he did not do it from settled choice). His deed is a breach of justice, and he would deserve punishment for the injustice, since he is at least legally guilty of adultery. Morally, however, he is not an adulterer, for he did not commit adultery qua adultery. We should, therefore, understand Aristotle to be using the term "adulterer" here to mean committing an act of adultery qua its being unjust and not qua its being pleasant.

These peculiarities of justice arise, as already noted, from the fact that it is a mean in the things and is determined as a mean by reference only to the equality of the things and not also by the how much or how little of the agent in doing or feeling it. The fact has indeed been made plain by the preceding discussion, that the just thing is determined by mathematical relations (geometrical, arithmetical, diagonal), for these are all a measuring of the thing in abstraction from the how of doing it. There is no like measuring in the case of the licentious thing, say, for the licentious thing is not in the what (as in an act of sex) but in the how (engaging in sex in the wrong way, and the wrong way is relative, in part, to the agent). Acts of injustice, like adultery, are wrong in the what, for that they are a taking of more than is equal is part of what they are (adultery, since it is sex with another's spouse, is by definition a more beyond the equal [cf. 2.3.1221b18–26]). The question therefore arises of what sort of relations may exist between acts and things in the case of justice such that, given the just or unjust thing, a just or unjust act may or may not be committed with respect to it. The like question does not rise in the other virtues where the thing is never determinable apart from the doing (the thing is always indifferent in itself and is only good or bad in how one does or feels it). The just or unjust thing, by contrast, is good or bad in itself prior to any doing of it or any how of doing it.

Consequently in order to answer the question about the relation of the thing to the act in the case of justice, Aristotle first has to specify the thing and then discuss the ways of acting in respect of it. He specifies the thing in chapters 6 and 7, and the ways of acting in respect of it so as to be just or unjust in the remaining chapters 8 to 11. These chapters thus have a clear and tightly logical structure. They are not an ill-assorted amalgam.

As for specifying the thing, it may seem that Aristotle has done it already in his discussion of the kinds of particular justice. In fact he has not, or only partially. For what he has said about particular justice is how to find the equal in each case (by geometrical proportion in distributive justice and by mathematical proportion in commutative). But one cannot find the equal in things until one has brought the things under a common measure. The point had already arisen with commutative justice in the case of buying and selling, that one could not find the equal in exchange of shoes and houses until one had brought shoes and houses under a common measure (the measure of money and ultimately of need, or supply and demand). In distributive justice reference was made to the principle of merit by which to determine the proportion (freedom, wealth, good birth, virtue [1131a27–29]), but with extreme brevity. More needs to be said. However, nothing more needs to be said about the common measure of exchange in commutative justice, for the point was dealt with at length in the discussion of reciprocity. Hence Aristotle makes a quick remark back to reciprocity and passes on (1134a23–24). This remark, therefore, is not out of place, as scholars suppose,[1] but exactly where it should be in the progress of the argument.

The matter that needs to be discussed instead is the determination of the just thing in distributive justice, namely the principle of merit. Aristotle turns to this question next and introduces it by saying that the object of search is both the simply just and the political just (1134a25–26). The political just, as is evident from the succeeding lines (1134a26–32), must be the legal just introduced at the beginning of the book (the just that embraces all the virtues in the common life of the city). The simple just, therefore, must be the particular justice dealt with in chapters 2 to 5 (which will be called simple because it is the justice that is a distinct virtue and not the justice that is the union and completion of all the virtues). The object of search embraces political or universal justice as well as simple or particular justice because, as has been made evident earlier, if only by the by, particular justice depends on political justice. Distributive justice manifestly does because the principle of merit is determined by the kind of city (freedom in democracy, wealth in oligarchy). But commutative justice will depend in the same way, because involuntary exchanges (as theft and murder) are matters of political law, and voluntary exchanges (as buying and selling) are matters of reciprocity between disparate persons, as cobblers and builders. But how a cobbler stands to a builder is a function of the city and of the household wherein the needs that people have for shoes and houses are concretely felt and concretely pursued. In some cities, for instance, cobblers may stand higher than builders and in others builders may, depending on variations in needs and desires and circumstances. Accordingly Aristotle passes immediately to a discussion of city and household in this chapter and then, in the next chapter, to a discussion of kinds of city, or of their regimes. This discussion enables him to explain the nature and kinds of just thing and thence to determine, in the light of this explanation, the kinds of just and unjust act and just and unjust agent in the succeeding chapters.

As for chapter 6 specifically, it is a summary statement of the fact and difference of the political and economic just. The political just is what belongs to those who share self-sufficient life together, where the just thing is obviously the common good. Hence rulers are just when they serve this good and unjust, or tyrants, when they distort it to their own advantage. The domestic just does not exist in the proper sense of justice for there is not sufficient separation between the members (slaves and immature children are as it were parts of the master and father). But to the extent there is separation, as in the case of husband and wife, the just does exist (the just of husband and wife not committing adultery, for instance, but organizing the household and educating the children for the common good [cf. *Politics* 1.12–13]). The domestic just, being improperly justice, is left for brief treatment in the last chapter of the book (11.1138b5–13).

Note

1. Rowe, ibid., Broadie and Rowe (2002: 346).

Chapter 7

The Political Just in Particular
Chapter 7 takes up the political just in more detail and draws a distinction between the natural just and the just by law. The distinction is multiple, because, as emerges, some of the things by law are natural and some are not, and of those that are not natural, some are initially indifferent and some are not. The legal things that are not naturally just but are indifferent are mentioned first. They are distinguished in that the natural is what is unchangeable and has the same force everywhere, while the legal is what is initially indifferent but ceases to be so when a law is laid down (as about what religious sacrifices to make to whom). There is no problem about these legal justs, either about how they relate to the natural just or about their justice (they relate and are just by legal fiat). Such law-created just, while it will vary indefinitely from place to place, is not arbitrary but rationally related to the common good (as honoring past benefactors by sacrifice is for the common good because it is naturally just to give thanks).

There is a problem, however, about the natural just, especially if the natural just is defined as that which is unchangeable and has the same force everywhere. There appears, in human affairs, to be no just of this sort but everything in them is changeable. Aristotle's point is obscure.[1] Part of what he means can be discerned from the parallel passage in *GE* (1.33.1194b30–95a4), where he makes it clear that by the natural just he means the things that it is normal for people to share in common in cities. The natural in this case is the normal, but nothing prevents this normal being changed in particular places and for particular reasons and being good, or even better, if so changed. The example of hands makes the point. Normally people are right-handed (or are skilled only with one hand, which for some may be the left hand), but they could, by practice, become skilled with both. Being ambidextrous is not normal and so, to this extent, not natural. But it is not unnatural either, if by unnatural is meant bad or unjust, for there is nothing bad or unjust about being ambidextrous. Hence Aristotle adds a remark about contracts and advantage in things just, that there are variations here according to variations in utility. These variations are good because they enable us to go on achieving what is advantageous despite changes in need and circumstance. The end, we may therefore say, is everywhere the same, namely the good of common life, but the ways of getting there, whether by sharing these things or also those, whether by using these measures or others, vary infinitely. Such variation in achieving the end is a feature of human life because human life is subject to change. It is not a feature, perhaps, of divine life (1134b28–30), for the gods are above the world of change and they and their state are always the same way.

Another part of what Aristotle means (and that is not in *GE*)[2] can be discerned from his closing remark about regimes (1135a3–5), that these too are not everywhere the same though one is everywhere according to nature the best. Regimes vary from place to place, but some regimes are correct and others deviant. The correct regimes (kingship, aristocracy, polity) are correct because they pursue the common good, and they pursue the common good because the ruling body in each case is virtuous (with complete virtue in the case of kingship and aristocracy, with military virtue in the case of polity). The deviant regimes (tyranny, oligarchy, democracy) are deviant because they do not pursue the common good, and their ruling bodies are not virtuous (*Politics* 3.6–7). These rankings are everywhere the same, and among them kingship is always best. Hence Aristotle is doubtless referring to kingship when he says that one regime is everywhere according to nature best. The regimes, however, that suit given cities are not everywhere the same, but for some kingship suits, for others aristocracy, for others polity; the deviant regimes may also suit some regimes, not by nature (for no deviant regime accords with nature [*Politics* 3.17.1287b39–41]), but because the citizens can only be got to choose a deviant regime and not a correct one (*Politics* 6(4).12–13).

In an extended sense, therefore, a deviant regime may be said to be natural for this or that city, if it will not tolerate a correct one.

A correct regime can, however, always in principle be set up, even in those cities that refuse a correct regime, for these cities will nevertheless have enough virtuous citizens in them to form the basis of a correct regime (whether a democratically leaning polity or an oligarchically leaning one [*Politics* 6(4).7–9, 11]). If they do not have enough virtuous citizens in them, then they are naturally slavish and may justly be subjected by force to a virtuous master (*Politics* 1.6–7), and under a master, if they do not have the political just, they will have the domestic just, for slaves share in the domestic just (earlier here, at 6.1134b8–17). Still, even where a correct regime can be set up, because the citizens are willing, the correct regime will not everywhere be the same. It will, however, everywhere be natural, for all correct regimes accord with nature.

Aristotle's position, then, on regimes and on the natural just steers a mean between the extremes of cultural imperialism and cultural relativism. It is not culturally imperialistic because it does not say that if some city does not have the regime that my city has, therefore I should say or think that that city is unjust or unnatural (for, on the contrary, if it has a correct regime, it will not be). The position is not culturally relativist because it does not say that all regimes everywhere are natural or just. On the contrary it says that some are natural and just and others unnatural and unjust.

If we interpret Aristotle's remarks in this way, what he does in the following chapters falls into place. For he has now shown what the just and unjust things are and in how many ways and differences they exist (by nature, as in the correct regimes, by necessary concession, as in deviant regimes, and by order, as in laws about things originally indifferent). So he can now turn to the question of the doing of just and unjust things and of the being just or unjust when doing so. This question could not properly be decided before the just things were decided. For if we do not know what the just things are, we will not know what acts and persons are just or unjust. We may, for instance, be tempted to say that those who sacrifice to Brasidas are unjust because we do not sacrifice to Brasidas, and since what we do is just, what they do, if it is different, must be unjust. But it is not. On the contrary it is just; only it is just for them and not for us (for they have a law about it and we do not). We may be likewise tempted to say that those who have a different regime from ours have an unjust regime, for our regime is just and since theirs is different it cannot be just. But, again, it can be just; only it is just for them and not for us (they have someone virtuous enough to be king, while we only those virtuous enough to be aristocrats or rulers of a polity). And even if it is not just (for it is a deviant regime), it may be the closest to justice they are currently willing or able to go. Nevertheless, despite all these relativities, we will still be able to rank all the just things that we find in different times and places according to a standard that is everywhere the same: the standard of nature that ranks kingship best and the others after it, some as correct and others as deviant (and the deviant as some more and some less bad [*Politics* 6(4).4–6]).

Notes

1. Dirlmeier (1959: 419–21); cf. Strauss who reviews the opinions of Averroes and Aquinas before offering his own corrupt interpretation (1953: 157–64).
2. For reasons explained in the commentary thereon (Transaction Publishers, forthcoming).

Chapters 8–9

Doing, Suffering, and Being Just or Unjust

In chapter 8 Aristotle decides the question of how one must do the just or unjust thing in order to be acting justly or unjustly (it has to be done voluntarily and with knowledge of the relevant facts; and there are several different ways in which people can do a wrong in communities and yet not be acting unjustly, as by committing a mistake or a misfortune; and there are several different ways in which doing a wrong is pardonable or not). In chapter 9 he decides the question of suffering justice and injustice and in particular whether it is possible to suffer injustice voluntarily. His answer here, which can seem peculiar, is that no one suffers injustice voluntarily because it is part of the definition of suffering injustice that it be involuntary (9.1136b3–6). The definition is not arbitrary even if it is stipulative. An injustice is a bad and no one wants a bad qua bad but only a bad that, in some way or at the time, he thinks a good. If we want what would ordinarily be an injustice, then we want it because in some respect it is a good, or thought to be a good, and then it automatically ceases to be an injustice. We may indeed by harmed by what we want (as masochists are by the pains they want inflicted on them), but we are not thus wronged. Likewise if we voluntarily allow ourselves to come off worse in an exchange of gifts (as Glaucon did with Diomedes [1136b9–14]), we are not wronged, for there must be another to do the wrong, and if we are willing he does not do any wrong (even if we suffer a loss). Chapter 9 also determines how we become unjust, as opposed to acting unjustly, namely by developing the habit. Hence arises an error that people easily fall into (1137a4–9). They judge that because someone acted unjustly, therefore he is unjust. But he need not be if, though he did it voluntarily, he did not do it from the habit but in some lesser way. Aristotle's insinuation seems to be, then, that we should not be so harsh in judging wrongdoers, for many of them, if acting unjustly, need not yet be unjust men. We should not, therefore, deprive them of all goods as if they were incurably wicked and incapable of benefiting from any good (1137a29–30). Rather, even though they should suffer some loss by way of punishment (so as to rectify the inequality that the injustice is), yet we should treat them as still in the human realm and as still up to a point needing and deserving goods.

Chapters 10–11

Equity and Wronging Oneself

Chapter 10 on equity has seemed to many to be out of place, but it naturally follows on. It is part of the question whether one can wrong oneself, which was one of the questions that the difference between unjust thing, unjust act, and unjust person naturally raises (those posed at 9.1136a10–b3). The equitable man is he who takes less and so he seems to be someone who wrongs himself by taking less than he should (9.1136b20–21). In fact, however, he is not, because the less he takes is not the less simply but the less relative to the universal rule. In particular cases the universal rule may be too universal and not have sufficient regard to the particular difference. The equitable man does have regard to the particular difference and takes what is equal in the particular case though less than the universal rule would allow. Hence it cannot be said that the equitable man wrongs himself, because, contrary to appearances, he does not take less in the first place. Further, in considering the question whether it is possible to wrong oneself, one must exclude the equitable man and equity, for these are not really instances of wrong.

One might, nevertheless, say that equity should have received treatment earlier, as in chapters 6 and 7, along with the discussion of the just and unjust thing, for the equitable is a certain sort of just thing (it is the just thing in a particular case). No doubt Aristotle could have dealt with it there, but there is also good reason to deal with it here, along with the question about wronging oneself. For even had it been dealt with earlier, it would have had to be dealt with here too, in the context of how just or unjust doing and suffering relate to the just and unjust thing. It is, after all, a just thing that raises a special problem relative to the question of wronging oneself. It is, therefore, sufficiently germane to the present context.

There are many ways to give fitting order to materials in a philosophical discussion, any one of which may reasonably be chosen. Aristotle chose this way. Perhaps we ourselves would have chosen another. But we cannot say, on this account alone, that he should have chosen our way, or that he really did, or that, given time and occasion, he would have, and that therefore the text as we now find it is unfinished or has been disrupted or is the incompetent work of a later editor. The available facts warrant no such conclusion. This chapter, as indeed the whole of Book Four, despite the doubts of scholars, follows an intelligible order, and one that makes sense of the virtue of justice both in itself and in the context of the treatise as a whole (whether the treatise is *EE* or *NE*).

Book Five: Prudence

That Book Five should, in *EE*, have the title of "Prudence" is plausibly deduced from Aristotle's own remarks (1.1.1214a30–b6, 1.4.1215a32–b14, 1.5.1216a27–b25), when he lists prudence, virtue, and pleasure as the three preferred candidates for the happy life. Books Two to Four are clearly about virtue, and Book Five, while it discusses all the intellectual virtues, is focused on prudence. The book could perhaps also have the same title in *NE* since, at 1.5.1095b14–96a5 in that work, the same division into three of the candidates for happiness occurs. A difference, however, is that there the three are introduced, not as pleasure, virtue, and prudence, but as the indulgent life (which concerns pleasure), the political life (which concerns honor, or virtue as true ground of honor), and the theoretical life (which is not further specified until Book Ten). The thematic division that guides *NE* seems rather to be into moral virtue and intellectual virtue (1.13.1103a1–10 and 2.1.1103a14–18). The same distinction is also found in *EE* (2.1.1220a4–15, and in the first chapter here, at 1138b35–39a3), but the division of Book One into prudence, virtue, and pleasure seems to take thematic prominence within the treatise as a whole. In the context of *NE*, a better title for this book might be "Intellectual Virtues." The content is the same, but the context of theme differs.[1] For as to content, the book is about prudence as one among several intellectual virtues. Since, then, prudence tends elsewhere in *NE* to be used for practical wisdom and in *EE* for both practical and intellectual wisdom, to give this book the title "Prudence" in *EE* is to give it a title that embraces all its content (right reason as well as intellectual virtue generally), but to give it this title in *NE*, and not that of intellectual virtues, is to give it a title that embraces only part of its content.

The division of the chapters of Book Five is clearer and less subject to scholarly disputes than those of Book Four. The aim of the book, as the opening chapter makes plain, is to determine what right reason is and what its mark (1138b34). Since definitions are found by a process of division, Aristotle begins with a division, namely of the soul and of the intellectual part of it. The division is clear and largely self-explanatory. It enables Aristotle to isolate all the virtues in the intellectual part of soul that may properly be called intellectual virtues. (A virtue being what makes a thing do its work well, and the work of thought being truth, all those intellectual states are virtues whereby thought thinks truth.) It also enables him, in chapters 1 and 2, to distinguish practical thinking from theoretical, practical truth from theoretical, and the virtues of the one from those of the other. The discussion that follows in chapters 3 to 7 of all these virtues is brief and schematic but straightforward. The point is evidently not to analyze all the virtues in detail but to set them out in summary form and thus give a complete review of them. For the aim of the book, as indicated at the beginning, is not the intellectual virtues as a whole but that one among them that concerns moral virtue, namely right reason or prudence. Hence all the succeeding chapters, 8 to 11, are about prudence, first in its differences from the other intellectual virtues as well as its several parts (chapters 7 to 11), and second in its operation in deeds (chapters 12 and 13). The organization of the book is reasonably clear and beyond serious dispute.[2]

A main puzzle that has exercised scholars is where the book answers the question about the mark of right reason or prudence, for the chapters and their divisions seem all to concern what right reason is and not what mark it looks to or follows in determining the right thing to do. The answer would seem to be that there is an error in thinking the mark of right reason to be something other or beyond the what of right reason.[3] The what of right reason is that it is not a reasoning power, or a power that deduces from some universal criterion what particular action best fits the criterion here and now (as in the utilitarian calculus of pleasure). Rather it is a discerning power. Prudence judges where the mean of virtue lies, not by referring back to some criterion or measure, but directly by seeing this mean in the here and now. Prudence does not *reason* about virtue; it directly *intuits* it (8.1142a23–30, 11.1143a32–b17, 12.1144a29–36). To look for a criterion of virtue that prudence is to follow is mistaken. To think a criterion is necessary is to think that prudence is a faculty that subsumes particular cases under general rules or applies general rules to particular cases. But if prudence intuits, rather than reasons out, such a faculty is precisely what it will *not* be.[4] Hence, once the "what" of right reason is seen (that it is a sort of intellectual perceiving of particulars), the mark of right reason is seen too (that it is the mean thus directly perceived in the particulars). At least the mark of right reason relative to particular acts of particular virtues on particular occasions is thus seen. Whether there is a mark relative to life as a whole, and if so what that mark is and how it is discerned and followed, are different questions, and are dealt with as different later (8.3 in *EE*; 10.7–8 in *NE*—though there is a brief anticipation of the answer here [13.1145a6–11]).

A second main puzzle about Book Five, at least in the context of *EE*, is how its treatment of prudence (*phronesis*) as an intellectual virtue distinct from wisdom (*sophia*) fits in with the treatment of prudence in the other books of *EE*. For these other books use the term in a different way and do not distinguish the two virtues but treat prudence as if it were a term that indifferently embraced both.[5] One plausible solution is to say that this difference in the use of the term is an indication that Book Five is not, after all, a part of *EE* but is proper only to *NE* (where a distinction between prudence and wisdom seems assumed from the start).[6] This solution tends to be associated with the further claim that *EE* is an earlier work than *NE* and betrays, by this fact among others, a less mature stage of philosophical reflection.[7] Another solution (to be argued for here) is associated with the claim that *EE* and *NE* do not differ by maturity of reflection or time of writing (even if the times were different), but by difference of audience and intention.

The use of prudence to refer to theoretical and not just practical wisdom is found in other writings of Aristotle's, as notably the *Metaphysics*, where Aristotle uses the term as equivalent to philosophy, or the highest science, in his opening discussion of wisdom and the wise man (1.2.982b24; he makes the like identification in his discussion of Plato later, 13.4.1078b15). He speaks similarly in *Politics* 6(4).1.1289a12 (drawing an equivalence with science [1288b22]), and the *Politics*, significantly, is the express continuation of *NE* (10.9.1181b12–23). Like instances are found elsewhere, as in the *Topics*, which speaks of the prudence that accords with philosophy (8.14.9–10; also 6.3.141a7), in the *Posterior Analytics*, which puts prudence into things of the theoretical class (2.2.54b14), and in the *De Caelo*, which speaks of prudence about things that do not come to be or change (3.1.298b23, 19). There is also a striking instance in the *De Sensu* (1.437a2–3), where prudence is expressly divided into a kind about intelligible things (*noēta*) and another about practical ones (*prakta*).

It seems, then, from these passages, that Aristotle is not particular in his use of the word prudence, at least when he has no special reason to be. Indeed only in Book Five of *EE* (Book Six of *NE*) does he seem to take any pains systematically and strictly to distinguish prudence from wisdom and science. In their other books, both *NE* and *EE* show a certain looseness of expression and usage. So, for instance, we find that the distinction insisted on elsewhere in *NE* is not between prudence and wisdom but between the political and the contemplative lives, and the contemplative life seems to involve moral virtue, and so prudence, no less than the political (1.5.1096a4–5, 10.7–8). The terms prudence and wisdom are used as distinct on occasion (1.8.1098b24, 13.1103a4–10), but the use of a similar distinction between wisdom and one of the parts of prudence (understanding [5.10]), as well as the moral virtues generally, is found in *EE* (2.1.1220a5–6, 11–12; also 8.2.1248a34–35). In addition, *EE* has one noteworthy passage where prudence is expressly said not to be science, and so, by implication, not wisdom either (if wisdom is the chiefest science, 5.7.1141a18–20). It is another kind of comprehending (8.1.1246b35–36). Yet elsewhere, *EE* speaks as if prudence referred to some kind of theoretical wisdom and was distinct from the political life and virtue (1.4.1215b1–4).

We cannot, therefore, put much weight on the fact that the common books maintain a strict distinction between the terms prudence and wisdom that is not observed outside those books. To discern Aristotle's meaning, we should look rather to the arguments he gives than to the terms he uses. So, for instance, as already noted, the argument in *NE* shows that, outside the common books, the distinction is rather between the theoretical and political lives than between wisdom and prudence. The man who devotes himself to the theoretical life will not need all the external occasions and goods that the political man needs, for the political man needs these, not so as to perform deeds of virtue, but so as to perform and display great deeds of virtue. The theoretical man will have the virtues and prudence no less than the political man, and he will no less act on them, but not for greatness or display; rather for the maintenance and preservation of human life and of community as devoted to theoretical activity (10.8.1178a23–b7, 78b33–79a29). There need be no fear, then, that the theoretical man, as Aristotle understands him, could be morally vicious and could commit crimes or ignore his fellows' needs so as to pursue a life of theory.[8] If he has need to live among others and depends on a supply of material goods so as to theorize, he has need of the virtues that govern living well among others and that determine the right use of material goods. Thus he will, if occasion demand, undertake deeds of moral virtue to support and preserve the community and its goods (as notably justice, temperance, and courage). He will, of course, want the community to be directed to the exercise of theory and will work as far as he can to that end. But a community that is at war with itself through crime, or incapable of defense against external enemies, or inadequately supplied with material necessities, cannot be directed to anything good, let alone to the goodness of the life of theory.

Aristotle's worry, unlike that of modern commentators, is not whether the theoretical man might turn out to be morally vicious, but whether the political man might turn out to be. For the political man, in order to display the moral virtues at their greatest, needs great possessions and occasions whereby to do so, as great wars in the case of courage, great power in the case of temperance, great conquest and the dispensing of great wealth in the case of magnificence (10.7.1177b6–18, 8.1178a25–b3). He will be tempted, therefore, to seek out great possessions and occasions, supposing that only so can he be best and happiest. He will be tempted, further, to think that such deeds are the goal of life and not, as they really are, for that goal's sake. If Aristotle is to counter this error of political men, he needs to make as evident as possible the inferiority of politics to philosophy—but not in such a way as to make the political life unattractive; for philosophers too are men and need the city and the goods of the city if they are to pursue philosophy. Only the rare few who are as gods can live beyond the city (NE 10.8.1178b3–7; Politics 1.2.1253a2–4).

Why, then, does Aristotle choose only in NE to subordinate politics to philosophy and to call the first a secondary happiness (10.8.1178a9–10)? Why does he not do the same in EE?[9] A natural answer is that NE is directed to legislators and has the Politics as its continuation, so that if Aristotle is to correct this error among political men he needs to make it plain to legislators, who give guidance to political men, that it is an error. Otherwise legislators may themselves err in setting up regimes and, instead of doing what they can to direct the city toward philosophy, may allow the regime instead to be directed, as so many other regimes were directed, to conquest and empire (*Politics* 2.9.1271a41–b10; 4(7).2.1324b1–22, 15.1334a11–b5). The Spartan regime was particularly at fault in this regard, and so also were the many legislators who took that regime as their model (*Politics* 4(7).14.1333b5–34a10).

EE, by contrast, is directed to philosophers who already know that philosophy is superior and do not need to be told either that the theoretical life is higher than the practical or that wisdom is higher than prudence. Hence Aristotle says nothing in *EE* comparable to what he says about the theoretical life in *NE*, nor does he much bother, outside Book Five, to draw attention to the difference between prudence and wisdom, or between the practical and the theoretical forms of wisdom. For philosophers do not need to be reminded of the fact. Legislators and politicians do. Still, Aristotle does say all these things in *EE*, and more forcefully, if also more briefly, in the end (8.3.1249b16–23). He includes a sharp repudiation of the Spartans as well, whom he does not hesitate to call "wild," because they chose virtue for its profits rather than for itself (8.2.1249a1, with similar sentiments about Spartan wildness in *Politics* 5(8)4.1338b9–38).

Book Five is as fully part of *EE* as *NE*, and fits the intention and teaching, as well as the audience, of both.

Notes

1. Rowe (1971: 114) holds the topic of this book to be prudence, even in the context of *NE*. He adverts to the fact that the book introduces itself in this way (that its object is to determine what right reason is, 1.1138b20, 34). But, as is evident, it soon broadens out to cover all the intellectual virtues for this purpose (1.1139a1–17). So even if, as he suggests, a title of "Prudence" would fit the context of *NE*, yet it fits better the context of *EE*.
2. Rowe (1971: 109–114).
3. Rowe (1971: 111–12), Broadie and Rowe (2002: 357–60).
4. Hardie (1980: 232–34), Cooper (1986: 58–76), Peterson (1988: 233–50).
5. Rowe (1971: 63–72), also in Moraux and Harlfinger (1971: 73–92).
6. The view of Rowe, ibid.
7. The view again of Rowe, ibid.
8. Kenny (1992: 89–93), Broadie (1991: 372–73).
9. Kenny (1992: 93–102) thinks *EE* preferable to *NE* because, as it seems, it does not subordinate politics or morality to contemplative philosophy.

Book Six: Pleasure

That Book Six should have the title of "Pleasure" in the context of *EE* is plausibly deduced from the division of topics for *EE* given in Book One (virtue, prudence, and pleasure). The book does deal first, and at length, with continence and incontinence but as subordinate to the overall theme of pleasure, with which theme its final chapters conclude. The new beginning that Aristotle mentions in his opening words (1145a15) must refer back to 1.5.1216a29–37, where two questions about pleasure are raised: whether bodily pleasure contributes to happiness and whether there are other pleasures that belong to the happy life to make it pleasant. Both questions, which were there postponed, are answered here: the first in chapters 1 to 10 (about continence and incontinence), and the second in chapters 11 to 14 (about pleasure). Within *NE*, by contrast, this beginning refers back to the end of Book Four (9.1128b33–35) where continence, in an aside, is referred to as a sort of mixed state, not a virtue, and something to be dealt with later. So, in the context of *NE*, this book has the theme of such mixed states (and so would plausibly have there the title of Continence and Incontinence). Its treatment of pleasure, then, instead of being, as in *EE*, the answer to the second of two questions expressly raised earlier, becomes simply subordinate to the treatment of continence and incontinence. The treatment proper of pleasure in *NE* comes later in its second discussion of pleasure in Book Ten. The double treatment of pleasure in *NE* is one of the features of that work that mark it as significantly different from *EE*. How and why it does and should differ over the treatment of pleasure will be discussed below.

Chapters 1 to 3

Continence and Knowledge

The main puzzles about Book Six that have exercised scholars are, first, precisely what answer Aristotle gives to the Socratic puzzle about how one can do something wrong while knowing or judging it to be wrong; second, how the several varieties or parts of incontinence fit in; third, what role in the book the treatment of pleasure is supposed to play. The third question has been briefly touched on already and more will be said about it shortly. About the first question nothing beyond a quick summary of the answer given in chapter 3 is necessary here:[1] the incontinent man does wrong knowing that what he is doing is wrong; however, either he knows it is wrong in general but does not exercise this knowledge at the time; or he does exercise it but does not know the particular or does not subsume the particular under the general; or he has and exercises the knowledge the way the drunk or asleep or mad do (mouthing the words but not knowing the meaning); or he exercises the knowledge and draws the right conclusion in thought but does not draw it in deed (passion intervenes first and he acts on the passion and not on the thought); or several of these are going on at once. Hence what Socrates thought impossible, that knowledge, which is stronger, could get dragged about by passion, which is weaker, does not happen: for if the knowledge is universal or unexercised or merely verbal, it is not dragged about; and if the knowledge is particular, it is either not dragged about but subsumed instead under a different universal; or if it is dragged about, it is so not as knowledge proper or science but only as sense knowledge. That this multiple answer is adequate in view of the puzzles Aristotle actually raises about incontinence seems plain. Whether it is adequate philosophically and in view of the whole phenomenon of incontinence as such, or whether more needs to be said, is a different question and beyond the present scope.

Note

1.   Broadie and Rowe (2002: 385–87), whose general interpretation is followed here.

Chapters 4 to 5

The Subject Matter of Continence
The second question, about the consistency of Aristotle's discussion of the varieties or parts of incontinence, is largely a matter of textual interpretation.[1] As regards the division of the text and the distribution of topics for discussion, the analytical outline of the book given at the beginning shows that this division and distribution does follow a clear and logical order. The order is anyway proposed by Aristotle himself when, after listing the phenomena and puzzles in chapters 1 and 2, he says, at the beginning of chapter 3 (1146b8–14), how he intends to examine them, namely first about the knowledge the incontinent have when they are being incontinent (chapter 3), second about the subject matter of continence and incontinence (chapters 4 and 5), and third about whether the continent man is the same as the man of endurance and also about the other puzzles (chapters 6–10).

With regard to what Aristotle says of the subject matter of incontinence, that it is the same as the subject matter of temperance and license, so that those incontinent in other matters (victory, honor, wealth, anger) are not incontinent simply but only in the relevant respect (the topic of chapter 4), his thesis seems plain. Those who are incontinent in these other matters do go to excess in some way, and so are to this extent blameworthy, but they do not have any of the vice incident to those who are incontinent in the pleasures of touch. For the latter, but not the former, are soft in how they behave. For not only do they yield to pleasure and flee pain when they should not, but the pleasures and pains, being those of touch, are matters of immediate feeling and not of calculation. The goodness, by contrast, of victory and honor and wealth is not felt by the senses (even if their effects are) but perceived by the mind. Thus there is nothing soft or blameworthy about these as such, whereas there is about the others. For the others conquer without reason and by immediate feeling. But to act without reason is blameworthy in man, and to yield to immediate feeling, qua felt and qua now, is soft.

Incontinence in spirit is rightly associated with incontinence in victory and honor and wealth because, although going to excess in spirit, as in these others, is a vice (the vices of anger, vanity, illiberality), yet incontinence in it is not, or not in the way incontinence in the pleasures and pains of touch is. Anger, unlike these pleasures and pains, does not work without reason or by immediate feeling. It works precisely by reason, if by faulty reason, for it works by some calculation of the just and unjust (anger is not a response to mere pain but to pain judged as wrong). The just and unjust are not sensed, as the pleasures and pains of touch are, but judged, for the just and unjust are the equal and the equal requires comparison and counting.[2] Hence incontinence in anger, like incontinence in honor and wealth, because of its use of reason, is not incontinence simply, nor does it involve vice, though it is blameworthy. Still, because anger is a passion, even if a passion that presupposes some act of reason (whereas wealth and honor and victory are not passions but objects of passion), incontinence in anger, but not incontinence in wealth or victory, can be used as a likeness for incontinence in passions that are extreme or unnatural (5.1149a1–4). Incontinence in anger is not incontinence simply, though it is incontinence in passion, so these others are not incontinence simply but incontinence in extreme or unnatural passion.

Notes

1. Extensive discussion in Rowe (1971: 93–99), whose interpretations of the text are questionable. The interpretations given here depart significantly from his.
2. Cf. *Politics* 1.2.1253a7–18, where Aristotle allows voice to animals for signifying pleasure and pain but denies them speech or logos for signifying the just and unjust.

Chapters 6 to 10

The Other Puzzles about Continence
As regard Aristotle's discussion of the other puzzles and topics (in chapters 6–10), it follows the phenomena and puzzles of chapter 2, though not exactly in the same order (the answers are expounded according to their connection with each other, not according to how the puzzles first get raised; the puzzle, for instance, about the subject matter of incontinence, which appears last in the list in chapter 2, is dealt with second overall, after the opening two puzzles about knowledge). So chapter 7 deals with the puzzles ([iv] and [v] in the summary to chapter 2 of the translation) about the identity or difference of continence and temperance and endurance. Chapter 8 deals with the puzzle ([ix]) whether the licentious man is worse or better than the incontinent. Chapter 9 deals with the puzzles ([vi] to [viii]) about the "continence" and "incontinence" of standing or failing to stand by a false opinion. Further, in view of what has been said about these puzzles, chapter 9 adds some other remarks about temperance and continence. Chapter 10 deals with a puzzle about prudence incidental to the question ([iii]) about what knowledge the incontinent man has when he acts incontinently. This chapter also suitably ends with a summary of the main points established in the preceding discussions.

A main problem here concerns the discussion in chapters 7 and 8, especially that about softness and endurance and how they relate to continence and license. Aristotle first draws a distinction between continence and incontinence, on the one hand, and endurance and softness, on the other, that the first pair concern pleasures and the second pains (7.1150a13–15). Hence, we may conclude, the man of endurance is he who is continent in pains and the soft man he who is incontinent in pains. The licentious man, in contrast, is he who by choice pursues necessary pleasures to excess (the insensible man goes to the opposite extreme, while the temperate man keeps to the mean [1150a15–23]). Aristotle then adds the same about the man who by choice flees pains to excess (1150a23–25). Presumably he means that such a man is licentious too, even if the license is more about pains than pleasures. The like does not seem to hold of those who pursue pleasures or avoid pains without choosing, for here the two, he says, are different (50a27). Hence, we may conclude, the licentious man, who acts by choice, is not different according to whether he concerns pleasures or pains (but the same man is licentious in both), while those who act without choice are different, and one of them concerns pains (the soft man) and other pleasures (the incontinent man proper).

Aristotle next adds, in a passage whose relevance to the context has been doubted,[1] that someone is worse if he does something bad from strong desire than from weak (1150a27–30). He thence concludes, first, that the licentious man is worse than the incontinent man and, second that, "of those mentioned, the kind may be more that of softness, but he is licentious" (1150a31–32).[2] The sense of this remark seems to be as follows: First, a man who, without choosing, gives in to weak passions is worse than a man who, without choosing, gives in to strong passions, and we say the licentious man is worse than the incontinent man for this reason. Because he is acting by choice, he acts to follow his passions even when they are weak, while the incontinent man only follows passions when they are strong. Second, of the two kinds of those who act without choice (the one kind following pleasure and the other avoiding pain), the kind of the latter (the one that avoids pain) is softness (for softness, as was said, is incontinence in pain), but he, the soft man, is licentious. He is licentious, we must understand, because, although he acts without choosing, he is being driven by weak passions and not by strong. That his passions are weak is presumably what Aristotle had in mind when he said of the soft man that he flees "the pain that is apart from desire" (50a26–27). The meaning of this remark may best be understood from the example Aristotle gives of the soft man who is self-indulgent and lets his cloak drag on the ground to avoid the pain of picking it up (1150b2–3). The pain does not come from any desire one is striving to resist (as with the continent man resisting a shameful pleasure), for he has, we may suppose, no desire with respect to his cloak. He simply cannot be bothered to pick it up. Avoiding this sort of pain, even if it is softness because done without choosing, makes him licentious because it is done without strong passion.

The following remarks about the superiority of continence to endurance (because continence is conquest while endurance is merely holding out [50a32–b1]), which have also been doubted, admit of a fair explanation. In the case of pleasure, which continence and incontinence are about, to resist it is to conquer it, for it has thereby been refused. The desire for the pleasure may, indeed, still be present, but the pleasure is not, for it has precisely not been taken. In the case of pain, by contrast, which endurance and softness are about, to hold out against it is not to conquer it, for the pain remains present however much one resists it. This point seems more a matter of logic than of ethics; yet it does have the moral conclusion Aristotle draws.

There do not seem, then, in any of these chapters of Book Six, whether those about continence and knowledge or the subsequent ones about the other puzzles, to be any difficulties of doctrine or interpretation that should require us to doubt either that they were written by Aristotle or that they are integrally part of *EE* (or indeed integrally part of *NE*).

Notes

1.　Rowe (1971: 95), with apposite references. In his translation (2002: 199, with Broadie's note, 396–97), he brackets the lines as out of place.

2. Rowe translates "of the types in question, then, one is more softness—of a sort, whereas the other is self-indulgence" (2002: 199), which is strictly inaccurate, since the Greek says "he" and not "the other [type]" (*ho* and not *to*), and "self-indulgent" (or licentious) and not "self-indulgence" (*akolastos* and not *akolasia*).

Chapters 11 to 14

Pleasure and Happiness

The final chapters of Book Six, as mentioned earlier, answer the second of the two questions postponed from Book One (1.5.1216a29–37): whether there are other pleasures, besides the bodily ones, that belong to the happy life and make it pleasant. Chapter 14 also adds further points about how bodily pleasures contribute little or nothing to happiness. These chapters, their teaching, and their place in *EE* are fairly straightforward and need little comment. Worth noting nevertheless is that while the treatment of bodily pleasures in *EE* serves primarily to answer the question posed in Book One, in *NE* it serves primarily to show why the incontinent are incontinent (because the bodily pleasures, though not best, are most obvious). Legislators have need especially to know such things, so as to be better able to educate the citizens in virtue. In *EE* the treatment shows the same thing, but as theory and not for practical use. Philosophers can be content to understand the world; they are not charged, unlike legislators, with the task of changing it.

The main peculiarity about *EE* in contrast with *NE* is the presence in the latter of a second treatment of pleasure (10.1–5). Why should *NE* have two treatments of this topic while *EE* has only one? The question has long been a matter of scholarly dispute.[1] In accordance, however, with the hypothesis assumed here, that *EE* and *NE* differ not by time of composition or maturity of development, but by intention and audience, the view will be proposed that a second treatment of pleasure is introduced in *NE* because of the needs of its audience.

Book Ten of *NE*, which has no parallel in *EE*, is striking in how directly oriented it is to the needs of legislators. It ends with the topic most proper to legislators: how legislation is needed for virtue and how the study that follows in the *Politics* is needed for correctness of legislation. The topic of legislation is preceded by the topic of contemplative happiness, and it was argued above that this other topic is also proper to legislators because it emphasizes the need to direct the city to philosophy and not to conquest and empire. One may reasonably conjecture, therefore, that the topic of pleasure, which precedes the topic of contemplation, is meant to fit the same pattern and is directed likewise to some concern proper to legislators. This concern can be conjectured to be the same as the concern with contemplation. For pleasure is inseparable from happiness, both in fact and in everyone's instinctive judgment, so that, if contemplation is happiness at its most complete, it must contain pleasure at its most complete. Most people, however, including political types as well as the vulgar many, find it hard to see how contemplation could be most pleasant, or even pleasant at all. Politicians think pleasure is found especially or only in the exercise of rule over others, and the vulgar many think pleasure is found in the exercise of certain functions of the body. Some morally virtuous men, by contrast, are inclined to think pleasure is bad (or that it should at least be presented as such), because most people are enslaved to pleasure (of the bodily kind) and can thus only be led to virtue if they are taught that pleasure is bad (points Aristotle expressly makes at 10.1.1172a27–33). All these views are erroneous.

The error of the vulgar was dealt with in the first treatment of pleasure in *NE* Book Seven (*EE* Book Six), but it is taken up again in Book Ten along with the error of the morally virtuous and of politicians. The error of the morally virtuous is plain, for no one, not even themselves, eschews all pleasure, and their attempt to reform the many by teaching that pleasure is bad is bound to backfire when they themselves are seen, as seen they will be, pursuing and enjoying it (1172a33–b7). The solution is to tell the truth, that pleasure is good, but that the best pleasures are not the vulgar pleasures of the body. Here next, then, arises the error of political men, who conceive the pleasures of political action to be these best pleasures. Their error is more subtle because political action is a kind of happiness and it does have many and fine pleasures. The problem is that this happiness and these pleasures are secondary to contemplation (the political life cannot be the final or complete end of man [10.7.1177b4–26]), and if legislators are to legislate correctly in cities, they need to be fully aware of the superiority in all respects, including pleasure, of the philosophical and contemplative life. Book Ten performs this service.

The teaching about the formal nature as such of pleasure is the same in Book Ten as in Book Six/Seven, save for being more fully developed and explained. Pleasure, it is there argued, is not a coming to be or a change (*genesis* or *kinēsis*) but an activity (*energeia*), or rather it is activity as complete and unimpeded (10.3–4, cf. 6/7.12). Hence any activity is pleasant the more complete and unimpeded it is; hence pleasures differ in kind as the corresponding activities do; hence those pleasures must be best and most desirable that are found in the best and most desirable activities. But these activities are those of contemplation. Hence, further and finally, the pleasures of contemplation must be simply best and most desirable (10.7.1177a22–27, b19–26, 8.1178b18–32). Armed with such a true and salutary teaching, and salutary because true, the legislator will be able more surely to aim the city toward philosophy, and more able to persuade political men, if not also some of the vulgar many, to do likewise and to direct themselves, their friends, and the whole city, as far as possible, toward the happy life of contemplation.

One might wonder, however, why the same teaching is not given in *EE*, or why this other work contents itself with one only of the treatments of pleasure, and with the lesser of the two in terms of fullness of treatment. The answer must be that philosophers, to whom *EE* is directed, do not need the fuller treatment. What is said in Book Six is sufficient by itself, for although briefer it says the same and, in saying the same, has the same implications about the superiority in pleasure of the philosophic life (6.12.1153a12–15, 13.1153b7–32). Legislators need the extra treatment and the extra emphasis, both for themselves and for those to whom they give their laws, so that they can perform their task as well as possible. Philosophers do not. Therefore while *EE* lacks anything comparable to Book Ten of *NE*, so *NE* lacks anything comparable to Book Eight of *EE*. Book Eight lauds divine chance and divine understanding, and sets divine worship as the mark and measure of happiness (2.1248a33–38, 3.1249b16–21). It thematizes God as the last book of *NE* thematizes the city, and the reason for the difference is in each case the difference of the audience: philosophers of *EE* and legislators of *NE*. For even if *NE* too does not fail to notice the role of God in serving as the standard of happiness (10.8.1178b21–22, 1179a22–29), yet it does so in view of legislators, for these, in directing the city to philosophy, must direct it to God.

Note

1. Review in Dirlmeier (1956: 494–96, 567–68); Broadie and Rowe (2002: 65–74) suitably argues that both treatments fit together in *NE* because they deal with pleasure in different contexts and from different perspectives.

Book Seven: Completion of Happiness: Complete Life

Chapter 1

Completion of Happiness
Complete Life
Friendship and Life
Reasons for Investigating Friendship

If Book Six may be viewed as answering the question from Book One about 1234b18/b31 pleasure and its role in happiness, and if thus the account of happiness as best and noblest (the virtues and prudence, Books Two to Five) and pleasantest (the pleasures of virtue and of intellect) has thus been fully gone through, Book Seven and Book Eight must be about the remaining aspect of the account, namely that happiness must be complete. If so, Book Seven on friendship can be viewed as about how it is complete with respect to living virtuously (as chapter 12, on the happy man's need of friends, shows in particular), and Book Eight on luck and gentlemanliness can be viewed as about how it is complete with respect to attaining and possessing all the virtues (as chapter 3, on the gentleman, shows in particular). The suggestion can be confirmed by how the argument in each book progresses.

The reasons Aristotle immediately gives here for examining friendship tie the discussion in with what has just gone before, that friendship must belong to happiness because it is both a great virtue and a great good. It is a great virtue because of its role in communal life where it achieves the same or better than justice. But justice was seen earlier (4.1.1129b25–30a10) to be the perfection of all the virtues in their relation to others. So if friendship is the same or better than justice (because it goes further than justice in making people love each other and treat each other well), it too must be such a perfection. Friendship is a great good because of the role of friends of all kinds in life and free choice (the sphere proper of virtue).

Puzzles about Friendship

Some eight puzzles, as based on prevailing opinion, are raised: 1235a4/b6

- (a) whether friendship is with the like
- (b) or with opposites
- (c) or only with the good
- (d) or with anyone who is dear (as children to mothers)

(e) or with the useful;
(f) whether it is easy
(g) or hard and requires luck
(h) or is self-interested, even when loyalty is shown in bad times.

Aristotle manages to save these conflicting phenomena by answering all the puzzles in the affirmative, but only because he first divides friendship into different kinds, for the opposite phenomena turn out to be true of opposite friendships.

Chapter 2

Nature and Kind of Friendship
The Three Basic Kinds
In General

1235b13/b24 The method, here as elsewhere, is to save the phenomena as much as possible or, in this case, the *legomena* (the things people say), so as to show how the opposing views are each right in a way. The clue is found in another puzzle, not so far mentioned, whether what people love is the good or the pleasant, since it appears that people love both and yet the two are not the same or always in harmony. Aristotle gives the telling example of erotic love where our desire is for the pleasant, but our wish is for the good. Lovers who are drawn to each other by mutual pleasure want to be together always, but, as time passes, the pleasure fades and the beloved turns out not to have the goodness that the lover would want always to be with. Yet at the beginning both lovers wanted each other as good and desired each other as pleasant. The explanation of this phenomenon is that the good includes also the apparent good and that appetite and wish can focus on both. The pleasant is always at least an apparent good, or a good for appetite, even if we do not also judge it good (as food and drink appeal to appetite even when we judge it bad to take more of either). Hence love, the love of friendship, can focus on both the good and the apparent good, and mistake one for the other too.

1235b30/36a7 The good is complex, not just in the sense that there are many goods (as goods of the body, of the soul, and external goods), but in the sense that there is the good simply and the good for but not simply, and that the simply good things are also simply pleasant. The case of health and the difference between things good and pleasant in health and those good and pleasant in sickness make the point clear. But so do the cases of moral habits and age, since what is good and pleasant for the childish in age or in habits is not what is simply good and pleasant.

The good then divides into that which is good because of what it is and that which is good because it is helpful or useful for someone. The pleasant falls into the same division, for, as was said, the same things are simply good and simply pleasant so that the simply pleasant is simply good and the pleasant for good for or an apparent good (as Aristotle now adds [36a10]). The division of goods is thus in a way fourfold and in a way threefold: either the four of the good simply, the good for (the useful), the pleasant simply, and the pleasant for; or the three of the good, the useful, and the pleasant. But the good simply and the pleasant simply are necessarily inseparable, while the pleasant for and the good for or the useful need not be, for things useful for a sick man need not also be pleasant to him. Aristotle insinuated this fact by glossing the pleasant for as also the apparent good and not merely as the good for. A useful but unpleasant thing, as medicine for the sick, is really good while a thing pleasant to him could be really bad. Thus, in terms of kinds of goods to choose between, the fourfold division collapses into the threefold one, and we can choose and love different men (as we can also things) for three different goods: for the simply good of virtue, for the useful, and for the pleasant. Accordingly, since friendship is a choosing and a loving (for it is a mutually aware loving and being loved back), there must be three kinds of friendship according to these three kinds of good.

The three kinds are, however, not coordinate kinds but subordinate or 1236a17
analogous ones. In illustration Aristotle uses the example of "medical." The first or primary sense of medical is medical in us, namely in those of us who are doctors and who possess in our soul or mind the medical art, the art of healing. Other things are called medical by reference back to this first sense, as a medical tool is called so because it is a tool that a doctor uses for his medical art. The first sense is thus first but it is not universal, for while the account of medical doctor falls into the account of medical tool, the account of medical tool does not fall into the account of medical doctor. But it would be absurd to say that a medical tool was not medical because it was not a doctor.

Friendship is the same, says Aristotle, so he presumably means that the account of the first friendship falls into the account of the others but not vice versa, and that all must therefore rightly be called friendships through reference back to the first. How they are so can be understood in the light of what he has just said about the useful and pleasant. Note, then, that the useful and the pleasant will only be distinct goods when they are not the same as the simply good. So, for instance, the useful is not the simply good insofar as those for whom it is useful are not simply good, as the sick, or the incomplete (like children), or things of an inferior nature (like the beasts). The pleasant is likewise not the simply good insofar as those for whom it is pleasant are not simply good. Moreover it need not then be the useful either, if it is in fact bad for those for whom it is pleasant (as drink is pleasant to drunkards but not good for them). The pleasant and the useful are, nevertheless, related to the simply good, because any good they are related to must itself be related to the simply good. For the useful that is good for the sick and is not simply good is for the sake of restoring health, which is simply good; the useful that is good for lesser natures (as beasts) is for the sake of the completion of the cosmic whole, which is also simply good; and the pleasant, which is really bad but apparently good, can only appear good because it appears to be the simply good. Hence the simply good enters into the account of the useful and the pleasant, but the useful and the pleasant do not enter into the account of the simply good (the simply good is useful and pleasant, but it is useful and pleasant because it is good; it is not good because it is useful and pleasant). So, by the same token, the three friendships must be related in the same way. The account of the first friendship, which is love based on the simply good, will enter into the account of the other friendships, which are loves based on goods that are referred to the simply good.[1]

1236a30   The three friendships, besides being of unequal status, are also found unequally among men. The friendships typical between most people are useful ones (even the virtuous, as transpires later [1238a7–10], have only useful friendships with most of the virtuous, because the number of people one can have a first friendship with is limited);[2] friendships typical of the young are pleasant; those of the best are virtuous (these will be first friendships as based on the simply good).

The First Kind

1236b1/b22   The first kind of friendship is thus clear: the reciprocal loving and choosing of each other by good men. Since animals, therefore, do not choose (though they do desire), they cannot have this kind of friendship. Nevertheless they can and do, to some extent, have useful friendships. Base men are similar, not because they do not choose, but because they choose only the pleasant or the useful and not the simply good. They can, therefore, love each other despite the fact that base people wrong each other and that the wronged do not love those who wrong them. The paradox is solved by their love not being that of the first friendship but rather a "suspicious" one.[3] They know their friendship is harmful and suspect each other of only behaving as they do because of the pleasure involved. Hence they suspect that, without the pleasure, they would behave very differently (as the incontinent would too if not overcome by pleasure). They are harmed, therefore, but not unwillingly (for they want the pleasure), and so they are not wronged, for wrong is an involuntary harm, and the harm they inflict on each other is not involuntary. The same goes for the fact that the friendships of the base are not lasting or stable, for again only the first friendship is such and theirs is not the first friendship.

These puzzles, then, and the way to resolve them give further proof that there is more than one kind of friendship (since to speak otherwise is to fall into manifest absurdity). But though there are several friendships they can nevertheless accord with one account, namely in the way stated, not as species of one genus but as related, by analogy, to one thing.

This doctrine of relation to one thing has so far only been give in general terms. What Aristotle does next is apply the general account to the friendship of virtue, to show how this friendship is first in the way stated, and also that it is simply pleasant and useful. The argument he gives, however, is complex and the Greek compressed. Scholars have therefore been induced to make numerous emendations to the text. But the text makes sense as it stands and no emendations are strictly necessary.[4]

1236b26

Aristotle begins with the following propositions:

(1) the same thing is simply good and simply pleasant, and is so at the same time (unless someone prevents it);
(2) the friend truly and simply is the first;
(3) such a person is he who is preferable because of his very self;
(4) there must be such a person, for as one wishes good things to exist for oneself so one must prefer oneself to exist;
(5) the true friend is also pleasant simply;
(6) hence it is held that any friend at all is pleasant.

Aristotle accepts all of these propositions up to and including (5) but demurs over (6). As for (1), the someone who prevents it (or makes it false as applied to himself) must be primarily the bad man, who finds pleasure in things simply bad. Proposition (2) is true more or less by definition, for the simply so must be prior to the relatively so and therefore the friend who is simply so must be the first sort of friend. Proposition (4) proves (3) because to desire good things for oneself is to desire oneself more, since one is oneself the reason for desiring the good things. Hence one must oneself be more desirable than the good things, and hence further, if the good things in question are simply good, one must oneself be simply good (only something simply good could be such that simply good things were good for it, or could be a reason for desiring simply good things). Therefore one must be good or preferable because of one's very self, which is (3). From (2) and (3), it follows (7) that the true and first friend is simply good; and from (7) and (1), it follows that the true and first friend is simply pleasant, which is (5).

The problem is the inference from (5) to (6), which is too quick and the result too vague. For that one friendship is pleasant does not entail that the others are too (unless one assumes, falsely, that all friendships are of one kind); and even if all friendships do involve pleasure, the pleasure need not be the same; and again, if all friendships involve pleasure, the one thing that they are all analogously referred to need not be pleasure, or not the same pleasure. There are, then, several questions here in need of sorting out, and Aristotle proceeds to the task in what follows. His analysis, however, involves him in a rather convoluted digression, so he expressly alerts the reader to the fact by saying that his drawing of further distinctions has an end (1236b33), and he alerts the reader again to the fact when the digression stops (1237a18–19).

He begins by posing two questions: is it the good for oneself or the good simply that is dear (or loved), and, second, is the act of loving accompanied by pleasure (so that the thing loved is pleasant) or not? The first question focuses on the relation of the good to the lover, and the second on the relation of the act of love, and therewith also of its object (for the act is active about the object), to pleasure. Both must be brought together to the same point, adds Aristotle, which means either that both questions must be brought together or that the good and the good for and the loving and the object loved must be brought together (or harmonized). Perhaps he means both. At any rate he says in explanation:

(8) what is not simply good but bad is to be avoided (if fortune permits);
(9) what is not good for oneself is nothing to oneself;
(10) the thing we seek after is that things simply good be good for oneself;
(11) the simply good is preferable, but for oneself the good for oneself is preferable;
(12) virtue harmonizes the simply good and the good for oneself;
(13) the job of politics is to make this harmony so for those for whom it is not yet so.

Proposition (8) is obvious enough, for what we want is not apparent or relative goods but real goods, things that, as Aristotle says, are simply good, like health, and not things that are good under some condition, like painful medicine if we are ill (for we do not want to be ill). The reference to bad things and fortune, or chance, is perhaps to this very fact, that we do not want bad things, like pain and ill health, but that it is not up to us but to chance whether we always avoid them. We avoid them as much as we can, of course, but, if chance compel, we choose some bad things, as painful medicine, for the sake of greater goods, as cure from disease. Premise (9) is more controversial, for can we not love what is simply good even if it is nothing to us? Perhaps the point is that even a thing simply good, if we are to love it, must become something for us at least to the extent that it becomes an object of our act of love, and an act of love, being our act, must be something for us. Moreover, it must be something good for us if we are to do it, for we should not do any act that is not good, either simply or for us. The object, then, may be simply and supremely good regardless of us and of what is good for us, as God perhaps is; but the act that focuses on this object, by serving it or worshiping it (as Aristotle says at the end of this work, 8.3.1249b16–21), cannot fail to be something to us and, if we are to do it, something good for us too. There need, therefore, be no objectionable selfishness implied in (9); for if the acts are ours and good for us, their essence is to be *from* us *to* the objects. In other words, an object does not become centered on us but rather we become object-centered.[5]

This point emerges from (10) and (11), that what we really want is simply good things but that it makes no sense for us to pursue these things if they are not good for us (just as it would make no sense for a sick man to pursue the simply healthy things but rather the things that are good for him now; he needs first to recover health so that he may then be able to pursue the simply healthy things). Propositions (12) and (13) express this thought, for virtue is to the soul as health is to the body, and as the latter makes the simply healthy things healthy for us, so the former makes the simply good things good for us. Hence if we have virtue, we can and will pursue the simply good things; but if we do not have virtue we need first to receive the discipline or education that will make us virtuous, which is the task of politics (*NE* 10.9).

Politics may be the way people are to be made virtuous, but certain con- ditions must be met, the first and most obvious of which is that one be a human being, since only human beings, and not the other animals, have a nature such that the simply good things can be good for them (as virtue and wisdom in particular, of which the animals are not capable). A second condition is being a man and not a woman. Aristotle is presumably thinking of the greater recalcitrance to prudence of the passions in woman, which does not mean that a woman cannot be complete in virtue but only that she needs the authority of a man to become complete.[6] The third condition, that one must be simple (*aphyēs*) instead of clever (*euphyēs*), seems to confirm this point. The remark initially looks odd since it would seem that the reverse should be true (hence scholars follow Fritzsche in altering the Greek to produce the reverse). But Aristotle is perhaps thinking of cases like the Spartan women (*Politics* 2.9.1269b12–70a11), who were too much still in their natural state (*eu-phyēs*) that the legislator could not impose his legislation on them (they were "too clever" for him), while the men, because of much military campaigning, were sufficiently educated out of that state (*a-phyēs*) that he could impose it on them (they were "simple enough" for him). 1237a3

Education to virtue, however, is through the pleasant, for virtue is about pleasures and pains, and education to virtue is education in feeling pleasure and pain in the right things, and the end of education, virtue, being simply good, must be simply pleasant too (as was at 1236b26–27). Before the process is completed, however, one cannot yet be completely virtuous, as is shown especially by the fact that incontinence is then still possible. Incontinence is when one's passions make one pursue the pleasant over the simply good, and so when one must still have a passion for pleasures that are not simply good. But to have passions for what is not simply good is not to be fully virtuous.

The first conclusion that Aristotle wants now follows from the above, namely that the first friendship, since it is good simply and pleasant simply, is the friendship that is based on or accords with virtue. But the precise bearing of this conclusion is not clear until the two questions posed at the beginning of the digression are also answered (whether the good for oneself 1237a9 or the good simply is what is loved, and whether the act of loving is accompanied by pleasure).

Note further, then, that it now follows that those who are friends with the first friendship will be themselves simply good, not because they are useful, but "in another way" (37a11), that is precisely because they are virtuous. The things of virtue are the simply good, and the simply good and the good for are, as such, distinct (the good for this or that man need not be the simply good, and indeed it will not be if he is not virtuous). The same distinction holds of habits, that the simply beneficial is distinct from the noble, which is the simply good. The simply beneficial is indicated later (1238a39–b1) to be that which is of help for getting the simply good and not for getting something that is so only in relation to a given choice. Its contrast, then, with the noble must be, not that it is not of help for the noble, but that what is of help for the noble is not, qua helpful, the noble.[7] The point is immediately illustrated with an example: physical exercise, which is an act that a healthy man does, is simply good, but being given medicine, which is an act that the sick man undergoes, is beneficial for the sick man but is not simply good.[8] The same holds of the habit that is man's virtue, that it is good simply and, as such, distinct from the good for, or from the simply useful and beneficial. The proof turns on supposing (as is anyway the case) that man is of his nature a good or virtuous thing, that is, on supposing that man's nature is to other and lesser natures (those of the irrational animals, for instance) as the healthy are to the sick. For the perfection or virtue of such a naturally good or virtuous thing must be simply good, while the perfection or virtue of something not naturally good or virtuous can only be good for it. Or, the perfection of a perfect nature is good *simply*; the perfection of an imperfect nature is only good *for*.

Accordingly the same must hold of the pleasant as of the good. For the simply good, as was said before, is also the simply pleasant (1236b26–27). Hence the pleasant for a perfect thing must be pleasant simply but the pleasant for an imperfect thing need be pleasant only for it; and likewise the good for an imperfect thing need not be pleasant (as taking medicine is good for a sick man but not pleasant). The simply good, in other words, is always simply pleasant and the simply pleasant always simply good, but when we come to the pleasant for and the good for, this connection between goodness and pleasure no longer holds. The pleasant for need neither be simply good nor good for (eating too much is pleasant to the glutton but is neither simply good nor good for the glutton); and the good for need neither be simply pleasant nor pleasant for (medicine is good for the sick but is neither simply pleasant nor pleasant for the sick man).

So understood, propositions (8) to (13) and the attendant discussion show how the two questions are to be answered and also at the same time how the good and the good for go together. For the thing that is dear or loved is the simply good, provided we have become virtuous enough that the simply good is good for us (the first question). Further, the act of loving and the object loved will both be pleasant under this same condition (the second question). For the pain of being disciplined to be virtuous is not pleasant and the act of loving such discipline is not pleasant; but we accept both in order to become virtuous, and, having become so, we are then such that acts of virtue and objects of virtue are good for us, and, being good for us, are necessarily pleasant at the same time.

The digression is now over, as Aristotle expressly remarks. But while it 1237a18 has prepared the way for understanding how (6) does and does not follow from (5), it has not yet given that understanding. Hence Aristotle proceeds to give the understanding now, but to do so he has to raise and answer further questions. The questions are: (a) whether there can be friendship without pleasure; (b) what difference this makes (or pleasure makes); (c) which of the two the loving is in (the lover or the loved); (d) whether someone good but not pleasant can be loved (though not because he is unpleasant).

These questions arise because it has just been shown that the first friendship of virtue is necessarily with pleasure for the virtuous. But nothing thereby follows about (a) whether the other friendships possess pleasure, which was the inference from (5) to (6), or whether they lack pleasure (though it does thereby follow that they lack the pleasure that is simply pleasure, for only virtue is such). Further, regardless of what follows from the truth about the first friendship, there is the question (b) what difference, if any, the presence or absence of pleasure makes to friendship, or what the importance of pleasure in friendship is; and this further question cannot be separated from the question (c) who is active in friendship, whether the lover or the loved (for, as argued at 6.12.1153a9–17, pleasure is activity); nor from the final question (d) whether, if pleasure is absent, goodness by itself is enough for a friendship.

Aristotle begins with the first question but through the idea of activity, for pleasure is by definition activity (it is unimpeded activity [1153a13–15]). Loving can be potential or actual, but pleasure, being activity, can only exist in loving when loving is actual. The question, then, if we are to find out if there can be friendships without pleasure, becomes whether actual friendship is pleasant because it is good. For since the lesser friendships are not good, or not simply so, they will not have pleasure if goodness is required for pleasure. The answer to this rephrased question is both yes and no.

The answer is no in the sense that any activity becomes intense (and to this extent therefore unimpeded) if it is concerned with things familiar and alike (even if those things are not good but only good for us, or taken to be so). Things we have just learned and studied are more perceptible to us, and so things we more intensely exercise our knowledge about, than what we learned or studied some time ago and need first to remind ourselves of. The same holds, and for the same reason, of recognizing someone who is alike in habits, that we are recognizing something familiar to us because we are the same ourselves. This fact, therefore, explains the delight that all like things, including incomplete or imperfect ones, take in each other. But it also explains, and especially so, the delight that the virtuous, who are complete or perfect, take in the virtuous, for virtue is not only pleasant simply (it is good simply, and the simply good is by nature simply pleasant), but also pleasant to the virtuous. Hence the answer to the question is also yes. Only the friendship of virtue is pleasant because good, for only in this friendship is there the simply good; in the others there is at most only the good for (and sometimes there may only be the bad that appears good to the people involved). Friendships other than the first friendship of virtue can, then, be pleasant even if they are not good, for the friends will be in some way alike or familiar (they will certainly be so qua both being men, if not also in other ways). Therefore the answer to the first question just posed, (a) whether there can be friendship without pleasure, is, strictly speaking, no: all friendships are pleasant because or insofar as all friendships involve some familiarity or likeness between the friends. But they are not all pleasant because good, for some of them are not good, or not simply so.

1237a30   If friendship is thus a mutual choosing, with pleasure, of knowing each other, the first friendship of virtue will be a choosing of things simply good and pleasant because they are simply good and pleasant (and not because they are merely good or pleasant for). This choosing, like all choosing, is activity, but it springs from a habit of so choosing (any friendship of any duration will, to that extent, have the character of a habit, but in the case of virtuous friendship it will also be the habit of virtue). The act or work of a habit, however, is an actuality within the thing or person that has the habit (it is the activating of a settled disposition to behave in a certain way). The work is, however, "outside" any power or potentiality, for it comes to a potentiality from without (the potential is actualized by something other that is actual, whether this other is simply other or is the thing itself qua other; self-movers, for instance, move themselves insofar as they have a first part that is moved and a second part that moves the first, and this second part is "other" to the first though within the same thing). Hence loving, which is the actuality of the lover's habit, is pleasant, for it is an activity in the lover; but being loved is not, for it is "outside" the one loved, being a potentiality that is actualized by and in another (hence being loved can even exist in things that are incapable of activity, as lifeless things).

Thus Aristotle has now answered the second and third of his four questions: (c) loving is an activity in the lover, not the loved, and (b) the difference pleasure makes is that, being unimpeded activity, it shows that the activity of loving in any given case is, as far as it goes, unimpeded (it has the intensity that comes from likeness and familiarity).

1237a40   We are left with the fourth question, (d) whether goodness, even without pleasure, is sufficient for friendship. In a way the answer has already been given, since it has just been shown that all friendship is with pleasure. But the point deserves express treatment, for perhaps the pleasure, even if present, is a derivative phenomenon and not something internal to friendship (so that it can be abstracted in thought if not in fact).

The act of love is the actuality of the loved thing in the lover, for a loved thing is actually loved when someone loves it, that is, when someone employs it precisely qua loved thing. So the friend, qua loved thing, is actual when loved qua friend and not in some other capacity. For if he is loved as musician or doctor, he is not loved precisely as friend; but he can only be an object of the love of friendship when he is loved as friend. The pleasure, therefore, that comes from this object, that is from him as him (as this friend), is the pleasure proper to friendship; for it is as friend to the friend who loves him that he is friend, and not because he is friend or pleasant to someone else.

In answer, then, to (d), the fourth question, there will be pleasure necessarily involved in friendship, the pleasure internal to the act of loving that actualizes the being loved of the friend qua friend. But this pleasure will vary according to the kind of friendship and, moreover, is not such that it cannot be overwhelmed by some accidental pain. For if the enjoyment the friend gets from his friend is not from him qua good, the friendship in question is not the first friendship but some other (first friends love each other qua good and not, as other friends do, qua merely pleasant or useful). Further, while this love and pleasure will not (at least in the case of first friendship) be hindered by any accidental impediment (the good friend will be loved for his goodness regardless of anything else), the accidental impediment may, nevertheless, be such as to prevent some of the acts of friendship, as the act of living together. The example Aristotle gives is of someone who smells very bad, for it is hard or impossible to live with someone who has that accidental impediment—not because he is not good, nor because he is not thereby pleasant too, but because the pain of the smell when in his presence is overwhelming. One would still love his goodness, of course, and so still embrace toward him all the good will or kindly disposition (*eunoia* [b7]) that one could (acts of friendship possible at a distance would still be done); but one would avoid his company. The story of Philoctetes (of whom Aristotle is likely thinking) is a striking example. The Greeks sailing to Troy left him on Lemnos despite still loving him and holding him in high regard, for his wound's smell had become unbearable.

Thus Aristotle has answered his four questions and thereby shown how (6) follows or does not follow from (5). Every friendship is indeed with pleasure and is so partly by inference from the first friendship and partly not. The first friendship is pleasant because it is an active loving of a friend who is simply good. Its pleasure is pleasant to the lover, for the loving is the lover's act about someone familiar to and like the lover, and is simply pleasant, for its object is simply good and the simply good is simply pleasant. The other friendships are also pleasant, but only pleasant *for* and not pleasant simply. They must indeed be pleasant because, by inference from the first friendship, the loving is the act of the lover and this act is pleasant for the lover insofar as the one loved is familiar to and like the lover. Their pleasure, however, cannot be the pleasure of the first friendship (and so their being pleasant cannot be inferred from the first friendship), because the one loved is not, as in the case of first friendship, pleasant simply but only pleasant for the lover (or if pleasant simply then not for this reason pleasant to the lover, as a virtuous man might be pleasant to a base man for his wealth, say, but not for his virtue).

The Other Kinds

1237b7 The preceding discussion began as a continuation and explanation of the claim that all friendships are friendships, not as being coordinate species of one genus, but as being analogously related to one thing, the first friendship. The discussion so far has established both that the first friendship is the friendship of virtue and that the other friendships are like and unlike the first friendship in how they are and are not good and pleasant (they are pleasant for and good for, or useful, but not pleasant simply and good simply). The next point, then, is to show precisely how this fact about pleasure and good makes the other friendships to be analogously related to the first friendship of virtue. Aristotle proceeds to this task now and also at the same time to the resolution of the puzzles about friendship posed at the beginning (for the way the several friendships are and are not friendships is the way to explain how those puzzles are and are not correct).

All agree to the first friendship, says Aristotle, by which he means presumably that all agree that it is a friendship, for doubtless not all would agree that it is first (especially not those who think all friendships are equal species of one genus). But since it is universally agreed to be a friendship, it can be used as a measure for other friendships, either to say that they are friendships or to say that they are not. Aristotle has argued that the other friendships are only friendships by reference to the first friendship; so he begins by showing how the other friendships fail to be first friendships. He then shows how they can nevertheless be friendships in some other way.

The first friendship, then, is firm or stable but the others not. He gives the following argument:

(1) what has passed judgment is firm;
(2) what does not arise quickly or easily is not rightly judged;
(3) there is no firm friendship without trust or trust without time (as Theognis's couplet illustrates).

The point of (2) is that it is hard to judge rightly things that are a long time coming about because, in contrast with things that happen quickly, what they really are takes time and much care to be noticed. Taken thus (2) when

346

combined with (3), that firm friendships rest on something that takes time to come about, namely trust, produces the conclusion (4) that firm friendships rest on something that it is hard to judge and easy to misjudge. But (1) says that things that have passed judgment are firm. Hence from (1) and (4) follows (5), that it is hard and takes much time for friendships to pass the judgment that makes them firm.[9]

Two things thus result from this argument about firm friendship: that it rests on trust and that it takes time. The first fact, trust, is what shows that only the first friendship can be firm because only the virtuous are trustworthy. The second fact shows, paradoxically, that virtue by itself is not enough for first friendship. Virtuous people who have not spent time getting to know and try each other cannot, despite their virtue, yet be virtuous friends. Friendships can fail, then, to be first friendships in two ways: lack of virtue and lack of time.

Aristotle illustrates this result by showing how both lack of time and lack of virtue make most relationships colloquially called friendships not to be the first friendships. As for lack of time, the wish to be friends, which arises quickly and in many people, is not friendship despite often being supposed to be so and despite the performance of many friendly services. "Wishing does not make it so," as we say and as Aristotle's example of wishing to be healthy but not actually being so forcefully shows. His further proof, that those are easily divided by slander, who think they are friends but have not gone through the necessary trial or judgment, has been made painfully evident to us in Shakespeare's *Othello*. 1237b17/b27

The problem in such cases is not, or need not be, lack of virtue, for, given time, they might perhaps have achieved first friendship (Othello and Desdemona would likely have achieved it, or something close to it, had not the malicious Iago intervened). Time, however, will never enable the base to achieve friendship, for, lacking virtue as they do, they are not trustworthy themselves and do not trust others (they judge others to be as bad as themselves). Further, what they want is not friends but the material or natural goods to be got by using or exploiting friends. The things of friends in their case never become common since friends for them are a means of getting things for their own exclusive use.

That the base cannot be first friends is an obvious and, by itself, a relatively uninteresting fact. More striking and important is that, because of the requirement of time, most of the virtuous cannot be first friends with most of the virtuous either. For to spend time living with someone to make trial of him cannot be done with many people. One should not, therefore, choose a friend the way one would a cloak, by taking the new and better one over the old and inferior. A new friend, even if he is a better man, cannot become a friend without time and trial, that is, without becoming an old friend. A friend, to be dear and our own, must not only be good simply but good for us, which he will not be if we have not been with each other long enough to be old friends. 1237b34

Now, however, something of no little interest follows. The virtuous man who is not, or not yet, our friend (because of lack of time and trial) is still simply good (he is virtuous, after all). He is not, of course, good qua virtuous friend for us, but he is still necessarily good for us, because his virtue is *useful* for us (lesser dealings with him, for instance, will be handled justly and honestly, for virtuous people are honest and just). Hence, as Aristotle says (38a7–8),[10] "what he is simply" (namely virtuous) "is a good for the person other than this" (namely for someone other than the person he has had time to become a first friend with), "because he is useful." Nay, further, he will be a good like this even for someone who is "not simply virtuous but other" (someone base, say) because virtuous people are as useful to base people as to virtuous ones. They will not only treat base people justly but also, by example and rebuke, serve to move them, if possible, from vice toward virtue (as Aristotle indeed notes later [1238b5–9]).

In other words, because virtuous friendship requires time and trial and not just virtue, a merely useful friendship (and not a first friendship of virtue) will arise from the very virtue of virtuous men. The lesser friendship of utility is unavoidably built in, as it were, to the virtue that, of its proper nature, generates first friendships. At least it is so when, as Aristotle immediately remarks (38a8–10), the impediments of numbers and time are factored in: "to be friends to many at the same time is to hinder loving, for it is impossible to be active toward many people at the same time." The friendship of utility is not, then, a degradation from first friendship as people typically think, and as those in particular must think who suppose that first friendship is the only one there really is. On the contrary, it is a result precisely of virtue itself. We need not suppose, therefore, that lesser friendships only arise because there are people around who are not virtuous. The demands of time and trial, or the limitations of human existence, will make them arise, paradoxically, even where everyone is virtuous.

1238a10 Still, a useful friendship, even one between virtuous men, is not a first friendship. So it is not, for instance, a stable friendship, because, of course, it is not based on time and trial of virtue. Nevertheless, friendships are rightly said to be something stable (as happiness is rightly said to be something self-sufficient), because the first friendship necessarily is such (it cannot exist without the time and trial that necessarily generate stability). The further remark (38a12–14), that nature is firm but money, or moneyed property, not, is also correct, for while a useful friendship could be about money (as say a business friendship), a first friendship could not be. It must be about nature, or rather, as Aristotle immediately says by way of improvement, about virtue. Virtue not only stands the test of time that shows what the loved one is really like, but also stands the test of misfortune. Friends who are so on the basis of virtue will stand by each other in misfortune and use their goods to help each other out, whereas useful friends (even useful friends who happen also to be virtuous) will not or need not. For friends on the basis of virtue are choosing each other as the men they each are and not, like merely useful friends, for the resultant benefits of the relationship. Or as Aristotle pointedly says, misfortune shows those who are friends "really" or "in being" (*ontōs* [38a19]), that is, who are friends because of their being as virtuous, and not because of some utility or other.

What is true of utility holds also analogously of pleasure, for there is a   1238a21
pleasure that people can get from each other that is not the simply pleasant, or not the pleasure of virtue. Pleasure also differs from utility in that we can get pleasure from someone quickly but utility takes time. However, pleasures differ too by time, since quick pleasures quickly cloy, as is obvious in the case of food and drink but is no less true of people. The pleasant has to be judged by time as well as by end or results, or it has to be judged by long term results, for first results can be deceptive.[11] Refined pleasures, as we call them, are subtle and take time to enjoy. Virtue is such a pleasure and friendships of virtue will be simply pleasant, but their pleasure will need as much time and trial to be perceived and enjoyed as the virtue itself. Hence, the pleasure proper to the friendship of virtue can no more be enjoyed by many than the friendship itself can exist among many.

The same interesting result, then, will follow in the case of pleasure as in the   1238a30
case of utility, that merely pleasant friendships will arise from the very virtue of the virtuous. The point should be obvious already of itself, but Aristotle draws special attention to it by recalling that the first friendship is that by which the others are called, and by adding that the first friendship accords with virtue and is on account of the *pleasure* of virtue (38a30–32). The virtuous are of course pleasing to those of the virtuous with whom they have first friendships, but, because of their very virtue, they must be pleasing also to those of them with whom they do not have such a friendship, for the virtuous are pleased by the deeds of virtue everywhere and anywhere. Moreover, they must, for the same reason, be pleasing to the non-virtuous with whom they may happen to have dealings, for everyone is pleased by the effects of virtue, such as not being cheated, receiving kindnesses, or listening to elegant and witty remarks. The non-virtuous will perhaps not be pleased by the rebukes of the virtuous, at least not at first, though they may be later when they see the benefit they have thereby received. The friendships of pleasure and utility, then, are called by reference to the friendship of virtue, as Aristotle says, because virtue will spread its utility and pleasure beyond the strict range of the friendship of virtue. These other friendships are, as it were, rays from the friendship of virtue that, because of the limitations of human existence, penetrate further than that friendship can properly do by itself.

In fact, as Aristotle now explains, these friendships can exist, not merely as effects of virtue, but even in total separation from it, as among children (who are too young to be virtuous), beasts (who do not have the nature to be virtuous), and the base (who have failed or refused to become virtuous). The reason, as he insinuates, is because of the possibility of separating what is *simply* so and what is so *for* someone. In the case of the virtuous these are always united (the simply good and useful and pleasant are also good and useful and pleasant for the virtuous), but not in the case of the non-virtuous. The base can be useful and pleasant to each other precisely in their baseness (they enjoy and mutually benefit from the wicked things they do with and to each other), or in neutral things, as a talent like singing, or a natural bent like thriftiness (which is not a virtue but matter for virtue, or vice, depending on how it is used), or in something or other good (since goodness exists to some extent in everyone). This separation of the *simply* so from the *for* someone can also exist, paradoxically, between the virtuous and the base, because the baseness of the base might incidentally serve the purposes of virtue (using a thief to catch a thief, as we say), or vice versa (as a courageous soldier might fight to preserve his city though it is run by the base). Or in any of the ways just listed for friendships between the non-virtuous.

We might say, then, as a general conclusion that the other friendships arise from the first friendship of virtue in two ways but in each case because of the difference between the *simply* so and the so *for* someone. The virtuous, by having the simply good of virtue, also necessarily have the simply pleasant (for the simply good is simply pleasant), and also the simply beneficial (the beneficial that promotes the simply good of virtue). But friendship, in any form, requires that the thing on which it is based be so *for* the friends. Thus the friendship of virtue must be based on the virtue of the friends being so for each other, and it cannot be that without the necessary time and trial. However, the pleasure and utility of virtue can exist for others without such time and trial. Hence it is possible for friendships of utility and pleasure to arise from virtue but without friendship of virtue. This separation is the first way that the other friendships can arise, and as such it is natural and harmless (the virtuous would be friends of virtue with all the virtuous if they had the time and capacity).

The second way is not so natural or harmless because it assumes the existence of the non-virtuous or the base. Here the pleasant and useful are no longer simply so but only for the persons, because the pleasures and utilities can be in something base and vicious. They are friendships, nevertheless, because they have the same character that the friendships of pleasure and utility among the virtuous have, namely being based on what is so *for* the persons involved. That this "for" is no longer also a "simply" makes them, as it were, depraved friendships but does not prevent them being friendships altogether. (We might note, by the by, that the poet quoted at the very beginning of *EE* could hardly be someone who was a virtuous friend, since for him the noblest and best and pleasantest were separate, but in a virtuous friendship they would all be the same thing.)

Aristotle has thus also answered several of the puzzles posed at the beginning, though since the fact is obvious he does not bother to say so explicitly. That (c) friendship is only with the good is true, but of first friendship; that (e) and (b) friendship is only with the useful, and so unlike, is true, but of useful friendships; that (a) it is with the like is also true, but of virtuous and pleasant friendships; that (f) friendship is easy is true, but only of certain sorts of pleasant friendships; that (g) it is hard is true of all other friendships and that it requires good fortune is true of useful friendships; that (h) friends who stay friends in bad times are self-interested is true, but again of useful friendships. Even point (d), about friendships with anyone who is dear (as children are dear to mothers), has been perhaps implicitly answered, in that a friend must in some respect be dear to the friend in order to be a friend. But something directly related to this point is mentioned later [6.1240a35–36].

Notes

1. See Owens (1989: esp. 136–37) and Ward (1995: esp. 202–205) for similar expositions, and review and critique of other and contrasting interpretations.
2. Hence we may keep the *dia* (between) with the *tōn pleistōn* (most people) at 1236a33 and not delete it as scholars wish, for the *dia* serves perhaps to make it clearer that useful friendships can exist also between the virtuous.
3. Most scholars follow Bonitz in emending "they are suspicious of each other" at 1236b16 to "they put up with each other" (discussion in Dirlmeier [1962: 388]). The emendation is unnecessary. Suspicion is what the comparison with incontinence calls for. Any loving that is harmful but is persisted in nevertheless must necessarily generate suspicion about what sort of love is really involved.
4. Dirlmeier (1962: 390ff.), who is criticized on this point by Von Fragstein (1978: 310–14). But Von Fragstein himself still unnecessarily accepts some of these emendations.
5. See further the comments on 7.12 below.
6. *Politics* 1.13.1260a10–13; cf. Simpson (1998: 67).
7. If we read the sense in this way, there will be no need to follow other scholars in emending the Greek; Dirlmeier (1960: 394), Von Fragstein (1974: 313–14).
8. The point is clearer in the Greek for at 1237a14–15 *gumnazesthai* (do exercise for oneself) is middle and *pharmakeuesthai* (be given medicine) is passive.
9. Bonitz' emendation to the MSS at 1237b11–2 (on which Dirlmeier [1962: 400]) deletes a "not" in (2) so as to make it mean: "where things are not done quickly or easily the judgment *is* made rightly." The emendation is required neither by the grammar nor by the logic of the passage.
10. If one keeps the MS readings, that is. If one changes them, as scholars do, one will lose the logic of this argument.
11. Dirlmeier's comments here (1962: 407–408), especially against the emendations to the Greek adopted in the translations of Solomon and Rackham, are exact.

Chapter 3

How These Kinds Can be Equal and Unequal

1238b15   The division of friendships into three kinds admits of further divisions within these divisions, and notably according to equality and excess. Those whose virtue is superior in kind can be friends of virtue with those whose virtue is inferior, but according to equality of proportion and not of number. Aristotle's examples where the virtue of the friends differs in this way are standard if not uncontroversial: god and man, ruler and ruled, benefactor and benefited, father and son, man and wife. There is not the same loving back here as in equal friendships, for the superior partner in each case confers on the other the benefit of his superior virtue and can receive nothing similar in return for which he might owe love. The superior's love is a love that by loving creates love (as a father, by generating and educating his son, creates loving in him). So it is a love where the benefactor is due the debt of being loved but owes no debt of loving (or at least not initially). It is loving "in another way," as Aristotle pointedly remarks (1238b29–30; which means, presumably, that it is gratuitous and springs from superfluity of goodness, not debt). The pleasure involved differs similarly.

1238b32   That the other two kinds of friendship can also exist in equality or excess is clear, since here too one of the parties can be initiator and benefactor. But since these other kinds are not based as such on virtue, the superiority, instead of being an occasion of reverence or worship on the part of the inferior (as in 8.3 on God and man), is an occasion of complaint on the part of the superior. The superior party wishes to receive back the same as he gives, not realizing that such does not become superiors but rather equals. So erotic lovers complain that the beloved does not enjoy enthusing over them as they do over him, whereas, in fact, it is the part of the lover to enthuse (since he loves the beloved for his beauty), but the part of the beloved to express thanks for benefits conferred.

Chapter 4

Equality and Loving Are More Proper to Friendship

1239a1   The points made in this chapter (a natural continuation of the previous one) seem relatively straightforward: that even if one can love and be loved by an inferior, one is friends, properly speaking, with one's equals; that some, the honor lovers, prefer to have friendships with inferiors (even with flatterers) because of the excess and honor involved; that others, the love inclined, enjoy

352

loving and prefer to love even if being loved back is not possible; that the latter sort are more like friends than the former. The final remarks, at 39b2–5, neatly summarize and conclude the content of chapters 2–4.

Chapter 5

Like and Unlike Friendships

A puzzle mentioned at the beginning is still in need of more treatment, the universal or extrinsic one, embracing lifeless as well as living things, that both the like and the unlike are said to be friends. The answer has in a way already been implied, that the like are friends on the basis of goodness and pleasure but the unlike on the basis of utility. This first point is straightforward and just needs express statement or restatement, which Aristotle immediately gives. 1239b6/b16

A second point is more complex. That opposites can be useful to opposites is obvious enough (as the examples show), but the utility is, of course, for the sake of the end and not itself the end. What is less obvious, but more important, is that appetite for the opposite is not of the opposite qua opposite but qua good, and is thus not strictly of the opposite but of what the opposite effects. The opposite brings the opposite into the mean (as the hot are brought to the mean by the cold and the cold by the hot), and it is the mean, not the opposite, that is wanted (hot people do not want to be cold but to be between hot and cold). Were they not opposites they would not want the opposite but would rejoice in the mean (the naturally pleasant state) without desiring anything further. Since, however, they are opposites, they want what will take them out of their natural state, which is precisely the opposite. Hence, they do *reach* the mean but they do not *become* a mean. For the opposites do not fuse into one; rather, by coming together, they supply each other's defects (which is the force of the sentence at 39b31–32, provided the manuscript reading is kept). 1239b23/40a4

The example of hot and cold already shows the fact. The hot in question does not cease to be naturally hot, for left to itself it would remain hot. Rather it gets cooled when in the presence of the cold (and the same analogously of the dry and wet). The examples about the austere enjoying the witty, and the hasty the sluggish, confirm the point. The austere and hasty are not changed in their nature by the unlike but are rather set in the mean by them. The result is that opposites and the unlike are not strictly friends of each other. They appear so (hence the common opinion to this effect), but on careful consideration they are only so accidentally and because of the good. For they are not of the opposite qua opposite, and therefore not of it qua bad either, but qua its being an instrument to bring them to the mean, which is of it qua good.

The final remarks at 40a4–7 again neatly summarize the contents of the preceding chapters 2–5. That Aristotle makes them stresses that he has now finished one part of his discussion (about the fundamental nature and kinds of friendship) and is moving on to a rather different one.

Chapter 6

Friendship with Oneself

1240a8   Aristotle begins the discussion of this next topic about friendship with oneself by giving reasons as to why such a discussion should next arise. These reasons are also the puzzles that guide it. Certainly, if it is possible not to be friends with oneself, as the incontinent, it should be possible to be friends with oneself, as the virtuous must presumably be. The key to the discussion is that friendship toward oneself is only friendship by analogy insofar as the soul, by having parts that can be or fail to be in harmony with each other, is a two between which a relation of friendship is possible. The clearest cases of such twoness are the continent and incontinent where desire and reasoned choice are in conflict, and they are friends to themselves both willingly and unwillingly (they do and do not want to do what is right and best for themselves). The same holds, therefore, of being an enemy to oneself and of wronging oneself (discussed earlier [4.11.1138b5–13]). But the same does not hold of any souls where such parts do not exist (as in the animals and small children mentioned later [40b31–33]).

1240a21   The interest, however, of the phenomenon of friendship toward oneself is less the basis in the soul of its analogical possibility than the way the analogy furnishes a pattern or model for understanding friendship as such, namely that friends are related to each other as a self to itself (which was the first question Aristotle began the chapter with). For friends wish well to each other for each other's sake, giving them good things, wanting their existence, wishing to live with them. These features naturally go together (and do when the friendship is the first friendship of virtue), but they need not (as in the case mentioned of fathers and children). Hence people can use them against each other, saying that they are not loved if they get one of them but not another; as that even if the other gives them good things, he does not really love them because he does not choose to live with them; and similarly with the others. But in fact each counts as a way of being loved even without the others. It is only in the first friendship of virtue that they are all present equally.[1]

1240a33   Friendship goes further in its imitation of a self's relation to itself, namely in feeling and wanting to feel exactly the same thing as the friend does, even voluntarily taking upon oneself the same pain (as thirst with his thirst, if one is not in a position to offer any other or immediate help), not to mention, of course, feeling the same joy; and such is how mothers in particular relate to their children, which responds to puzzle (d) raised at the beginning, that mothers love their children regardless. Two friends, in fact, seem to be most perfectly friends when their friendship is equal and moreover, when it is one, that is, either when it is just of one kind (of virtue or utility or pleasure) and not mixed (as with the friendships mentioned later [10.1243b15–37], where there are many complaints), or better, when it is of the virtuous kind (for in this kind the good, the useful, and the pleasant all go together in the same direction, and there is no possibility of conflict or inequality between them). There is thus parallel after parallel between such equal and single friendship and the way a self relates to itself.

But if friendship with oneself is possible, then so is enmity, and such   1240b11
enmity is what exists in the bad man who is not one with himself, nor even the same from moment to moment. Thus only the good man is really a friend to himself; the bad man is by contrast always in conflict with himself. So, the good man is one in the way "Coriscus" and "virtuous Coriscus" are one. The second term does not add to the first anything that conflicts with the first but rather something that perfects and completes it. Hence virtuous Coriscus is just Coriscus understood at his best. Further, when people bring accusations against themselves, it is themselves they are "slaying," whether metaphorically (they slay their bad self by the criticism) or literally (they commit suicide out of despair and self-disgust).

Such badness, where one wishes oneself not to exist, is unnatural, for by   1240b27
nature the self is a good to itself and is not a two that can be separated in such a way that one exists and the other not (if a bad man kills himself, his good self does not survive his bad self but both perish together). Only the good man is what he naturally is and wants his self to be one with itself and never separated. He is, then, both a two and a one: he is a two insofar as he has parts, and he is a one insofar as his parts are in accord and he is a friend to himself. Things that do not have such parts can be a one but cannot be a two; hence they cannot be friends to themselves either. Animals and small children are of this sort (they have desire but not choice as well). They are selves by themselves but not selves that are friends to themselves (b31–33). A child only becomes a two when he develops choice and can find his choice discordant with desire, and so when he can, by training in virtue, bring desire and choice into harmonious friendship. Such friendship will be most necessary because, as Aristotle adds, one cannot escape being related to oneself any more than one can escape being related to one's family. To fall out with them is not thereby to dissolve the relationship or the duties attaching to it (as one can dissolve the relationship with one's other friends). One's relationship with oneself is even more intimate. Hence the incidence of suicide among the bad who despair of ever making up for their crimes; it is the only way they have to escape themselves.

Note

1.   So Dirlmeier (1962: 424–25), whose interpretation is exact.

Chapter 7

Kindly Disposition and Oneness of Mind

1241a1/a10 This chapter is fairly straightforward. It follows on naturally enough because both kindly disposition and oneness of mind are related to friendship (and by some identified with it). The first, kindliness, can only exist, as Aristotle explains, in the friendship of character. The utility and pleasure that the other two friendships are based on have features that, as such, are incompatible with kindliness. Such friends could, no doubt, be kindly disposed to each other (the virtuous would be thus disposed to those, whether virtuous or not, with whom they could not have a friendship of character),[1] but their kindliness would not be internal to their friendship of utility or pleasure. It would belong to a possible friendship of character. For, as Aristotle immediately remarks, kindliness is not friendship but only its beginning; all friends are kindly but not all the kindly are friends. Hence, the kindliness that friends in utility or pleasure might have would be the beginning of friendship in character, but it would not be such friendship.

1241a15/a21 The section on oneness of mind seems to begin abruptly and hence some scholars think there is a lacuna in the text. The positing of a lacuna is unnecessary.[2] The logical connection (marked by "for" at a15) is that while friendship may get its start from kindliness, oneness of mind is needed to complete it. Aristotle thus naturally passes from one to the other. Naturally too he explains how oneness of mind, if it is to complete friendship, has to be understood. First, it cannot be about everything, but it is only about what friends are actually to do together and about what contributes to their common life (otherwise there would not yet be friendship)—the implication is, then, that kindliness could be about everything (it is a wishing of goods, and need not be confined to goods that friends are to do together). Second, the oneness cannot just be in thought or appetite (though kindliness could presumably be), but it must be in both as united together (and not as divided, the way they are in the incontinent). Third, it must be in good things (as kindliness too must be). Thus the base cannot really be of one mind, since the things they choose are harmful to them. If the base can be said to be of one mind, it is only in a secondary sense. They can agree on choosing and desiring the same things (even if the things are bad), provided these things can be possessed jointly by them all. For the base are selfish and will fight to keep for themselves and to deny to others what only one or a few of them can enjoy.

1241a30/a32 Rule is the obvious case in point. The base will want to rule exclusively and to make others serve them, so they cannot be of one mind about rule. Oneness of mind about rule is to agree on the same person or persons as ruler and not to fight to be ruler oneself. Such oneness of mind will, therefore, be what characterizes political friendship, where the citizens agree with each other on who should rule. If they do not agree they will fall to faction, as they typically do in base regimes (the rich fighting for oligarchy against the poor, the poor for democracy against the rich, the one powerful man for tyranny against all).

Notes

1.   A point not altogether accurately explained by Dirlmeier (1962: 430).
2.   Von Fragstein rightly (1978: 329–330), against Dirlmeier (1962: 431).

Chapter 8

Love of Benefactors and Benefited

This chapter is introduced by a puzzle that effectively relates it to what has just been discussed, for since friendship is a matter of doing (and not of wishing merely) one might wonder why, when doing does occur, those who did good to receivers are more loving than those who received good from doers. This puzzle, however, only arises if one considers the question form the point of view of justice. For justice would seem to require that receivers owe doers more because of the good they have been done. The puzzle, therefore, anticipates the topic of the next several chapters (which are all about justice in friendship). However, if instead one considers the question from the topic of the preceding chapters, namely friendship as such and its kinds, the greater love of doers is obvious and natural.

To begin with, a problem arises over the Greek. If the manuscript reading is followed, the remarks at a37–39 are serving to explain why doers love more than receivers (the justice of the opposite being taken as self-evident). If the emendation is followed, the remarks are serving to explain why justice requires receivers to love more than doers. An argument in favor of the former reading (besides its being what the manuscripts have) is that the next remarks, at a39ff., seem to be continuing, and not contrasting, what has just been said and to be adding (through the "not only" at a39–40) a *further* explanation of why doers love more. The first explanation Aristotle gives turns on the fact that one loves a good deed that one does more than a good deed that one receives (because, perhaps, it is a manifestation of one's own goodness, or perhaps too because it brings honor and praise from the recipient). Hence, for this reason, a good deed done is more useful or helpful to the doer (it helps him see and enjoy his virtue). The second explanation he gives complements the first by adding that doing is anyway preferable. Activity is like work in being realization of an end; and the receiver of a benefit, since he is the one in whom the act of giving is realized, becomes as it were the work of the giver.

1241a35

1241a37

1241b2   The phenomenon is a natural one, as is evident in the way that parents, human and animal, love their offspring more than offspring love their parents. For producing offspring is activity and a realization of one's natural powers. Similarly mothers, or females generally, love their offspring more than fathers, because childbirth is difficult and painful (even we call it labor), and this difficulty defines the child as more her work. (We may, then, regard this point as a further answer to puzzle (d) from the beginning.)

1241b10   The concluding sentence indicates that the first part of Aristotle's discussion about friendship, with oneself or others (everything from chapter 2 onward), is complete. What now follows (to the end of chapter 11) concerns friendship and justice.

Chapter 9

The Justice of Friendship
Summary Statement

1241b12/b16   The connection between friendship and justice, and political community, was stressed at the beginning of this book and given there as the main reason for studying friendship. In addition the first or true friend has in the meantime been shown to be the virtuous man. Hence, to summarize: justice is a virtue, the friend fully speaking is the virtuous man, living together with others is natural, and all three together are integral to happiness. In what follows Aristotle first states in summary form, in chapter 9, that (and how) friendship and community and so justice go together, and next, in chapters 10 to 11, he gives the detailed particulars.

     The present chapter opens with an argument, the first propositions of which, at b12–14, run:

(1)   the just is something equal;
(2)   friendship exists in equality;
(3)   all regimes are a form of justice.

From (1) and (3) the obvious conclusion follows that (4) regimes are a form of, or exist in, equality, like friendship. Further, since (1) is logically convertible (the just is by definition the equal in relations with another, so that the equal in relations with another is just), then it follows from the converse of (1) and from (2) that (5) friendship exists in something just. From (4) and (5) it also follows that (6) regimes and friendship are found in the same thing, namely the equal and the just. But, as is evident from what follows, at b15–16, Aristotle wants more than (6) alone, for he also wants to establish that forms of friendship are forms of justice and of community, and (6) does not warrant that conclusion.

The next statement, at b14:

(7)   they are a community

is ambiguous, and indeed the Greek elliptical. All it expressly says is "For a community . . .," and the words "they are" have to be supplied. Supplying them is easy and grammatically justified, but the ambiguity is whether the "they" refers back only to regimes or also to friendship. The statement is true in either event, but if the reference is taken to be also to friendship the logic of Aristotle's argument is clearer, for then (7) will do double duty. First, as referred to regimes and as taken along with the next statement, at 42b14–15:

(8)   everything common is based on the just

it will prove (3). Second, as referring also to friendship, it will expressly state (9) that friendship is community, which, while perhaps too obvious to need stating, nevertheless, along with (5), proves the conclusion Aristotle now states (b15–16):

(10)   the forms of friendship are also forms of justice and community.

The puzzles are, first, that (10) does not establish how forms of friendship are or are like forms of regime (but some likeness between friendship and regimes is what Aristotle is now concerned with and exploits in what follows); and, second, that proposition (6), which admittedly Aristotle implies rather than states, is redundant, for it is not needed to get to (10). Yet it does state how friendship and regime are similar (they are found in the same thing), and it would therefore seem a necessary step in showing how (10) can be made to apply to regimes as well.

These puzzles receive some answer in what Aristotle does next when he says, at 41b16:

(11)   all these border on each other and have the same differences.

The reference of "all these" is presumably to everything he has just mentioned (friendship, justice, community, and regime), for his succeeding remarks concern how these four are indeed close to each other and have the same differences. This statement, then, seems to be a continuation or refinement of (10). In explaining it, Aristotle first repeats something he had explained in the case of friendship with oneself, that such friendship can only be said of the self insofar as the self is a two (and thus cannot be said of animals but only of men). Hence, in the case of friendship with others too, it can only be spoken of where the things related are a two. Soul and body are not a two, nor are artisan and tool, nor master and slave. To be a two, each would have to be a one, but each is not a one; only the first item in each case is a one, while the second, by contrast, is not a one but *of* a one.

Aristotle does not here give an account of this fact, but an obvious one is that the first item in each case is the actuality or activation of the second (the soul actualizes the body so that it is alive, and the artisan and master activate tool and slave so that each performs its work), and actuality and potentiality are together a one and not a two. This obvious, but unstated, account is a metaphysical one. Aristotle himself adds a political account, namely that the members of these pairs do not each have a good of their own that they share, or make common, by coming together; rather the good of both is the good of the one for the sake of which this good is (for soul and body are together for the sake of the soul, and likewise for artisan and tool and master and slave).

Such things, then, are not communities and do not, taken precisely as such, involve friendship.[1] As regards communities proper, however, Aristotle next adds (b24–25):

(12) the other communities are a part of the city's communities.

The fact is obvious about subordinate communities like clans (the so-called phratries of ancient Athens) and sacred associations (for celebrating religious festivals); but it is no less true of business associations. Such associations may, it is true, transcend political boundaries and not be between fellow citizens alone, but unless one intends to dignify them with the title of regimes, which would be absurd (they do none of the things distinctive of cities), they should be regarded as communities for the sake of, and so subordinate to, the community of the city (they provide it with the materials and tools of life).[2]

The statement that communities are a part of the city's communities subordinates all communities to the city, and if we add (10) from above, that the forms of friendship are also forms of justice and community, we get the conclusion (13) that the forms of friendships are a part of the city's communities, and moreover parts of it as forms of justice. But justice in the city is expressed in its regime (for the regime, by determining rule, determines justice in the city), and (6) above said that regimes and friendship are found in the equal and the just. Hence, (14) the forms of friendship, being part of the city's communities, exist in that in the city that regimes also exist in, namely its justice. They will not exist in it as regimes proper (for, by supposition, they are subordinate to the city and so to the regime of the city), but they will exist in it as inchoate or quasi-regimes, as forms of justice that, when complete, are regimes. Thus (14) is equivalent to (11), provided (11) includes regimes in its reference to "all these."

One should expect, therefore, to find in the forms of friendship likenesses to the forms of regimes. Moreover, one should, for the same reason, treat these likenesses seriously and not as matters of mere accident or curiosity. They reflect something of the essence of friendship, for they reflect its form as something just (and the same result, indeed, will hold of all communities generally).

Accordingly Aristotle proceeds to state how these subordinate communi- 1241b27/b32 ties manifest the forms that are present at the political level. So kingship and aristocracy and polity (as well as their deviations) are found between the several divisions of the family. For, clearly, the relationship of father to sons is not that of husband to wife nor that of brothers to brothers, and these different relationships or communities do also reflect the different kinds of justice (from Book Four), some having the justice of numerical equality and others of proportional equality. Aristotle attributes the proportional equality of kingship and aristocracy to the communities of father and son and husband and wife, and the numerical equality of polity to the community of brother and brother. These forms are indeed those that do naturally arise in the several family relationships, and it takes considerable force and effort, still today, to introduce different forms.

Notes

1. There can be friendship with a slave insofar as he is also a man but not insofar as he is a slave, so *EN* 8.11.1161b5–8, on the details of which see Lockwood (2007).
2. The argument is made with some force and clarity in *Politics* 3.9 and also 1.4, 8–11.

Chapter 10

Particular Discussion
The Household

What has just been said in summary or general form (that all communities 1242a1/a11 are forms of friendship and justice, and mirror the forms of regimes), is now stated and explained in detail of each case: friendships in the family, among companions, and in the city. But certain preliminaries are in order. Political friendship is primary, for, as has just been said, all communities are logically part of and subordinate to that of the city. In explanation of the details, therefore, Aristotle begins with remarks about political friendship, and then applies them to the several cases. He states two things about it: that it is founded on utility and that it involves common sharing and not, as in the other communities, some sort of superiority.

The utility of political friendship is the utility of self-sufficiency, but to say that survival and political friendship are founded or set up in accord with this utility is not to say that the city does not have the life of virtue or the noble as its end (the teaching of the *Politics*, as 3.9). The utility is not a vulgar one. The city exists for the good life of virtue but, because citizens are many, the friendship of every citizen with every citizen cannot be one of virtue; it can only be of what is useful for friendship of virtue, namely sharing and setting up together a political community. Within this community, there will be friendships of virtue, and it is this community that most makes such friendships possible (for it provides all with the self-sufficiency that allows the concern with virtue as opposed to survival to become real). But these friendships of virtue, since they will not be with all citizens, will not be with citizens qua citizens but only with those few among them one can spend time with.

Political friendship is also essentially sharing in common, for it is friendship between equals. The others, by contrast, are between unequals, and sharing would seem to be at its most complete between equals rather than superiors and inferiors. There will, however, be no friendships at all with things related as user and tool, for, as was said in the previous chapter, such things do not have a good common that is shared but a single good, that of the user, for which the tool is tool. Hence a tool is at its best when it is in actual use and not when it is merely available, since actual use is what it is for and it is looked after in view of its use. There is no question of justice here (or of injustice either), because there is no question of a two who have a common good to share. By contrast, the relations of friends are a question of justice. Hence to look for how friends should associate is to look for what is just.

1242a20 As confirmation and proof of this point Aristotle next states the converse, that not only is the relationship of friends a matter of justice but that matters of justice are relations with friends. In other words he makes the connection between friendship and justice reciprocal: friendship is a matter of justice, and justice is a matter of friendship. Two premises are given for this claim:

(1) the just is for or between sharers;
(2) friends are sharers, in family or in way of life.

These premises as stated do not prove the reciprocity of justice and friendship, but they do prove it if each premise is converted in turn. The converse of (1), namely that what holds between sharers is justice, proves, with (2), that what holds between friends is justice; and the converse of (2), namely that sharers are friends, proves, with (1), that the just is what holds between friends.

That these propositions and their logical conversions are correct seems to be what Aristotle argues next. First he shows that (2) and its converse are correct. In stating (2) he said that friends are sharers in family or way of life. By way of life Aristotle seems to mean life in the city, for he contrasts city and household in the next lines. But, as he said in the previous paragraph, sharers in the city are friends (with the political friendship of utility). Here he speaks of someone who is "friend of a man alone and does not belong to a city" (a22–23),[1] by which he must mean someone who is friends with one or a few and not with many in a city. But such a person, even if he is not part of a city, must at least be a sharer in family. For, Aristotle continues, man qua man is, unlike other animals, a household animal, and sets up permanent relations with another and does not pass from one chance encounter to the next. Aristotle mentions male and female here but his remarks are sufficiently vague, and deliberately so it would seem, to include relations both with the opposite sex (for the sake of children) and with the same sex (for the sake of companionship, whether in work or leisure, as philosophy in particular). Should there be some men who are not friends and do not share even in this way, they are presumably either beasts or gods (*Politics* 1.2.1253a3–4) and so can, for present purposes, be excluded from consideration. So if all men are either part of a city or not, and if they are sharers and friends in both cases (friends and sharers of utility at least), then, necessarily, all friends are sharers and all sharers are friends, which is (2) and its converse.

As for (1), its truth, that justice is between sharers, was established at length earlier in Book Four. To be established here is the converse, that what holds between sharers is justice. What Aristotle says is a continuation of what he has just said, that man is an animal that shares with others, or has relations with those he is naturally akin to. Hence he has some sort of community with them (to share is to be in community in some way with those one shares with); hence, further, he has some sort of justice with them (for justice is about shares in some community or other even if not in that of the city); hence, finally, sharers are united in some bond of justice, or what holds between sharers is justice, which is the converse of (1).

Having thus set out the reciprocity between friendship and justice, Aristotle explains how it applies to what he said in his summary statement. So in the case of masters and slaves and the art and its tools there is no justice save by analogy, for here there is not a two but a whole and only a likeness to a two insofar as the whole has parts. There is friendship, and community, in the case of man and woman because they are a two useful to each other (for offspring); there is friendship of father and son as a two of benefactor and benefited or of natural ruler and ruled; there is friendship as equal comradeship of the two of brother and brother. These relationships arise naturally and necessarily from the very fact of how people sexually generate and produce families. Hence families and the communities they naturally form within themselves are the natural beginnings and origins of friendships and regimes and justice: the latter extend and complete what has already existed in the former. 1242b2/b11/ b16

Of these friendships, only the last, that of brothers, is according to equality, while the others accord with excess. Thus the just in the case of these others will also accord with excess: that the greater gets more than the lesser. In the case of brothers the just is the numerically equal. The fact and the difference are clear enough in business partnerships where the proceeds are proportional to the investment: equal if equal, differential if differential. Since, however, the lesser in a friendship cannot return to the greater a service equivalent to

1242a27

the service rendered, honor is fittingly given in its place: from ruled to rulers, from men to god.

The City

1242b21/43b1 Friendship in the city, as stated before, is of equality and utility (if attention is confined to citizens who are, as such, equal parts of the city). So citizens are like cities in caring for each other as long as the utility is there and not otherwise (though the utility need not be construed as vulgar, for the city is also instrumental to the good life of virtue); and they are equals in sharing rule by turns. Because the friendship is of utility and equality, regulation by law is better since thus mutual obligations are made clear. Complaints arise if such useful and citizen friendships are based on virtue and not on law. For friendships of utility are not, as such, friendships of virtue and to combine the two is unnatural. Those involved are at cross purposes from the start.

Virtuous friendships are, by definition, beyond complaint (the friends would not be virtuous otherwise); pleasant friends part when they give and get the desired pleasure; useful friends would do the same if their friendship was by law (as soon as the legal and financial obligations are fulfilled on both sides the friendship will cease). Problems will arise, of course, if a useful friendship is not regulated by law but is treated, if falsely, as one of virtue. Were it truly one of virtue, there would be no complaint, because good men are naturally just and do not need courts to adjudicate between them. Since, however, it is not one of virtue, but since, too, it is not one of law, the just man who is called on to adjudicate is faced with whether he should look to the thing done or to the persons, whether the cost to the doer or the benefit to the receiver (complaints can be and are fitted to suit the interest of either side, as Aristotle neatly illustrates).

Where, then, the friendship is political and useful the legal agreement and the deed are what count. Where, by contrast, the friendship is of character, the choice is what counts (for character is in the choice). The latter is more just, because it takes account of more things (both the person and the thing), and it is also more noble, because virtue of character is noble. If these two kinds were kept separate, there would be no ground for complaints. But people do not keep them separate: they unite as if for virtue but really they have an eye on utility, and if they do not get the utility, they care nothing for the principles of virtue. The way to determine what is just here is to require that the parties determine whether virtue or utility was the basis of their friendship. If it was of virtue, they must be content that their choices were equal (they each chose the other as a friend of character) and dismiss questions of how much benefit each gained or lost. If it was of utility, they must be content with the terms of what a reasonable contract would say. If they cannot agree, they should have recourse to an arbitrator, tell the truth, and accept whatever they get.

In explanation of the difference between choice and utility, Aristotle notes, in the case of choice, that it is enough to make return as one can and not as one received. The other party, as noble, will be content with the choice, that as he gave the best he could, so the first returned the best he could (or as we sometimes say, "it is the thought that counts"). In the case of utility, as with seller and buyer and lender and debtor (or in the city generally), equality of choice is not enough but rather equality of payment.

The problems that arise when a friendship of one kind (utility) is treated as if it were one of another kind (character) arise also and more so where a given friendship is not of a single kind to begin with, as when one is friend for pleasure and the other for utility, or one for this utility and the other for another. Here the friends are not "in a straight line" for each is looking in different directions or seeking equality in different things (pleasure or utility).

The stories Aristotle refers to make the point vividly enough. The stories also point to how ubiquitous the problem is, as well as how to solve it. Equalizing wisdom and money, or judging how much a certain learning is worth, is like equalizing the shoes made by the cobbler with the food produced by the farmer, or any exchange of anything in the city. The measure here is not the one thing of equality but the one thing, or the complex thing, of proportion: as the cobbler is to the farmer so shoes are to food, or as the wise man is to the rich man so learning is to wealthiness. But what is this proportion? It will obviously depend on times and occasions, for perhaps sometimes food will be more necessary than shoes or wealth than learning, so that a little food will be worth many shoes or a little wealth much learning; and sometimes it may be otherwise. As Aristotle said earlier (4.5.1133b20) the only measure is need or, as we say, supply and demand. Still even here there are absurd extremes, as if one party pays much and the other nothing. Exchange of utilities (provided such was the relation to begin with) requires that there be giving and taking on both sides, even if supply and demand always relativize the amounts.

Note

1. Provided we follow the MSS and not Casaubon's emendation. The MSS reading is peculiar but it makes grammatical sense. More to the point it makes logical sense. The emendation does not, or less so.

Chapter 11

In Multiple and Changing Friendships

This chapter continues the theme of the previous section in that it discusses other cases of friendship not "in a straight line." Here the cases are of obligations to different friends, or changing obligations to changing friends. They are found both in the household and the city.

A first question concerns whether to give assistance to the virtuous man or to a friend who can pay one back. For it would seem one should help a virtuous man because he is better, and that one should help one's friend because he is a friend. There is no problem, of course, if the same man is equally both virtuous and friend, but if he is not the problem is compounded by the question of time: either as friend or virtuous he could be so now or in the past but not in the future; or he could be in the future but not now; or he could be actually becoming so now but not yet be so (for becoming both friend and virtuous take time); or, hence and finally, he could be now and neither in the past nor in the future.

These combinations could no doubt be increased: for the change involved could be in friendship or virtue alone or in both, and if in both in the same or different directions; again, the friendship involved could be of virtue, or utility, or pleasure, or two or all of them. No wonder, then, that Aristotle adds that the thing is rather wearisome (a10). For not only is it now obvious how to work out all the alternatives (even if the working out is involved), but also these alternatives make no difference to the answer, which is neatly provided through a quotation from Euripides: if the relationship has progressed to deeds (if the other is already virtuous or friend) then respond with deeds; if it is only in promise (if the other says he will be friend or virtuous), then respond with promises.

1244a12　So much concerns the case where the same man is or will be or was virtuous and friend. In the case where the man is not the same, let the deeds (and promises) correspond to the kind of man and friendship. For it is not the case, as the opening question implied, that duties are always to the better (and so to the virtuous rather than to a friend who is not virtuous or not as virtuous): some things are due to the lesser, as to a mother rather than a father (the father is head of the household), and to other gods besides Zeus, though Zeus be chiefest among them. Likewise, one owes useful things to useful friends (as money for food and necessaries), but not virtuous things (as sharing one's life with them). To think and act thus is to be infatuated but not to be just.

1244a19　The variations in the kinds of friendships and the kinds of things due to each mean that the several marks of friendship by themselves give no help. They do not say which is due to which or to whom. Judgment must be made according to what is reasonable in each case, as that to some friends it is proper to wish good things, to others existence, to others living together, to others feeling together. Once the kinds of friends are distinguished, discerning what is due to each is not hard.

1244a30　Some of course will do wrong no matter what, as those who do not love their friends but what their friends possess. So they take the thing to the detriment of their friend, judging the thing more useful, which it may indeed be. Hence the friend gets annoyed, since he has been judged of less worth than his possessions. But if they were friends for utility's sake such behavior, even if deserving of complaint, is hardly surprising. A useful friend is a useful friend and a pleasant friend a pleasant one; neither, as such, is a good man and cannot be expected to behave like one.

Chapter 12

Friendships and Self-sufficiency
Need of Friends

The topic of friendship was introduced as belonging to the completion or perfection of the happy life. Since friendship's nature and kinds and justice have now all been discussed, the question remains of how many friends the happy or complete life needs. But this question at once raises a puzzle, for the happy man is supposed to be complete in his happiness and, if he is, he could be in need of nothing, and so could not be in need of friends (whether useful ones to benefit from, pleasant ones to be cheered by, or virtuous ones to live with). Hence happiness and friendship seem to be incompatible. Not surprisingly, therefore, does Aristotle introduce his discussion as being about the powers in respect of each other of self-sufficiency and friendship, namely what each can do for the other (whether friendship contributes to self-sufficiency, or self-sufficiency to friendship, or something else). 1244b1

To focus the question Aristotle begins by arguing on both sides, and first he argues against the need for friends by taking the extreme case of God. For, by definition, God does not need anything (other things depend on him, while he depends on nothing); so he will not need a friend and will not have a friend. At least he will not have a friend who is his equal (for who but God could be equal with God?), and if it be said that he can have inferior friends (for he is ruler of all and is friends of those he rules as a father is friend of his children), it could not be said that he has *need* of such friends. For God's rule is not that of a master who, qua master, needs slaves to do necessary labors for him (he who has no physical necessities has no need of slaves and no need to be a master). His rule is a gratuitous extra whereby he benefits others not whereby they benefit him.[1] If we take God, then, as the model of happiness, we must say that the happy man will only have need of friends to the extent he is not yet self-sufficient. Consequently the happier he becomes, and so the more self-sufficient, the fewer friends he will need, the less eager he will be to have friends, and the less he will think of any of them, including virtuous ones for living with. But such a result is utterly paradoxical (if not indeed inhuman). 1244b7

Arguing next on the other side, in favor of having friends, Aristotle first points out that the argument from God only shows that there will be no place 1244b15 in the happy life for useful friends; it does not as such show that there will be no place in it for virtuous ones. On the contrary, in self-sufficiency we most need friends to indulge with, not so as to have people to get things from but so as to have people to give things to (as kings, for instance, love to shower gifts on their courtiers and subjects). Further, our judgment of people is better when we are self-sufficient than when in need (we are at leisure then to weigh people as they really are and not as need may compel us). So since we can in self-sufficiency better judge who is worth living with, we will in self-sufficiency have more need of such people to live with.

1244b21 These arguments are not all equally compelling, but they are enough to show that there is a puzzle here that needs sorting out. The problem, as Aristotle now suggests and goes on to show, lies in the comparison with God. The things said about God are indeed fine and noble, but comparing our self-sufficiency with his is making us fail to notice something. What we are failing to notice, Aristotle continues, will be clear if we consider what living in its actuality and its end is (such actuality is happiness, as argued before [2.1]). There then follows an argument that, though involved, focuses on two main points: what the goodness of living consists in, and what role living with others plays in this goodness. For it turns out that while the goodness of living is the same for us and for God (some kind of knowing or awareness), this good life is possessed by God on his own but by us only along with others, and the latter fact is what the comparison with God is making us fail to notice. Accordingly Aristotle's explanation proceeds in two stages, first about the goodness of life, and then, from 1255a11 on, about the role in this goodness of living with others.

On the goodness of life, Aristotle lays down the obvious statement that life as actuality or end is in perceiving and knowing (these acts are distinctive of life among animals and men), and hence that living together must be, in its actuality, perceiving and knowing together. But, he pointedly adds, it is the very perceiving and knowing that is preferable to each and because of which all have an appetite for life. For, as he also adds, to live is to *handle* knowledge,[2] to manage it or deal with it. He immediately explains what he means by this remark through a thought experiment. The experiment is to cut off the knowledge from the handling and put it by itself, and also not to do this. The only difference one thereby makes, he says, is to posit someone else knowing instead of oneself and so someone else living instead of oneself. In other words, to separate the knowing from the handling of it by the knower is really to make that knower cease to be a knower and posit someone else as knower in his stead.

Aristotle adds that this fact escapes notice in the way it has been written in the argument but need not do so in the thing. What has been written in the argument is the cutting off of knowledge from the managing of knowledge, so it would seem that what escapes notice is what one has thereby done. As far as the words of the argument go, it would seem that one has separated two things (knowledge and handling knowledge). As far as the thing itself is concerned, that is one's act of knowing, one has not separated two things but destroyed one thing. For to separate in an act of knowing the knowledge from the handling is to make the act of knowing altogether cease to be in that knower and to place it instead in some other knower. Take, for instance, any given act of knowing or perceiving, as knowing a mathematical theorem or perceiving a tree. In any such act there is an object known or a piece of knowledge (the theorem, the tree), and an act of knowing it. The two are integrally part of the same act. So if one separates in thought the object known from the act of knowing, one is left neither with an object known nor with an act of knowing; rather one is left with nothing at all. Or, if one thinks the object known as still a *known* object (for it is as "known object" that one has separated it), one is perforce thinking it as known by someone else in his act of knowing and no longer by oneself in one's own. Accordingly, if an act of knowing is to be kept as one's act, then one's being the handler of the knowledge has to be internal to the act, or has to be something one knows along with the object.[3]

The point obviously requires more explanation, and Aristotle proceeds to give it shortly (when he shows how, in an act of knowing, the knower, no less than the object, is actualized as a thing known). First, however, he draws the important, and necessary, conclusion that what we choose when we choose perceiving and knowing is not some separated act (for, as just shown, there can be no such act in cases of perception and knowledge), but our own act of perceiving and knowing.

The next argument is complex and made more complex by the peculiarity of the Greek. First, when Aristotle says that "there is, at the same time, need" (b34), he is clearly indicating that at least two things are necessary, and it initially appears that the two things are what he next immediately says (b35), about putting two things together in the argument. These two things themselves then appear to be two propositions, each introduced by a "that" (*hoti* [twice in b35]): 1244b34

(1) that living is in fact to be preferred;
(2) that the good is—or possibly (the Greek is ambiguous): (2a) that living is the good.

There then, however, follows another *hoti* (b36), which appears to introduce another "that" proposition, and a proposition said to be "from these," and so, one presumes, a proposition drawn from the two just stated. What this third proposition is, however, is unclear because the Greek lacks sense as it stands, and how it should be emended is disputed.[4] Let it however be stated indeterminately;

(3) [some proposition somehow to be inferred from the others].

By way of sorting out these problems, one should note, to begin with, that proposition (3), whatever it says, cannot include the verb *hyparchein* (to be available) at b36, for this verb would then have to be in the indicative and not, as it is, in the infinitive. One solution would be to change it to the indicative (from *hyparchein* to *hyparchei*); another is, with Fritzsche, to change *tois* in b36, which is unintelligible as it stands, into *dei* (there is need); a third is to supply *dei* from the beginning of the sentence at b34. This last suggestion, however, suggests another one, namely to read *hyparchein* as directly dependent on that initial *dei* and treat it as the second of the two things Aristotle there says are needed. The sense, then, will be that the two things needed are, first, putting together the two positions (1) and (2) and, second, whatever it is the final clause says.[5] However, if the *hyparchein* is read as dependent on the initial *dei*, it cannot be part of the final *hoti* clause, for this clause requires a finite verb that falls within it and not without it. The obvious verb to supply, since none is stated, would be the same as has to be supplied for the first two *hoti* clauses, namely the verb to be. That problem, however, is secondary, because if *hyparchein* is not to be taken as part of the final *hoti* clause, what that clause says becomes even more obscure, for the emendations proposed to the Greek all make *hyparchein* to be a part of it.

The Greek that needs emending, because it lacks sense as it stands, is the phrase *[hoti] to auto tois* ([that] the same to the . . .). On the supposition that *hyparchein* falls outside the *hoti* clause, this phrase must be emended so as to constitute a *hoti* clause all by itself (and note that *hoti* may mean "because" as well as "that").[6] A clue to a suggestion is to look at the way *to auto tois* might appear to a scribe as he was copying it and how accordingly he might have misread it (since some misreading must have occurred to produce a senseless phrase). Since in antiquity and for several centuries thereafter manuscripts were written in capitals without word divisions, hence *to auto tois* would appear as ΤΟΑΥΤΟΤΟΙΣ. Now ΤΟΑΥΤΟΤΟΙΣ looks very like ΤΟΑΥΠΟΤΟΒ, and might look even more like it depending on how carefully formed the letters in the original manuscripts were. But ΤΟΑΥΠΟΤΟΒ in turn becomes, when written out with proper word divisions, *to A hypo to B*, which means "the A is under the B" (a common form of expression in Aristotle's logical works, and the sort of thing meant by "ordered series" or *sustoichia*, which appears in the next line). Such a suggestion may initially appear farfetched if not indeed bizarre. It does, however, have the signal advantage here of producing (with the verb "to be" supplied) a *hoti* clause all by itself. If, then, we adopt this proposal, however bizarre, the translation will become (including the *hyparchein* part):

(3) [there is need], from these (because the A is under the B), for this sort of nature to be available.

This translation, however, may seem to replace the obscure with the more obscure, for what does it mean? First, as regards the A and B, these will refer to the content of propositions (1) and (2), or (2a), and the sense will be that "living as to be preferred" is under "the good as to be preferred," or under "living as the good." The living that is to be preferred is, as the earlier argument showed, the living that is our living, the living that we experience as us being alive (a point stressed in the Greek by the addition at b35 of *kai*, "indeed" or "in fact"). However, when Aristotle first introduced this whole present discussion, at b23–24, he said that the thing will be plain if we take life "in actuality and as end," and life taken as end is happy life, for happiness is the end and the good. We should probably, therefore, read (2a) in place of (2), and so understood the "sort of nature" that must be "available" as the sort of living that is the good, namely happy living. The argument will thus be that it is necessary to put "life as preferable" together with "life as the good," and then necessary, because life's being preferable is under life's being the good, that such a life is available to us for living ourselves. So what the argument is requiring us to do is to show, first, how the life that is preferable for us (because we are aware of it as us living) is, or can become, the life that is the good, and so, second, how this good is available to us as a life for us to live, because the life preferable for us to live is included under it.

Interestingly enough, what Aristotle does in the next paragraphs can be shown, with little difficulty, to be precisely these two things. For first he explains how the life that is preferable for us is a life of perceiving and knowing, and how such a life is perfected, or becomes the good, through sharing with friends. Then, second, he shows how such sharing with friends is the human equivalent of the divine life, which is the simply good life. Hence, as he said, the life that is preferable for us does indeed fall under the good, because it falls under the good when perfected with friends, and this good life is necessarily available to us as a life for us to live for the good life thus lived with friends is precisely us living. The argument is lengthy and involved, but it is ultimately clear. It also shows, as Aristotle was intending from the beginning, how the comparison with God is leading us astray about the need of friends. For the good life, which is available to God all by himself, is only available to us through sharing with friends. Thus the self-sufficient man (as opposed to the self-sufficient God) will need friends as constitutive of the happy and self-sufficient life, and not as an extrinsic extra.

The first thing, then, that Aristotle does is use the idea of one thing falling under another thing to make a further point about life as preferable. He states (45a1–5):

(4) if it is always the case that in an ordered series one thing is in the same column under another, and
(5) if the known and the preferable are the sharing of determinate nature (or are under the determinate in the same column),
(6) then wanting to perceive oneself is wanting to be of this sort (namely determinate).

Here (4) is a logical truth about the subsumption of terms under each other, that if X is in the same column under Y, and Y is in the same column under Z, then X is in the same column under Z. Proposition (5) basically uses the logical truth of (4) to subsume the A just introduced (life as preferable) under the term determinate. For life was earlier said to be a knowing, so that to say life is preferable is the same as to say some sort of knowing is preferable. Hence, if the known and the preferable are determinate (they are definite actualities), life as preferable must be determinate. Or, to put it schematically: A (life as preferable) is in the same column under C (knowing as preferable), and C is under D (knowing and preferable as determinate), so A must be in the same column under D too (life as knowing and preferable must be in the column of the determinate). Consequently, from (5) so understood, (6) follows, because wanting to perceive or know oneself, which is what wanting to be alive means (for life is preferable and to live is to perceive or know), is wanting to be determinate oneself (for only the determinate is perceptible and knowable).

1245a5 The next stage in the argument is more straightforward. It points out that we are not determinate of ourselves but only when actually using our powers in perceiving and knowing. The reason is that we become ourselves actualized in our actual perceiving, that we become perceived to the extent and respect we perceive, and in the way and as to what we perceive. The point may seem initially peculiar, for it is saying that if we perceive a tree we are perceived to the extent and in the way we perceive a tree, as if we ourselves became the tree in perceiving it. The meaning, however, is not quite so crude. We only perceive by perceiving something, and by perceiving it attentively or inattentively, and with one or more of our five senses, and as far off or near by, and obscurely or clearly, and the like. For our perceiving is not actual of itself but has to be actualized by the object, and it is actualized by it to the extent the object is able to act and we are able to be acted upon. This object, however, whatever it is, has a special nature. It is first of all some definite thing in the world, as a tree, but, second, it is also, in the act of perceiving, an object of that act. The tree as a thing in the world is not changed in its proper being by the act of perceiving (the tree stays as it is both when perceived and when not perceived), but it is, as perceived, changed in its relative being, for it is now made to be in relation to a perceiver when before it was not. Perceiving a tree is primarily perceiving the tree in its proper being, but it is at the same time perceiving the tree as object, as perceived thing. We perceive the tree, for instance, from here and from this angle and with these spectacles and in this light and so forth. Or, as we say, we see the tree in this or that perspective.[7]

The tree has, of course, no perspective in itself; it gets perspective only in an act of perception, or only in reference to a perceiver. But since the tree, when perceived, is perceived in some perspective, it is necessarily perceived in some reference to the perceiver, namely to oneself. Consequently one is oneself necessarily part of the object perceived. Or, rather, only by receiving the addition of "reference to self" does an object of perception or knowledge become such an object instead of staying itself by itself. Self-knowing, therefore, is always necessarily part of knowing, because the object known always includes reference to self as part of what the object qua object is. Such reference does not change anything in the object (perspective is not distortion),[8] because reference is all it is, and referring one thing to another does not change the thing. But, by the same token, if the object only contains the self as reference to self, then the self is actual in the object only as such reference. So the self is only actual, and only known, with the actuality of the object. Thus it is indeed in a way true that when one perceives a tree one becomes a tree, not in substance, but by intentional reference. One becomes, so to say, actual as tree-knower.

Such actuality of self is, as such, very limited, but it will become greater the more acts of perceiving and knowing one performs. To these will then be added acts of memory, of imagination, of anticipation, and of addition and combination (as with inductive experience). Further, there will, eventually, be added acts of knowing that take other acts of knowing as object. For, after one has perceived a tree, one can think about the act of perceiving a tree by a process of self-reflection. These acts of self-reflection will be second-order or higher-order thoughts (as they are called), and will take the self as direct object and no longer as mere reference. Of course such reference will also necessarily be involved, for reference to self is built into the idea of object, and so built into the idea of self as object too. Hence acts of thinking of self can also become objects of acts of thinking, and these acts objects of further acts of thinking, and so on indefinitely.

The point, nevertheless, remains that any act of perceiving or knowing includes within it, on the side of the object, reference to and actualization of self prior to any further or later acts of self-reflection. It is such immediate reference to self that is Aristotle's focus here, and on the basis of it he concludes that we want always to live, because we want always to know, and that because we wish ourselves to be the known. For, as he said earlier, living is a perceiving and knowing, and living is something we want to the extent it can be identified as us living, and we identify it as us living to the extent we are actualized in knowing, that is, to the extent we become known in the known object.

What Aristotle has shown thus far, then, is how we become determinate   1245a11
in acts of knowing by becoming ourselves known, and hence, that life, being preferable as determinate, is preferable as self-actualization, or self-presence, in acts of knowing. Presumably, therefore, one will be as determinate and as actual, and one's life as preferable, as the acts of knowing are that one performs. The present topic, however, is friendship and how having friends to live with is part of the happy and self-sufficient life. Thus the next question

to discuss is the sort of acts of life, the acts of knowing and perceiving, that one performs or can perform with others.

As is his wont, Aristotle first argues on both sides, and first against living together. So, at one level, living together is trivial, as with animals and in acts of eating and drinking, for there is, in these cases, no need for being together since the acts can be done as well apart as together, at least once one removes speech or the sharing together that is distinctive of man. But even sharing speech is trivial if it is itself trivial. Further, the speech of student and teacher, while it gets beyond the level of the trivial, does not establish the living together that is friendship, for student and teacher are not equals and friendship, at least at its fullest, is between those equal and alike.

1245a18 Next, arguing on the other side, in favor of living together, Aristotle points out the increase in pleasure that we all get from doing things together, whatever these things are and however good they are, from bodily pleasures, to music, to philosophy. These things are not on the same level, to be sure, but we each enjoy doing together the best we can and are pained when the friends we enjoy things with are far away. The fact is especially manifest in the case of erotic lovers whose desire for each other is focused on physical presence, since it is the feel of the other that eroticism focuses on (rather than the good of the other that is proper to friendship).

1245a26 These dialectical considerations help to focus the question but they do not answer it. Even those considerations on the side of friendship fail to give friendship much importance, for they relativize it to personal taste. One enjoys with friends whatever takes one's fancy as it were, whether it be sex or philosophy. But an argument that puts sex and philosophy on the same level hardly carries much weight. Indeed it conflicts with the facts, which we are all more or less aware of, that friendship has in it something great and noble (even erotic lovers, provided they are not crude about it, sense that there is something special about being with their friend over and above the sharing of touch). A better approach, then, is to begin with something great and noble, namely that a friend is, in the words of the proverb, another Heracles, another self (the friendship of Heracles with Iolaus, who was to him like another Heracles, was celebrated in story as something great and noble). Finding another self may be difficult, of course, since no given individual mirrors oneself in all respects, but this person here mirrors one in this respect and that person there in another. Still, a friend is properly another self, and this fact is what explains the phenomena adduced in the dialectical arguments, namely the enjoyment even in vulgar things that we take when being and living with others, for we perceive the other at the same time and, accordingly, perceive ourselves in the other too.

This friendship and the enjoyment will be better the more divine the things enjoyed together are. The reason is not the relativistic one, that those who are turned on by divine things will enjoy doing them together. The reason rather is that the divine things are simply better, and to see ourselves in divine things, because we see ourselves in our friends in the doing together of divine things, is itself simply better (it is the attainment of the best good, the true human end). Since such sharing will be complete, it will involve feelings (we feel with our friends in being with them), doings (we contemplate the divine together), and anything else the community of friendship involves. So it will even involve dining together, not for the pleasures of taste and indulgence, of course, but for these pleasures as subsumed into the pleasures of relaxed conversation about divine things. At least the best will enjoy this kind of friendship. Others will enjoy the best they are capable of, and if their friendships are not cases of enjoying the end, they will at least have friends for the giving and receiving of benefits (one of the points mentioned at the beginning of the chapter [1244b17–19]).

The argument thus proves the need we all have for friends. More to the point it shows how the preferable life, the life that we can prefer as ours, becomes the good, which was the aim of the argument asserted earlier. In sum it runs more or less as follows: life is preferable as determinate or actualized; life becomes determinate or actualized through acts of perceiving and knowing in which we ourselves become perceived and known; doing things with friends who are other selves is perceiving and knowing oneself in one's friend; the better the friend and the things one does together the better the perceiving and knowing; everyone wants the greater actualization and determination that comes from acts done with friends; the best acts are those about the most divine objects; the happiest and best man is he who acts about the most divine objects; these acts reach their greatest determination in being done with friends who are themselves happiest and best; a life of such most determinate acts is the happiest life; therefore the happiest and best man will most have these acts; therefore the happiest and best man will most have and most need the friends with whom alone such acts are achieved. Hence, as the argument presented earlier required, the life that is preferable because it is ours is shown to fall under the good and to be thereby available to us, because it is the life shared with friends in doing the most divine things. 1245b9

We can now see what was wrong in the earlier comparison between the happiest man and God. The error was not in what it supposed the best life to be, for the life of God is indeed happiest and the happy man is happy by becoming most like God. The error was in supposing that because the life is the same in both cases therefore the way of achieving it is the same. But it is not. God has this life all by himself because he is most determinate all by himself and does not need friends with whom to be made determinate in joint acts of perceiving and knowing. We, however, achieve it only by and with friends. To remove friends from us is to remove the happy life from us. We achieve happiness in relation with others; God has it by his very nature.

An interesting result follows from this argument, that it dissolves the question of altruism and egoism. The complaint is often leveled against systems of ethics like Aristotle's, that to make happiness the good and the point of the virtuous life is to make one's own personal good the point of virtue and so to subordinate the good of others to the good of oneself. The complaint assumes that there is a "self" and an "other" who can be the object of the egoism and the altruism. But Aristotle's argument about how life becomes determinate, and hence how it becomes the good, requires that there be no difference between self and other, or at least between self and the other of a virtuous friend. The self that is happy in the happiest life is the joint self constituted by the joint acts of virtuous friends. As substances each friend may be distinct, but as actors they are one because their action is one; and it is one because they each become the other in acts of perceiving and knowing; and they each become the other in these acts because knowing is a becoming actual of the knower in the object known. Hence we become actual in our friends and vice versa. Our actuality, our becoming determinate, is one, though the substances that act are many. There is thus no self and other left to be the focus of any egoism or altruism. The question between the two disappears because the two themselves disappear.[9]

At least the two disappear in the case of virtuous friends. They may even disappear, if to a lesser extent, in lesser friendships (for the fusion of self with self is characteristic in some degree of all friendships). In the case of God, of course, the fusion is complete because he is not two substances to begin with. He is his own best friend, as it were. The friendships of virtuous men with virtuous men, who are active together about divine things, is the closest that men can reach in imitation of God. The further implication, then, is that virtuous friends can have no better object to be active together about than God himself. Indeed if we only become actual and determinate in knowing, and in knowing something other than ourselves (for our "self" is not anything before it perceives and acts), and if the best knowing is about the best thing, which is God, then we become best and happiest when, along with our friends, we are active together in knowing God. Indeed if we receive our determinateness and actuality from the object known, and if God is the object we know, the determinateness and actuality that is happiness is in a way the determinateness and actuality of God himself, insofar, at least, as it can be made present to us in acts of knowing. There is already here, then, an anticipation of what Aristotle says at the very end of this whole work, that the best and happiest life is the worship of God, the best knowing of God that we can perform.

Number and Treatment of Friends

1245b19 We can perhaps also see now what is wrong with supposing that the life of happiness, even though it be one of contemplation, can be separated from the practice of the moral virtues. The moral virtues reach a unity in their relation to others in justice, and justice is the same as friendship, and the greatest justice must exist in the greatest friendship. Hence, since the happy life is a life of activity with friends, the happy life is impossible without the activity of the moral virtues that are friendship. What friends do together is contemplation; how they do it together is moral virtue. Or at least it will be the moral virtue that is internal to virtuous friendship, and since virtuous friendship transcends the friendship of the city (which is a friendship of utility), the moral virtues of friendship must, to this extent, transcend the moral virtues of the city. Since the moral virtues, as they are focused on in the *NE*, are directed toward perfection of life in the city, they are there focused on in their political reality, and hence are focused on in that reality that is transcended in contemplation. In *EE*, by contrast, they are focused on in their philosophical reality, and hence they are not here transcended by philosophy but incorporated in it. The moral virtues, therefore, differ in their status and role in each work: in *NE* they are political moral virtues; in *EE* they are philosophical moral virtues. The difference is not in the what (hence the descriptions of the virtues in each work are more or less the same), but in the context in which the what is put.

These points are implicit in what Aristotle does now, which is discuss the number of friends the happy man will need. The answer is in a way simple: as many as possible (for it is through and with friends that life is best). However the number possible is not great because of the limitations of human nature. Time is needed to test friends and time is limited; attention is needed to use friends, or to be and live with them as friends, and attention too is limited. These limits show that friends cannot be many, but how few they will be must be left to individuals and circumstances to decide according to their own dispositions of time and attention.

Aristotle could have perhaps ended his discussion here. That he continues 1245b26/6a2 is because of what was just said, namely that moral virtue is internal to the practice of friendship, and friends must use each other justly. There are limitations imposed on friendship, or rather on being with friends, by the demands of justice. Friends do and must want to be together, but if having our friends by our side is unjust to our friends, we should not want them there. It will or may be unjust if by wanting or keeping our friends with us we deny them something better. So Heracles' mother would obviously want her son to be with her, but if he is thereby made worse (because he is made a slave instead of being a god), she should not want him to be so. In general, in fact, it would be unjust to want to make things worse for our friends by involving them in our troubles. On the other hand, it is just for friends to support a friend when he is in distress.

The demands of justice, therefore, are in tension. But they are not in conflict. A resolution is possible. It is better to be together sharing a lesser good than apart enjoying separately a greater one, for friendship means being together. The friend in trouble, however, should not want to involve his friend in pain, for that is contrary to the love of the other that friendship is. On the other hand, the friend of someone in trouble should want to relieve him in his trouble. Since both these views are correct, there is no simple right or wrong answer. The friends should decide for themselves case by case. The benefit of the doubt, however, should go with being together, as the extreme case makes clear, that it is better for them, as friends, to be together sharing great trouble than apart enjoying great success.

1246a10/a18 Conversely, if our friends can do us no further good in our misfortunes but will only be the more pained thereby, we should not want their presence, despite the pleasure it brings, for as we flee pain in our own case we should in justice flee it for our friends too. The question is one of weighing pros and cons, which is the necessary work of prudence in justice as in anything else. The fact and need of such weighing is illustrated from the example of the bad, who may indeed decide the question badly but they do nevertheless decide it and think too that they need to decide it.

Notes

1. That the reference to master at 1244b9–10 is appropriate and can be kept and not, as some scholars wish (e.g., Von Fragstein [1978: 344]), emended away, is rightly argued by Dirlmeier (1962: 457–58).

2. Bonitz' emendation at 1244b28 of *diatithenai* (to handle) to *dei tithenai* (one must set down [living as a sort of knowing]) may be philologically plausible, but it is repetitious and destroys the sense. Aristotle has just said, at 1244b23–25, that living is knowing, so he hardly needs to say it again so soon. What he is now saying is that living is the actual handling of knowledge, as his following thought experiment indicates. Osborne (2009: 11, 19) rightly keeps the MSS reading in her rendition and analysis of this passage. She also translates *to auto aisthanesthai* and *to auto gnōrizein* at 1244b26–27 as perceiving or feeling "the same" and as knowing or observing "the same," rather than as "the very" perceiving and "the very" knowing. The translation is grammatically possible but not contextually so, for the argument in the context, as the preceding and subsequent lines make clear, is not about what is perceived or known but about our living being our perceiving and knowing and not someone or something else's perceiving or knowing. Osborne's larger point is indeed right, that for us perceiving and knowing is perceiving and knowing along with others, but it is not the point of this passage.

3. The interpretation just proffered bears some resemblance to the interpretation of Von Arnim (1928: 11–17), but without his unnecessary textual emendations, which Dirlmeier rightly criticizes (1962: 460).

4. Discussion in Dirlmeier (1962: 461–62), also Von Fragstein (1978: 345–47), Susemihl and *OCT* app. crit. ad loc.

5. So Dirlmeier (1962: 91, 462).

6. So Dirlmeier ibid.

7. Cf. Osborne (2009: 12–13).

8. Unlike what the tradition of German Idealism from Kant onward would have us believe.

9. Osborne (2009) gives a similar analysis of the bearing of Aristotle's argument here.

Book Eight: Completion of
Happiness: Complete Virtue

Chapter 1

Complete Virtue
Using Virtue: Supremacy of Prudence
The connection of this book, or this chapter (there is question whether a
new book begins here or not), to the previous one is puzzling. It is not really
about friendship, though it begins, at least according to some manuscripts,
with a question about friends (b26–27): "... whether it is possible to use each
thing that is dear—or each friend—on the basis natural to it and otherwise."
It deals, instead, with a question about whether virtue can be used viciously
or vice virtuously, and this question seems more appropriate in a discussion
about the use of virtue than the use of friendship (such a place is where
Aristotle puts it in *GE*, 2.7.1206a36ff.). However, perhaps here precisely is the
clue to an answer. Friendship is in a way the same as virtue (for, as argued at
the beginning of chapter 10, it is the same as justice). Hence a question about
how to use friends is also a question how to use virtue. Moreover, the previous
chapter, or book, has just ended with a discussion of friends who use friends
badly, namely bad men who kill their friends along with themselves. Therefore, a question about whether we can really use friendship badly naturally
arises. This question is heightened if we also retain the word for "pleasant"
at a27 instead of emending it. For bad men do bad things because they think
them pleasant, or less painful, and thus do they kill their friends along with
themselves. For if bad men can use friendship badly, can virtuous men do the
same? If they can, then it must be possible to use virtue badly; if they cannot,
then it must be impossible to use virtue badly. In either case, the question
about the bad use of virtue, or the good use of vice, naturally arises, and this
question is what is dealt with in this chapter.

Accordingly, we have reason to retain the words "dear" and "pleasant"
in the opening sentence and not delete or emend them. The deletion and
emendation are plausible, to be sure, and the sense they produce is attractive; moreover not much will change in the philosophical point Aristotle
is making if they are accepted. All that is lost is the connection with the
immediately preceding discussion. For, if we keep that connection, we can say,
in answer to the question whether this chapter starts a separate book or not,
that it both does and does not. It does not insofar as it continues the topic of
friendship from the previous book; it does insofar as it takes that topic in a

different direction. In fact it takes it in the direction of finalizing the idea of completeness of happiness. For as the topic of friendship completes happiness by completing the life of happiness, so the topics in this book of luck and the gentleman complete happiness by completing the virtue of happiness. Since happiness is virtuous living, the completion of happiness requires completeness in both respects. Both books therefore deal with the same topic but in different respects. Hence they are both one book and also two books.

1246a26 Aristotle begins with a question that, if we suppose this chapter directly follows on the previous one, does pick up on what was just said there. The question, to repeat, is whether it is possible to use friends, or anything dear, on the basis natural to them (because they are dear or friend), as well as in some incidental way, because they are pleasant. The bad just mentioned, for instance, kill their friends from friendship because of the pleasure, or the absence of pain, they think is thereby involved. For even if the bad have friendships of pleasure, the pleasure they would kill their friends for would be incidental; it would not be the pleasure of being with their friend, but the imagined pleasure, or absence of pain, of not having them live on beyond themselves.

In illustration Aristotle takes the eye but gives three uses, not two.[1] The first use is using an eye to see; the second is using it to mis-see; the third is using it to sell or eat. The first two uses will be of the eye on the basis natural to it, which is seeing (for even mis-seeing is a case of seeing). The third is an incidental use, because selling or eating an eye[2] is not using an eye to see with.

1246a31 The example of the eye is now applied to knowledge (it is applied to moral virtue, and so to friendship shortly), but only two uses are mentioned, not three. The first is to use knowledge in a true way and the second to use it to make mistakes. The second is then glossed as using knowledge as ignorance, and the further examples are given of contorting the hand and of dancing girls using their hands as feet and their feet as hands. This second use, therefore, seems to be parallel to the third or incidental use just mentioned in the case of the eye (where the eye is not used as an eye but as edible or pleasant to eat).[3] For to use feet as hands and hands as feet is not to use either as feet or hands but incidentally, as the opposite. Hence to use knowledge as ignorance when making mistakes is to use knowledge incidentally. The other and third use of knowledge, the one equivalent to using the eye to mis-see, is not mentioned. It reappears directly but Aristotle's focus here is on uses of a thing that are not really but only incidentally uses of it qua it (and not on uses that, though misuses, are still uses of it qua it).

At all events, if we take knowledge in these two uses, as knowledge and incidentally, and if the virtues are instances of knowledge, then we should be able to use justice as injustice (that is, in an incidental way), and so we should be able to do wrong from justice in the same way as we can do ignorant things from knowledge. If, however, we cannot use justice as injustice, then the virtues would not be instances of knowledge.

Aristotle has so far assumed, for the sake of argument, that one can use   1246b1
knowledge incidentally, as ignorance. But this assumption is not in fact correct.
Knowledge cannot make one ignorant and one cannot be ignorant from knowledge. What one can do is imitate the effects of ignorance. One can, that is, make
the same mistakes as ignorance but, if so, one will be acting deliberately or of
set purpose, as when a teacher makes a deliberate mistake to test the learning
of his students. Here the mistake, being deliberate, springs from knowledge
and not from ignorance. Hence, in this sense, incidental use of knowledge (as
in the case of using an eye for eating or selling) is impossible. All that is possible is misuse of knowledge or using knowledge to make deliberate mistakes
(as in the case of using an eye to mis-see by distorting it so as to see double).

In the case of justice, however, or the moral virtues generally, not even
deliberate misuse is possible. One cannot misuse justice as one misuses
knowledge and do deliberately from justice what one might do from injustice.
Aristotle needs only to assert this point here because he had in fact stated
and proved it earlier (4.8–9). The unjust man is precisely he who does unjust
things deliberately, whereas not to do an unjust thing deliberately is not, or
not yet, to be unjust. What then of prudence, which is intimately connected
with moral virtue (it is the knowing and commanding of the virtuous thing to
be done here and now)? Since prudence is a sort of knowledge, and since it is
possible to misuse knowledge (though not moral virtue), one should be able
to misuse prudence and do deliberately from prudence what the imprudent
man does. Hence, since "the use of each thing, insofar as it is such, is simple"
(b7), that is, since any use, for instance, of knowledge qua knowledge is a case
of knowing (even the misuse of knowledge is a knowing, as a misuse of the
eye is a seeing), and hence since a deliberate misuse of knowledge is a making
mistakes knowingly, then it must follow that a deliberate misuse of prudence
is a doing imprudent things prudently.

This result is bizarre, but it follows from the argument so far. The error   1246b8
must lie somewhere in the analogy with knowledge, that it is not exact. If one
considers, then, the case of knowledge, one sees that the misusing of knowledge is done by another knowledge that controls the first. So the knowledge
of teaching controls how and where and when to use one's knowledge to
make deliberate mistakes so as to aid the teaching of students. Likewise, if
there can be a deliberate misusing of the knowledge of teaching, there must
be a higher knowledge in control of it, and so on. But if all knowledge can be
misused, then the highest or most controlling knowledge, which controls all
the others (as politics is said to be in the first chapter of the *NE*, for instance),
cannot itself be controlled or misused by some higher knowledge (for, *ex
hypothesi*, there is none), nor, accordingly, by anything of intellect. Neither
can it be controlled by virtue, or not moral virtue, for prudence uses virtue
by ruling over it (as argued in 5.13), and if this highest controlling thing is
also in control of prudence, it will be in control of virtue and not be virtue.

1246b12 Another answer, then, if this controlling thing is not knowledge or virtue, can perhaps be found from the model of the incontinent man. For the incontinent is like the virtuous in having intellect (he judges rightly what the temperate thing to do is), but he is also like the licentious in having passions that get the control and make him do the licentious thing instead. Hence one could say that the controlling thing in the case of knowledge is passion of some sort. This other answer, however, has problems too, because it leads to results that contradict what has already been said and that are generally absurd.

Since the answer relies on the model of incontinence, this model must be examined in more detail. Incontinence is a case of vicious passions conquering sound thinking (or, schematically, it is a case of vice in the passions conquering or misusing virtue in the intellect). But if vice in the passions is powerful enough to distort or misuse virtue in the intellect, then vice in the intellect should be powerful enough to distort or misuse virtue in the passions. So we have, from the same phenomenon, two cases of vice misusing virtue: first, the case of the phenomenon of incontinence itself and, second, as Aristotle himself concludes now, the case of justice having a bad use (when vice in the intellect misuses virtue in the passions), alongside its just use (the use the just man makes of it). This case will also, of course, be a case of intellect thinking imprudently (for the intellect will be commanding unjust things). But it was said earlier that justice cannot have an unjust use, so this result is already contradictory.

1246b18 The model of incontinence produces other oddities. For in addition to the two cases already mentioned, Aristotle now says there will be the opposite cases when, instead of vice in one part of the soul misusing virtue in the other, the roles will be reversed and virtue in one will misuse vice in the other.[4] Here there are also two cases and both can again be inferred by analogy from incontinence. For if vice in the passions distorts virtue in the intellect to a bad use (as in the case of incontinence), then, first, virtue in the passions should be able to distort vice in the intellect to a good use and make it judge correctly; hence we will have the prudent use of imprudence. Second, virtue in the intellect should be able to distort vice in the passions into a good use; hence we will have the temperate use of license (as with continence or endurance, where we correct through intellect our licentious passions and make them act temperately). There are four cases, then: the two just mentioned of incontinence and of bad use of justice, and now the two cases of prudent use of imprudence and of temperate use of license.

The third case here, prudent use of imprudence, is particularly odd. It is a case of acting prudently with a virtue that comes from ignorance. For there is folly or ignorance in the intellect and yet we behave prudently because virtue in the passions distorts folly and makes us do the virtuous thing. It is, indeed, the contrary case to the one the discussion began with. That initial case was one of using prudence to act imprudently; this case is one of using imprudence to act prudently.

All these results are odd or absurd, and especially the last mentioned, that 1246b25 of behaving prudently from imprudence or ignorance. For such a thing, that vice can achieve the effects of virtue, is not found in other cases of knowledge (and the assumption here is that prudence is a kind of knowledge). All that vice can do is distort knowledge; it does not make what is not knowledge to become knowledge. License, for instance, can make someone with the art of medicine or grammar misuse the art (when he makes deliberate mistakes), but it cannot do the reverse and make someone without these arts into someone who has them. The point is almost one of logic: the capacity includes the incapacity but not vice versa. A man possessed of the art of grammar can write as badly as a man who lacks it, but someone who lacks it cannot write as correctly as someone who possesses it.

We must say, then, that anyone who acts prudently is acting with prudence 1246b32 after all, and is not, as the model of incontinence suggested, using imprudence prudently. Consequently we must also reject the incontinence model as a way to explain how prudence, if it is a sort of knowledge, can, like other knowledges, have an imprudent use. On the contrary, we must reject the supposition that prudence is knowledge, at least in the way the other knowledges are. We must also say that the good cases just talked about (where virtue in one part of the soul overcomes vice in the other) are not cases of prudence, or indeed of virtue properly speaking, but of continence or endurance or the like.

In sum, therefore, we must both agree and disagree with Socrates. We must agree with him when he said that nothing is stronger than prudence (for prudence cannot be overcome and misused as imprudence), but we must disagree with him when he said that prudence was knowledge. We must instead say that it is a virtue like justice (which also cannot be misused as injustice), and is not strictly a knowledge but some other kind of comprehending things (for prudence is at least a comprehending or grasping of the right thing to be done here and now). As Aristotle argued in Book Five (and also at the end of Book Two), prudence is a knowing or grasping that essentially includes the moral virtues within it as an integral part, for they give it its end.

Accordingly too, if we return to the beginning of the chapter, we must say the same thing about friendship insofar as it also is virtue, that it cannot be misused. On the contrary, when the bad man kills his friend along with himself, he is not using friendship, not even the friendship of pleasure, but something else, as say the vice of injustice. For it must be as unjust to use a pleasant friend for a pleasure contrary to the friendship as it is to use a useful friend for a utility contrary to the friendship, or to give him pleasure when what is owed is utility (instances mentioned in 10.1243b22–38).

Notes

1. If we accept the alternative reading of the text and omit the reference to friendship and emend the reference to pleasant, these three uses will be

differently characterized. Seeing correctly will be the use of the eye on the condition natural to it, and the other two will be uses of it in another way, either as itself, which will be using the eye to mis-see, or accidentally, which will be using it to sell or eat; Von Fragstein (1978: 357).

2.   This example of eating an eye has seemed so peculiar to scholars that they think the text needs emending, as Dirlmeier (1962: 473) and Moraux (in Moraux and Harlfinger [1971: 257]). But if we retain "pleasant" at 1246a27 (as in the translation), the example falls neatly into place, for there are indeed people who find eyes pleasant for food (as the eyes of fish and sheep in particular) and who might buy or sell them for this purpose.

3.   So Woods (1992: 158–59).

4.   Woods (1992: 162).

Chapter 2

Acquiring Virtue: Good Fortune
What It Is
Discussion of Puzzles

Two questions are naturally raised by the end of the previous chapter: where does prudence come from (or what controls it) and who are these others who are morally good without wisdom (for he who is good without moral virtue, the continent, is already a known case). An obvious answer to the first question is chance or fate, but this term is ambiguous and the sense in which it could be cause is the sense in which it is identical with God. An answer to the second question is similar. Those who have virtue in the passions but no wisdom in the intellect can still act well if they act well by some natural impulse derivative from God. Further, those truly virtuous may or perhaps must become virtuous in an analogous way: by divine influence through the passions. Such divinely favored individuals are likely founders of cities (like Lycurgus in Sparta or Theseus in Athens [*Politics* 1.2.1253a29–31]), where their divine virtue exercises rule in the city and hence where the virtuous upbringing of others in virtue and prudence can do for others what divine favor did for the founder (*NE* 10.9, esp. 1179b18–80a24).[1] But this process cannot be completed without philosophers who will develop and teach the true art of legislation. Philosophers too, like founders, will get their first movement from God (1248a22–39). There are thus, as is effectively argued through this present chapter, two sorts of divine people: heroes like Theseus whose divinely infused virtue founds the city, and philosophers like Aristotle whose divinely derived wisdom perfects it. Hence, further, this chapter leads naturally into the final chapter of this book, which is about how the best life must be a return to the beginning by having God as the express object of worship.

Aristotle begins the chapter with the empirical observation that well doing and virtue are produced not only by prudence but also by good fortune. The good fortune in question, as becomes clear in the course of the discussion, is the sort that must have fashioned the ancient heroes, whose surpassing virtue seems to have been inborn in them (as with Heracles) or also received from some divine teacher (as with Achilles, who was taught by Chiron). But such good fortune is still visible in those people who, despite folly of thought, succeed much in matters where fortune is in control. One is naturally reminded of Alexander the Great, Aristotle's pupil, who took personal risks in battle that a more experienced general would have considered foolish, and yet he conquered the whole Persian Empire and founded many and great cities, some of which survive to this day.[2] The question is whether their fortune is not more a matter of nature (for it is so constant) than of mere luck.

In answer Aristotle goes through a series of dialectical arguments on either side of the question. First, then, there are the facts that:

(1) people do have certain characters by nature as they have thus certain bodily features;
(2) such people do not succeed by prudence, for prudence can give an account of itself but they cannot;
(3) their folly is in matters where they are fortunate;
(4) this success of theirs is like always winning at dice and is viewed (the way it was in Alexander's case) as a sort of divine favor or assistance coming from outside themselves;
(5) it is odd, nevertheless, that God thus favors the foolish rather than the best and most prudent.

From these considerations Aristotle draws an initial conclusion, that since the good fortune of these people is not by intellect (points [2] and [3]), nor from the guardianship of God (point [5]), but is continuous (point [4]), it must be by nature.

The problem with this conclusion is that (6) nature is cause of what happens always or for the most part, whereas (7) luck is not, so that the fortunate, since (8) fortune is a matter of luck, cannot be successful always or for the most part. Hence, if the fortunate are fortunate by nature, they are not fortunate by luck (point [7]), and hence not fortunate at all properly speaking (point [8]).

The question has thus shifted to the causality of luck, whether it is a cause at all or a cause only in some limited sense. If it is not a cause at all then nothing happens by luck, but luck or chance is just a name we use when we do not know what the real cause is. Hence the definition people give of luck, that it is a cause "irrational to calculation" (b7). This question, however, while it has thus naturally arisen, is not the same as the question what fortune is and the latter needs answering first. Aristotle therefore leaves the question of causality aside until 1248a15, and returns to pursue the question of fortune's nature.

1247b8 The previous discussion has ended in the paradoxical conclusion that the fortunate are not fortunate (because not fortunate by luck). However, it is plain that (9) some people are fortunate by luck. Thus, if the fortunate are fortunate always or often, then those fortunate by luck should go on being lucky time and time again, for (10) the same cause is cause of the same thing. But if they are thus lucky, then luck cannot after all be the cause but rather something we could learn about (point [7], repeated here more at length). Certainly we could not learn luck from experience because then one could become lucky by experience, and so become experienced, say, at always throwing high scores in dice. But manifestly nothing of the sort happens.

1247b18 The dialectical discussion has again reached an impasse: good fortune is and cannot be a matter of luck. Aristotle shifts, therefore, to the other facts about good fortune, not that they often succeed (point [4]), but that people have some characters by nature (point [1]) and that the fortunate succeed without reason (point [2]). For, in the case of human beings at any rate, if action does not spring from reason it springs from desire or impulse. But there are two sorts of impulse: some we generate ourselves from calculation (when we deliberate what to do and decide to do this thing rather than that) and others are there by irrational appetite. The latter are also prior in time (they are present in children from birth but reason is not thus present in them). If these latter are by nature, then they will naturally tend to the good. The good of each thing is the end to which it naturally tends, so that if nothing damages or disrupts nature (no outside interference or no direction otherwise from reason), then nature must naturally go toward the good. Those naturally endowed, therefore, will go right without reason because their desires will be naturally right, even though their intellect is foolish (the example of people being able to sing well without any training nicely illustrates the idea of the thing). Such people will be fortunate (they will go right without or despite reason), but they will be so by nature (their desires by nature will be directing them).

1247b28 The result of this final piece of dialectic is that there must be such a thing as good fortune by nature, for those who have naturally good desires are fortunate by nature. Consequently if fortune is also a matter of luck and not of nature, the only way out of the puzzle is to suppose that good fortune has more than one sense and that the problems are arising because of failure to distinguish these senses.

Aristotle proceeds to distinguish two such senses using what he has just said about impulses as clue. So there are things people do from impulse and choice and others not so. Fortune happens in the case of the former if people go right despite bad reasoning, and there is fortune in the case of the latter despite good reasoning or, as Aristotle puts it here, if the good they intended to take was a lesser good (but they somehow chanced not to take it but a better one). The former can be cases of good fortune by nature because they

386

are cases of going right, without reason, by natural appetite. The latter cannot be good fortune by nature for here people are following reason, not appetite, and they are reasoning well. The trouble is that, despite their best efforts, they have come to an unlucky decision (many things are hidden to reason so that even good reasoning can fail), and had they carried out their decision they would have failed. However, some chance event has intervened and they do another thing instead that happens to be successful. Experienced travelers, for instance, reasonably decide to go to town by one road, but a chance event forces them to go by another, and so they avoid the thieves waiting for them unbeknownst on the first road. Contrariwise, suppose the chance event merely forced them to reconsider their first decision, and they do reconsider it but conclude, again for good reasons, that they should continue with it. Reason again leads them into disaster.

These two cases of good fortune are evidently quite different ways of being lucky. Are they, however, instances of the same kind or of two different kinds? Clearly fortune against reasoning cannot have reasoning as cause. Hence those who go right because of desire go right because of things not subject to human reasoning. Their desire is, however, not altogether without reason, for it naturally desires what it should and to desire what one should, even if one does not know why, is to be led by something in principle rational (nature in this case). Something is lacking to it, of course, namely its capacity to be penetrated by human reasoning (whether of the agents themselves or others). Thus it has one characteristic of luck, that it is not a matter of reason or knowledge, though it cannot really be from luck (for luck is not continuous). The upshot, then, is twofold: first, some of the people we call fortunate are fortunate by nature and not luck; second, there is such a thing as luck, but it is not cause of all cases of fortune. It is not cause of the first kind but only of the second kind. (Aristotle does not say here how this luck is a cause; he does that in the *Physics*, which is perhaps one of the speculative matters not part of this treatise [cf. 1.1.1214a8–10].) *1247b38*

How Luck Is and Is Not a Cause

The distinction just drawn solves the puzzles that were driving the earlier dialectic, but it leaves still unanswered Aristotle's other question, how luck is or is not a cause (1247b8–9). He deals with it here, and first with the first kind of fortune, that through desire. If luck is cause here it will be cause of everything, for we think and deliberate in response to desire (if we always have to think in order to think there will be an infinite regress). Hence if desire is caused by luck, thinking and deliberation will be so caused too, and everything we do will be caused by luck. *1248a15*

The answer to this puzzle turns on what is the first principle in the soul (the principle of desire), and this principle must be in the soul what God is in the cosmos, namely an unchanging principle of change, and such a principle *1248a22* will be something greater than reason and not, like luck, something inferior to it. Only the divine intellect or God can be this principle (virtue cannot be because, as recalled in 8.1.1246b10–11, virtue is instrument of reason). Thus the fortunate who are fortunate by impulse are in fact fortunate by intellect but by God's intellect and not their own. For it is the divine intellect that, in moving the whole cosmos, moves the powers that give some people one nature and others another and so give some people desires that tend naturally to go right.

1248a33/b3 Other people do not have this kind of divine fortune, nor do they have any inspiration; they must follow their own reasoning and they will fail if they do not. They are nevertheless divine in a way, or they have a sort of divination, because reason is this, being a capacity in the wise and prudent for swift discernment, acquired in some cases by experience and in others by familiarity (the sort of way, one imagines, that Anaxagoras had it, or Philip, Alexander's father, though not Alexander himself who seems to have had the other sort of divination). So what the fortunate have by natural desire, the wise and prudent have by experience and learning. Both, therefore, have access to God and are using his superior insight into things present and to come, save that the one do it without reason (they are thus more open to divine influence through their natural desire), and the others do it with reason. The first are the fortunate who are moved by God through natural desire and not reason. The second are not the fortunate but the wise. They may be fortunate on occasion, in that chance sense of fortune where it means mere happenstance and is, unlike the former and divine kind, not continuous.[3]

There are clear implications here in these remarks of Aristotle's, especially toward the end, that the God who rules the cosmos exercises a providential care over human things. He does so because, as Aristotle expressly remarks, he sees what is to come as well as what is. Hence he can guide and prepare what is in view of what is to come. His guidance and preparation also take two forms. One is by human reason whereby the wise discern, through their experience of and familiarity with things divine, things to come in the light of what now is (as Thales did with respect to the coming olive harvest; *Politics* 1.11.1259a6–19). The other is through the naturally good who, even if they lack wisdom, do possess virtue. Their desires are good and they always pursue the good regardless of knowledge. The latter are also typically the first initiators of human goods, being the heroic founders of forms of civilized existence (as Alexander famously was in Asia). The former will typically be the perfecters of what the latter create, as the family of the Ptolemies perfected Egypt, or as the schools of the philosophers perfected first the Greek and then the Roman world. Hence, further, to the extent that fortune is a divine gift it only goes to the best and most prudent (as implied by the argument at 1247a28–29). For the naturally good who are naturally fortunate are the best in the irrational powers of the soul, and their lack in the rational powers is supplied, in their own case, by God himself and, in the case of their successors, by the wise and prudent among men.[4]

Notes

1. See Simpson (1998: 9).
2. Plutarch *Life of Alexander* and *Fortune of Alexander*. We ourselves might also be reminded of Cyrus the Great who, unbeknownst to himself, was especially favored by God to perform many great deeds for the people of Israel (*Isaiah* 41–48).
3. Kenny (1992, chapter 5) has a long discussion of this chapter but adopts readings of the MSS and corresponding interpretations of the argument that are at a tangent to the alternative interpretation offered here (for instance, he wants to distinguish four kinds or candidates for luck instead of two, p. 74). See also Johnson (1997), who follows Kenny in this regard, and Kenny's own later and briefer discussion (2011: 186).
4. Van der Eijk (1989: 31–33, 41–42) explains the fortune of the naturally good people not as a matter of divine care but as a simply natural phenomenon: such people just happen to be constitutionally more susceptible to the influence of universal divine causality than others. The point about natural constitution is of course correct (it is what Aristotle says); but the inference that no divine care need therefore be involved is unwarranted. The periodic emergence of such naturally good people (or heroic founders) may be precisely how God provides for the moral and material advance of mankind.

Chapter 3

The Quality of the Gentleman
What It Is

The previous chapter has ended talking of the two kinds of good fortune in   1248b8
the context of the two kinds of men who have divination through contact with God. Both kinds of men are good, but one by good fortune from God and the other by reason that relies on God. Since the emergence of the first kind is not within human control, there is nothing further that can be said of it. One should gladly receive and follow such men when or if they arise, but there is, even so, something deficient about them, for they lack the perfection of reason. This lack is supplied by God, to be sure, but it is in them still a lack. The perfect man must be perfect in all his faculties. He must have all the virtues individually, including all the virtues of reason. He must be of himself both noble and good.

Goodness comes from the virtues, but perfection comes from all the vir-   1248b16
tues together. The notion of the gentleman, the man both noble and good, is the notion of such a perfect man. He will have all the goods, because he is

389

good, but he will have them as noble, because he is noble. Goods are noble when they are ends or for their own sake, and are deserving of praise both in themselves and in their deeds. Health and strength, by contrast, are goods but are not deserving of praise. Their deeds need not be praiseworthy, as they will not be when used in the service of tyranny. Virtue and its works, by contrast, are to be praised, for these, as the first chapter of this book showed, can never be misused.

1248b26   Two sorts of goods are in play here: goods as such and praiseworthy goods. Goods like health and strength, as honor and the goods of fortune, are goods as such or natural goods, and they are the goods that people fight over. But they are not good for everyone since they will harm those who cannot use them well (as the food of the healthy will harm the sick). The good man is he for whom such goods are good. The gentleman, by contrast, is not only good in this sense but has the virtues for their own sake and does the deeds of virtue for their own sake.

1248b37   The distinction is significant. There are certain people, the Spartans in particular, who are of the sort to be benefited by the natural goods, for they have and pursue the virtues, but who are nevertheless not noble. The reason is that, while possessing and practicing the virtues, they do not do so for the sake of virtue but for the sake of the natural goods. Consequently, despite being good, they are also wild, like the beasts of the field.[1] They have noble things, the virtues and deeds of virtue, but not as noble or not for their own sake. They are not gentlemen. One might wonder, therefore, if they can really be virtuous if they are not virtuous for its own sake, or for the sake of the noble. The answer must be that virtuous acts, like most acts, can have two ends: the immediate end that is internal to the act, and the remote end that is the sort of life for which the act is done.[2] A Spartan soldier, for instance, is brave in battle for he holds bravery to be a noble thing. He is thus really brave (for intending the nobility of the act is the mark of virtue), and is not like the experienced soldier or the citizen soldier (whom Aristotle distinguished earlier as only possessing a likeness of bravery). But a Spartan soldier is brave so that he and his fellow Spartans can live a life of dominance over others in enjoyment of the natural goods, whether the others be helots at home or Greeks abroad (Aristotle's discussion of the Spartans elsewhere makes the point plain [Politics 2.9, esp. 1271a41–b17, and 4(7).15.1334a40–b3, 5(8).4]).

The problem, as Aristotle remarks (Politics 2.9.1271b3–6), is that Spartans only practiced with a view to war and did not know how to be at leisure; hence, while they had the virtues of occupation (courage, endurance, justice, moderation), they did not have the virtue of leisure, philosophy (Politics 7.15.1334a19–34). In other words, they knew only of the secondary happiness of the political life and not also the primary happiness of the contemplative life (for the sake of which, however, politics exists [NE 10.7.1177b4–6, 12–15]). So they were drawn, as simply political men are, to covet the material goods and occasions in which the virtues of the political life are best displayed (*NE* 10.7.1177b6–12, 8.1178a28–b7). The gentleman, by contrast, is brave for the sake of a life of virtue and not for the sake of dominance over others in enjoyment of the natural goods. He intends not only, like the Spartan, the nobility or beauty of each act of virtue, but also the nobility or beauty of a whole life of virtue, and especially of the virtue of philosophy. Hence the Spartan is wild because he is wild in the way he treats those subject to him as well as in the way he treats himself when he has the natural goods. The gentleman never is. We should say, therefore, that the Spartan has virtue piecemeal (for he has the virtues to do with war and not those of leisure), but the gentleman has it in its fullness.

The Spartan seems to be typical of the man who pursues the secondary life of happiness discussed in *NE* 10.7–8 and who, for the sake of doing glorious deeds, might be tempted even to commit crimes so as to generate occasions for glory (7.1177b6–15). These sort lack the orientation to the first happiness of philosophic contemplation that would save them from such one-sidedness and that Aristotle expressly lays down for the true legislator to follow (*Politics* 4(7).15.1334a11–b5). Thus his placing it in *NE* where he does and his putting so much stress on it. For he needs to make it clear to political men, especially legislators, that politics is not the best life. To think it is so is almost inevitably to think one should commit great crimes so as to achieve superiority in political deeds (*Politics* 4(7).2–3).

We should say of the gentleman, by contrast, that he has the virtues of leisure as well as of occupation. Hence, when he has the natural goods, which are not in themselves noble, he makes them to be noble by his use of them, for he uses them, not for their own sake, but for the sake of virtue. Thus his use of them makes it both just and fitting that he has them, and what is just and fitting is noble. So his use of them makes them noble both in use and in possession. 1249a3

The gentleman differs, therefore, from both the many and from the Spartan. The many are harmed by the natural goods because the natural goods are not good for them; these are only good for the good man, and the gentleman is of course good. But for the gentleman these goods are also noble because he does noble deeds through them. The Spartan also does noble deeds through them but qua useful for obtaining external goods and not qua noble. Therefore he only does noble things incidentally, for when he has the external goods, he will not do noble deeds but rather wild ones. The gentleman will do noble deeds when he has the external goods, and even to a greater extent since their possession enables him to do further noble deeds. One has to assume, therefore, that the gentleman will be a philosopher, for contemplation of the highest things, and not the slaying or enslaving of captured enemies, is the activity par excellence of leisure (cf. *Politics* 4(7).15.1334a22–34). The gentleman will do this contemplation, of course, along with friends like himself. 1249a11

1249a17   The life of the gentleman, therefore, will be best, because it is a life of deeds of virtue (unlike the life of the many), and noblest, because it is a life of deeds of virtue for their own sake (unlike the life of Spartans). But it will also be pleasantest. The simply pleasant things are the noble things, and the simply good things, which for the gentleman are noble, are also pleasant. Hence the gentleman, in possessing the noblest things, will possess the pleasantest things, and possess them in activity. But pleasure was earlier said to be activity, so the gentleman will possess the pleasantest things, when he possesses them, in acts of pleasure. That he has, then, all the best and noblest goods means he must be the truly happy man, and that he has them in acts of the greatest pleasure, means the truly happy man lives most pleasantly (as men all claim must be the case with the happy man). The gentleman philosopher, then, will be the man who meets the criterion Aristotle set down for happiness in the first chapter of this treatise: he will live the best, noblest, and pleasantest life all at once.

What Its Target Is

1249a21   Aristotle has thus proved the claim he set down in response to the person who inscribed the contrary opinion on the propylaeum of the temple to Leto's son. His opinion has been backed up, moreover, by the extended and elaborate proof that is *EE*. But on the propylaeum of which temple is the *EE* inscribed and in honor of which god? Leto's son, Apollo, was patron of health among other things, and the inscriber on the propylaeum of his temple declared health to be best. Doctors are those who have the science of health, and doctors judge how to apply their science by reference to a certain mark, the mark of health, and they judge the things for health in view of health. So likewise the virtuous man, who is as it were the doctor of the soul, must have a mark for choices and actions about the natural goods that are not, unlike virtue and the deeds of virtue, things to be praised.

1249b3   This mark, to keep to the analogy with health, must be the noble. The noble is virtue and the deeds of virtue, but these are virtues and virtuous deeds when they are as reason says. The mark of the natural goods should be the same, therefore. But what reason says in the case of the virtues is clear (it is the mean that prudence perceives in the here and now). It is not clear what reason says in the case of the natural goods. The perception of prudence in the here and now does not determine how much and which of the natural goods one should have on hand, just as the doctor's perception of what medicine to give in what quantity to which patients does not determine how much and which medicines and other instruments he should keep in store ready for use. The doctor evidently determines this question by reference to the number and kind of patients he has, or expects to have, the care of, and the resources available for securing needed supplies. The gentleman must do something analogous. He will presumably, therefore, judge by reference to the number and kind of virtuous deeds his life is to consist of (for he will need more natural goods and of more varieties if his deeds are the sort that need much equipment for their completion). The key to the answer is that the gentleman should follow the same principle as holds in other cases, namely to live by reference to the ruling element and its virtue, not the ruled element; for the ruled element is for the ruling element, as the slave is for his master.

The ruling element is either that which rules or that which it rules for,   1249b11 as the medical art rules for the sake of restoring and preserving health. The ruling element in man is reason and specifically reason in its contemplative activity (for the work of this part is in leisure while that of the practical part is in occupation [*Politics* 4(5).15.1334a22–34, *NE* 10.8]). The contemplative part does not give orders but has orders given by prudence for its sake, as prudence also gives orders for the sake of God but not to him (*EE* 5.13.1145a6–11). God is the object of these orders not as being benefited by them but as being the end of them, or as the goal aimed at.[3] The choice and possession of natural goods, then, must be judged by reference to this mark of God, and hence by reference to that activity of man that most has God as object. This activity is contemplation (the contemplation praised at the beginning of *EE* in the mouth of Anaxagoras). Hence contemplation of God is best, being the best life of the best part of the best man, of the gentleman and the philosopher.[4] Any choice of natural goods that gets in the way of such worship and contemplation of God must be base, for it will get in the way of the simply best life, and nothing could be baser than what prevents the best.[5]

The mark then for the choice of natural goods is clear, the contemplation   1249b21 and worship of God. But this mark entails that the soul too dispose itself accordingly and that the life it lives, or the knowing and perceiving that constitute what it is to live (7.12.1244b23–29), be the knowing and perceiving that is contemplation, and hence that the other part of the soul, the part not involved in contemplation, be perceived as little as possible. Accordingly one should choose a life as little involved in political cares as possible, whether simply or for oneself or for one's city (*NE* 10.8.1178b28–79a16, *Politics* 4(7).3.1325b14–30). The mark, therefore, subordinates all natural goods to the life of contemplation. But it does not subordinate moral virtue to intellectual virtue, save insofar as the moral virtues are exercised in political cares not required for the needs of contemplation (as is especially true of Spartans, for instance, and of those like them). For the gentleman, being complete in happiness, will be complete in and through sharing with friends like himself (were he able to be complete by himself he would be a god). But friendship is justice and justice is complete moral virtue. The supremely contemplative life is the supremely just life—precisely the vision of moral purity and intellectual perfection Aristotle attributed to Anaxagoras at the beginning of *EE* (1.4.1215b11–14). It is also precisely the vision that has animated religious and mystics of all traditions throughout the centuries.[6]

1249b23   *EE* ends where *NE* ends, before its transition to the *Politics*. It ends with the supremacy of the contemplative life. But here is where it differs. *EE* makes no transition to politics. It does in its closing paragraphs, however, make a reference to what has been said elsewhere, namely about the meaning of "for the sake of." The reference is to Aristotle's contemplative or theoretical writings in philosophy, in particular the *Metaphysics* and *Physics* and *De Anima*. These would seem to be the theoretical questions mentioned at the beginning of this treatise as to be discussed when the right time arrives. The right time now seems to have arrived. The transition made by *EE* is not to the *Politics* but to the *Metaphysics*. The temple on whose propylaeum *EE* stands inscribed is the temple, not to Leto's son, but to the cosmic God, the unmoved mover that moves all things, and moves especially the intellect of the wise and prudent gentleman.

Notes

1. At 1249a1 all the MSS say "wild" (*agrioi*) but scholars universally accept the emendation of it to "good" (*agathoi*). The emendation is understandable but unnecessary and even obscures Aristotle's point. Whiting (1996) has an extensive discussion of this chapter, 8.3, which, with the help of certain Kantian ideas, nicely thematizes the difference between the Spartan character and that of the gentleman, but unfortunately lessens the force of the difference by accepting the emendation.

2. The distinction is noted by Allan (in Moraux and Harlfinger [1971: 70]) who uses it precisely to explain the relation between individual virtuous acts and an overall plan of life.

3. Dirlmeier (1962: 502).

4. Cf. Buddensiek (1999: 255–57).

5. The involved scholarly dispute (especially between Jaeger and Von Arnim and their students) about whether the "God" referred to here is, as Jaeger thought, the cosmic God or rather, as Von Arnim contended, the divine element in us (the "god in us" that is our intellect) is fully reviewed and summarized by Wagner (1970: 14–51). Dirlmeier (1962: 502–504) adopts the view that it is the divine in us, as does Wagner himself (in a long discussion, ibid. 52–150), and also the editors of the *OCT*, who follow Robinson in writing at 1249b17 and b20 *theion* (divine [element]) in place of the MSS *theon* (God). But Verdenius (in Moraux and Harlfinger [1971: 288–94]) has well exposed the flaws in this reasoning and he is rightly followed by Kenny (1992: 96–102; 2011: 187–88). Both Verdenius and Kenny adopt the natural reading that the God in question is the cosmic God. Certainly the MSS, the context, and the sense are all on their side.

6. Cf. La Croce (1985): 40–41.

Bibliography

Allan, D. J. "*Magna Moralia* and *Nicomachean Ethics*," *Journal of Hellenic Studies* 77 (1957): 7–11.

———, "Quasi-Mathematical Method in the Eudemian Ethics," in Mansion (1961): 318.

Aquinas, Thomas, *In Decem Libros Ethicorum Aristotelis ad Nicomachum*, ed. Spiazzi, Marietti, 1964.

Barnes, J., ed., *The Complete Works of Aristotle : The Revised Oxford Translation*. 2 vols. Princeton University Press, Princeton, 1984.

Bekker, I., *Aristotelis Opera*. The original Prussian Academy Edition, Berlin, 1831. Available for download from Google Books at (for volume 2 with the ethical works): http://books.google.com/books?id=OnEShWI0kNwC &printsec=frontcover&dq=aristotelis+opera&hl=en&ei=yyfpTKWIEsW t8AbSjonVCQ&sa=X&oi=book_result&ct=result&resnum=7&ved=0CD 4Q6AEwBg#v=onepage&q&f=false; and at (for multiple volumes): http:// www.google.com/search?tbs=bks%3A1&tbo=1&q=aristotelis+opera&btn G=Search+Books#hl=en&sa=G&tbo=1&tbs=bks:1&q=editions:8AP0Mh Dvk18C&fp=2c7b41253d4bc886

Bendixen, J., "Bemerkungen zum siebenten Buch der Nikomachischen ethik," *Philologus* 10 (1855): 199–210, 263–292.

Bodéüs, R. "Contribution à l'Histoire des oeuvres morales d'Aristote," *Revue philosophique de Louvain* (1973): 451–467.

Bonitz, H., *Observationes Criticae in Aristotelis quae feruntur Magna Moralia et Eudemia Ethica*, Berlin, 1844.

Brink, K. O., *Stil und Form der pseudarist. Magna Moralia*, (Diss. Berlin 1931), Ohlau, 1933.

Broadie, S., *Ethics with Aristotle*, Oxford, 1991.

———, "Aristotelian Piety," *Phronesis* 48 (2003): 54–70.

Broadie, S., and C. Rowe, *Aristotle Nicomachean Ethics*. Translation, Introduction, and Commentary. Oxford, 2002.

Buddensiek, F., *Die Theorie des Glücks in Aristoteles' Eudemischer Ethik*. Hypomnemata 125. Vandenhoeck & Ruprecht. Gottingen, 1999.

Burnet, J., *The Ethics of Aristotle*, Methuen, London, 1900.

Caesar, I., *Why We Should not be Unhappy about Happiness via Aristotle*, PhD diss., City University of New York, 2009.

CAG = Commentaria in Aristotelem Graeca, vol. xix ed. Heylbut, Berlin, 1889; vol. xviii ed. Busse, Berlin, 1900.

Case, J., *Reflexus Speculi Moralis qui commentarii vice esse poterit in Magna Moralia Aristotelis.* Joseph Barnes. Oxford, 1596. Available online in the original Latin and in English translation at http://www.philological.bham. ac.uk/reflexus/

Cooper, J. M. "The *Magna Moralia* and Aristotle's Moral Philosophy," *American Journal of Philology* 94 (1973): 327–349.

———, "Friendship and the Good in Aristotle," *Philosophical Review* 86 (1977): 290–315.

———, *Reason and the Human Good in Aristotle* 2nd ed., Hackett, Indianapolis, 1986.

Décarie, V., *Aristote. Éthique à Eudème.* Bibliotheque des Textes Philosophiques. Vrin, 1978.

Diogenes Laertius, *Lives of Eminent Philosophers*, 2 vols., ed. and trans. R. D. Hicks, the Loeb Classical Library, Harvard, Heinemann, 1942.

Dirlmeier, F., *Aristoteles, Magna Moralia, übersetzt und erlaütert*, Berlin, 1958.

———, *Aristoteles, Nikomachische Ethik, übersetzt und kommentiert*, Berlin, 1956.

———, *Aristoteles, Eudemische Ethik, übersetzt und kommentiert*, Berlin, 1962

———, *Merkwürdige Zitate in der Eudemischen Ethik des Aristoteles*, Heidelberg, (1962): 5–43.

Elorduy, E., "Los Magna Moralia de Aristóteles," *Emérita* 7 (1939): 6–70.

———, Besprechung von E. J. Schächer 1940, *Emérita* 13 (1945): 364–368.

Fahnenschmidt, G., *Das Echtheitsproblem der Magna Moralia des Corpus Aristotelicum.* Diss. Tübingen. 1968.

Flashar, H., "Die Kritik der Platonischen Ideenlehre in der Ethik des Aristoteles," in *Synusia, Festschrfit Schadewalt*, Pfulling, 1965.

Gaiser, K., "Zwei Protreptikos–Zitate in der *Eudemischen Ethik* des Aristoteles," *Rheinisches Museum für Philologie* 110 (1967): 314–345.

Gauthier, R. A., and Jolif, J. Y., *L'Ethique à Nicomaque* (Paris, 1958/59, 2nd ed. 1970).

Gigon, O., "Zwei Interpretationen zur Eudemischen Ethik des Aristoteles," *Museum Helveticum* 26 (1969): 204–216.

———, "Die Socratesdoxogragphie bei Aristoteles," *Museum Helveticum* 15 (1959): 174–212.

Gohlke, P., "Die Entstehung der aristotelischen Ethik, Politik, Rhetorik," *SB Wien* 223 (1944).

———, *Aristoteles. Grosse Ethik.* Schöningh. Paderborn, 1949.

———, *Aristoteles. Nikomachische Ethik.* Paderborn, 1956.

Hall, R., "The Special Vocabulary of the *Eudemian Ethics*," *The Classical Quarterly* 9 (1959): 197–206.

Hardie, W. F. R., *Aristotle's Ethical Theory*, 2nd ed. Clarendon, Oxford, 1980.

Helms, P., *[Aristoteles], Populaere Forelaesning over Etik. Den "store Moral," Magna Moralia*, trans. and intro., Copenhagen, 1954.

Jaeger, W., *Aristoteles. Grundlegung einer Geschichte seiner Entwicklung*, Berlin, 1923.

Johnson, K., "Luck and Good Fortune in the *Eudemian Ethics*," *Ancient Philosophy* 17 (1997): 85–102.

Jost, L. J., "Owen and the 'Single-Science' Argument in the *Eudemian Ethics*," *The Southern Journal of Philosophy* 39 (2001): 207–218.

Kenny, A. J. P., *The Aristotelian Ethics*, Clarendon, Oxford, 1978.

——, *Aristotle on the Perfect Life*, Clarendon, Oxford, 1992.

——, *Aristotle. The Eudemian Ethics*, Oxford World's Classics, Oxford, 2011.

Kraut, R., *Blackwell Guide to Aristotle's Nicomachean Ethics*. Blackwell, Oxford, 2006.

La Croce, E., "Etica e Metafisica nell' *Etica Eudemia* di Aristotele," *Elenchos* fasc. 1 (1985): 19–41.

Leighton, S., "*Eudemian Ethics* 1220b11–13," *Classical Quarterly* 34 (1984): 135–138.

Lieberg, G., "Die Lehre von der Lust in den Ethiken des Aristoteles," *Zetemata* 19 München, (1958): 2–15, 117–123.

Lockwood, T., "A Topical Bibliography of Scholarship on Aristotle's *Nicomachean Ethics*: 1880–2004," *Journal of Philosophical Research* 30 (2005): 1–116.

——, "Is Natural Slavery Beneficial?," *The Journal of the History of Philosophy*, 45 (2007): 207–221.

Mansion, S., *Aristote et les Problèmes de Méthode*, Louvain, 1961.

Mills, M.J., "The Discussions of Andreia in the *Eudemian* and *Nicomachean Ethics*," *Phronesis* 25 (1980): 198–218.

Mingay, J., "How Should a Philosopher Live? Two Aristotelian Views," *History of Political Thought* 8 (1987): 21–32.

Moraux, P., *Der Aristotelismus bei den Griechen*, 2 vols., Berlin, 1973.

Moraux P. & Harlfinger D., *Untersuchungen zur Eudemischen Ethik, Akten des 5. Symposium Aristotelicum*. 1971. Berlin: Walter de Gruyter.

Mueller-Goldingen, C., "Aristoteles uber die Methode in der Ethik (*EE* 1.3 und 1.6)," in Steinmetz, 1990.

Natali, C., *The Wisdom of Aristotle*, trans. G. Parks, SUNY, Albany, 2001.

——, "Rhetorical and Scientific Aspects of the *Nicomachean Ethics*," *Phronesis* 52 (2007): 364–381.

——, "Posterior Analytics and the Definition of Happiness in NE I," *Phronesis* 55 (2010): 302–322.

Osborne, C., "Selves and Other Selves in Aristotle's Eudemian Ethics vii 12," *Ancient Philosophy* 29 (2009): 1–23.

Owens, J., "An Ambiguity in Aristotle, *EE* VII 2 1236a23–4," *Apeiron* 22 (1989): 127–137.

Pakaluk, M., "The Egalitarianism of the Eudemian Ethics," *Classical Quarterly* 48 (1998): 411–432.

Peterson, S., "*Horos* (Limit) in Aristotle's *Nicomachean Ethics*," *Phronesis* 33 (1988): 233–250.

Plebe, A., *Grande Etica. Etica Eudemia*. Editori Laterza. Bari, 1965.

——, "La Posizione Storica dell 'Etica Eudemia' e dei 'Magna Moralia,'" *Rivista Critica di Storia della Filosofia*, (1961): 131–152.

Rackham, H. Aristotle. *The Athenian Constitution. The Eudemian Ethics. On Virtues and Vices*. Loeb Classical Library. Harvard, Cambridge, MA, 1961.

Rose, V., *Aristoteles Pseudepigraphus*. Teubner, Leipzig, 1863.

Rowe, C. J., *The Eudemian and Nicomachean Ethics: A Study in the Development of Aristotle's Thought*, Cambridge, 1971.

——, "A Reply to John Cooper on the *Magna Moralia*," *American Journal of Philology* 96 (1975): 160–172.

——, "De Aristotelis in tribus libris Ethicorum dicendi ratione: particles, connectives and style in three books from the Aristotelian ethical treatises," *Liverpool Classical Monthly* 8 (1983), Part I, 4–11; Part II, 37–74.

Schächer, E. J., *Studien zu den Ethiken des Corpus Aristotelicum, I und II*, Paderborn, 1940.

Schleiermacher, F., *Über die ethischen Werke des Aristoteles, gelesen am 4.12.1817* = *Sämtliche Werke*, iii.3, Berlin, 1835.

Schmidt, E. A., *Aristoteles. Über die Tugend, übersetzt und kommentiert*, Berlin, 1965.

Simpson, P. L. P., *A Philosophical Commentary on the Politics of Aristotle*, Chapel Hill, NC, 1998.

Spengel, L., "Über die unter den Namen des Aristoteles erhaltenen ethischen Schriften," *Abhandl. der Bayer. Akademie* 3. 1841 and 1843.

Steinmetz, P., *Beiträge zur Hellenistischen Literatur und ihrer Rezeption in Rom*, Stuttgart, 1990.

Stock, St. G., Translation of the *Magna Moralia* in *The Complete Works of Aristotle, The Revised Oxford Translation*, vol. II, ed. J. Barnes, Princeton, 1984. Originally published under the editorship of W. D. Ross, Oxford, 1915.

Strauss, L., *Natural Right and History*, Chicago, 1953.

Susemihl, F., *Aristoteles. Magna Moralia*. Teubner, Leipzig, 1883.

——, [*Aristotelis Eudemia Ethica*] *Eudemii Rhodii Ethica*. Teubner, Leipzig, 1884.

Thomas, W., *De Aristotelis Exōterikois Logois deque Ciceronis Aristotelio More etc.*, Diss. Göttingen, 1860.

Van der Eijk, Ph. J., "Divine Movement and Human Nature in *Eudemian Ethics* 8.2.," *Hermes* 117 (1989): 24–42.

Von Arnim, H., "Die Drei Aristotelischen Ethiken," *SB Wien* 202 (1924).

——, "Arius Didymus' Abriß der peripatetischen Ethik," *SB Wien* 204 (1926).

——, "Die Echtheit der Grossen Ethik des Aristoteles," *Rheinisches Museum* 76 (1927): 113–137, 225–253.

——, "Eudemische Ethik und Metaphysik," *SB Wien* 207 (1928).

————, "Nochmals die Aristotelischen Ethiken," *SB Wien* 209 (1929a).

————, "Die neueste Versuch, die Magna Moralia als unecht zu erweisen," *SB Wien* 209 (1929b).

Von Fragstein, A., *Studien zur Ethik des Aristoteles*. Amsterdam, Grüner, 1974.

Wagner, D., *Das Problem einer Theonomen Ethik bei Aristoteles*, PhD diss. Heidelberg, 1970.

Ward, J. K., "Focal Reference in Aristotle's Account of *Philia*: *Eudemian Ethics* VII 2," *Apeiron* 28 (1995): 183–205.

Whiting, J., "Self-Love and Authoritative Virtue: Prolegomenon to a Kantian Reading of *Eudemian Ethics* viii 3," in *Aristotle, Kant, and the Stoics: Rethinking Ethics and Duty*. Eds. Engstrom and Whiting, Cambridge, 1996.

Wilpert, P., "Die Lage der Aristotelesforschung," *Zeitschrift für philos. Forschung* (1946): 123–140.

Woods, M., *Eudemian Ethics*. Books I, II, VIII. Aristotle. Translated with a commentary. 2nd ed. Clarendon Press, Oxford, 1992.

Zeller, E., *Die Philosophie der Griechen. 2.2. Aristoteles und die Alten Peripatetiker*. 2nd ed. Tübingen, 1862.

Zürcher, J., *Aristoteles' Werk und Geist*, Paderborn, 1952.

Index

Readers should consult the Analytical Outline for detailed contents of the translation, which the commentary also follows. Page numbers for most entries below refer to the translation only since the corresponding sections of the commentary can then be readily found by use of Bekker numbers or chapter headings. Page numbers and entries specifically for the commentary are printed in italics.